Antique Trader®

Advertising
PRICE GUIDE

Editor **Kyle Husfloen**
Contributing Editor **Rich Penn**

Published by
Antique Trader Books, A Division of

**krause
publications**

700 E. State Street • Iola, WI 54990-0001
Telephone: 715/445-2214
www.krause.com

Please, call or write us for our free catalog of antiques and collectibles publications.
Our toll-free number to place an order or obtain a free catalog is 800-258-0929
or please use our regular business telephone, 715-445-2214.

Library of Congress Catalog Number: 2001091060
ISBN: 0-87349-224-2

Printed in the United States of America

Table of Contents

Photography Credits

Photographers who have contributed to this volume include: Susan N. Cox, El Cajon, California; Susan Eberman, Bedford, Indiana; Scott Green, Manchester, New Hampshire and Eileen Rosnick, Manchester, Massachusetts.

For other photographs, artwork, data or permission to photograph in their shops, we sincerely express appreciation to the following auctioneers, individuals and shops: American Social History and Social Movements, Tucker, Georgia; Autopia Advertising Auctions, Woodinville, Washington; Charles Casad, Monticello, Illinois; Collectors Auction Services, Oil City, Pennsylvania; Daniel Auction Company, Sylvester, Georgia; DeFina Auctions, Austinburg, Ohio; Fink's Off the Wall Auction, Lansdale, Pennsylvania; Gary Metz's Muddy River Trading Company, P.O. Box 1430, Salem, Virginia; the Gene Harris Antique Auction Center, Marshalltown, Iowa; Glass-Works Auctions, East Greenville, Pennsylvania; Green Valley Auction, Mt. Crawford, Virginia; International Toy Collectors Association, Athens, Illinois; Jackson's Auctions, Cedar Falls, Iowa, James Julia, Fairfield, Maine; Peter J. Kroll, Sun Prairie, Wisconsin; Russ McCall Auctioneers, Inc., Onawa, Iowa; Wm. Morford Auctions, Cazenovia, New York; Richard Opfer Auctions, Timonium, Maryland; Pacific Glass Auctions, Sacramento, California; Past Tyme Pleasures, San Ramon, California; Pettigrew Auctions, Colorado Springs, Colorado; Sandy Rosnick Auctions, Manchester, Massachusetts; Skinner, Inc., Bolton, Massachusetts; Slawinski Auction Company, Felton, California; Sotheby's, New York, New York; and Stanton's Auctions, Vermontville, Michigan.

Special Category Contributors

Richard A. Penn
Author of *Mom and Pop Stores*
Pennyfield's Publishing
Box 1355
Waterloo, Iowa 50704-1355

Calendars
Sharon and Bob Huxford
Authors of *Huxford's Collectible Advertising,* Collector Books

Coca-Cola Collectibles
Allan Petretti
21 South Lake Drive
Hackensack, New Jersey 07601
Author of Petretti's *Coca-Cola Collectibles Price Guide* and *Petretti's Soda-Pop Collectibles Price Guide,* Antique Trader Books/Division of Krause Publications

Mr. Peanut Collectibles
Richard Reddock
914 Isle Court
N. Bellmore, New York 11710
(516) 826-2247
e-mail: NB887929@nassaunet.org

Spice Tins
Joan M. Rhoden,
edited by Connie Rhoden
8693 N. 1950 East Road
Georgetown, Illinois 61846-6264
(217) 662-8046
fax: (217) 662-8223
e-mail: rhoden@soltec.net
Co-author of *Those Wonderful Yard-Long Prints* and *Yard-Long Prints*

On the Cover

Left to right, top to bottom: "Whistle" soft drink tin sign, 6-3/4" x 9-3/4", $715; "Red Bell 5¢ Cigar" paper sign, 15" x 20", $853; Rare "Aunt Jemima Pancake Flour" cardboard string toy, $7,590; "Turkey Brand Coffee" 3 lb. tin, $1,650; "Roaster to Customer Coffee" 2-1/2 lb. tin, $578. Courtesy of Past Tyme Pleasures, San Ramon, California and William Morford Auctions, Cazenovia, New York.

Introduction

In our continuing effort to offer the broadest coverage of the antiques and collectibles marketplace, Antique Trader Books is proud to present this new *Advertising Price Guide.*

The field of Advertising Items is one of the broadest, most active and popular collecting areas today and we have worked diligently to bring together the widest range of advertising-related materials available on the marketplace today. Organized into twenty-four major chapters, covering everything from Automotive Collectibles to Watch Fobs, we have also divided several of these chapters into focused subcategories. For instance, under the "Clocks" heading we are providing separate sections on various types of advertising clocks such as Key-wind, Electric or Neon types. This format will make it even easier for the reader to locate a specific types of items under our chapter headings.

Drawing from many sources, our nearly 3,000 detailed listings provide a comprehensive overview of items from common to extremely rare. Prices will generally reflect an actual sale price for a piece in "Good" or better condition as well as a price bracket where a variety of market factors would influence what the advertising piece might sell for. The following special feature will provide excellent guidelines for learning to understand and evaluate the materials you choose to collect.

For his tremendous help with organizing and preparing material for this new guide we are deeply indebted to our Contributing Editor, Rich Penn. His extensive experience and knowledge in the field of advertising memorabilia proved invaluable in preparing this guide and including a tremendous range of listings and great illustrations. Rich's credentials include the authoring and publishing of a fine reference book on this theme - "Mom and Pop Stores - A Country Store Compendium of Merchandising Tools for Display and Value Guide." Released in 1998, this attractive volume is full of important historical information and collecting guidelines to all things related to that great American institution of years gone by - the small country store.

In addition to our extensive price listings which are highlighted by over 1,000 black and white illustrations, we are also pleased to provide a special sixteen page all-color supplement which dramatically presents the wonderful graphic appeal of many choice advertising collectibles.

My staff and I hope you will find this handy volume a wonderful resource, whether you are a collector, dealer, appraiser or decorator. Be sure and take it along on all your antiquing forays and it should prove invaluable in helping you to become a confident and knowledgeable connoisseur of our wonderful merchandising heritage.

— Kyle Husfloen, Editor

Please note: Though listings have been double-checked and every effort has been made to insure accuracy, neither the compilers, editors nor publisher can assume responsibility for any losses that might be incurred as a result of consulting this guide, or of errors, typographical or otherwise.

Advertising Items - Guidelines to Understanding Values and Collectibility

By Rich Penn

Author, "Mom and Pop Stores, A Country Store Compendium of Merchandising Tools for Display and Value Guide" and Co-author, "Mom and Pop Saloons, A Compendium of Saloon Statuary Tools for Display and Value Guide"

The field of Advertising Items is one of the largest and most diverse in the world of collecting today. With such a huge array of interesting material to draw from we have decided this guide will focus on two dozen of the most widely popular areas of collecting. That will allow us to present the widest possible cross-section of today's marketplace.

For collectors in any field there are a number of factors to consider when buying and selling pieces. The "value" of any given item is determined by these factors and should be taken into account when using this price guide.

A great majority of the items listed in this book reflect actual "sale" prices for that piece, that is, a "retail" valuation, often based on an auction result. In other instances we've included a value range. That range reflects a bracket within which that pieces will usually sell. The market factors we'll discuss here are what determine where - within the "value range" - a specific piece may fall. We also need to remember, however, that there is another level of price and/or value: the wholesale level. If you're selling - and there's urgency to sell - you may have to sell in the wholesale market to a dealer. This market can reflect a different set of considerations and different prices. To sell to a dealer, you must ex-pect to sell at something below top retail values. The only incentive for a dealer to buy something is because he or she has a potential profit margin. Many times wholesale prices are half of retail. Sometimes, for items that may require considerable time and effort to find a retail buyer, wholesale prices might be even less. These margins are required to make the marketplaces work.

To better understand value you must begin from a very simple premise: *things are without value until someone wants to buy them.* Then value becomes a function of a number of variables. Those variables could be divided into at least four major areas: Market Factors, Product - or item - Factors, Buyer Factors and Seller Factors.

Market Factors

These are factors we can't control as a buyer or a seller, but they can impact our assessment of value:

* *Cost of capital* impacts both the buyer's ability to buy and the seller's ability to sell.

* *Geography* can affect the number of buyers and sellers. Certain things have stronger demand in certain areas. Some things gave greater supply in certain areas.

* *Seasonality* can affect both the buyer's willingness to buy...and the seller's willingness to sell.

* *Publicity* can also affect the buyer's and seller's interests in certain antique and collectible categories.

* *Decorator trends* can quickly stimulate interest and demand in certain antique categories, they can also direct interest away.

* *What's happening* in films and the "Arts."

Product Factors

These are among the most important determinants in any field of collecting and always need to be carefully considered in the purchase or sale of a piece. They include:

* *Condition* - Without knowing condition and other factors, it's difficult to determine what is the appropriate value. There are basically five levels of condition which are used in the marketplace: Mint - Excellent - Good - Fair - Poor. In this guide we will consider most items to be in at least "Good" condition, a base level. We have provided detailed descriptions with nearly all of our listings. Plus those items of greatest rarity are so indicated. Use the descriptions to better evaluate the "condition" as well as the other factors discussed here.

Mint: Means a piece is in perfect or near perfect original condition. This should not be a restored piece.

Excellent: Much of what we find that is restored probably falls in the excellent condition category. Still, the piece should be complete, with all original parts or exact replacements.

Good: This generally means "average." Good condition can show the wear and tear of the years but must generally be nearly complete and not seriously worn or damaged.

Fair: This level of condition means the piece needs attention. If refinishable, it is probably worth considering. It may have missing or damaged pieces and the artwork is probably incomplete and metal parts may show some rust or pitting. Wood parts may have a worn finish or some dry rot. Restoration would be called for and might bring the value level to "Good."

Poor: This level of condition usually indicates a basket case or a parts piece. It's substantially incomplete, meaning, it's missing key components.

* *Rarity* - This can influence value upward, if there's sufficient demand. But rarity doesn't always mean something is worth more...or anything for that matter. Again, someone must want to buy it first. However, rarity can have a major impact on determining what a realistic price would be. For examply, if you look at tobacco tins, you see a good illustration. There are literally hundreds - perhaps thousands - of different examples of some of the more common tins: the Lucky Stroke Flat Forty for example. It's not likely that you would expect to see dramatic changes in the value of that tin since there are so many. It is NOT rare. Most collectors should be able to find a very good example at quite a reasonable price. The Orcico tobacco tin is a different case. It's uncommon and some would consider it rare. It's also very attractive with its colorful Native American graphics and is highly sought after. When one comes up for auction, it's selling price is more a function of nuances of condition and who will spend the most, rather than someone's - even an expert's - opinion on what it is worth.

* *Quality* - This factor ties in closely with Condition and Rarity and also has a great influence on value. Early advertising pieces were often well constructed of good quality, durable materials which have withstood the test of time.

* *Location* - Where an item is offered for sale can also influence its market demand and can vary regionally. For example, in the Midwest and areas where there's a

strong agricultural base, you see that reflected in strong prices for advertising items related to agriculture. Veterinarian medicine and supply cabinets, cream separator parts cabinets, feed and seed advertisements and all materials relating to such products. As you move North and West you can see stronger demand for sporting good material. Ammunition items, shot cabinets, fishing equipment, trapping and hunting supplies...all seem to have demand that varies geographically. There are also geographic differences resulting from the way our nation grew...from East to West. You would expect to find earlier advertising pieces in the East, and more of them.

Buyer Factors

As a buyer, these are the elements in your domain. You can have a direct impact on them. You can control them.

* *Ability to buy:* Not all buyers have the financial ability to buy what they want.

* *Authority to buy:* Sometimes purchases are joint decisions.

* *Willingness to buy:* Even though buyers might have both ability and authority, they must then be willing to buy something. These three previous factors can translate into economic demand.

* *Experience:* A buyer's experience with the market, the category and his or her experiences as a negotiator can influence selling price.

* *Knowledge:* Knowledge within a category can impact both willingness and buying urgency. The more you know...the more likely you are to act on intuition or qualified judgement.

* *Urgency to fill a collection:* This can include the desire to get a piece in particularly good condition and can effect the need to act decisively.

Seller Factors

* *Economic Issues:*
  - Cost of Goods: Often when a dealer has a generous margin, he/she has more pricing flexibility.
  - Inventory Carrying Costs: The amount of revenue tied up in inventory can influence a seller's need to sell, discounting merchandise may cost less than borrowing operating capital.

* *Ability to Replace Inventory:* When it comes time to sell, dealers always worry about their ability to replace quality merchandise.

* *Knowledge:* A dealer's level of knowledge, just like the buyer's, can influence willingness to negotiate prices...up or down.

* *The "Like" Factor:* This can be one of the most illusive factors in the market. A seller sometimes likes something at a level much higher than it might realistically be worth. That makes price more firm.

Most of these factors are beyond the buyer's control. But all have an impact on both value and buying dynamics. In fact, the *Buyer Factors* are only variables here that can be controlled by the buyer.

As you can see, establishing a value is a complex issue and it involves a wide variety of factors. If you study and continually review these factors it will help you develop a keener collecting sense. It will also help you become a better shopper and/or buyer and - when necessary - a better seller. Both of which will provide a greater appreciation and understanding of how to build a collection that will bring you years of pleasure and fulfillment.

Chapter 1

Automotive Collectibles

Arno Air Meter

Air meter, "Arno" white stepped base w/tapering cylindrical body, rectangular red meter at top, air hose & two air gauges, by Romort Mfg. Co., Oakfield, Wis., cracked glass face, older restoration, 9 x 12", 62" h. (ILLUS.) **$1,210**

Air pump stand, "Gilbert & Barker," cast iron, a square stepped base below gently curved paneled sides supporting a slender tall fluted pedestal w/square top, painted red, earliest known base for a Gilbert & Barker Gilbarco Air Meter, No. 4-6598X, restored, 12" sq., 41" h. **303**

Ashtray, "Allstate," tire-form, glass & rubber balloon-style, outside rubber tire w/glass center, 5 3/8" w., 2 1/4" h. **11**

Mobil Ashtray w/Figural Pegasus

Ashtray, "Mobil," round metal ribbed ashtray w/curved extension mounted w/figural Pegasus logo, original felt base, minor nicks & wear to base, 3 3/4 x 4 x 5 1/2" (ILLUS.) **385**

Attendant's cap, "Mobil," light brown cloth w/black plastic rim & visor, red, white & blue Mobil patch on the front, 10 x 11", 5" h. (some soiling, wear to inside edge) **149**

Attendant's hat, "Gulf," dark blue cloth w/woven blue border band & orange braid above black plastic visor, orange & blue Gulf cloth logo patch on front, size 7 1/4, original packing paper inside **297**

Mobilgas Hat with Badge

Attendant's hat, "Mobilgas - Mobiloil," tan cloth hat w/black plastic rim band & bill, die-cut enameled company badge on front w/Pegasus logo & wording in red & blue, size 6 7/8, very minor wear & soiling on hat, moderate nicks & scratches on badge (ILLUS.) **275**

Gas Station Attendant's Hat

Attendant's hat, "Phillips 66," tan cloth top w/embroidered black & orange logo patch & black vinyl bill, side loops hold advertising plastic mechanical pencil w/name & address of gas station, minor wear & cracking on pencil decal, hat size 7 3/8, 2 pcs. (ILLUS.) **231**

Attendant's hat, "Texaco," dark green material w/green woven border band & braid cord above black plastic bill, white, red green & black Texaco cloth logo patch on front, size 7 3/8 (minor wear & fading) **209**

Attendant's shirt, "Phillips 66," white w/emblem above left pocket, red trim above both pockets, size 14, 14 1/2" (some soiling) **22**

Effecto Auto Finishes Color Wheel

Auto finish color display, "Effecto Auto Finishes," figural spoked wheel, metal rim w/wood inner, spokes display various finish colors, Pratt & Lambert, minor bends to tin signs on each side, some flaking & chips on spokes, 25" d. (ILLUS.)...................... **385**

Baby Feeding Dish with Auto Scene

Baby feeding dish, china, rounded w/flattened rim transfer-printed w/red letters of the alphabet & small animals, the center w/a scene of two young boys driving an early red open auto, marked by Three Crown China, Germany, minor scratches & soiling, early 20th c. (ILLUS.)...................... **182**

Badge, "Mobil/Socony Vacuum," nickel-plated w/red & blue painted detail, large pin/clasp, die-cut five-point shield form, w/"1939 - Clinic Member - Socony - Vacuum," 2 x 2 1/8" (minor scratches)................ **242**

Bank, "Fire Chief" metal figural gas pump w/trap & paper label, 5 3/4" h. (minor paint chips) **303**

Shell Plastic Bank

Bank, "Shell," plastic, double-sided yellow shell-shaped w/red letters reading "Shell," 2 x 4 x 4" (ILLUS.) **138**

Shell Gasoline Pump-form Bank

Bank, "Shell Premium Gasoline," molded plastic bank, model of a gas pump in red & green w/sticker labels in red, white & yellow, very minor soiling, hose tip broken off, heat-stamped on the back "Mankato Oil Co.," 1 1/4 x 1 7/8", 4 5/8" h. (ILLUS.)... **264**

Banner, "Esso," cloth, depicts red-gloved hands holding can marked "Esso Motor Oil Unexcelled" reads "Change Now!" in white lettering, all on navy blue background, 64" w., 33" h. (soiling & wrinkles) **127**

Banner, "Ford," cloth w/gold fringe at bottom, white lettering, "1942" on blue at top, "Ford SIX 90 Horsepower" on red center & "America's Most Modern SIX" on blue at bottom, 40" w., 60" h. **187**

Banner, "Gargoyle - Mobiloil," long narrow lithographed canvas banner, a red ground w/a red & white Gargoyle logo at the left end & a white & red can of the product at the right end, "Mobiloil - Make the chart your guide" in white letters in the center, 24 x 117" (minor soiling & wear, one grommet torn, couple of small holes) **495**

Sunoco Banner w/Donald Duck

Banner, "Sunoco," cloth w/cloth backing, colorful scene depicting Donald Duck driving red hot rod near road sign reading "Change Now to summer type Oil and Grease Sunoco" & "Unexcelled Lubrication" & "Form A700 15.5m 3-39 Litho in U.S.A. Copyright 1939 Walt Disney Productions" at bottom, soiling & fading, touch-up in spots, 56" w., 35 1/2" h. (ILLUS.) **770**

Banner, "Texaco," white cloth showing two Scottie dogs w/heads to one side & "Drain—Fill—then LISTEN" in black & red letters, The Texas Company Sweeney Litho Co. Inc. Belleville, NJ, 80" w., 36" h. (soiling, creases) **209**

Banner, "Winter Richlube," cloth, reads "Safety, Instant Lubrication at Zero and Below, Winter Richlube 100% Pure Pennsylvannia Motor Oil," marked "Sweeney Litho Co. Belleville N.J.," white & yellow lettering on navy blue background, 70" w., 36" h. **198**

Blotter, "Gargoyle Lubricants," leather rocker-type, the flat top stamped in gold "Gargoyle Lubricants" w/gargoyle logo, foreign-made, 2 x 6 3/4", 3 1/4" h. (minor scratches & soiling) **66**

Oilzum Ink Blotter

Blotter, "Oilzum," rectangular, white & yellow w/black images of checkered flags & sprint cars, top reads "1951 Oilzum Champions," dealer information at bottom, 3 3/8 x 6 1/4" (ILLUS.) **39**

Blotter, "Socony," cold test motor oil & winter gear oil, 1920s **28**

Blotter, "Texaco," heavy paper, depicts race car driver, older model race car & two attendants & reads "Under The Rack And Strain Of Racing Wise Drivers Use Texaco Motor Oil, Protect Your Car The Same Way, Brennen & Canney, 124 Market Street Lowell, Mass.," 6" w., 3" h. **187**

Book ends, cast metal, three slender long bars joining hinged end rectangular pierced metal panels w/arched & rounded top above a side view of a man driving an early open auto, early 20th c., 7 1/2 x 11 3/4", 5" h. (some rust spotting, scratches & soiling) **143**

Booklet, "The Arizona Sheriff," ca. 1925, Studebaker Corp. **48**

Havoline Oil Bottle Rack

Bottle rack, "Havoline Wax Free Oil," rectangular metal framework w/raised center section & conforming porcelain side signs in black, white & red, chips at mount holes, 19 x 29 1/2", 22 1/2" h. (ILLUS.) **825**

Bottle rack, "Imperial," eight clear quart bottles marked "Hep" above decaled logo, each w/metal screw-on nozzles, wire-rack carrier w/handle, 17 1/2" w., 9" d., 15 1/2" h., the set (soiling, wear to tops) **303**

Bottle rack, "Mobil Oil," w/porcelain sign & six complete bottles **325**

Mobiloil Bottle Rack

Bottle rack, "Mobiloil," composed of two porcelain signs bolted to a steel frame w/original green paint, the small sign at the top reads "Property of Vacuum Oil Company," the larger sign w/the image of a large red gargoyle in the center, black

& red letters reading "Authorized Service - Genuine Gargoyle - Mobiloil," tiny edge flecks on signs, 20 3/4 x 25 x 30" (ILLUS.) **1,870**

Bottle rack, "Mobiloil," rectangular metal crate on wire stretcher legged base painted dark orange w/white wording "Mobiloil 'AF'" or "Mobiloil 'AF' Filpruf," holds eight diamond-shaped clear glass quart bottles w/metal tops but no caps, 10 x 18 3/4", 22" h. (one bottle repainted, crate w/some paint chipping, denting, rust spotting, scratches & soiling) **1,210**

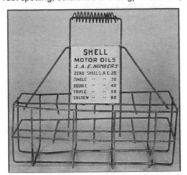

Shell Motor Oil Bottle Rack

Bottle rack, "Shell Motor Oil," metal rectangular rack designed to hold eight one quart bottles, w/attached yellow porcelain sign, black letters reading "Shell Motor Oils - S.A.E. Numbers" w/list of various oils, rack w/overall wear, bends & rust, sign 5 1/4 x 6 3/8" (ILLUS.) **187**

Bowl, "Mobil," china, red & navy blue Mobil emblem on cream background w/navy blue stripes around upper & lower parts of bowl, marked "Shenango China, U.S.A.," 5 3/4" d., 2 1/4" h. (scratches, chips on lower rim) **55**

Brochure, 1958 Plymouth, colorful illustrations **55**

Cane, "Gulf Refining Co.," wood w/rubber base, "Gulf Refining Co." debossed on front top, 39" l. (minor scratches, small chips at bottom, rubber tip worn on one side) **28**

Charcoal briquets picnic kit, "Ford," metal box w/bail handle, marked "Ford Charcoal Briquets" **193**

Chauffeur's badge, 1922, Illinois **28**
Chauffeur's badge, 1922, Kentucky **60**
Chauffeur's badge, 1931, Virginia **45**
Chauffeur's badge, 1948 Illinois **35**

Cigarette lighter, "Buick," metal, car-form desk-top model, pull hood ornament to open, made in Occupied Japan, loose headlight & grill, 5" l., 1 3/4" h. **165**

Cigarette lighter, "Cities Service," plastic, model of 8-ball, top lifts to expose lighter, logo at base, w/original packet of flints & box, 3 1/2" d. **77**

Cigarette lighter, "Dodge," chrome w/Dodge pickup truck imprint & "From Pickups to Diesel Power" on one side, "Dodge Builds Tough Trucks" & semi

truck on other side, 2 3/8" h. (rust spotting on bottom) **33**

Cigarette lighter, "Husky," pocket-size, metal w/emblem, lettering & dog above "Husky," 1 1/2" w., 2 1/4" h. **83**

Cigarette lighter, "Mobil Oil," desk-top style, clear plastic panels w/red Pegasus logo, brass component, 2" w., 3 1/2" h. **93**

Mohawk Gasoline Lighter

Cigarette lighter, "Mohawk Gasoline," pocket-type, metal w/cloisonné die-cut image of American Indian head w/feather & marked "Mohawk," Penquin brand, 3/8 x 1 1/4 x 2 1/4" (ILLUS.) **242**

Cigarette lighter, "Sinclair Gasoline," debossed metal, Sinclair logo above "Powell C. Heiskell - Sinclair Products," 2 1/4" h. (scratches) **105**

Richfield Oil Co. Cigarette/Cigar Box

Cigarette/cigar box, "Richfield Oil Co.," copper flashed over chalkware, model of racing car on cover, "Richfield" on side, ca. 1920s-30s, 4 x 4 3/4 x 10" (ILLUS.) **743**

Creamer, porcelain, bulbous ovoid form w/a wide rim & small rim spout, C-form handle, white decorated w/a color transfer of a lady & gentleman riding in an early open auto w/various animals running to get out of the way, early 20th c., 2 1/2" h. **99**

Credit card, "The Texaco Company," paper, pale bluish green w/recipient's name & address, issued for May, June, July & August 1940, tire & battery purchase coupons still attached, 3 1/2 x 6 1/4" (some soiling & staining) **176**

Cuff links, "Sunoco," metal, blue lettering on yellow triangles, original box, 1" w., 1/2" h., pr. **176**

Old Indianapolis Speedway Item

Desk accessory, "Indianapolis Motor Speedway," plaster model of a race car molded into a domed oblong base w/raised wording, gold paint, back side of base embossed w/"500 Mile Race - May 30, 1931," some scratches, soiling & edge wear, 3 x 7 1/2", 3" h. (ILLUS.) **237**

Desk accessory, "Texaco," wooden base, two metal Scottie dogs on one end, recessed cup holder on other, 6 5/8" w., 2 1/2" h. **242**

Door push, "Texas Punch," tin, 4 x 10" **140**

Fan, "Hudson Gasoline," two-sided cardboard w/wooden handle w/scene of gas station w/electric pumps & tanker trucks, "Economical Transportation with Hudson Gasoline and Oils" & "'Always Less' (logo) At This Sign," company blurb on reverse, 8" w., 13 1/2" h. (staining & soiling, minor paper separation at top of fan, minor chips to fan) **176**

Fan, "Sinclair," cardboard, funnel shape, depicts mechanic & old car w/young girl sitting in front seat & sign reading "Garage Storage Parking Car Oil Service Accessories," 7 1/2" w., 10 1/2" h. (one ragged edge) **94**

K C Pistons Figure

Figure, "K C Pistons," yellow & black smiling figural, nodder/bobber-type, base marked "Let Casey Go to Bat For You," in original box, 7" h. (ILLUS.) **154**

Fire chief's hat, "Texaco," child's size, mint in box **195**

Mobilgas-Mobiloil First Aid Kit

First aid kit, "Flying Red Horse - Mobilgas-Mobiloil First Aid Kit," flattened rectangular tin w/a dark blue lid printed in the center w/a large red flying Pegasus logo w/white wording at the top & bottom & a red banner w/blue wording, features the Good Housekeeping seal of approval, denting & wear on lid, 3 x 3 1/2" (ILLUS.) **209**

Flag, "Mobilgas," linen cloth w/wooden pole, black & white checkered flag w/red Pegasus logo, 35" w., 36" h. **176**

Flag, "Texaco," sewn wool, 48 x 75", rare **500**

Floor display rack, "Pennzoil, Outboard Motor Oil, 100# Pure Pennsylvania, Safe Lubrication," two-sided sign above two-tier metal rack, marked "A-4-60," 39" h. (scratches & dents on sign, slight rusting on rack) **154**

Fly swatter, "Socony Oil," wire handle & bound wire mesh, "Socony Kerosene Oil - Safest and Best," 17" l. (edge wear) **55**

Gas pump globe, "Ashland Kerosene," wide hull body w/two milk glass lenses, red & black lettering, 13 1/2" d. (very minor inside rim chips) **605**

Gas pump globe, "Clark," round white milk glass w/painted orange, black & white "Clark" emblem, 13 1/2" d. **270**

Gas pump globe, "Elreco," Gill body, one premium & one regular lens **600**

Gas pump globe, "Esso," round, milk glass lens w/"Esso, Extra (logo emblem) Extra," red low profile body, marked "Made in Canada," 16" d. (some fading to lens) **385**

Figural Crown Pump Globe

Gas pump globe, figural crown-shaped, milk glass crown painted in gold design, metal base, minor paint loss at top, 16" w., 16 1/2" h. (ILLUS.) **413**

Ford Pump Globe

Gas pump globe, "Ford," round milk glass, marked "Ford (winged-logo) Service" in black, metal base, repainted, 16" w., 16 1/2" h. (ILLUS.) **4,950**

Frontier Gasoline Globe

Gas pump globe, "Frontier - Rarin' To Go" w/black & red image of man on rearing horse, single Gill body lens, minor edge soiling (ILLUS.) **3,080**

Gas pump globe, "Frontier," round three-piece milk glass, black horse & rider on white background above, "Frontier, Rarin' - To - Go" in white lettering on red background below, 14" d. (soiling) **990**

Gas pump globe, "Gulf," round one-piece milk glass w/"Gulf" in navy lettering on orange backgound w/navy trim, metal base, 16" w., 18" h. (fading to lens) **495**

Guyler Pump Globe

Gas pump globe, "Guyler" round glass, marked "High-Tech Guyler Brand Gaso-

line" in white lettering on red background, red ripple body, 13 1/2" d. (ILLUS.) **2,178**

Hudson Gasoline Globe

Gas pump globe, "Hudson Regular," single globe lens, black, white & red w/image of tank truck marked "Hi-Octane Gas - Hudson Oil Company," chipping at mounting hole areas & below w/material loss, 13 1/2" d. (ILLUS.) **880**

Rare Independent Gasoline Globe

Gas pump globe, "Independent Gasoline," high profile metal body w/two milk glass lenses, red frame, black lettering in ring around central round color scene of marching Minutemen based on "The Spirit of '76," minor flaking on one lens, other w/water stain & paint loss, very rare, 15" d. (ILLUS.) **5,500**

Gas pump globe, "Indian Gas," round, three-piece white glass, "Indian" above & "Gas" below in blue lettering, red center circle, metal base, 13 1/2" d. **770**

Gas pump globe, "Kyso" (Standard Oil Kentucky), three-piece, wide body glass, rare **800**

Gas pump globe, "Loreco," round, marked "Loreco Gas" in red lettering around "Ethyl" emblem, low profile light yellow metal body, 15" d. **495**

Gas pump globe, "Mobil Premium" w/original Capcolite body, 13 1/2" d. **250**

Gas pump globe, "Mobil," round, milk glass lens w/"Mobil Kerosene" below Pegasus logo, high profile white metal body, 16 1/2" d. (paint loss & wear to body, slight rust to base) 770

Gas pump globe, "Mobilgas Ethyl," high profile metal body w/two milk glass lenses, red Pegasus logo above blue & red wording, 16 1/2" d. (minor fading, paint chips & soiling to body).................... 495

National White Rose Gas Globe

Gas pump globe, "National White Rose Gas," wide round milk glass hull body, dark blue & red printing, minor chips inside base rim, overall interior spotting in the making, 13 1/2" d. (ILLUS.).................... 413

Figural Red Crown Ethyl Globe

Gas pump globe, "Red Crown Ethyl," crown-shaped one-piece milk glass, embossed lettering painted red around the lower rim, minor scratches, 17 1/2" d. (ILLUS.).................... 1,210

Gas pump globe, "Red Indian," high profile black metal body w/two milk glass lenses, profile of Native American w/full headdress, red, white & black, black lettering, 13 1/2" d. (newer body) 605

Gas pump globe, "Red Pepper Ethyl," metal body in blue mounted on a wooden light-up base, two milk glass lenses w/"Red Pepper" in red above "Ethyl" & other printing in a black & yellow triangle, label on base reads "Cinti Ball Crank Co. Balcrank Cincinnati, Ohio," 15 1/2" d. (scratches on body).................... 1,788

Gas pump globe, "Red Star," round, milk glass lens painted "Red Star Valvoline Gasoline" in black lettering, high profile black base (base repainted) 1,430

Gas pump globe, "Rice Oil Co. - Johnstown, O.," high profile metal body w/two milk glass lenses, black wording in outer ring around center monogram of colored, overlapping letters, red frame, 15" d. (display lens w/paint loss & fading to edges, reverse lens w/cracks & two glued pieces, soiling to both) 1,320

Gas pump globe, "Richfield," round, milk glass lens painted "Richfield, Hi-Octane" in black lettering below, bird logo above, black painted low profile metal body, 15" d. (paint chipping & rust to body) 770

Gas pump globe, "Shamrock," plastic body w/two milk glass lenses, green shamrock, white lettering, 13 1/2" d. (melting at base of body, chips to mounting areas on lenses) 231

Gas pump globe, "Shell," milk glass in figural shell shape, "Shell" w/red decal lettering, marked "Property of Shell Mex & BP Limited/2-4-53" inside base, 19 1/2" w., 20" h. (dime-size chip on reverse side base) 770

Gas pump globe, "Sinclair Pennant," narrow hull body w/two milk glass lenses, red ground w/white fluttering pennant & lettering in white & black, 13 1/2" d. (lenses glued in) 990

Gas pump globe, "Sinclair Power-X - The Super Fuel," white glass in original Capco frame, green & red wording, from original deteriorated box, 13 1/2" w. 270

Gas pump globe, "Sinclair," round, milk glass w/wide body, marked "Sinclair, Marine, Gasoline" in orange & green lettering, scratches, 13 1/2" d. 523

Gas pump globe, "Sinclair," round, one-piece milk glass w/black striped center, outer rim marked "Sinclair Gasoline" in white lettering on painted black background, 16" w., 16" h. (fading & paint loss to sides).................... 847

Socony Motor Gasoline Globe

Gas pump globe, "Socony Motor Gasoline," low profile metal body w/one embossed milk glass lens, shield form also marked "Reg. U.S. Pat. Off. - Standard

Oil Co. of New York," flanked by "N - Y" w/"SO" white letters on blue, minor yellowing & scratches to lens, paint chips to body base, 16 1/2" d. (ILLUS.) **1,980**

Solene Gasoline Pump Globe

Gas pump globe, "Solene No-Knock Gasoline," wide milk glass round body w/two lenses, printing in red & green, cracks in back lens, body scratches, 13 1/2" d. (ILLUS.) **880**

Gas pump globe, "Spur Gas," round milk glass, navy train gas tank marked "Spur Gas" w/"Spur" above & "Gasoline" below in painted red lettering, 13 1/2" d. (some paint chipping) **1,485**

Gas pump globe, "Standard Oil Gold Crown," one piece globe w/original mount ring/base, all original **450**

Gas pump globe, "Sterling," round, wide white globe w/"Sterling Gasoline" in black lettering on gold background, "A Quaker State Product" on affixed porcelain sign above, lens 13 1/2" d., sign 16 1/2" w., 5" h. **825**

Gas pump globe, "Stoll's," round, marked "Stoll's" above & "Gasoline" below w/arrow marked "Golden Tip," painted canary yellow high profile body, 15 1/2" d. (repainted body, reverse lens cracked) **550**

Gas pump globe, "Super Kant-Nock Gasoline," wide milk glass hull body w/two lenses, black & red printing within thin yellow ring, 13 1/2" d. (soiling)....................... **468**

Texaco One-piece Globe

Gas pump globe, "Texaco," one-piece milk glass w/raised letters & copper base w/"Pat. No. 1604773," 16" d. (ILLUS.) **1,238**

Gas pump globe, "Texaco," round milk glass, "Texaco" above Texaco star w/black circle trim, wide body, marked "B-57," 14" d. **715**

Gas pump globe, "Tydol," double-sided glass inserts in glass frame, 17" h. **550**

Union Gasoline Globe

Gas pump globe, "Union Gasoline," high profile metal body w/one milk glass lens w/shield-form design, blue top & red & white striped bottom, "Property of Union Oil" bottom of globe, newer metal body, cracking to paint around edge, minor scratches, 15" d. (ILLUS.) **1,870**

Gas pump globe, "Vickers," round, lens w/"Vickers" & "V" logo, red plastic body, 13 1/2" h. **468**

Gas pump globe, "Zephyr" two milk glass lenses w/red ripple frame, red lettering 13 1/2" d. (soiling on body & lenses, paint chips on metal rims) **1,320**

Rare Early American Oil Gas Pump

Gasoline pump, "American Oil Pump and Tank Co.," cast-iron, sheet metal & glass, front slides up & down to expose pumping mechanism, glass tank at top, completely restored, one BB hole in glass tank, 17" d., 99" h. (ILLUS.) **2,365**

Gasoline pump, American Oil Visible Pump Standard No. 70730, cylindrical red base w/black trim, side slides open to expose interior, round glass top, w/Flying A reproduction globe, restored w/original parts, 18" d., 102" h. (BB hole in glass cylinder) **1,540**

Early Atlantic Gasoline Pump

Gasoline pump, "Atlantic," tall upright red metal casing w/rounded top & stepped sides w/two porcelain name plates above the meter dial on each side & the name in red lettering in white stripes down the front, back name insert cracked, well restored, 15 x 28", 79" h. (ILLUS.) **1,540**

Gasoline pump, Bennett Model 646 B/W, restored to Dino Gasoline, curved top, painted white border & green center w/a small round dial over the gas metering face, lights up, reproduction globe, 18 x 29", 73" h. (small chips to "Contains Lead" signs) **880**

Crown Gas Pump

Gasoline pump, "Crown," Model No. 117, Pump No. 20-5531, original round white glass globe marked "Crown" in red letters, white body marked w/"Fry" decal, red base, completely restored (ILLUS.) **1,650**

Eco Meter Gasoline Pump

Gasoline pump, "Eco," red roof-shaped top over round glass clock dial-style gallon register w/white dial, dial No. R2, tapering red body w/black trim, no identifying numbers, restored w/one original & one replaced new glass face, 19 x 20", 84" h. (ILLUS.) **6,160**

Gasoline pump, "Essolene," No. 711, red metal body, round globe, all original parts (holes in globe, paint loss & wear) **770**

Restored Early Pennsylvania Pump

Gasoline pump, Pennsylvania Pump Co. model, red-painted metal body w/"Tydol Ethyl" pump signs, black domed top & metal dial within black ring, chips to pump signs, fading to face, lights up, reproduction globe w/"Flying A" symbol on lens, 18 x 24", 68" h. (ILLUS.) **1,045**

Gasoline pump, "Sharmeter" by Neptune Meter Co., black roof-shaped top overhangs the red-painted body w/black rectangular plate w/half-round ribbed "roof" projecting over the round clock dial-style gallon register, white dial w/black numbers & "Sharmeter" in red, smaller black rectangular plate below reads "Motor," restored, 22 x 25", 68" h. (plate not attached, reproduction globe w/Flying A symbol) **1,210**

Gasoline pump, Wayne Model 60, restored to Atlantic gasoline, rounded top & step-sided Art Deco style, red body w/a white arched dial face w/two "Hi-Arc" insert signs, white vertical stripes down the front w/"Atlantic" in red, 18 x 27", 75" h. (chips & staining to pump signs) **935**

Gasoline pump globe lens, "Gulf Coast" (New Orleans Tenneco Affliate), 15" d. **200**

Gasoline pump globe lens, "Kyso" (Standard Oil Kentucky, 16 1/2" d. **375**

Gasoline pump globe lens, "Red Indian," 13 1/2" d. **890**

Gasoline pump globe lens set, "Ben Franklin," depicts Ben Franklin w/yellow & black Ethyl logo at bottom center, "Ben Franklin" in white lettering w/black border on red outer rim, minor scratches, 13 1/2" d., the set.......................... **5,500**

Gasoline pump nozzle, heavy metal, raised marking "K-721-1," 14" l. (wear, scratches) **66**

line," red, white & blue chevron logo at base, overall surface scratches, rubs & nicks, paint loss at bottom tip of logo, 11 x 13 3/4" (ILLUS.)...................................... **303**

Douglas Blend Gasoline Pump Sign

Gasoline pump sign, "Douglas Blend Gasoline," rectangular, white w/red & blue lettering, left side w/wing atop a red heart, wear, 10 x 14" (ILLUS.) **550**

Gasoline pump sign, "Pate Challenge," one-sided porcelain, rectangular, design in red, black & white of knight's helmet above a large shield w/"Pate" above a black narrow rectangle w/"Challenge" in white, 12 x 15" (some fading, minor edge chips & scratches) **495**

Gasoline pump sign, "Shell Gasoline" die-cut porcelain, 12 x 12 1/4" **925**

Gasoline pump sign, "Sky Chief Su-preme," one-sided porcelain, rectangular, upper band w/"Sky Chief Su-preme" in red & black on white over a green ground w/large red wing & "Texaco" star logo & "Gasoline," bottom white band printed in black & red "Super-Charged With Petrox," 12 x 18" (minor chips & water stain) **110**

Chevron Gasoline Pump Sign

Gasoline pump sign, "Chevron Gasoline," die-cut tin, round top, white w/red & blue letters reading "Chevron Supreme Gaso-

Socony Motor Oil Pump Sign

Gasoline pump sign, "Socony Motor Oil," curved circular porcelain, white shield form in center, edged in red w/blue letters reading "Socony - Motor Oil - Standard Oil Co. of New York," white letters "SO - N - Y" on blue around border, small chip at bottom, tiny edge & surface flaws, 15" d. (ILLUS.)... **1,073**

Gasoline pump sign, "Sunray D-S Petroleum Products," porcelain, 9" sq. **1,000**

Gasoline pump sign, "Texaco Fire-Chief Gasoline," rounded porcelain w/logo & fire hat & marked "Made in USA 9-20," 10" w., 18" h. (waterstain, chips & cracking) **176**

Rare "Wings" Gas Pump Sign

Gasoline pump sign, "Wings Regular Gasoline," one-sided porcelain, rectangular, blue & red on a white ground, "Wings" printed in red across the top above a blue design of three geese flying in formation above clouds above "Regular Gasoline" in red at the bottom, chips at edges & mounting holes, minor scratches, 6 x 7" (ILLUS.).. **1,870**

Gasoline station floor display, "Mobil," painted wood life-sized cut-out figure of a gas station attendant in uniform, easel-backed, red logo on his cap & jacket pocket, 21" w., 72" h. **715**

Early Shell Station Soap Dispenser

Gasoline station soap dispenser, "Shell," silvered cast metal, a deep rounded container w/paneled sides & notched corners w/a matching domed cover w/hinged flap w/Shell logo over dispenser opening, swings between knob-topped end bar uprights joined by a flat rectangular base, some pitting & minor rust on base, 5" h. (ILLUS.).. **165**

Glasses w/carrier, "Mobil Pegasus," metal carrier w/six white glasses w/red Pegasus logos, 6" h., the set.............................. **226**

Grease can, "Sambo Axle Grease" above face of black man & "Nourse Oil Co., Kansas City, Mo., Business Is Good," black lettering on white label w/checkerboard wrap, tin w/contents, 3 1/2" d., 4 1/2" h. (dents, fading, paint chipping, rust & soiling).. **198**

Texaco Gas Pump Gumball Machine

Gumball Machine, "Texaco" gas pump form w/battery-operated plastic light-up sign at top, side handle dispenses gum ball stored in glass top, Olde Tyme Reproductions, Inc., Serial No. 90-012183, 21" h. (ILLUS.) **121**

Hand cleaner, "Cleanzum," painted orangish yellow tin, depicts "Bucky" character w/mask & red attendant hat on lid & round, White & Bagley Co., 3" d., 2 1/2" h. **1,540**

Hat, "Sunoco Laceby Dealer," beige & brown, gasoline station attendant-style, vinyl bill, cloth top w/metal enameled badge, size 7 1/4"... **237**

Hat badge, "Mobilgas/Mobiloil," cloisonné w/original hat **300**

Hat badge, "Tydol/Flying A Gasoline" cloisonné over nickel, 1 3/4" **500**

Union Oil Company Badge

Hat/uniform badge, "Union Oil Company," cloisonné five-point shield-shape, blue top w/"Union Oil Company" above red & white stripes, by Whitehead & Hoag, small repair in white at bottom center, minor cracks, 1 3/4 x 1 3/4" (ILLUS.) **798**

Hood ornament, "Mustang," metal, painted dark red Mustang on primitive cylindrical capped base, 7 1/2" h. (denting & rust at bottom) **55**

Hood ornament, "Pierce Arrow," die-cut metal w/raised lettering, a ring w/wording pierced w/a hexagonal opening showing the front of a car, a small wing at the top of the ring & an arrow tip & feathered end on each side, 5 1/2" w., 4" h. (some soiling & use wear) **187**

"The Wiggler" Hood Ornament

Hood ornament, "The Wiggler" spinner-type, metal w/rubber-coated base, composed of a large shiny top center orb above half-round cupped orbs w/alternating red or green center 'jewels' & mounted to spin on a central short rod above a domed foot, marked "The Wiggler Co., Buffalo, N.Y. , Pat. Dec. 8, 1925 - June 29, 1926 Made in U.S.A.," some rust spotting, scratching & soiling, wear on base, 4" d., 3 3/4" h. (ILLUS.) **253**

Hood ornament, "Thomas Flyer," cast silvered metal, spread-winged eagle perched atop a realistic globe on a base ring atop a notch-edged cap, 2 3/4 x 5", 4 3/4" h. (some edge wear & scratches) **380**

Horn, 1912 Model T, fine condition **110**

Union 76 Inkwell & Pen

Inkwell w/fountain pen, "Union 76," Bakelite w/logo etched into lid, minor wear to gold paint, inkwell 3 x 3 1/4 x 4", the set (ILLUS.) **55**

Key holder, "Texaco, Registered Rest Rooms," plastic, rectangular, white & black w/red "Rest Rooms" seal on front, black & white background & printing on reverse **132**

Lamp, "Mobiloil Special," figural oil can in gold, blue & red w/Mobiloil logo, celluloid, metal & cardboard, 7" d., 9 1/2" h. (soiling, cardboard peeling on top) **275**

Lantern, "Dietz Nightdriver's Friend," large clear lens w/small red lens on other side **100**

License plate, 1911, New Jersey, one-sided porcelain, rectangular w/white ground & red lettering "10846 - NJ - 11," embossed tin medallion w/registration number at one end, stamped on back "Horace E. Fine Co. Ing-Rich Auto Tags, Trenton, N.J.," 6 x 13" (chips, edge rust, water stain, scratches) **143**

License plate, 1915, California, porcelain **50**

License plate, 1915, New Jersey, w/tags **150**

License plate attachment, "Boston Police," porcelain, one-sided cylindrical form, outer circle marked "Police" above & "Boston" below in red lettering on white background, black center marked "CD" in white diamond w/"Mass." below, 4" w., 5 1/4" h. (small chips to edge) **50**

License plate attachment, "Chamber of Commerce" above & "Pittsburgh" below in black lettering on gold background in oval, "Safety League" in white lettering on black background below oval, one-sided porcelain, 4" w., 5 1/2" h. (chips to edge & mounting hole) **66**

License plate attachment, "Harold's Club," one-sided die-cut metal, depicts man walking in front of oxen pulling covered wagon reading "Harold's Club or bust! Reno, Nevada," scratches & minor denting, 13 3/4" w., 8 " h. **61**

License plate attachment, "Jaguar," embossed metal, oval-shaped w/crown on

top & jaguar cat in center, marked "Jaguar Clubs" above & "Of North America,
Inc." below, 4" w., 5 1/2" h. **28**

Mobil Pegasus License Plate Attachment

License plate attachment, "Mobil," die-cut
embossed tin, red Pegasus logo, overall
light   soiling,   wear,   scratches,
4 1/2 x 6 1/4" (ILLUS.) **77**
License plate attachment, "Mobil," em-
bossed tin, red Pegasus logo above,
"Drive Safely" on band below, 6 1/2" w.,
5 3/8" h. (some scratches & soiling) **143**
License plate attachment, "Motorola Auto
Radio," oval, embossed tin, yellow & red,
marked on red banner at top "Drive Safely " w/black letters reading "Motorola
Auto Radio" in black letters in center,
4 5/8 x 4 3/4" (minor scratches & rubs) **143**

*Peacock Ice Cream License Plate
Attachment*

License plate attachment, "Peacock Ice
Cream," rectangular, white, red & black,
image of smiling Indian w/crown on head
indicating a World Series championship
& marked "Follow the Indians - Peacock
Ice Cream," nicks & scratches, some
paint thinning, 4 3/4 x 9 7/8" (ILLUS.) **220**

Pioneer Club License Plate Attachment

License plate attachment, "Pioneer Club,"
die-cut aluminum, image of man smoking
cigarette & wearing red neckerchief &
white cowboy hat, the hat marked "The
Famous" & white letters across bottom
reading "Pioneer Club - Downtown Las
Vegas, Nevada," surface & edge wear,
dings, 7 3/8 x 10 5/8" (ILLUS.) **275**

Tydol Motor Oil License Plate Attachment

License plate attachment, "Tydol Motor
Oil," die-cut embossed tin "Running
Man," scattered nicks & wear,
4 1/2 x 6 5/8" (ILLUS.) **121**

Die-Cut Tin License Plate Attachment

License plate attachment, "Washington
Chief," die-cut tin, a long narrow rectangular plaque w/slits for mounting, a red,
white & blue circle w/arched panel at the
top on the upper right end reads "New
Polyform - Washington Chief," the plaque
below in red & blue w/white wording
reads "It's Great To Be An American!,"
very minor nicks & wear, 4 7/8 x 10"
(ILLUS.).. **143**

"Florida" License Plate Alligator

License plate decoration, figural cast metal alligator w/open jaws, glass eye,
marked "Florida" in red script, by Erskine,
Tampa, Florida, original paint, 14" l.,
4 1/2" h. (ILLUS.) **171**

Shell Oil License Plate Reflector

License plate reflector, "Shell Oil Co." tin lithograph, shell-shaped w/three flags in the center, 1 x 3 1/4 x 5" (ILLUS.)................. **121**

Light bulb kit, "The Pep Boys Handy Bulb Kit," rectangular tin w/advertising on the lid w/cartoon depictions of "Manny, Moe & Jack," advertising for Cornell Tires on one side & Cadet Batteries on the other, red ground w/red, white & black printing, 2 1/4 x 4", 2 1/2" h. (minor fading, scratches & crazing of paint) **83**

Lighter, "Wayne Gas," metal, figural gas pump w/"Wayne" in gold oval on front, top lifts to expose lighter, 2" w., 1 1/4" deep, 3 5/8" h. **121**

Lighter fluid dispenser, "Shell Gasoline," metal w/glass cylinder, figural gas pump, clear upper w/white lettering, red bottom on cylindrical footed base, side penny slot, 19" h. **198**

Nourse Motor Oil Sign

Lubester sign, "Nourse Motor Oil," double-sided tin, image of warrior in center below "Guaranteed Motor Oil," blue border w/white letters reading "Nourse - Business is Good," w/original clamp, overall wear, scratches & paint loss, 6 1/2 x 8 1/2" (ILLUS.) **385**

Lubester sign, "Pennzoil," rectangular, double-sided tin, yellow w/logo & "Pennzoil" in center, upper left corner reads "Supreme Pennsylvania Quality" w/"Safe Lubrication" in lower right corner, 3 7/8 x 9 1/2" (scratches, nicks & wear)........ **121**

Lubricant dispenser, "Socony," metal & glass top dispenser, red base w/Socony logo & "SAE 50" decals, 9 1/2" w., 16" deep, 47" h. **495**

Lubricant oil can, "Shell," cone-shaped 1 qt. tin, "Golden Shell" logo above "Shell Oil," yellow background, 6 1/2" w. base, 11" h. (scratches overall, missing top) **176**

Lubricant oil can, "Texaco Home Lubricant (Texaco star logo) The Texaco Company" in label on green background, long pointed nozzle, 2 1/2" d., 6 1/8" h. (denting, scratches & soiling)................................ **479**

Mailbox, "Standard Oil," metal, Santa Claus-type, rectangular upright green box w/curved-back letter slot at the top, locked fold-down front opening, letter slot reads "Be Sure Your Letters Are Stamped," a red, white & blue Standard oval logo above the fold-down door w/a yellow frame around red & green wording "Santa Claus Mailbox," side w/white circle at the top reading "Santa Claus, Ind. - Dec. 25 7 A.M.," lower rectangular scroll frame around wording "Letters mailed here will be postmarked with the famous Santa Claus, Ind. Postmark," contains form letter from Santa, 7 3/4 x 12 1/2", 17" h. (some spotting, scratches, soiling)..... **253**

Map, 1928, "Fyre Drop Gasoline," motor trails, 4 x 9".. **210**

Map, "Michelin" map of Ireland, tin, reproduction Michelin Map No. 986, 25" w., 34 1/2" h. (scratches)............................ **55**

Map rack, "Conoco," painted black metal w/decal at bottom, marked "M2-33-Made in U.S.A.," includes 13 newer brochures, 11 1/8" w., 26 3/8" h. (scratches, nail holes).. **187**

Mechanical pencil, "Mopar," metal & plastic, includes parts & accessories, "Allied Motors, Inc. IA 7500 Kansas City, Mo," piston floats in oil, 5 1/2" l................................ **55**

Shell Household Memo Pad Holder

Memo pad holder, "Shell," metal holder w/cardboard backing, full paper pad & slot to hold household bills, receipts, etc., together w/pencil w/Super Shell & Golden Shell logos, minor wear & soiling, 5 1/4 x 8" (ILLUS.) 110

Gilmore Lion Head Mileage Card

Mileage card, "Gilmore Motor Oil," rectangular, cardboard, red & yellow, image of lion head on left w/"Gilmore Lion Head Motor Oil - The Most Highly Filtered Motor Oil in America," reverse w/mileage chart for California cities from Los Angeles, minor edge & surface wear, 2 1/2 x 4 1/8" (ILLUS.) 39

Monogram Car Kit

Monogram kit, paper decals in wooden box, ornamental borders, includes lodge emblems & letters, soiling & water stain, 12 3/8" w., 10" deep, 1 5/8" h. (ILLUS.) 154

Motor oil can, "Ace High," 1 qt. tin, orange wrap w/navy, orange & white label depicting a motor car & airplane in clouds, minor denting & soiling, 4" d., 5 1/2" h. 523

Motor oil can, "Husky," 1 qt. tin, depicts jumping Husky on yellow background below "Husky Heavy Duty Motor Oil," marked "Western Oil & Fuel Company Minneapolis, Minnesota," 4" d., 5 1/2" h. (denting, scratches & rust spotting at top & bottom) 413

Motor oil can, "Pennzoil," yellow 1 qt. tin, "Pennzoil Lubricates All Transcontinental Streamliners," depicts transcontinental streamliner w/three owls on back w/largest owl wearing conductor's hat, 4" d., 5 1/2" h. (denting & scratches) 360

Motor oil can, "Red Indian," 5 qt. tin, red American Indian in full headdress on white background above, "Red Indian

Motor Oil" in white lettering on red band below, 6 1/2" d., 9 1/2" h. (scratches) 193

Motor oil can, "Shell," cylindrical w/pouring spout, yellow w/red letters reading "Shell Handy Oil" w/image of auto & logo at bottom, additional graphics & text on reverse, 3 1/2 oz. (minor scratches & wear) 231

Motor oil can, "Workingman's Friend," green 1 qt. tin, depicts worker w/hard hat & tool box on white background, 4" d., 5 1/2" h. (denting, scratches & soiling) 204

Conoco Motor Oil Can Rack

Motor oil can rack, "Conoco," painted steel, two porcelain red & blue company logo signs at the top, arched top bar over wide cylindrical body fitted w/slots for oil cans, complete w/18 empty one-quart cans, rack repainted, some fading on signs, cans range from good to fair condition, overall 43" h., the group (ILLUS.) 770

Esso Oil Figural Oil Containers

Motor oil containers, "Esso," yellow figural plastic Esso Happy character forming the container w/a pointed spout top w/small white cap, in original countertop point of purchase display box, complete w/blue, yellow, white & red die-cut cardboard die-cut cardboard marquee, 20 containers, 5 3/4" h., the group (ILLUS.) **250-350**

Motor oil jar, "Longlife Motor Oil," 1 qt., features airplane.. 230

Name badge, "Conoco," nickel-plated brass, Art Deco design, rectangular frame w/fanned top w/the Conoco logo beside "Conoco" in red enamel letters, encloses original celluloid insert over the name typed on paper, 1 1/4 x 2 3/8" (chip to first "C," minor scratches of plating) 220

Name badge, "Sunoco," die-cut brass w/cloisonné detail, by Galfour, 1 3/4 x 3" 200

Navigator tin, "Michelin," cylindrical, depicts Michelin man smoking, white design on red background, 1 1/4" d., 5 1/2" h. 105

Trop-Artic Oil Cup

Oil cup, "Trop-Artic Auto Oil," cylindrical tin form w/wide strap handle, printed in color around the sides w/landscape scenes w/an early open touring car in the summer & winter, advertising in red & also marked "Manhattan Oil Co.," very minor scratches, 3 3/4" d., 2 3/4" h. (ILLUS.) 440

Oil dispenser, "Associated Oil Company," 1 qt. w/swingspout 70

Oil dispenser, metal floor model, pedestal flared base below the clear glass tall cylinder for oil below a tall pumping mechanism w/the spigot near the top of the glass cylinder, S.F. Bowser & Co., Inc., Fort Wayne, Indiana, Pump No. 46077, Figure 115, repainted red, 11 x 18", 55" h. (minor scratches & soiling) 303

Oil dispenser, "Union Oil Company," 1 pt., copper w/swingspout 110

Early Bowser Oil Pump

Oil pump, "Bowser Self Measuring Oil Pump," wood & metal, wooden casing encloses the oil pump & bulk oil tank, ca. 1900-12, restored, 21 3/4 x 29 3/4", 50 1/2" h. (ILLUS.).. 468

Owner's guide, 1953 Buick 20

Padlock, "Sinclair," metal, embossed lettering, marked "WB 622," 2" w., 3" h. (some scratches, no key) 11

Padlock, "Socony Mobil Oil Co. Inc. Padlock," metal w/debossed lettering, marked "WB 620," 1 1/2" w., 2 1/2" h, (no key) 39

Pamphlet, 1967 Ford taxicab.............................. 25

Paper clip, "Packard," brass, bell-shaped, embossed w/Packard radiator logo, floral decoration at sides, 2 1/2" w., 3 1/4" h. (some tarnish) 363

Parts book, 1928, Indian Motorcycle.................. 40

Mobil/General Petroleum Pen Holder

Pen holder, "Mobil/General Petroleum," desk-type, five-point shield form w/figural Pegasus logo, 15-year service award, brass plate not engraved w/name of recipient, pen missing, 4" h. (ILLUS.) 303

Pencil, "Lion Head Motor Oil," plastic & metal, yellow & red w/"Lion (logo) Head," sample of oil sealed in top, 5 1/2" l. (wear to pocket clip, scratches)................................... 66

Pennant, "Gilmore (head of lion) Lion Head Motor Oil," paper, red background w/printing on both sides, marked "Permit No. 232," 10" w., 21" h. 468

Picnic set, running board-type, a rectangular black leatherette-covered trunk holding six knives, six white graniteware plates, five graniteware cups, two graniteware coffee mugs, three tin cups, two tin compartments w/leather straps, one spoon, six various forks, one sharp knife & one can opener, outside straps for attaching to the car, made in Sweden, early 20th c., the set.. 330

Pin, "Lion Motor Oil," metal, cloisonné design of man in black barrel, brown base, marked "The Oil With the Right Body In It," 5/8" w., 1" h. 28

Pin, "Mobiloil," metal, Pegasus logo design w/clear coating, 1 1/8" w., 7 1/8" h. 176

Pin, "Mobiloil," metal w/cloisonné design, stick pin-type, oval head w/gargoyle & "Mobiloil, 5/8" w., 2 1/8" h. **66**

Pin, "Shell Oil," metal, seashell-shaped, silver, 1" w., 1" h. **11**

Shell Oil Pin

Pin, "Shell Oil," plastic, round w/fluted edging, yellow & gold Shell logo in center, black outer trim reading "Tractor Lubrication" in yellow lettering, 1 1/4" d. (ILLUS.) **17**

Pin, "Standard Oil," Standard Oil emblem in cloisonné design w/diamond at bottom, 5/8" w., 1/2" h. **138**

Pin, "Sunoco," celluloid over metal, round, depicts lamb jumping over fence, reads "Change Over Now!" above & "to summer Oil and Grease Sunoco" below **132**

Pin, "Texaco," metal cloisonné design in Texaco Oil Company star logo, round, 7/8" h. **176**

Pin, "Texaco," shield-form, cloisonné logo & small diamond on detailed 10k gold base, marked "Appreciation Award - Twenty-Five Years," minor wear, 5/8 x 5/8" **66**

Texaco Star Club Award Pin

Pin, "Texaco - Star Club - New York District," round award pin, gold-filled pin w/white, red, green & gold enameled company logo in the center, embossed letter in gold border band, 1/2" d. (ILLUS.) **259**

Union 76 Pinback Button

Pinback button, "Union 76," round celluloid, orange w/Minute Man logo & "I'm Fast!," soiling, light surface scratches, dimple dent at center, 2 1/4" d. (ILLUS.) **149**

Esso "Drip" Pins

Pins, "Esso," enameled metal, figural "Happy" & girlfriend waving, pr. (ILLUS.) **94**

Plates, 8" d., "Esso," ceramic, center cartoon illustration of dog w/small Esso logo by front paws, black & white, pr. (minor soiling & small chips on back) **55**

Postcard, "Mercury," advertising-type depicting 1967 Mercury **3**

Poster, "Quaker State," paper, depicts police officer w/whistle directing traffic & reads "Keep 'Em Rolling..., Change Now To Quaker State Motor Oil For Summer Driving," some soiling **66**

Program, 1933 Elgin National Auto Races **46**

Program, "Indianapolis Speedway," 1926, front reads "Official Program Indianapolis Motor Speedway Company" below picture of driver, car & tower, includes advertisements from Coca-Cola, Richfied, Lockhead, Delco, Polarine, Sinclair, Auburn, Olzum, Chrysler & others, black, white & orange pages (tears & soiling) **176**

Racing pennant, felt, long pointed red felt w/white wording "Nat. Road Races - Aug. 29-30, 1913 - Elgin," w/printed blue & white scene of a speeding race car, 29 1/2" l., 11 1/2" h. (piece missing from one letter, some fading) **385**

Bardahl Rack Topper

Rack topper, "Bardahl," die-cut tin, man in black opening his jacket to reveal can marked "Bardahl," w/"Try it!" on right, wear & some rust, 10 x 10" (ILLUS.) **220**

Radiator cap, "Chevrolet," cast metal, oblong, bust of woman holding figural plane & medallion w/Chevrolet insignia & "Quota Trophy" on front, marked "October 1927" on side, wooden base, 6" w., 4" h. (repainted, some minor cracking) **330**

Goodrich Radiator Grille Attachment

Radiator grille attachment, "Goodrich," porcelain, circular, yellow center marked "Goodrich - Tourist," the white border marked "Safety - First," minor edge wear, chip & scratches, 4 x 5" (ILLUS.) **303**

Radiator shield, "Mobilgas," two-sided Socony vacuum shield w/Pegasus & "For Friendly Service," 1920s, rare, 12 x 19" **125**

Radio, "Champion Spark Plug," plastic model of spark plug on pyamid-shaped base, working condition, 5 x 8 1/2", 15" h. **220**

Chevron Gas Transister Radio

Radio, "Chevron," transister-type, model of a rectangular gas pump w/AM radio tuner dial where the pump numbers would be, front w/label "Chevron Custom" & logo, made in Hong Kong, ca. 1950s, 2 1/2 x 4" (ILLUS.) **110**

Road map, "Marland Road Map of North Central United States," three-fold printed paper in white, red, pink & grey, the three panels showing a continuous lakeside resort landscape w/people camping, ca. 1920s, minor wear at folds, corners & edges, 9 x 12" **341**

Road map, "Official Road Map of California - Washington - Oregon - Union Oil Company of California," two-fold color-printed paper, the top of the two panels w/a rectangular color scene of a period gas station w/a roadster being serviced by attendants in red, blue, green, black & white, wording below in dark blue & red on white, dated 1926, 8 x 9 3/8" (very minor edge discoloration, small edge bumps) **385**

Shell Motor Road Guide

Road map, "Shell Motor Oil - Gasoline Motor Road Guide - Roxana Petroleum Corp., St. Louis, Missouri," three-fold color-printed paper, the cover of the three panels w/a continuous color landscape scene of an early gas station w/autos & couple playing golf in the foreground, Shell logos in gold & red, wording in red & dark blue, edge & fold wear, minor scattered soiling, 9 x 12" (ILLUS. of cover) **413**

Unusual Mobil Safety Award

Safety award, "Mobil Oil," a brass model of a ship's wheel on an oval platform base, the glass face includes a thermometer & humidity indicator, 1955, some soiling & scuffs, 4 1/2" d., 4 1/2" h. (ILLUS.) **55**

Sales award pin, "Texaco," sterling silver, star-shaped w/scroll trim on the lower half & set w/a pearl below the star, star centered by a green "T," Balfour maker's mark, 1/2" d. **303**

Salesman sample kit, "Gulf," metal box containing lighter fluid, household lubricant, rejuvenator, preservers, electric motor oil, penetrating oil & insect killer samples, all w/Gulf colors & logo (missing one can, some scratching) **275**

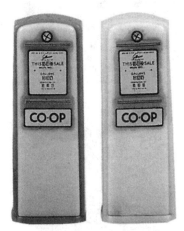

Plastic Gas Pump Shakers

Salt & pepper shakers, "Co-Op Gasoline," plastic gas pump-shaped, one pale green, one cream, each w/advertising

decals on the sides, one side resembling a gas pump, the opposite side reading "See your Co-Op first," ragged edges to decals, 2 3/4" h., pr. (ILLUS.) **143**

Salt & pepper shakers, "Conoco," plastic, gas pump shape w/orange Conoco logo on white background, black base, marked "Primary Oil Company New London Iowa" on back, 1" w., 3/4" d., 2 3/4" h. pr. **50**

Salt & pepper shakers, "Esso," model of gas pump, plastic, 2 3/4" h., unmarked, pr. **37**

Salt & pepper shakers, "Firestone," model of tire w/"Firestone" on one, "U.S. Rubber" on other, pr. **57**

Salt & pepper shakers, "Mobilgas," plastic, figural gas pump, "Central Oil Co., Plainview, Nebraska," 2 3/4" h., pr. **200**

Salt & pepper shakers, "Mobilgas," plastic, gas pump shape w/Mobiloil logo, one w/red background & one w/red & white background, marked "Basha's Service Station Main St. Westminister, Mass. Tel Tr. 4-9977," 1" d., 2 3/4" h., pr. (overall soiling) **99**

Salt & pepper shakers, "Phillips 66," plastic, gas pump shape, orange w/black base & Phillips 66 logo, marked "Compliments of Key City Oil Co. Mankato, Minn." on back, in original box, 1" w., 1" d., 2 3/4" h., pr. (wear to box) **61**

Salt & pepper shakers, "Richfield Ethyl" plastic, figural gas pump, stamped "Boise, Idaho," 2 3/4" h., pr. **425**

Salt & pepper shakers, "Richfield," model of gas pump, plastic, yellow, 2 5/8" h., pr. ... **50-60**

Salt & pepper shakers, "Richfield," plastic, figural gas pump w/Richfield decals, one w/orange lettering & one w/black lettering, marked "Eagle Oil Co, Fort Plain, N.Y.," 1" w., 2 5/8" h., pr. **132**

Standard Crown Gas Pump Shakers

Salt & pepper shakers, "Standard Crown," model of gas pump, plastic w/decals, marked "T.E. Gessele Your Standard Oil Agent Phone Gl 7-4140 Mercer N.D.," 3 1/4" h., 1" w., soiling & small pieces missing to decals on both, pr. (ILLUS.) **171**

Texaco Gas Pumps

Salt & pepper shakers, "Texaco Sky Chief & Fire Chief," model of gas pump, plastic, silver & red, 2 3/4" h. pr. (ILLUS.) **50**

Union 76 Salt & Pepper Shakers

Salt & pepper shakers, "Union 76," ceramic, gas pump shape w/logo at center, dealer information at bottom, minor crazing, 3 1/2" h., pr. (ILLUS.) **385**

Scale-tool, "Valvoline Oil Company," flat stainless steel bar etched w/numbers & w/a bolted-on swiveling arm w/etched wording, w/original leather pouch, ca. 1920-40, 5 3/4" l. (minor tool wear, pouch worn & soiled) **33**

Service pin, "Wasatch (Refining Company) 5 Years," round gilt-metal w/a central bust profile of a Native American chief, red enameled band w/brand name, other wording embossed in outer ring, single screw back, 5 /8" d. **413**

Service pin/necktie bar, "Texaco Oil Co." rectangular bar marked "14k" on back, octagonal center enameled pin w/star logo & "20 Years Service," 1/2 x 2" **77**

Service station map rack, "Cities Service Road Maps - For People - Going - Places!," painted tin, upright five-tiered rack in dark green w/a yellow, white & green

company logo at the top & other wording in white, two hanging holes near the top, 7 x 8 1/4", 19 1/4" h. (overall minor to moderate nicks, scratches, rubs & ding, few small rust spots, some adhesive residue) **220**

Sign, "Boyce Moto Meter," painted metal cut-out depicts woman in red dress & hat pointing to emblem, reads "Boyce Moto Meter Authorized Service Station" in white & red lettering on black background, rare, 21" w., 18 3/4" h. (some fading & paint chipping) **1,980**

Sign, "Esso," circular metal sign w/cast-iron base, curb-side style, "Aviation Products" in white lettering on black background below "Esso" logo on obverse, "Stand Clear" in white lettering on red background above "Esso" logo on reverse, black base, marked "A22124-38," scratching & soiling, 24" w., 62" h. **1,100**

Sign, "Fisk Tire," one-sided tin w/attached hanger, model of clock, logo in center, w/movable hands to show when attendant will return, H.D. Beach Co., Coshocton, Ohio, 6 1/8" d. (minor scratches, denting & soiling) **330**

Sign, "Igol," die-cut plastic, figure of an attractive young blonde woman walking & holding a can of the product aloft in one hand, wearing white short shorts & tight short-sleeved shirt w/wide black belt, red lace-up sandals, 11 1/2" h. (minor scratches) **275**

Sign, "Mobil," one-sided die-cut porcelain, painted red Pegasus logo, 54" hoof to wing **1,100**

Sign, "Pennzoil," curb-side style, "Supreme Pennsylvania Quality Pennzoil (brown bell) Safe Lubrication" on two-sided porcelain, cast-iron base & lollipop, 20" w., 5' h. **935**

Sign, "Pure-Pep," one-sided porcelain, reads "Pure-Pep, (logo), Be sure with Pure" in navy blue & orange on white background, orange trim, marked "I.R., 46-712," 10" w., 12" h. (scratches) **60**

Sign, "Sunoco" two-sided porcelain w/iron hanger, "Rest Room," 22" w., 14" h. (few chips to both sides & edges, wear to hanger) **825**

Signs, "Fina" porcelain "Rest Room," 4 x 9", pr. **450**

Old Shell Soap Dispenser

Soap dispenser, "Shell," heavy cast metal w/silvered finish, a deep rounded octagonal covered container swiveling in a metal mount, the Shell logo riveted on the cover, minor overall wear, new wood stand, 6 1/2" w. (ILLUS.) **468**

Speedometer, 1912 Model T, w/new brass cable **83**

Rare Texaco Stained Glass Window

Stained glass window, "Texaco," round w/wire frame, large red logo star w/green "T" surrounded by white & w/"Texaco" painted in black across the top, some cracks to glass "T," one piece of star replaced, 21 3/4" d. (ILLUS.) **1,375**

Stationery, "Standard Oil Company," linen paper, letterhead reads "Panama Pacific International Exposition San Francisco, California, 1915," includes envelope (yellowing) **66**

Phillips 66 Stovepipe

Stovepipe, "Phillips 66," tall metal cylinder printed w/orange ground w/thin white pinstripes & wide white band printed in black "Motor Oil" below white circle w/orange & black company logo, denting, rust spotting, scratches, soiling, 8" d., 21 1/4" h. (ILLUS.) **110**

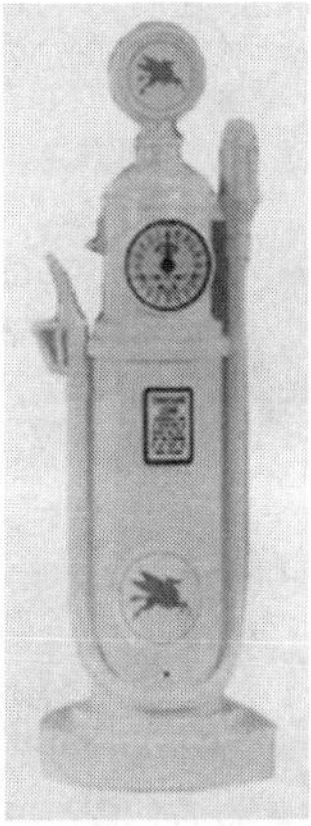

Mobilgas Telephone

Telephone, "Mobilgas," plastic, figural gas pump, cream color w/red emblems, black lettering on dial, marked "Copyrighted 1984 Synanon Made in Taiwan," 3" d., 9 1/2" h. (ILLUS.) **94**

Ticket brochure, 1935 Indianapolis Speedway **32**

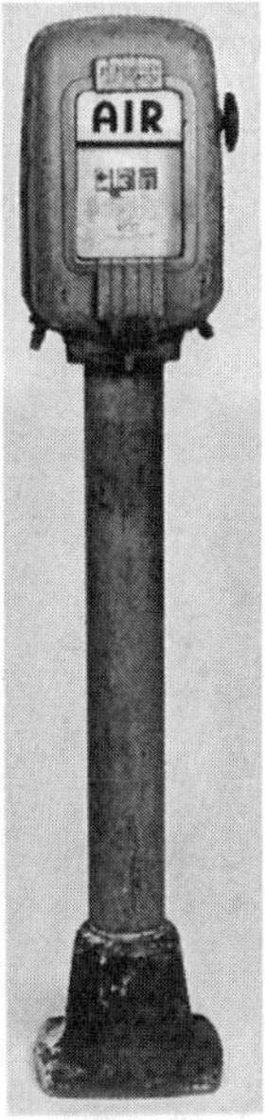

Early Eco Tireflator Pump

Tire air pump, "Eco Tireflator," painted metal & glass, a heavy iron base supporting the round red-painted pedestal & top meter compartment w/a glass dial cover below the word "Air," original condition w/overall paint loss, early 20th c. (ILLUS.) **721**

Tire inflator, "Eco," red metal casing, chrome-trimmed glass on front, reads "Air (meter numbers) Eco Tireflator," restored, 9" w., 10" deep, 16 1/2" h. **468**

Tire inflator island, "Eco," service-station type, white over-head lamp w/upright red cast-iron body, glassed-front meter reads "AIR," 98" h. (restored)............................... **2,420**

Early Michelin Tires Stand

Tire stand, "Michelin Tires," die-cut tin, an upright panel outlining the Michelin man beating a large drum, heavy metal rack for tire, in dark blue, gold & white, fold-out supports, ca. 1920s, moderate peppering, nicks, scratches & overall edge wear, rusty on back, 10 x 19 x 20 1/4" (ILLUS.)..................................... **1,540**

Toy car, "Mobil," fiberglass, metal steering mechanism & rubber tires, Mobil logos & number "1" on front, back & sides, white w/red & blue stripes, 53" l., 19" h. (some scratches & soiling) **143**

Texaco Fire Chief Hat

Toy fire chief hat, "Texaco," plastic w/microphone & speaker attached, shield in front w/logo & "Texaco Fire Chief" held by eagle on top of hat, original box & instructions, box w/tears, faded & pieces missing on edges, 14 1/4" l., 8" h. (ILLUS.) **110**

Toy tea set: cov. teapot, cov. sugar bowl, creamer & four cups & saucers; porcelain, each piece decorated w/a chauffeur-driven open auto w/two ladies in the back seat in red, yellow & green, a running boy on the reverse, marked "Made in Japan," the set (various minor damages) **242**

Texaco Toy Truck

Toy truck, "Texaco," metal, red w/"Texaco" decals on tank sides, Texaco logo on doors (ILLUS.)................................. **183**

Uniform badge, "Chevron Station Manager," 1 1/4 x 1 1/2" **230**

Uniform badge, "Shell" die-struck brass w/cloisonné detail, 2 1/2 x 2 5/8" **450**

Uniform badge, "Signal Trucking," cloisonné on brass, 2" w. **450**

Vase with Early Auto Scene

Vase, china, a flattened ovoid body tapering to a short flaring neck flanked by ornate scrolled handles, cobalt blue ground w/a front reserve w/pointed white floral clusters forming a ring around an oval reserve w/a color scene of seashore w/two women, a boy & a dog in an early open automobile, early 20th c., worn gilt trim, 4 1/2" h. (ILLUS.)........................... **275**

Water bag, "Pep Boys," metal & cloth w/plastic cap, marked "The Pep Boys" above three men in vehicle, "Drinking Water Bag Keeps Water Cool Fresh Palatable" below, all on cream cloth background, metal top closure & hanging holes, 10 1/2" w., 16 1/2" h. **44**

Water can, "Mobilgas," metal, red w/Mobilgas logo in circle, 23" w., 17" h. (professionally restored) **110**

Chapter 2

Breweriana

Advertisement, "Fort Pitt Brewing Co., Pittsburgh," lighted, counter or wall mount, metal w/glass face, decorated w/fort in circle near top flanked by hops & banners reading "Choicest Malt" & "Finest Hops" w/"Fort Pitt - Special - Beer" in center w/"Fort Pitt Brewing Co., Pittsburgh, 15 Pennsylvania Epp-13," black & red lettering, 14 1/2" d. (minor scratches) ... **$330**

Advertisement, "Special Kaier's Beer," diecut cardboard w/3-D effect, depicts a light tan horse w/glossy coat standing on green ground & against dark brown background, brown frame w/"Special Kaier's Beer" at top & "First Prize Winner" on bottom & in white lettering at one side "Kaier Brewing Co. Mahanoy City, Pa. - Brussels 1950 Belgium," clear coating, 19 1/2" w., 16 1/2" h. **99**

Advertisement, "Al. S. Schorrs City Brewery," Hannibal, Missouri, embossed scene of clutch of dead game birds, lithograph by Gast, St. Louis, Missouri, ca. 1905-1910, matted & framed, 11 x 23" **308**

Backbar display, "Altes Golden Lager Beer," white chalkware, molded as an upright round disk w/writing above a narrow rectangular base w/a round indent at the right end holding an amber bottle of the product, printed in red & gold, 1950s, 11 x 11 1/2" (some corner chips) **95**

Backbar figure, "Blatz Beer," metal & plastic, seated banjo player w/barrel body beside a large model of a Blatz beer bottle, upright back w/sign across the top reading "It's Draft-Brewed - Blatz," colorful, 1950s (some scuffs to bottle label) **87**

Backbar figure, "Cooper's Beer," figural chalk standing bartender w/towel over one arm & holding up a large bottle of beer in front, 1940s, 7 x 15" (lots of wear, chips, missing bottle labels) **150**

Miller High Life Beer Bar Figure

Backbar figure, "Miller High Life Beer," hard rubber figure of a standing girl wearing a large round red hat & short flaring red skirt w/blue & yellow trim, high-top black boots, flaring rectangular red & white base, 1930s, some overall scratches, 6" h. (ILLUS.) **115**

Neuweiler Beer Backbar Figure

Backbar figure, "Neuweiler Beer - Ale," molded plastic figure of an older bartender holding up glass of beer, printed in yellow, black, white, red & pink, 1950s, some worn & chipped paint, 8 1/2 x 12" (ILLUS.)..................................... **77**

Backbar light, "Schmidt Beer," model of a covered wagon, metal, wood & cloth, wooden wagon & wheels w/a cloth cover in white printed in red "Schmidt" above a blue banner printed "The brew that grew with the Great Northwest," electric light inside, cord extends from base, 1950s, 10 x 17" (cloth yellowed w/some stains) **102**

Bank, "Metz Beer," ceramic, barrel-shaped, tan glaze, embossed "Premium Metz Beer," 1950s, 6 1/2" h. (light crazing & some small base rim chips) **25**

Bar light, "Peerless Amber," glass panel fitted into a metal base, features an elf w/white beard, dressed in red w/a green cap & shoes & holding a glass & a bottle of Peerless Amber Beer, large white letters read "Peerless Amber" & in red lettering below "The Beer of Good Cheer," new old stock, 12" w., 11" h. **149**

Beer can, "Fitzgerald's Pale Ale," cone-top crown closure type, cylindrical, oblong front label printed in red w/white & black design, an emblem at the top above "Fitzgerald's Pale Ale," address in white border band, white ground, 1940s, 12 oz. (rub mark between faces, ding in shoulder)... **125**

Gluek's Beer Can

Beer can, "Gluek's Beer," cone-top crown closure type, cylindrical, printed w/a squared label reading "Gluek's" in blue on a white band flanked by dark blue bands w/"Beer" in white below, all within a thin red border, narrow red base band printed in white "Gluek Brewing Company," 1940s, 12 oz., few tiny humidity spots on spout (ILLUS.) **96**

Beer can, "Hanley's Lager Beer," cone-top w/crown closure type, cylindrical sides, fine black on silver check ground, central red oval w/small reclining lion above white wording "Hanley's Extra Dry Lager Beer," cigarette lighter in neck, 1940s, 12 oz. (few dings in spout) **377**

Rare Hudepohl Chevy Ale Can

Beer can, "Hudepohl Chevy Ale," cone-top crown closure type, cylindrical, silver ground w/round front label w/wavy border enclosing a pale blue ground w/dark blue, red & white wording, narrow wavy blue & red stripes around the shoulder & base, 1940s, 12 oz., small scattered scratches (ILLUS.) **726**

Beer can, "Jung Pilsener Beer," cone-top crown-closure stype, cylindrical, silver ground w/a large green hop leaf on the front printed in white & black "Jung

Pilsener Beer," 1940s, 12 oz. (rusty rim, small rust spot on one face) **227**

Milwaukee Club Beer Can

Beer can, "Milwaukee Club Beer," cone-top, low profile-type, black background w/wide yellow stripe w/black lettering, reads "Keg Beer Flavor - Milwaukee Club Beer," minor scratches in black, 1930s (ILLUS.) **507**

Beer can, "Neuweiler's Pilsener Beer," cone-top, high-profile style, yellow ground w/ornate silvery blue, red & black design, minor nicks, tiny scratches, 1940s (ILLUS. right, below) **1,000**

Beer can, "Pacific Lager Beer," cone-top, low profile-style, dark blue upper portion w/white wording, narrow bluish green lower band w/white waves & small sailing boat, 1930s (overall small rust spots, lacquered) **75**

Rare Piel's and Neuweiler's Cans

Beer can, "Piel's Special Light Beer," cone-top, low-profile style, red ground w/silver oval ribbon reserve enclosing black & red wording, few small nicks, some minor dings, 1930s (ILLUS. left) **427**

Beer can, "Schmidt's First Premium Lager Beer," cone-top, high-profile style, colorful printing, 1940s (some small nicks & scratches) **187**

Various Beer Glasses

Pilsner Beer Glasses

Beer glass, "Atlas Prager" & image of bottle in red, Chicago, Illinois (ILLUS. far left, top photo) **31**

Beer glass, "Bevo The Beverage," ovoid shaped, wording in red, St. Louis, Missouri (ILLUS. second from left, top photo) **40**

Beer glass, "Bonn Pilsner" & logo in red & black, Random Lake, Wisconsin (ILLUS. second from right, top photo) **57**

Beer glass, "Bud Light," tapering footed form w/colorful "Spuds" decoration, Budweiser, (ILLUS. far left, second photo) **33**

Beer glass, "Calumet Beer," cylindrical form, name in red, Calumet, Wisconsin (ILLUS. far right, top photo) **99**

Beer glass, "Drewry's," Drewry's logo in black & red above red enamel lettering, South Bend, Indiana & Chicago, Illinois (ILLUS. second from left, second photo) **61**

Beer glass, "Edelweiss" on black enamel, Chicago, Illinois (ILLUS. second from right, second photo) **88**

Elder Brau & Old Dutch Tumblers

Beer glass, "Elder Brau," clear glass cylindrical form, gold wording, Arizona (ILLUS. left) **336**

Etched Beer Glasses

Four Collectible Beer Glasses

Beer glass, "Elgin Eagle Brewing Co. - Elgin, Ill." & logo, yellow etching (ILLUS. left, top photo) **440**

Beer glass, "Esslinger's Premium Beer" & logo in red, Philadelphia, Pennsylvania (ILLUS. far left w/collectible glasses) **35**

Beer glass, "Falstaff" logo in yellow, red & black, St. Louis, Missouri (ILLUS. second from left w/collectible glasses) **198**

Beer glass, "Famous Old Lamp Beer" within scrolled border, red enamel, East St. Louis, Missouri **33**

Beer glass, "Fox Brew" on red w/head of fox, Waukesha, Wisconsin (ILLUS. second from right w/collectible glasses)................ **55**

Beer glass, "Goebel's," Detroit, Michigan (ILLUS. far right w/collectible glasses) **99**

Beer glass, "Grain Belt Beer" on red enamel bottle cap logo above red enamel "the friendly beer," Grain Belt Brewing Co., Minneapolis, Minnesota **193**

Beer glass, "Koppitz-Melchor Brewing Co.," clear glass cylindrical form w/gold rim band & white printing reading "Koppitz-Melchor Brewing Co. (below logo w/"Pale Select") - Detroit, U.S.A." (ILLUS. left) **45**

Beer glass, "Lubeck Royal Beer" on black enamel w/logo, wide red band flanked by narrow black band around glass, South Bend, Indiana & Chicago, Illinois **242**

Beer glass, "Mundus West Side," clear glass cylindrical form w/white printing reading "Mundus West Side Brewery Co. - Detroit, Mich." w/logo at the top (ILLUS. right).. **32**

Beer glass, "Old Dutch," clear glass cylindrical form w/red wording reading "Pennsylvania Best - Old Dutch - Happy Holiday" (ILLUS. right with Elder Brau) **36**

Beer glass, "Old Milwaukee Light," frosted w/logo & circle, red enamel, Milwaukee, Wisconsin (ILLUS. far right w/pilsner glasses on page 35)... **33**

Old Reading & Schepps Beer Glasses

Beer glass, "Old Reading Pale Reserve," clear glass cylindrical form w/red & white wording (ILLUS. left) **256**

Two Early Detroit Beer Tumblers

Beer glass, "P.O.N. Porter" printed in blue enamel on opaque white, Newark, New Jersey 33

Beer glass, "Ritschler and Tiesse Malting Co., Clinton, Iowa," clear glass w/heavy gilt decoration depicting a lion & shield, ca. 1910-1920, 4 3/4" h. 61

Beer glass, "Schepps Xtra Beer," clear glass cylindrical form w/red & blue design & silver rim band, Dallas, Texas (ILLUS. right)... 40

Beer glass, "Terre Haute Brewing Co.," cylindrical w/etched name & etched logo flanked by "Trade" & "Mark," Terre Haute, Indiana (ILLUS. right w/etched glasses, top photo, page 36) 54

Beer glass, "The Moerschel Spring Brewing Company - Brewers and Bottlers of Fine Beers.," ovoid shape w/etched name & logo, St. Charles, Missouri (ILLUS. center w/etched glasses, top photo, page 36) 66

Two Early Beer Tumblers

Beer glass, "Utah Brau," clear glass cylindrical form w/white wording reading "The Standard Brewerys (over eagle logo) - Utah Brau - & Standard Malt Extract," Chicago (ILLUS. left)....................... 253

Beer glass, "Zang Brewing Co.," clear glass cylindrical form w/white wording reading "P.H. Zang (below logo) - Denver, Colo. - The G.A. Lammers Bottling Co." (ILLUS. right).. 77

Schlitz Beer Cab Light

Cab light, "Schlitz Beer," reverse-painted glass & metal, a flat arched glass plate w/"Schlitz" in red on a gold ground, set upright in a rectangular silvered metal base, 1930s, some oxidation on the base, few rust spots on rear cover, 7 1/2 x 13" (ILLUS.)....................... 406

Anheuser-Busch Calendar

Calendar display, "Budweiser," tin over cardboard w/chain to hang, "Budweiser" above tray holding a beer bottle & a pilsner glass filled w/beer, "Preferred Everywhere" below, cardboard calendar months & days included, red & gold, Anheuser-Busch, Inc., minor scratches, denting & rust spotting, 12" w., 22 1/2" h. (ILLUS.)... 248

Cigar box, "Budweiser Perfecto Cigars," wooden, w/labels, 1910, 5 1/2 x 9 1/4" (warped lid, tears, wear, grime on paper)....... 28

Coaster, "A-1 Pilsner Beer," tin, round tip-tray form, red outer rim w/white center marked "A-1 (below motif of eagle) Pilsner Beer Thank You," 3 1/2" d...................... 33

Coaster, "Valley Forge Special Beer," lithographed tin, round, tip tray-form, bottle in center flanked by "Valley Forge Special Beer" & "A Beer for Unsurpassed Quality" w/"Bottled Only at the Brewery" below, black, yellow & red, Adam Scheidt Brewing Co., Norristown, Pennsylvania, ca. 1954, wrapped in original paper, 4" d. 94

Dart board, "Pabst Blue Ribbon," Masonite printed in color, square, cartoon caricatures of Hitler & Tojo in upper corners, the remainder of the board printed in color w/a deck of playing cards laid out in rows, "Pabst Blue Ribbon" banner across the top, blue borders w/white printing including "Poker - Black Jack" at the bottom, made w/dart holes, 1940s, 18" sq. (some soiling & water stains, dinged corners)............. 58

Budweiser Fairy Lamp by Fenton

Hamm's Beer Bear Decanter

Decanter w/stopper, "Hamm's Beer," ceramic figural Hamm's bear in black & white, colored Hamm's label at front, head forms stopper, like new, 1972 (ILLUS.) **37**

Display mug, "Consumer Brewing Company," w/reverse on glass trademark of man holding American flag amid a variety of Consumer Brewing products, 10" h. (some paint loss & cracking in label, rim chips) **690**

Fairy lamp, "Budweiser," creamy frosted glass shade w/transfer decoration of the Budweiser team of horses pulling a wagon, cupped matching footed base w/scalloped rim, Fenton (ILLUS.) **110**

Foam scraper holder, "Ballantine Ale - Beer," plastic, a cylindrical tumbler above a flaring short conical base printed w/wording, 1950s, 7" h. (overall light scuffs & scratches, mostly on tumbler) **29**

Silver Spring Brewery Barrel End Label

Label, "Silver Spring Brewery," paper barrel end label, round w/center image of uniformed fireman holding glass below "The Life Saver," in white letters, blue border w/red letters reading "Silver Spring Brewery Ltd - Victoria, B.C.," yellow oval at each side reading "6 Doz." & "Quarts," framed under glass, ca. early 1900s, minor wrinkles, 13 x 16" (ILLUS.) **99**

Letterhead, "Lebanon Valley Brewing Company," 1945, one sheet (creases, staple holes) **10**

Letterhead, "Terre Haute Brewing Co.," letter dated 1906, one sheet (creases, staple holes) **20**

Mug, "Budweiser," ceramic, color logo of the "Budman" w/"Hero No. 1" below, white ground (ILLUS. third from left, top photo, page 39) **50**

Stegmaier's Beer Door Push Sign

Door push, "Stegmaier's Beer," long rectangular lithographed tin, gold ground w/a large grey shield at the top printed in white & black "We Serve Stegmaier's Gold Medal Beer," a bottle & can of the beer in color at the bottom, appears unused, minor face dirt, hole scratched, 3 1/2 x 8" (ILLUS.) **94**

Various Newer Budweiser Mugs

Various Budweiser Mugs

Mug, "Budweiser," ceramic, figural commemorative w/gold Budweiser logo &
"New Hampshire" (ILLUS. far left, top
photo).. 46

Mug, "Budweiser," ceramic, footed tapering
cylindrical form, view of the Brew House
above "Budweiser" in red, gold band trim
(ILLUS. far right, top photo) 33

Mug, "Budweiser," ceramic, slender tapering cylindrical shape, color printed Clydesdales & wagon design, Ceramarte
CS12 (ILLUS. far left, second photo) 176

Mug, "Budweiser," ceramic, tapering cylindrical shape, color printed Clydesdales &
wagon design, made in U.S.A. (ILLUS.
second from left, second photo) 36

Mug, "Budweiser," ceramic, tapering cylindrical shape, color printed Clydesdales &
wagon design, made in U.S.A. (ILLUS.
third from left, second photo) 36

Mug, "Budweiser," ceramic, tapering cylindrical shape, color printed Clydesdales &
wagon design, made in U.S.A. (ILLUS.
far right, second photo)..................................... 36

Mug, "Budweiser," pottery, Budweiser series, Bud Girl, purple dress, no filigree,
CS20 (ILLUS. second from left) **650**

Mug, "Budweiser," pottery, cylindrical
shape, Budweiser "Wurzburger" label
model, CS39 (ILLUS. far right) **363**

Mug, "Budweiser," pottery, "Grant's Farm,"
cylindrical shape, green ground
decorated w/scene of brown & white
horses & green trees in background,
CS15 (ILLUS. right)... **294**

"Grant's Farm" Mugs

Mug, "Budweiser," pottery, "Grant's Farm,"
wide cylindrical shape, tan & brown decorated w/colorful scene of brown & white
horses & green trees in background,
CS15, small (ILLUS. left) **340**

Mug, "Budweiser," pottery, "Label" model,
CS18 (ILLUS. far left w/series mugs) **605**

Budweiser Mugs

Mug, "Budweiser," pottery, Budweiser series, Bud Girl, blue dress, w/filigree,
CS20 (ILLUS. second from right) **457**

Budweiser Mugs & Stein

Pre-prohibition Mugs

Miniature German Pilique Mug

Mug, "Budweiser," pottery, miniature German Pilique-style, tapering cylindrical form w/molded narrow bands around the top & base, in tan & brown, decorated w/tavern scene on dark blue background, CS5 (ILLUS.) **402**

Mug, "Budweiser," pottery, slightly tapering cylindrical shape w/molded narrow bands around the top & base in tan & brown, "Grant's Cabin" w/horses in foreground, CS83 (ILLUS. second from right, top photo) **65**

Mug, "Budweiser," pottery, tapering cylindrical shape w/colorful castle scene & "Oktoberfest" & "The Old Country" in red, CS42-variation (ILLUS. far left, top photo) **330**

Mug, "Busch Bavarian Beer," pottery, Budweiser, name & eagle logo in blue, CS44-variation (ILLUS. second from left, top photo) **295**

Mug, "Kuebeler-Stang Brewing Co., Sandusky, O," pottery, footed cylindrical shape w/shield decoration above name & "We use crystal rock spring water," Sandusky, Ohio (ILLUS. second from left w/pre-prohibition mugs, second photo) **220**

Mug, "Original Fabacher's," pottery, barrel-shaped w/name & grain sheaf, New Orleans, Louisiana (ILLUS. far left, second photo) **110**

Mug, "Rochester Brew. Co.," pottery, barrel-shaped, w/narrow blue bands above & below name & "Rochester, N. Y." (ILLUS. second from right, second photo) **87**

Mug, "Stroh's Beer," bulbous barrel-shaped w/name above logo, Detroit, Michigan (ILLUS. far right, second photo) **152**

Two Wurzburger Beer Mugs

Mug, "Wurzburger Hofbrau," miniature, ceramic, Budweiser product, label in green, black & yellow (ILLUS. left) 17
Mug, "Wurzburger Light Beer," miniature, ceramic, Budweiser product, label in dark blue (ILLUS. right) 61
Mugs, "Budweiser," ceramic, stacked cylindrical mugs w/embossed logo on top one & embossed wording on lower one reading "Pick A Pair of 6-Paks - Buy Bud," tan glaze, pr. (ILLUS. second from left w/newer mugs, top photo on page 39) 52

Centlivre's Nickel Plate Beer Poster

Poster, "Centlivre's Nickel Plate Beer," rectangular, color lithograph scene of railcar interior, man & woman seated at table w/glasses & bottles, waiter standing nearby, white border reads "Centlivre's Nickel Plate Bottled Beer - Manufactured By C. L. Centlivre Brewing Co. - Fort Wayne, Ind.," image of bottle in lower right corner, oak frame, 26 3/4 x 31" (ILLUS.) 440
Print, "Westward Ho," lithographed paper by Oscar Berninghaus for Anheuser Busch, colorful scene of wagon trains, matted & framed, 13 x 21" 99
Promotional set, "Piel's Light Beer," boxed, three compartments, two holding six round coasters & center one w/a metal bottle opener, 1940s, the set (overall light wear & slight yellowing) 6

Brewers Association Pin

Pin, "United States Brewers Association (1897)," convention souvenir w/embossed buffalo head in center, surrounded by enamel work & set stones, suspended from a scrolled bar pin inscribed "1897," Heintz Bros., Buffalo, New York, 1 1/2" l. (ILLUS.) 110

Hamm's Beer Bear Radio

Radio, "Hamm's Beer," stuffed cloth Hamm's bear in black & white w/red tongue, Hamm's cloth label on his chest, radio inside works, 16" h. (ILLUS.) 60

Salinas Brewing Company Plate

Plate, "Salinas Brewing Company," ceramic, round plate w/tightly scalloped rim, center printed w/a brown & white horse head against a white ground bordered in dark brown, made by the Sterling China Company for a California company, dated 1904, 9" d. (ILLUS.) 55

Iroquois Beer Sign

Schlitz Globe Radio

Radio, "Schlitz," modeled as a globe, plastic & metal, w/"Schlitz" on circular band, switch is dirty, battery compartment at mounting hole is broken, not working, 5 1/2" d., 8" h. (ILLUS.) **44**

Sign, "Iroquois," porcelain, self-framed, curved corner depicts trademark Iroquois Indian, some chipping in frame around border & where bracket is attached to sign, 16 1/4 x 24" (ILLUS.) **2,300**

Sign, "Grain Belt," center of cardboard sign depicts dog having just retrieved a duck, border of various firearms & game, artist-signed, ca. 1947, Inland Lithography Company, 23 1/2 x 27" (overall soiling, scratching w/chipping & tearing around border) **230**

Sign, "Kamm & Schellinger Brewing Company," paper, depicts company logo of lion climbing atop the world, wood frame, 29" w., 38 1/2" h. to outside of frame (some staining, tearing & paper loss around edges, minor crease near lion's mane) **403**

Schlitz Salt & Pepper Shakers

Salt & pepper shakers, "Schlitz," miniature bottle-shaped, plastic w/plastic lids, 4" h., pr. (ILLUS.) **15**

Sign, "Drewry's," self-framed tin over cardboard, entitled "The Thrill of a Lifetime," depicting frontiersman & Mountie shooting the rapids w/beer-laden canoe while trying to avoid a cougar ready to attack a porcupine, Drewry's logo on sides of canoe, artist-signed, American Art Works lithography, 17 x 23" (some minor inpainting, overall spotting & soiling) **460**

National Brewing Co. Stamp Holder

Stamp holder, "National Brewing Co., San Francisco, Cal.," flat celluloid sleeve printed in blue w/a racing cowboy holding up a bottle of beer, red lettering, top reads "The Best in the West," 1 1/2 x 2 1/2" (ILLUS.) **110**

Various Busch Gardens Steins

Stein, "Bud Natural Light," miniature pottery, white ground w/blue, red, gold & white logo label (ILLUS. right) **180**

Two Miniature Pottery Steins

Stein, "Busch," miniature pottery, white ground w/blue, gold & white Busch mountain logo label (ILLUS. left) **180**

Stein, pottery, blue & white relief-molded Balmoral Castle, Busch Gardens (ILLUS. far left, top photo) **176**

Stein, pottery, cylindrical w/slightly domed hinged metal lid, "Bald Eagle," CS106 (ILLUS. far right w/Budweiser mugs, top photo on page 40) **375**

Stein, pottery w/colorful scene of wild animals & reads "Busch Gardens, 1st Extinction is Forever" (ILLUS. far right, top photo) **85**

Stein, pottery, white & blue, reads "Busch Gardens, Tampa/Williamsburg/Los Angeles" & decoration of amusement park ride (ILLUS. second from right, top photo) **55**

Stein, pottery, white w/blue geometric design border & blue wording "Busch Gardens, Los Angeles, Tampa" (ILLUS. second from left, top photo) **134**

Altes Lager & Arrow Beer Knobs

Tap knob, "Altes Lager," plastic w/enamel insert, green w/dark green & white insert, 1950s (ILLUS. left, above) **66**

Tap knob, "Arrow Beer," chrome w/printed enamel insert, red & white insert, 1930s, small hairline in insert, bubbles in chrome (ILLUS. right, above) **35**

Tap knob, "English Lad," black Bakelite w/enamel insert, 1930s (minor wear & scratches) **437**

McCoy & Michelob Beer Tap Knobs

Tap knob, "McCoy Beer," chrome w/enamel insert, insert w/red & black wording on white, reads "It's the real McCoy," light wear, 1940s (ILLUS. left, top photo)............. **110**

Tap knob, "Michelob Beer," Bakelite w/enamel insert, black knob w/red insert w/center gold band w/"Michelob" in white, 1940s, wear, small chips to rim (ILLUS. right, top photo) **60**

P.O.C. & Pabst Beer Tap Knobs

Tap knob, "P.O.C. Beer," Bakelite w/printed metal insert, black knob w/white insert & red wording, 1940s, small spots on insert, wear (ILLUS. left).................... **100**

Tap knob, "Pabst Breweries," chrome w/enamel insert, red, white & blue insert w/blue maple leaf & "B" in center surrounded by "Pabst Breweries," 1930s, light wear (ILLUS. right).................... **28**

Tap knob, "Rainier," black Bakelite w/a white enamel disk w/red wording, 1940s (few small cracks in white) **140**

Tap knob, "(Star) Pilsener Special," chrome w/red, white & blue enamel insert w/a blue star & red & blue wording, overall light scratches, few small rim dings, Star Union Company, Peru, Illinois. ca. 1940s (ILLUS. right with Walter's knob)................... **155**

Walter's and Star Pilsener Tap Knobs

Tap knob, "Walter's Pilsener Beer," black Bakelite w/red & white enamel insert, lists both Wisconsin & Colorado breweries, minor wear, few small spots on face, 1940s (ILLUS. left) **147**

Old Ranger Thermometer

Thermometer, "Old Ranger Beer and Ale - Hornell Brewing Co., Inc., Hornell N.Y.," metal w/glass front, center w/hunter holding rifle, soiling & minor rust spotting, 10" d. (ILLUS.) **55**

Toy, "Budweiser Beer," HO scale railroad reefer car, plastic, applied weathering, 1970s (some wear to print) **27**

Toy, "Coors Beer," HO scale railroad reefer car, plastic, 1970s.. **21**

Chapter 3
Calendars

Airline, 1953, "TWA Airline," rectangular, six double-sided pages, each w/a different month & picture from around the world (minor edge & surface wear, light rolls at top) **$33**

Winchester Ammunition Calendar

Ammunition, 1899, "Winchester Ammunition," lithographed rectangular form w/a large color top scene of hunters in a rocky winter setting w/a large bear in the distance, a bottom color scene of a hunter & dogs in an open field, partial date pad, some creases, 14 1/4 x 27" (ILLUS.) **1,650**
Ammunition, 1900, "DuPont," battle scene of Santiago, Cuba, full pad, matted & framed, 14 x 28" **495**
Ammunition, 1900, "DuPont," tall narrow rectangular form w/a large upper color scene of a naval battle viewed from a battleship, full date pad at bottom, minor creases, minor stain at bottom left, both bands, 14 x 28 1/4" **358**

1913 Selby Calendar

Ammunition, 1913, "Selby Loads," colorful scene w/California quail by Edward Wilson Currier, Olsen Litho Co., S.F., December page only, complete bands top & bottom w/minor cracks from rolling, 21 x 27 1/2" (ILLUS.) **4,455**
Automobile, 1920, "Chevrolet Motor Cars," green w/white lettering & lined border, farm scene w/car & family above, full pad, 16 x 31" **145**

Bemis Bros. Bag Co. Calendar

Bags, 1903, "Bemis Bros. Bag Co.," rectangular, lithographed cloth, red w/white & yellow lettering, center w/white circle depicting head of a buffalo in black & white & surrounded by a circle of white dots, flanked by torches above bags & marked above "Animals that Are Hunted," Bemis Bros. Bag Co., St. Louis, Missouri, each page features different animal & colors, ca. 1903, 11 x 16" (ILLUS.) **450-650**

Baking company, 1911, "Collins Baking Co.," child on edges, full pad **130**

First National Bank Advertising Calendar

Bank, 1899, "First National Bank," pictures sailing ship, 'First National Bank, Moravia, NY' in red, full pad (ILLUS.) **230**

Biscuits, 1922, "Sunshine Biscuits," girl in yellow & pink gown w/brown stole ready for an evening out, June sheet, worn, 9 x 15".. **50**

Bottling company, 1895, "Edward Heuer Bottler," waitress beside large bottle surrounded by flowers, full pad, matted & framed, image 12 x 19".................................... **975**

Bread, 1909, "Collins Celebrated Bread," diagonal version w/product name above girl in bonnet w/holly leaves, full pad, 8 x 8"... **25**

Bread, 1918, "James V. Cardi Italo - American Bread Co.," features bakery w/baker serving customers, full pad, 15 x 21 1/2"....... **75**

Brewing company, 1895, "Consumers Brewing Co.," elegant woman in blue dress & hat, full pad, framed, image 14 1/2 x 19" (water staining & soiling) **400**

Brewing company, 1896, "F.L. Ober Brewing Co.," die-cut, dog holding monthly calendar sheets in front of palm trees, framed, image 9 1/2 x 17" **350**

Brewing company, 1897, "Lorenz Schmidts' Estate Mt. Carbon Brewery," paper, girl w/dog at her feet, December sheet only, framed, image 15 x 19 1/2" **350**

Brewing company, 1898, "F.A. Poth & Son Brewers," paper, hunter & dog pausing to look at billboard, full calendar, framed, image 20 1/2 x 30".................................... **800**

Brewing company, 1898, "Louis Bergdoll Brewing Co.," Bavarian couple on royal carpet flanked by men w/flagons, full pad, framed, image 20 x 27"..................... **1,000**

Brewing company, 1898, "Oriental Brewery," boating scene w/logo & lettering above, framed, image 19 1/2 x 27 1/2" (minor creases) **1,100**

Brewing company, 1898, "Prospect Brewing Co.," inset of three children w/floral border, framed, image 16 x 20 1/2" (minor creasing & soiling) **1,100**

Brewing company, 1899, "Geo. Ringler & Co. Brewers," paper, girl wrapping herself in American flag, 12 calendar sheets below, framed, image 16 x 24".................. **2,500**

Brewing company, 1899, "John Kress Brewing Co.," U.S. fleet leaving for war in shield w/eagle atop, framed w/metal strips, full pad, 30 x 32" **700**

Brewing company, 1899, "Keystone Brewery," barmaid enticing fellow w/beer, Otto Eyring above, February pad, framed, image 15 1/2 x 30".. **900**

Brewing company, 1899, "Lauer Brewing Co.," paper, girl w/upheld tray serving drinks to three men, full pad, framed, image 17 x 22 1/2".. **900**

Brewing company, 1899, "Muhlenberg Brewing Co.," paper, girl presenting seasons greetings, Lager Beer & Porter, April pad, framed, image 15 x 19"............... **900**

Brewing company, 1900, "Jno C. Stocker Brewer," girl behind fence surrounded by knotted rope, September sheet, framed, image 16 x 22" **750**

Brewing company, 1901, "Olympia Beer," six individually matted cards picturing women surrounded by flowers, framed, image 10 x 13" **500**

Brewing company, 1902, "Berdoll's Beer," elderly man & woman w/glass of beer, circular logo in upper corners, framed, image 16 1/2 x 22".. **400**

Brewing company, 1903, "John C. Stocker Brewer," elegant woman seated in ornate gold chair, February sheet, framed, image 14 1/2 x 19"... **550**

Brewing company, 1903, "Pabst Extract," paper, babies from all nations holding calendar sheets, stork at bottom, framed, image 11 x 28" **375**

Brewing company, 1903, "Weisbrod & Hess Brewery," vignettes of parks, seashore scenes, display of products, etc., full pad, framed, image 20 x 28" **1,050**

Brewing company, 1904, "David Stevenson Brewing Co.," Uncle Sam toasting residents of New York above factory inset, framed, image 19 1/2 x 28" **2,300**

Brewing company, 1905, "Lauer Brewing Co.," factory scene above insert of Porter's Lake Hunting & Fishing Club, framed, image 19 1/2 x 27 1/2" **650**

Brewing company, 1906, "Grand Rapids Brewing Co.," paper, little girl in red shawl & bonnet w/open book, pad missing, framed, image 9 1/2 x 14 1/2"...................... **550**

Brewing company, 1907, "Adam Scheidt Brewing Co.," man standing beside two women in sailor attire, floral border, full pad, framed, 21 x 29 1/2" **600**

Brewing company, 1907, "Hudson County Consumers Brewing Co.," pictures factory scene surrounded by hops & wheat, logo upper right, framed, image 12 x 17" (pad missing)...................................... **900**

Brewing company, 1907, "Mathie Brewing Co.," die-cut cardboard, cherub & flowered beauty in gondola, full pad, framed, 14 1/2 x 15 1/2".............................. **1,300**

Brewing company, 1907, "P Barbey & Son Brewers," cardboard, oval image of girl in fur-trimmed jacket flanked by logo, May pad, framed, 19 1/2 x 24" **975**

Brewing company, 1907, "West End Brewing Co.," paper, girl at table sampling brew w/factory out window, full pad, framed, image 16 x 23 1/2" **600**

Brewing company, 1908, "Adloff & Hauerwaas Breweries," die-cut cardboard, fishing scene w/brewery inset below, full pad, matted & framed, image 13 x 20"...... **1,250**

Brewing company, 1908, "Ballantine's Breweries," cardboard, brewery inset at top, decorative border, December sheet framed, image 12 1/2 x 20" **320**

Brewing company, 1908, "David Stevenson Brewing Co.," Uncle Sam toasting residents of New York above factory inset, framed, image 19 1/2 x 28" **2,300**

Brewing company, 1908, "Lion Brewery," lion w/front paws on barrel surrounded by factory insets, no pad, framed, image 13 x 16 1/2".. **220**

Brewing company, 1909, "Geo. Zett Brewery," embossed die-cut cardboard, two children in hay surrounded by puppies, framed, 20 x 20".................................... **1,000**

Brewing company, 1910, "E. Robinson's Sons Pilsener," oval image of girl w/roses above product & factory insets, matted & framed, image 11 x 22"...................... **350**

Brewing company, 1910, "E. Robinson's Sons Pilsner," oval image of girl w/roses above product & factory insets, matted & framed, image 11 x 22"...................... **350**

Brewing company, 1910, "Independent Brewing Co.," paper, girl in elegant dress & bonnet holding basket of flowers, framed, image 14 1/2 x 19 1/2" **475**

Brewing company, 1912, "Lykens Brewing Co.," mother & child w/dog walking across creek on a board, full pad, framed, image 16 1/2 x 23"............................ **300**

Brewing company, 1912, "Penn Beer," paper, girl in green & black outfit & hat, Consumers Brewing Co., full pad, framed, image 16 x 31" **400**

Brewing company, 1913, "Ebling Brewing Co.," paper, factory scene w/casino & restaurant in foreground, full pad, framed, image 21 x 28 1/2".......................... **500**

Brewing company, 1913, "Ebling Brewing Co.," paper, factory scene w/casino & restaurant in foreground, full pad, framed image 21 x 28 1/2".. **500**

Brewing company, 1913, "Lykens Brewing Co.," paper, baby walking to mom & dad on table, full pad, matted & framed, image 16 x 18" **115**

Brewing company, 1914, "Rieger & Gretz Brewing Co.," bust-length portrait of a girl in wide-brimmed hat, logo upper left, full pad, framed, 16 1/2 x 22"...................... **450**

Brewing company, 1915, "Bernheimer & Schwartz Pilsner Brewing Co.," large brewery image, lettering above, full pad, framed, image 20 1/2 x 29".......................... **800**

Brewing company, 1915, "Crown Beer," paper roll-down, girl holding rose, crown logo in each corner, full pad, 10 x 34".......... **305**

Brewing company, 1916, "Geo. Ringler & Co. Brewers," factory image w/bottle insets below, store inset above, March pad, framed, image 13 1/2 x 19".................. **650**

Brewing company, 1928, "Iroquois Brewery," profile of young Native American squaw w/feathers & beads in her hair, full pad, framed, image 13 1/4 x 27 1/2" **850**

Brewing company, 1935, "Royal Style Ale," Indian princess picking water lilies, Globe Brewing Co., full pad, framed, image 14 x 28"...................................... **425**

Brewing company, 1947, "Jno C. Stocker Brewer," girl behind fence surrounded by knotted rope, September sheet, framed, image 16 x 22" **750**

1891 Gus Becht Butchers Supply Calendar

Butchers supply, 1891, "Gus Becht Butchers Supply - St. Louis," bright colored graphic of bull's head, full calendar pad, litho by Gast, St. Louis & New York, unused condition, framed, 10 x 14" (ILLUS.) **1,045**

Candy, 1909, "New England Confectionery (Necco)," three-section die-cut cardboard fold-out, chromolithographed scene of children in Colonial costume **85**

Candy, 1911, "Orange Candy Kitchen," die-cut cardboard, little boy playing violin while kittens play, matted & framed, 15 x 19" **100**

Candy, 1917, "Hall's Chocolates," paper, "Hall's Chocolates Tease the Taste" above a colorful scene of a man seated & writing at a table w/a plate of chocolates nearby, a young woman leaning over his shoulder, calendar pad December only, signed, newer frame, 16 3/4" w., 30" h. (soiling & scuffs along right side) **121**

Candy & grocery store, 1925, "Sherwood's Confectionary and Grocery," rectangular aluminum mount w/a printed label w/a black & white scene of American Indians on horseback titled "The Buffalo Hunt," partial date pad across the bottom, 7 x 9 1/2" **110**

"Squeezers" Playing Cards Calendar

Card company, 1899, "Consolidated Card Co.," die-cut cardboard, depicting a clown holding fanned-out playing cards marked "Squeezers" w/"The N.Y. Consolidated Card Co. - 222 to 228 West 16th St. New York - Sole Owners & Makers of 'Squeezer Playing Cards'" marked on lower body, foldout marked "The N.Y. Consolidated Card Co's. Playing Cards - 1899 - Playing Card Novelties" measures 5 1/2 x 6" (ILLUS.) **413**

Rare & Early U.M.C. Calendar

Cartridges, 1894, "Union Metallic Cartridge Co. (The)," long rectangular form w/color scene of a mother hunting dog & her pups w/an open package of the cartridges, partial date pad, excellent condition, 14 x 28 1/4" (ILLUS.) **5,005**

Cartridges, 1895, "Winchester Cartridges," large rectangular form w/an upper color scene of two hunters in a winter landscape beside a dead bear, the small date pad in the center above a small landscape of hunters at a rocky lake shore, partial date pad, based on artwork by A.B. Frost, 14 1/4 x 26 1/2" (both bands pinned to matte board, tack holes, missing piece, small tears) **935**

Cartridges, 1898, "The Union Metallic Cartridge Co.," paper, depicts Molly Pitcher priming cannon during Revolutionary War, entitled "Molly Pitcher at Monmouth June 28 - 1778" by "The Knapp Co. Litho.," original metal bands on top & bottom, 22" w., 34" h. (minor creasing & chipping to outer edges) **2,875**

Cartridges, 1917, "Peters," a tall rectangular format w/most of the page decorated w/a color scene of two hunting dogs in a field of corn shocks, small partial date pad at the bottom flanked by panels of advertising, based on artwork by G. Muss Arnolt, professionally mounted & framed, wrinkles from being rolled up, 13 5/8 x 27 1/8" **550**

Cartridges, 1922, "U.S. Cartridges," a tall narrow form w/a very long upper color picture of a standing, growling brown bear holding a crate of the product in a snowy landscape, only January date page, wrinkles due to rolling up, few splits, top band glued to mat board top & bottom, 15 x 35 1/2" **468**

Cartridges, 1929, "Western Cartridge Co.," pointer sitting in chair, original mailing promo price still attached, full pad, 14 x 27" **600**

Cartridges, 1931, "U.S. Shot-Shells & Cartridges," titled "Opportunity," man beside dog w/dead game, full pad, framed, 16 x 31 1/2".. **650**

Chicken feed, 1920, "Globe Feeds," pictures children & chicks, full pad..................... **110**

Clothing store, 1919 "Browning, King & Co.," celluloid pocket-type, center oval depicts small nude baby flanked by a man in a soldier's uniform & one in sailor's uniform, marked at the top "'I Want My Clothes' And It's Gotta Be A Uniform'," the bottom marked "Browning, King Co. - A National Institution," 2 1/4 x 3 3/4" **55**

Libby, McNeil & Libby
Corned Beef Calendar

Cream separator, 1908, "DeLaval Cream Separators," oval image of girl & cow, yellow lettering above, calendar never opened, framed, 17 1/2 x 24 1/2".................. **650**

1909 Bennett & Hall Calendar

Commission merchants, 1909, "Bennet & Hall, Commission Merchants," color lithographed paper, a rectangular sheet w/advertising at top on a dark blue ground above a keyhole reserve w/the bust portrait of a smiling dark-haired young girl below an arch of large pink & red roses, small pad at the bottom, January-May sheets missing, soiling, 12 x 18 1/4" (ILLUS.)..................................... **100**

Corned beef, 1905, "Libby, McNeil & Libby Corned Beef," little girl in front of pink flowers, corned beef can beside calendar below, 11 x 16 1/2" (ILLUS.) **45**

United States Cream Separator
Advertising Calendar

Cream separator, 1910, "United States Cream Separator," girl in profile w/cows beyond, Vermont Farmer Machine Co. below, March/April pad, framed 20 x 30" (ILLUS.) **200**

Cream separator, 1915, "DeLaval Cream Separators," product name above boy giving calf pan of milk, scrolled courtesy panel below, full pad **1,500**

Cream separator, 1918, "DeLaval Cream Separator," paper lithograph shows woman standing w/horse, full pad, framed under glass, 17 1/2" h. (minor stains & tears) **550**

Cream separator, 1918, "DeLaval Cream Separators," product name above girl standing w/horse, courtesy panel at right, full pad, framed 12 x 24"............................... **695**

Cream separator, 1920, "Sharples Separator," tall rectangular form w/a large color top picture of a young girl giving her little brother a drink from a pot, their mother in the background walking into a porch w/the separator, complete calendar pad, top band, 12 x 22" (minor tears & creases in upper right)............................ **237**

Cream separator, 1941, "DeLaval Cream Separators," four-section, color scene of Native American in a canoe by R. Ewell **165**

1916 DeLaval Calendar

Cream separators, 1916, "DeLaval Cream Separators," color lithographed paper, a long rectangular scene w/advertising across the top above an indoor view of a young girl seated on a crate w/a young boy holding a bouquet of wild flowers, calendar at the bottom, full pad, edge tear at top & bottom, wrinkles, 12 x 24 1/2" (ILLUS.) **303**

Farm equipment, 1908, "Deering Harvesting Machines," shows hunter & two bird dogs, 1908 stamped over two rows of six months each at bottom, no pad...................... **160**

Farm equipment, 1910, "Osborne Harvesting," paper lithograph showing woman standing by grazing horse, framed under glass, image 15 1/2" h. (minor creases) **400**

Farm equipment, 1913, "Deering," paper lithograph of boys playing baseball, matted & framed, 19" h. (minor creases & stains).. **2,300**

1944 John Deere Calendar

Farm equipment, 1944, "John Deere," color-printed paper, a rectangular scene at the top of a young boy & girl standing in front of a John Deere dealer's storefront, name & locale of business below picture w/calendar pad at bottom, soiling, bent corners, 10 3/4 x 16" (ILLUS.)......................... **66**

Farm equipment, 1955, "John Deere," wildlife book, full pad... **25-35**

Listers Animal Bone Fertilizers Calendar

Fertilizer, 1898, "Listers Animal Bone Fertilizers," Dutch farm scene, full pad,
framed, 18 1/2 x 29" (ILLUS.) 175
Fertilizer, 1906, "Frank Coe's Fertilizer
Co.," pictures three lads at field's edge
w/plow & fence, full pad, 9 x 13" 35
Fertilizer, 1908, "Parmenter & Polsey Fertilizer Co.," paper, bust-portrait of elegant
girl in oval surrounded by fancy border,
full pad, 13 1/2 x 21" 375
Fertilizer, 1914, "Lowell Fertilizer Co.," pa-
per, girl seated in profile w/bouquet of
roses, full pad, framed, image
14 1/2 x 21 1/2" 95
Fertilizer, 1914, "New England Fertilizer
Co.," paper, girl seated in window sill
w/flowers in background, full pad,
framed, image 15 x 23" 75
Fertilizer, 1949, "Royster Fertilizers," baby
girl w/segmented wooden doll,
"Charlotte Becker," full pad, 4 3/4 x 8" 16
Firearms, 1907, "Harrington & Richardson
Arms Co.," wintry scene w/running
mountain man, full pad, framed, 14 x 27" .. 2,000

Winchester 1914 Calendar

Firearms, 1914, "Winchester," large rectangular color image of a hunter & dogs stalking through an autumn field of corn shocks
at sunset, full date pad, dry-mounted,
bands missing, 15 1/4 x 30 1/4" (ILLUS.) 528

1913 Winchester Calendar

Firearms, 1913, "Winchester," half-length
portrait of bearded hunter w/gun on
shoulder, by noted artist Robert Robinson, bands top & bottom, November
page only, American Litho, New York,
dry-mounted, few wrinkles (ILLUS.) 935

Stunning 1915 Winchester Calendar

Firearms, 1915, "Winchester," tall rectangular form w/large color image at the top
showing a large condor-like bird attack-
ing a white mountain goat, brand in large

red letter at bottom above the partial date pad, picture based on artwork of Lynn Bogue Hunt, bands pinned to mat, roll creases, 15 1/4 x 30 1/4" (ILLUS.) **1,155**

Winchester 1916 Calendar

Firearms, 1916, "Winchester Guns and Cartridges," rectangular, colorful scene of two men w/a dog climbing a rocky hillside trail (ILLUS.) **1,925**

Dramatic 1923 Winchester Calendar

Firearms, 1923, "Winchester" tall rectangular form, a tall full-color picture at the top w/a brand in red above a panoramic mountainous landscape w/a hunter perched high on a craggy rock, based on artwork by Phillip R. Goodwin, a large partial date pad at the bottom, top band pinned to mat board, a minute pin hole, 13 3/4 x 25 5/8" (ILLUS.) **990**

1927 Remington Calendar

Firearms, 1927, "Remington," showing older gentleman cleaning gun, seated before fireplace w/a dog sitting on a rug near his master, by Henry Watson, 14 calendar pages, top 2" glued to mat board, 15 x 27" (ILLUS.) **660**

Firearms, 1979, "Ruger Firearms," 30th Anniversary, scene of hunting moose in a canoe, full pad **65**

Fishing rods, 1918, "Bristol Fishing Rods," paper, depicts fishing scene w/lady catching fish, signed by artist Philip R. Goodwin, lithographer "Horton Mfg. Co.," original metal rims at top & bottom, 22" w., 37 1/2" h. **3,450**

Tyee Tackle 1928 Calendar

Fishing tackle, 1928, "Tyee Tackle," rectangular, printed in color w/a large image of a pretty lady getting ready to fish standing on the right, landscape in background, small dated pad in lower left corner, includes a 1927 California game laws booklet w/same advertising, calendar 12 x 16 1/2", 2 pcs. (ILLUS. of calendar)... **605**

Gasoline, 1929 "Socony Gasoline," partial pad, 13 1/4 x 26 1/2" (cleaned & repaired) **425**

Sinclair Gasoline Calendar

Gasoline, 1946, "Sinclair Gasoline," full pad, image of beautiful girl w/jump rope wearing purple shorts, yellow sweater & red head scarf, titled "A Jump Ahead!" by Earl Moran, minor rolls, 16 x 33 1/2" (ILLUS.) **110**

Gasoline, 1947, "Gilmore Gasoline," red lion logo, 7 x 17" **19**

Glass company, 1920, "Glenshaw Glass Co.," scene of woman sitting by water w/note in her lap, reads "Glenshaw Glass Co., Inc., Glenshaw, Pennsylvania Manufacturers of Flint, Green and Amber Bottles," picture titled "From Over There," 17" w., 32" h. (minor deterioration) **83**

Hazard Smokeless Powder Calendar

Gunpowder, 1903, "Hazard Smokeless Powder - The Trophy Winner," color

scene at the top w/a dog & youth walking home w/his rifle & dead game, titled "Return of the Hunters," dark grey ground w/gold & white wording, partial date pad, some scuffs around edges, 3 1/2 x 6 1/4" (ILLUS.)... **495**

Early DuPont Powder Calendar

Gunpowder, 1904, "DuPont Powder Co.," a large color image at the top of a group of hunters waiting on a railroad depot platform w/a young black boy holding the collar of one of the hunting dogs, deep maroon background w/"DuPont" in large gold letters, partial calendar pad at bottom (ILLUS.)... **3,080**

Gunpowder, 1938, "Hercules Powder Company," tall narrow rectangular form, a long color scene at the top showing interior of medieval chemist's shop w/a young pretty female alchemist kissing the forehead of a handsome young man in front of an open window, titled "The Alchemist," based on art by N.C. Wyeth, partial date pad, minor cracks from being rolled up, bright colors, 11 3/4 x 30 1/2" **77**

1940 Hercules Powder Calendar

Gunpowder, 1940, "Hercules Powder Co.," color lithographed paper, scene of young family in covered wagon, picture titled "Pioneers," copyright Hercules Powder Co. Inc. 1939, Litho in U.S.A., unused, minor creases & soiling, 14 1/2" w., 31 1/2" h. (ILLUS.) **358**

1950 Hair Dressing Calendar

Hair dressing, 1950, "Pinol Tar-mange Shampoo - Southern Rose Hair Dressing," tall rectangular form w/a large color picture at the top showing a young fisherman standing in a stream & holding up a net w/a large fish, a scowling young woman w/fishing rod standing beside him in the water, scene titled "Happy Ending," based on artwork by J.F. Kernan, advertising section below w/small date pad flanked by color images of the products, 17 x 35" (ILLUS.) **121**

1891 Simmons Hardware Calendar

Hardware, 1891, "Simmons Hardware Co., " rectangular, cardboard w/paper pad, wood frame, portrait of young woman w/"Simmons Hardware Co. - St. Louis,

Mo. - J.I.C. Horse Nails - Finished and Pointed and Made From Best Norway Fillets," 13 x 16 1/2" (ILLUS.) **225-325**

Insurance, 1891, "Aetna Insurance Co.," port scene w/mountain beyond, full pad, matted & framed, image 6 1/2 x 9 1/2" (glass cracked) **25**

Insurance, 1893, "John Hancock Insurance," horse-drawn carriage w/building beyond, full calendar, matted & framed, image 12 1/2 x 16" **45**

Insurance, 1893, "Prudential Insurance Co.," round w/girl holding insurance policy surrounded by months of the year, 9" d. **75**

Insurance, 1894, "Prudential Life Insurance Co.," April, May & June sheet on the diagonal shows girl w/hand at mouth & halo of flowers, 6 x 6" **45**

Insurance, 1894, "Prudential Life Insurance Co.," July, August & September sheet on the diagonal showing boy in billed cap, 6 x 6" **40**

Insurance, 1900, "United States Fidelity Guaranty Co.," cardboard, shield-shaped, children in uniform & portrait inserts, April pad, framed, image 16 x 20" **300**

Insurance, 1902, "John Hancock Life Insurance Co.," company name & year above girl asleep beside large dog, two rows of months below, 8 1/2 x 10 1/2" **185**

Insurance, 1906, "Connecticut General Fire Insurance Co.," general on horseback carrying document, full pad, matted & framed, 13 1/2 x 19 1/2" (stains & creases) **70**

Insurance, 1910, "First American Life Insurance Company," paper, round, depicts bust of American Indian on front, calendar on reverse, signed by artist H. Vos, 13" d. (some overall staining & chipping **288**

Insurance, 1922, "Western & Southern Life Insurance," shows girl in bonnet w/flowers, two rows of six months each below, 9 x 9" **21**

Livestock company, 1906, "Dode Meeks Company Livestock," diamond-shaped w/a round center color print of a pretty lady in a large red-feathered hat & a red gown, small date pad at the bottom, framed, overall 11" sq. **154**

Lumber company, 1956, "Grogan Robinson Lumber Company," paper depicts autumn scene of man hunting pheasant, entitled "Up & Ready," original metal rims at top & bottom, 18" w., 30" h. **86**

1904 Youth's Companion Calendar

Magazine, 1904, "Youth's Companion," fold-out die-cut cardboard printed in color, left & right panels w/scenes of birds in blossoming branches, center scene of a young family standing under blossoming trees, minor blemishes mostly on reverse, 12 x 21" (ILLUS.) **187**

Dr. Miles Remedies Advertising Calendar

Medicine, 1908, "Dr. Miles Remedies," child holding a rose, 'H.H. Alley & Co. Druggist...,' calendar never opened, minor edge wear (ILLUS.) **50**
Medicine, 1928, "Lydia E. Pinkham Vegetable Compound," paper in newer frame w/mat, "Bringing You Health" above beautiful color illustration of airplane flying over countryside, Lydia Pinkham's portrait in center below w/short history of her background, full calendar pad, "Ask Your Neighbor" at bottom border, Litho U.S.A., 15" w., 22 3/4" h. (minor water staining on edges) **121**
Milk, 1940, "Hood's Milk," pictures happy baby face w/bottle, October pad, 10 x 14" **35**

Texaco Advertising Calendar

Petroleum products, 1922, "Texaco," "The Texas Company Petroleum & Its Products" surround star logo atop calendar, full pad, 25 x 13" (ILLUS.) **185**

1946 Atlantic Petroleum Calendar

Petroleum products, 1946, "Atlantic Petroleum Products, The Atlantic Refining Company," color-printed paper, "Atlantic" in large white letters on red across the top, long calendar pad below, creases, edge tears & soiling, 16 x 28 1/2" (ILLUS.)...................................... **50**

Union Oil Company Pocket Calendar

Motor oil, 1921, "Union Oil Company of Arizona," celluloid, pocket-type, colorful image of yellow & black early convertible auto & service station marked "Union Oil Company," logos on reverse, minor wear & light bends, 2 3/8 x 3 3/4" (ILLUS.) **198**

Printing supplies, 1906, "Berger & Wirth," color lithographed paper, a scene of a native woman, reads "Berger & Wirth Manufacturers of Fine Dry Colors. Lithographs and Printing Inks, Office and Factory Centre & Broome Sts. New York," 14 3/4 x 29 3/4" (edge tears, hole in shoulder of woman) 55

Pump supply company, 1906, "Horrigan Supply Company," large central color bust portrait of a pretty lady w/brown hair wearing a choker necklace & a low-cut deep red gown, black & white wording & small pictures of pumps around the sides, small partial date pad at bottom, bands w/wrinkles, 15 x 20"................ 259

Railroad, 1937, "Chesapeake & Ohio Railroad," scene of infant waking & stretching, toy bunny near foot, black kitten tucked in bed, four pages, each w/three months, complete w/original mailing tube, 13 1/2 x 16 1/2".......................... 66

Railroad, 1942 "Burlington Railroad," rectangular, image of "Silver King" at top last page w/three months printed on main poster, missing the previous months (heavy crease side to side at top, rip at top right side, minor edge creases & tears)........................... 83

Railroad, 1945, "Great Northern Railway," titled "Custer's Last Fight," decorated w/American Indian 575

Railroad, 1950, "Great Northern - Streamlined Empire Builder," a large color portrait at the top of Tom Dawson, a famous early mountain man & explorer, a vignette of two train engines just above the date pad, w/both bands, 16 x 33 1/2" 77

1956 Pennsylvania RR Calendar

Railroad, 1956, "Pennsylvania Railroad," colorful landscape scene of trains passing on tracks, calendar pad below, signature of agent at top corner of calendar, write-up about the "Truck Train" on the back, framed, scratches at top, overall creases, minor frame wear, 30 1/2" sq. (ILLUS.) 275

Railroad supplies, 1895, "American Railway Supply Co.," pocket-style, metal case w/calendar sheets, marked "Compliments of American Railway Supply Co. 24 Park Place New York" on front, calendar sheets on reverse, 2 1/8" w., 2 3/4" h. (some soiling) 22

Restaurant, 1890, "Feldstein's Restaurant, New York City," in fancy embossed slipcover 30

1924 Snyder Restaurant Calendar

Restaurant, 1924, "Thos. C. Snyder - Restaurant - Confectionary - Ice Cream - Fruit," large color scene at the top of Little Red Riding Hood & the wolf, large partial date pad across bottom, great colors, band at top, 12 x 21" (ILLUS.) 242

Roofing products, 1952 "Texaco," die-cut paper & cardboard, circular top w/logo, top of calendar w/"Texaco Asphalt Roofing Products," full pad, 15" w., 26 1/2" h. (creases & some soiling) 358

Sarsaparilla, 1886, "Hood's Sarsaparilla Calendar," large profile bust portrait of a pretty young Victorian girl w/blonde hair wearing a flower-trimmed white bonnet w/blue ribbons, advertising date pad across the bottom, slight crease, 4 3/4 x 7".. 77

Sarsaparilla, 1888, "Hood's Sarsaparilla," die-cut paperboard, young girl's head portrait wearing blue bonnet, full pad, 9 3/4" 180

Sarsaparilla, 1892, "Hood's Sarsaparilla," round, eight children w/various sewing projects surround complete calendar pad, 7 3/4" d. 85

Sarsaparilla, 1897, "Hood's Sarsaparilla," die-cut paper, pretty child in lilac hat, October pad, 4 1/2 x 7" (top corner bent & facial creasing) 38

1898 Hood's Coupon Calendar

Sarsaparilla, 1898, "Hood's Coupon Calender," top of cover w/a color bust picture of a pretty golden-haired child in a circle framed by white daisies on a pale blue ground, unused condition, 4 1/2 x 7" (ILLUS.) **100-150**

Sarsaparilla, 1900, "Hood's Sarsaparilla," die-cut cardboard, pictures two little girls, complete **75-85**

Sarsaparilla, 1901, "Hood's Sarsaparilla," entitled "Patience," heavy paper, full pad, matted & framed, "Hood's Sarsaparilla - Calendar 1901" in corner above young girl w/blonde bangs & curly hair dressed in white long-sleeved ruffled dress sitting w/hands folded in lap & leaning against a white & blue ruffled pillow w/floral decoration, "Copyright 1900 by C.I. Hood & Co. Lowell Mass." in bottom corner, 9 3/4" w., 6 3/4" h., w/frame 10" w., 13 1/2" h. (small creases & tears to edges & corners, very minor rust to staples) **110**

1903 Hood's Sarsaparilla Calendar

Sarsaparilla, 1903, "Hood's Sarsaparilla," color-printed paper, scene depicts young girl in a pink dress w/a bow in her long blonde hair playing w/two dogs & a horse, full pad w/top cover sheet missing, wooden frame w/glass front & back, w/advertising information on back, picture titled "Four Friends" & marked "Copyright 1902 By C.I. Hood Company, Lowell, Mass.," edge wear & tears, fold mark across center, 6" w., 16 1/2" h. (ILLUS.) **99**

Shoes, 1903, "Snag-Proof Shoes," colorfully lithographed scene of Old Woman who lived in a Snag-Proof shoe, pad incomplete, 7 x 10" **110**

Soap, 1900, "Larkin Soap Company," colored lithograph, oval, a scene of a seated woman in a white & blue dress below an American flag, wording across top "Rah, Rah, Rah - Columbia," attached football-form calendar to side w/full pad, signed by Ellen Clapsaddle, 19 x 24" **176**

Plate-shaped Fairbanks Calendar

Soap, 1903, "Fairbanks Fairy Soap," die-cut cardboard w/a plate shape w/gently scalloped rim, wide blue border band w/gold banded trim enclosing months, center color scene of a lovely young fairy maiden w/flowing hair seated on blossoming branches, based on art by Paul Moran, 9 1/2" d. (ILLUS.) **33**

Soft drink, 1893, "Hires Root Beer," color lithographed cardboard in pastel tones showing two young children w/a black & white cat, complete w/full pad, 7 x 9" **700**

1896 Coca-Cola Calendar

Soft drink, 1896, "Coca-Cola," color lithographed cardboard, color bust portrait of a beautiful lady holding a mug of Coca-Cola, rare, 6 1/2 x 10 1/2" (ILLUS.) **20,000**

Soft drink, 1899, "Coca-Cola," color lithographed cardboard, central oval reserve of lovely lady seated at table writing a letter, pink roses along one side, calendar below, rare, 7 3/8 x 13" **10,000**

1901 Coca-Cola Calendar

Soft drink, 1901, "Coca-Cola," color lithographed cardboard, lovely lady wearing feathered hat & holding a glass of Coca-Cola in a scroll-trimmed central reserve surrounded by yellow & purple pansies, 7 3/8 x 13" (ILLUS.) **7,500**

1905 Coca-Cola Calendar

Soft drink, 1905, "Coca-Cola," picture of Lillian Nordica standing next to pedestal holding a large feather fan, "Coca-Cola At Soda Fountains - 5¢" at top, 7 3/4 x 15 1/4" (ILLUS.) **6,000**

Soft drink, 1906, "Coca-Cola," color lithographed cardboard, bust portrait of pretty young lady wearing a lacy white blouse w/a corsage of violets & drinking a glass of Coca-Cola, calendar below, 7 3/4 x 14 1/4" **6,500**

Soft drink, 1908, "Coca-Cola," lady w/dark hair, red dress, long black gloves & feathered red hat, ballet stage in background, matted & framed under glass, 12 1/2 x 19 1/2" **4,200**

Rare 1909 Coca-Cola Calendar

Soft drink, 1909, "Coca-Cola," color lithographed cardboard, portrait of a young lady seated at a table w/a glass of Coca-Cola, the lights of a World's Fair in the background, rare, 11 x 20 1/2" (ILLUS.) .. **16,100**

Soft drink, 1910, "Coca-Cola," color lithographed cardboard, Hamilton King artwork w/the head of a young lady wearing a large feathered hat, 8 3/4 x 17 1/2" **6,500**

Soft drink, 1912, "Cherry Smash," color lithographed cardboard w/a tall scene of a young lady seated in a large swing holding a glass of the product, small monthly calendars scattered around the bottom section, 7 1/2 x 15" **600**

Soft drink, 1913, "Coca-Cola," color lithographed cardboard, lovely lady seated & leaning on a railing while sipping from a bottle of Coca-Cola, wearing large white & red hat & a white dress trimmed in red, bottlers' calendar, 16 x 28" **8,500**

Soft drink, 1914, "Coca-Cola," color lithographed cardboard, three-quarter length portrait of young lady "Betty" wearing a pink & white dress & bonnet, 13 x 32" **2,000**

1915 Coca-Cola Calendar

Soft drink, 1915, "Coca-Cola," color lithographed cardboard, full-length portrait of a young lady wearing a pale pink dress & hat seated on a large boulder, holding a glass in one hand & leaning on a closed parasol w/the other, 13 x 32" (ILLUS.) **4,800**

Soft drink, 1918, "Coca-Cola," color lithographed cardboard, beachside scene of a young lady in white carrying a glass & open umbrella & standing beside a second young lady seated wearing a yellow & red bathing outfit, 13 x 32"....................... **5,000**

1919 Coca-Cola Calendar

Soft drink, 1919, "Coca-Cola," young lady wearing frilly pink dress & hat w/large brim & holding a glass, airfield in background, 12 x 31" (ILLUS.)............................ **4,500**

1922 Coca-Cola Calendar

Soft drink, 1922, "Coca-Cola," color lithographed cardboard, three-quarter length portrait of a young lady wearing a pink dress & hat & holding a glass while leaning on a bench, baseball players in background, 12 x 32" (ILLUS.)............................ **2,400**

Soft drink, 1923, "Coca-Cola," "Flapper Girl," beautiful smiling woman w/short dark hair, wearing blue dress & white fringed stole, holding glass, 12 x 24"......... **1,000**

Soft drink, 1926, "Chero-Cola," color printed long scene of a young woman seated in a wicker armchair in a garden holding a book in her lap & a bottle of the product in one hand, complete w/pad.......................... **500**

Soft drink, 1927, "Nehi Beverages," color-printed paper, a scene of a young flapper wearing an orange dress seated on the edge of a rowboat on a beach & drinking a bottle of soda, marked "Copyright Chero-Cola Co.," framed, 11 x 21" **231**

Soft drink, 1928, "Coca-Cola," color lithographed cardboard, a seated flapper in a satiny gown & a wrap w/a white fur collar holding a glass of Coca-Cola, 12 x 24" **1,200**

1931 Rockwell Coca-Cola Calendar

Soft drink, 1931, "Coca-Cola," color lithographed cardboard, Norman Rockwell artwork of a young boy in straw hat seated by tree eating sandwich & drinking from a bottle, his dog watching, 12 x 24" (ILLUS.) **1,000**

Soft drink, 1936, "Coca-Cola," color lithographed cardboard, coastal scene of old fisherman, girl & basket of clams by a rowboat, 12 x 24" **900**

1936 Nehi Soda Calendar

Soft drink, 1936, "Nehi," color printed paper, a long bust portrait of a pretty dark-haired lady wearing a bright red wide-collared blouse & red kerchief, calendar at bottom (ILLUS.) **250**

Soft drink, 1937, "Coca-Cola," "Fishin Hole," depicting young barefoot boy w/fishing pole on his shoulder & carrying two bottles, his dog running at his side, by N.C. Wyeth, full pad w/cover sheet & metal strip, matted & framed under glass .. **2,200**

Soft drink, 1937, "Dr. Pepper," long color scene of a young woman seated on a round hassock & wearing an elegant gown, holding a bottle of Dr. Pepper in one hand, complete w/full pad **800**

Soft drink, 1942, "Pepsi-Cola," color-printed paper, large winter landscape scene of snow-covered hills w/a road in the foreground, calendar at the bottom, 17 x 23" **60**

1943 South American Calendar

Soft drink, 1943, "Coca-Cola," color lithographed cardboard, half-length portrait of pretty dark-haired lady surrounded by flowering branches & holding a glass of Coca-Cola, text in Spanish for the South American market, 14 x 29" (ILLUS.) **500**

Soft drink, 1945, "Coca-Cola," young boy in Boy Scout uniform, Boy Scout oath written in background, by Norman Rockwell **550**

1946 Boy Scout Rockwell Calendar

Soft drink, 1946, "Coca-Cola," color lithographed paper, Boy Scout version w/Norman Rockwell artwork of a Boy Scout teaching a Cub Scout to tie a knot, 6 1/2 x 11 1/2" (ILLUS.) **375**

Soft drink, 1947, "Coca-Cola," color lithographed paper, bust portrait of a pretty young lady holding skis, two months on each page, six pages **350**

Soft drink, 1954, "Coca-Cola," color lithographed paper, a month at the top & bottom w/the bust portrait of a young lady holding a bottle of Coca-Cola in the center w/a background portrait of a leaping basketball player to the right, six pages **165**

1958 Rockwell Boy Scout Calendar

Soft drink, 1958, "Coca-Cola," color printed paper, Boy Scout version w/Norman Rockwell artwork showing a Cub Scout, Boy Scout & Eagle Scout standing & saluting, 11 x 23" (ILLUS.) **400**

Soft drink, 1960, "Coca-Cola," color printed paper, scene of a young couple standing & holding skis, each w/a bottle of Coca-Cola 60

Soft drink, 1966, "Coca-Cola," color printed paper, color photo scene of a couple working in a flower garden, a wheelbarrow full of flowers, he drinking from a bottle, six pages 60

Soft drink, 1972, "Coca-Cola," color printed paper, a large photo close-up of a yellow daisy, six pages 20

Coca-Cola Wall Calendar

Soft drink, 1972, "Coca-Cola," tin, button-style wall calendar, complete pad w/cover, light wear, 8 x 19 1/4" (ILLUS.) 523

Soup, 1980, "Campbell's Soup," paper 10

Steamship agent, 1908, "SP Lapcevic Steamship Agent," die-cut w/embossed cowgirl & vignettes of horses, full pad, framed, 11 x 21" 550

Steamship line, 1912, "Cunard Line Dock," lithographed ceramic tile, black & white scene of steamers on front, calendar on the back, printed "Cunard Line Dock New Boston," 4 5/8" w., 3 1/4" h. (minor edge chips) 44

Tea company, 1901, "Lipton's Teas," embossed paper, girl w/cup of tea surrounded by months, floral ground, framed, image 10 x 12" 55

1907 Grand Union Tea Co. Calendar

Tea company, 1907, "Grand Union Tea Co., Brooklyn, NY," die-cut, large colorful scene of small girl wearing a white dress, red shoes & large red hat, seated & holding a small puppy, litho by Sackett & Wilhelms, professionally framed, overall 14 x 32" (ILLUS.) 385

1908 Grand Union Tea Co. Calendar

Tea company, 1908, "Grand Union Tea Co.," rectangular die-cut, large scene of young girl w/doll standing before a china cabinet & near a small table set for tea, flanked at the bottom by months of the year, minor ding top center, 11 x 29" (ILLUS.) 440

Clark's Mile-End Spool Cotton Calendar

Thread, 1886, "Clark's Mile-End Spool Cotton," girl seated under Oriental parasol above January page showing advertising, framed 20 x 30" (ILLUS.) 650

1951 Goodyear Tire Calendar

Tires, 1951, "Goodyear Tires," color-printed heavy paper, a large rectangular color picture at the top of a giant Uncle Sam launching bomber airplanes w/a pilot & Boy Scout in the foreground, signed "Dean Cornwell," full pad, minor creases, minor edge tears, 20 1/2 x 28" (ILLUS.) **66**

Toys, 1901, "Daisy & Sentinel Air Rifles," paper, child holding rifle, full pad, rare, framed, image 15 1/2 x 22 1/2" **3,200**

Trading company, 1928, "Hudson's Bay Company," long horizontal rectangular format w/a color image on the left of two trappers getting ready to climb into a canoe, nice landscape scene titled "Starting a Canoe Trip" by artist Phillip R. Goodwin, text in red & black on the right side includes "We Want Your Raw Furs" above the company name, w/original mailing envelope, 6 1/2 x 11 1/2" **468**

Weed Chains Advertising Calendar

Tire chains, 1916, "Weed Chains," four colorful vignettes of women in hats above full calendar, minor wear, small edge tear 13 1/2 x 34" (ILLUS.)...................................... **550**

Trucking Company Calendar

Trucking company, 1937, "Waldron & Solberg, Algona, Iowa - Independent Jobber," die-cut tin, the upper section w/a billboard behind a 1930s tanker truck all in white, dark blue, red & green, a long narrow paper calender pad below, minor scratches, thin paint at center, few small bends, missing stand tabs on back, 4 3/8 x 6" (ILLUS.).. **61**

Yeast, 1911, "Fleischmann's Yeast," pocket-type, celluloid cover, pictures lady w/long hair, calendar & product name on reverse, 2 x 3".. **26**

1949 Kelly Tires Calendar

Tires, 1949, "Kelly Tires," color-printed paper, a long rectangular form w/a pale green background w/a sketched-in front end of a car w/a full-length color portrait of a pin-up girl seated on the front bumper wearing a short white tennis outfit & holding a racket, dealer advertising below picture & above calendar pad, full pad, picture signed "Medcalf," wrinkles, 16 x 34" (ILLUS.) **176**

Chapter 4
Clocks

Battery-operated

Champion Steering Wheel Clock

Spark plugs, "Champion," plastic w/glass front, die-cut steering wheel w/clock in center w/Champion trademark & Spark Plug illustration, by "Spendia - Paris," minor scratches, soiling & staining w/corrosion in battery compartment, 11 1/2" d. (ILLUS.).. **$380**

Electric

Phillips 66 Light-up Electric Clock

Auto service station, "Phillips 66 Tires - Batteries," round plastic light-up type w/'double-bubble' dial cover, white background, large company shield-shaped logo in black, white & red in the center w/black wording above & below, an outer ring of Arabic numerals, sweep seconds hand, light not working, 15" d. (ILLUS.) **688**
Automobile, "Oldsmobile," wall-type w/light, glass front w/heavy metal body, white background, 15 1/4" w., 17 3/4" h. (scratches, soiling).. **303**

Rare Packard Presentation Clock

Automobile, "Packard," presentation model, cloisonné on metal, rectangular front w/rounded top & notched bottom corners, white enamel outer band w/black wording across the bottom "Master Salesman - 1926," grey enamel central panel w/inlaid Packard logo above the round brass bezel & steel dial w/the numbers replaced w/incised letters spelling "Packard Motor," plate below the dial engraved "J.E. Land," Seth Thomas model, four jewels, small chip at bottom corner & one at "P" in dial, 4 x 5 1/4" (ILLUS.)......... **2,750**
Automobile service, "Pontiac Service," wall-type, round molded plastic, outer rim w/white lettering on blue background, blue lettering on blue background, blue letttering on yellow clock in center, metal hands, 15" d. (fading & paint chipping to lettering & numbers)...................................... **275**
Automotive supplies, "Atlas Tires," metal & glass, octagonal, reads "Atlas Tires - Batteries - Accessories" in white lettering on blue, 18 1/4" x 18 1/4" (restored glass on front).. **880**
Beer, "Fort Pitt Beer," wall-type, tin clock face, glass cover & reverse painted glass advertising at top w/"Fort Pitt Special Beer," metal housing, 25" w., 16" h. (face paint cracked, scratches & dents) **110**
Beer, "Schaefer Beer," wall model, plastic, barrel-shaped w/lighted advertising, clock on one end, Schaefer logo on other, 9" d., 12" h. **55**
Beer, "Southern Select Beer," red, blue & white w/chrome bezel, ca. 1940s-early 1950s, Pam Clock Company, Brooklyn, New York for Galveston-Houston Brewery, 14 1/2" d. (some rusting to chrome, minor paint drips on back).............................. **303**

Vernors Soda Advertising Clock

Beverage company, "Vernors," round, wall-mount, glass dome w/metal case marked "Drink Vernors - deliciously different" above head of bearded man, 19 1/2" d. (ILLUS.) **145**

Brewing company, "Duquesne," w/light, Art Deco style, rectangular bar w/"Duquesne - The Finest Beer in Town" above stepped frame enclosing octagonal clock, reverse-painted glass w/metal housing, old clock starting mechanism, black & grey w/red numerals, red & yellow lettering, 5 1/2 x 24 1/2", 18 1/2" h. (very minor paint chips to hands, minor scratches & soiling & minor staining to white background) **468**

Brewing company, "Iroquois Beer-Ale," wall model w/light, round molded embossed plastic w/metal back & hands, depicts embossed white bust of Indian in full headdress on red arrowhead design & advertising "Iroquois Beer-Ale" & marked "Since 1842," red & white lettering, 17" d. (paint chips to hands & soiling) **440**

Leinenkugel's Beer Clock

Brewing company, "Leinenkugel's," wall model w/light, round glass & metal, white w/black Arabic numerals & hands, red seconds hand, bust of Indian over wide red banner w/"Leinenkugel's" & "made with Chippewa Water from the Big Eddy Springs" in black, Advertising Products, Inc., Cincinnati 23, Ohio for Jacob Leinenkugel Brewing Co., Chippewa Falls, Wisconsin, some scratches & soiling, 15" d. (ILLUS.) **534**

Coal company, "Liberty Coal," glass dome w/metal case, by Gillco Mfg., 19 1/2" d. **450**

Dairy products, "Borden's," wall-type, metal body w/glass face & cover, center w/flower petals surrounding decal of Elsie, "Borden's - Milk & Cream Sold Here" in red lettering around edge, black hands & 3, 6, 9 & 12 marked on face, working, 20 1/2" d. (soiling & scratches, part of decal missing, overall yellowing) **171**

Farm equipment, "International Harvester," square wall model w/glass face & front & metal body, square white dial w/black Arabic numerals around the border, large black & red "IH" logo in center over "International Harvester," marked "Pam Clock Co., Rochelle, N.Y.C. '60," sweep seconds hand, 15 1/2" sq. **358**

Farm equipment, "John Deere (motif of deer) Quality Farm Equipment," wall-type w/light, glass & metal, round w/yellow & green John Deere emblem on white background, marked "John Deere-2 Telechron Inc. Ashland, Mass, U.S.A. Ng. Co.," 14 3/4" d. (wear to cord & casing, soiling) **660**

Gasoline, "Mobil Pegasus," wall-type, glass dome w/aluminum case by American Time Corp. (new movement/motor & matching hand set) **625**

Gasoline, "Phillips 66," round glass & metal 'double bubble' type, Arabic numerals around the outer ring border, the inner circle w/a large orange & black "Phillips 66" shield logo w/"Tires" in black above & "Batteries" in black below, w/sweep seconds hand, by Advertising Products, Inc., Cincinnati, Ohio, 15" d. (small scratch above shield, paint flaking near "6," seconds hand worn) **990**

Chico's Ice Cream Clock

Ice cream, "Chico's Ice Cream," plastic body & face w/glass front, lights up, reads "Chico's Dairy Co. - Ice Cream - Milk" in center w/"It May Be Good And Not Be Ours" in border above & "But It Can't Be Ours And Not Be Good" below, paint speckles, minor wear to face, small crack to side, working (ILLUS.) **75**

Harley-Davidson Advertising Clock

Motorcycles, "Harley-Davidson Motor Cycles," square wall model w/glass face & dial & metal body, square dial w/numbers only at the "12," "3," "6," & "9," the other numbers represented by small company logos, a large orange, black & white company logo across the center, sweep seconds hand, minor body wear, 15 1/4" sq. (ILLUS.)... **770**

Time Oil Company Electric Clock

Oil company, "Time Products - Time Tested," round metal w/glass dial cover, white dial w/blue, orange & white logo in the center & blue Arabic numerals around the sides, very minor scattered nicks & wear, 14 1/2" d. (ILLUS.).............................. **303**

Petroleum products, "Gulf," plastic, triangular, orange, blue & white Gulf colors, 22" w., 22" h. (small hand broken)............... **187**

Hastings Piston Rings Electric Clock

Piston rings, "Hastings Piston Rings," round w/plastic domed cover, white ground w/black Arabic numerals w/wording in the top center above the red, white & black Hastings Piston man logo, works, minor wear, retention ring missing tabs, 14 3/4" d. (ILLUS.)... **176**

Shock absorbers, "Monroe-Matic Shock Absorbers," round 'double bubble' wall-type, glass face & front, metal body, the dial w/an outer band of Arabic numerals on white, yellow center w/black wording "Monroe-Matic Shock Absorbers - Monroe - Load Levelers," like new, 16" d. **550**

Clicquot Club Clock

Soft drink, "Clicquot Club," round w/center image of young boy wearing fur-trimmed parka holding large green bottle, black Arabic numerals & black-tipped hands, Telechron, ca. 1940s, composite case repainted, metal plate installed near hanging hole, 15" d. (ILLUS.) **495**

Soft drink, "Coca-Cola," counter-type, rectangular metal w/reverse-painted glass, "Lunch With Us" in embossed green lettering at bottom, "Drink Coca-Cola" in white lettering next to dial, gold Arabic numerals, lights up, hook for hanging, working condition, 5 x19", 9" h. (edge wear, scratching & soiling) **1,018**

Soft drink, "Coca-Cola," wall-type, metal w/glass face & cover, black outline of bottle in red center w/"Drink Coca-Cola" in white lettering, green border w/Arabic numerals, Pam Clock Co. Brooklyn 1, NY, U.S.A, working, 15" d. **550**

Soft drink, "Coca-Cola," wall-type, square wooden frame, "Drink Coca-Cola in Bottles," 1939, 16 x 16" **500**

Dr. Pepper Clock

Soft drink, "Dr. Pepper," 1930s Deco style, red & black w/gold trim & "Drink Dr. Pepper 5¢" (ILLUS.) **5,750**

Soft drink, "Enjoy Canada Dry," wall-type w/light, glass & metal, Canada Dry logo on white clock face, marked "Copyright 1962 Pam Clock Co. Inc. New Rochelle NY," 15" d. (minor scratches) **550**

Nesbitt's Orange Electric Clock

Soft drink, "Nesbitt's Orange," back-lighted metal & plastic w/domed plastic cover, black Arabic numerals & orange dots form dial, central logo design in black, white & orange in a bold geometric design, two bottles & oranges shown in the lower left, very minor nicks & wear to reverse face, Canadian origin, working, 16 1/4" d. (ILLUS.) **495**

Soft drink, "Pepsi-Cola" beneath "Say Pepsi Please," wall-type w/light, glass & metal, 4" w., 14 3/4" l., 15 3/5" h. **121**

Pepsi-Cola Clock

Soft drink, "Pepsi-Cola," wall-mount, glass front, large blue numbers on white light-up background, center logo, working condition, one of the hands slips, ca. 1940s, by Telechron, 15" d. (ILLUS.) **209**

Soft drink, "Pepsi-Cola," wall-type, round, metal & glass, ca. 1944, 15" d. (scratches, denting & paint loss to hands) **358**

Pepsi Electric Wall Clock

Soft drink, "The Light Refreshment - Pepsi," round wire grill-form background mounted w/large gold teardrops serving as numbers, the white round center printed w/a gold sunburst & wording in black w/a red, white & blue Pepsi bottle cap, white openwork dial hands, ca. 1950s, very minor wear & scratches, minor paint loss & bends to hands, 17 1/4" d. (ILLUS.) **171**

Soft drink, "Whistle," back-lighted metal & plastic w/plastic domed cover, round w/blue Arabic numbers & dots with musical notes around the outside border of the dial, blue, orange & white design in center w/a large musical note printed w/"Thirsty? - Just Whistle," orange printing just below center reads "Sparkling Orange Goodness," sweep seconds hand, 14 1/2" d. (frosty dirty look w/some tiny flecks) **231**

Electric Light-up Coppertone Clock

Sun tan lotion, "Coppertone," square plastic & metal light-up model, two-sided, the white ground w/a large full color image of the Coppertone girl & her dog, the boxed clock dial in the upper right, slogan in black in the bottom right "Don't Be A Paleface," 8 x 36", 36" h. (ILLUS. of one side) **1,760**

Dunlop Tire Clock

Tires, "Dunlop Tires," black metal tire frame w/"Dunlop" in yellow plastic letters, tin face, iron bracket to side for mounting, minor scratches, soiling & paint chips, 48" w., 36" h. (ILLUS.) **770**

Fisk Tires Clock

Tires, "Fisk Tires," desk-type, clock w/"Time to Re-Tire - Get Fisk," little boy logo at bottom, mounted in black rubber tire w/airplane on it, tire is hardened & out of round, clock missing stand-up support bracket & adjuster knob, appears to keep good time, 6 1/4" d. (ILLUS.) **187**

Key-wind

Automobile, "Oldsmobile," mantel-type, metal & wood w/beveled glass front, marked "The Ansonia Clock Co. Manufacturers U.S.A.," 4" w., 6" l., 7" h. (soiling & scratches) **165**

Baking powder, "Calumet Baking Powder," reverse painting on glass front panels, 31-day face, 34 1/4" h. (minor flaking) **650**

Bitters, "Lewis Red Jacket Bitters," wall-type, white, black & red face w/lithograph on paper of Indian chief in center, ca. 1890-1910, 14 1/4 x 21 1/4," clock face 9 1/4" d., (some chipping of paint on clock face) **743**

Gum, "Honeymoon Chewing Gum," cast iron, wall-mounted **2,860**

Motor oil, "Veedol Motor Oil," square, metal, Veedol logo w/black lettering on pale yellow background, signed "Japy," 9 1/8" x 9 1/8" **154**

Patent medicine, "Mishler's Herb Bitters Purifies The Blood Improves The Appetite Sold Here," wall-type, wood w/raised plaster embossing, marked "Made by Baird Clock Co. Plattsburgh, N. Y. U.S.A.," ca. 1880-1900, 18 1/2" x 31" (letter "T" in "Appetite" is missing) **3,300**

Planters Peanuts Alarm Clock

Peanuts, "Planters Peanuts," alarm clock, round yellow face, red clock body, Mr. Peanut, clock hands & numbers in black, Mr. Peanut's arms serve as the hour & minute hands, ca. 1960s (ILLUS.) **250**

Shoe polish, "Black Cat Shoe Polish," rectangular tin advertisement w/wooden frame, illustration of black cat below clock & near product containers w/"Black Cat Shoe Dressing & Superba Polish Challenges the World - The Nonsuch Mfg. Co., Limited Toronto. McDonald Mfg. Co., Limited Toronto," 17 1/2" w., 23 1/2" h. (soiling & paint loss overall, minor touch up, key missing) **990**

Coca-Cola "Contessa" Clock

Soft drink, "Coca-Cola," "Contessa" anniversary-type, glass dome & wood base, two figural bottles form rotary pendulum, 1950s, 3 1/2 x 5" (ILLUS.) **750**

Sidney Advertising Clock

Tin and hardware company, "John H. Hough - the Leader in Tinware - Hardware - Stoves & Ranges," wooden wall-type, rectangular case shelf & drawer, arched top w/advertising, corner spire finials, Sidney Clock Co. (ILLUS.) **6,000**

Tobacco, "Lucky Strike," wooden schoolhouse-style case w/octagonal top w/wood graining surrounding the brass bezel opening to the round dial w/Roman numerals around a red center dot reading "R.A. Patterson Tob. Cos. - Lucky Strike," short drop below w/gilt-trimmed glass door over the pendulum, late 19th - early 20th c., original key, chimes, 12 1/4" w., 19" h. **660**

Whiskey, "Duffy's Pure Malt Whiskey," wall-type, wording around clock face, pendulum door w/reverse-painted glass decoration depicting an alchemist & the words "Absolutely Pure & Unadulterated Trade Mark," clock works made by "The New Haven Clock Co., New Haven, CT," 32 1/4" h. (reverse-paint shows some separation & loss, repainted face lettering) **1,348**

Whiskey, "Green River The Whiskey Without a Headache, J.W. McCulloch Distiller Owensboro Kentucky," table model, cast brass, depicts two men shaking hands over a bottle, stamped "Pat. Sep. 22 85 Other Pat. Apld. For" on back, ca. 1885-1900, 13" w., 15 3/4" h. **770**

Whiskey, "Lewis 66 Rye, The Strauss, Pritz Co. Cincinnati, O," wall-type, white, silver & black reverse-painted decoration, ca. 1890-1920, 12" d. (some separation & discoloration of paint, minor chipping along edge) **176**

Neon

Automotive parts & accessories, "Mopar," metal & glass, octagonal, reads

"Mopar Parts & Accessories Use Chrysler Corporation Parts Division Products," red, yellow & white lettering on clock face, neon trim, 18 1/2" w., 18 1/2" h. (soiling & fading) **605**

Farm equipment, "International Harvester," square, wall-mount, metal body w/tin face & glass cover, neon light tube around edge, 15 1/2" (scuffs to body) **715**

Price's Milk Neon Clock

Milk, "Price's Milk," neon w/glo-dial, chrome-plated case, black face w/blue border, white hands & Arabic numerals, keeps good time, minor wear to reverse glass detail, hands may have been repainted, 14 1/2" d. (ILLUS.) **523**

Motor oil, "Quaker State, Oils & Greases," wall-type w/glass & metal, white background & green trim & lettering, new chrome ring holding glass face, 19" w., 16" h. (scratches, new neon) **605**

Motorola Radio Neon Clock

Radio, "Motorola Radio For Home and Car," neon spinner-type, white face w/blue Arabic numerals & red lettering, keeps good time, repainted case, wear to reverse glass, minor wear & rust to face, 1 1/2" d. (ILLUS.) **550**

Soft drink, "Dr. Pepper," octagonal, black numbers w/red 2, 4 & 10, late 1930s, soiling, (stains & wear w/light rusting on interior of case) **688**

Chapter 5

Coca-Cola Items

Advertisement, cardboard, brightly colored scene of a couple at masquerade party, man wearing mask, lady holding her mask, wood frame, 19 1/2" w., 28" h. (scratches, denting & soiling)...................... **$198**

Advertisement, round, celluloid over metal w/cardboard backing for hanging or standing, red w/bottle of Coca-Cola in center, reads "Coca-Cola" across diameter, 9" d. (scratches & soiling)...................... **198**

Advertisement, stand-up cardboard, autographed picture of baseball player Ernie Banks swinging a bat & reading "Swing to the Real Thing!," 1960, 10" w., 20" h. (minor chipping at edges & some fading)..... **303**

Ashtray, clear glass, six-sided w/cigarette rest at each side, round red center w/logo & advertiser's name, ca. 1950s...................... **20**

50th Anniversary Ashtray

Ashtray, porcelain, marked "50th Anniversary Coca-Cola 1886-1936," w/signature on rim, 1936 (ILLUS.).................... **700**

Bag holder, metal w/"For Home Refreshment - Coca-Cola" & the Sprite boy, ca. 1949, 16 x 40"...................... **650**

Bank, plastic, vending machine-shaped, marked "Drink Coca-Cola - Work refreshed - Ice Cold," 1950s, 5 1/2" h. **125**

Barrel-shaped Coca-Cola Pottery Bank

Bank, pottery, barrel-shaped, red w/white embossed wording, Haeger Pottery (ILLUS.)... **225**

Red Tin Dispenser Bank

Bank, tin, battery-operated, painted red, designed to look like Coke dispenser, window at top front to view money, reads "Drink Coca-Cola" on window, other lettering reads "Refresh Yourself" & "Ice Cold," 1950s (ILLUS.).................... **440**

Banner, canvas, "Drink A Bottle of Coca-Cola Delicious and Refreshing," 1911, 16" x 11"... **2,500**

Banner, cloth, bottle on blanket of snow & covered by icicles, 1950, 18 1/2 x 56"......... **425**

Baseball bat, aluminum, marked "Coca-Cola Baseball Bat," 1970s.................... **60**

Bell, brass, pictures cow w/"Our Only Competitor" on front, "Coca-Cola" on back, 1920s, 3 1/4" h. **425**

Blotter, 1906, "Delicious - Refreshing - Invigorating - Drink Coca-Cola - The Most Refreshing Drink In The World," in rectangle flanked by glasses being filled by a soda fountain dispenser **125**

Blotter, 1923, "Drink Coca-Cola - Delicious and Refreshing" within a shield, flanked by bottles... **30**

Blotter, 1929, "One little minute for a big rest," pictures radio announcer holding bottle **225**

Blotter, 1940, pictures a clown, "The greatest pause on earth" & "Drink Coca-Cola - Delicious and Refreshing"................................ **65**

Book, "When You Entertain - What To Do And How," 1932, by Ida B. Allen, 124 pp. **8**

Book ends, bronze, bottle-shaped on flat base, ca. 1963, pr. **275**

Booklet, "Know Your War Planes," w/Coca-Cola advertising, 1943.................................... **50**

Booklet, "The Truth about Coca-Cola," 1912, 16 pp. **35**

Bookmark, 1898, celluloid, heart-shaped, beautiful woman w/glass in center, "Drink Coca-Cola - Delicious ... - 5¢ - Refreshing" in border, 2 x 2 1/4" **700**

Hilda Clark 1903 Bookmark

Bookmark, 1903, "Drink Coca-Cola - 5¢" w/Hilda Clark pictured below, 2 x 6" (ILLUS.) **375**

Lillian Nordica 1904 Bookmark

Bookmark, 1904, "Drink Coca-Cola 5¢," dark red ground w/Lillian Nordica pictured, wearing white dress trimmed w/large red ribbon & streamers, one hand resting on chair back, pansies & leaves at top & upper sides w/glass in

holder in upper center, scrolled edge, 2 x 6" (ILLUS.) **325**

Bookmark, celluloid, two-sided, owl on branch holding book marked "What - Shall -We - Drink" on one page & "Drink - Coca - Cola - 5¢" on the other, reverse w/"Compliments of The Coca-Cola Co. - Atlanta - Philadelphia - New York - Chicago - Boston - Dallas - Los Angeles," 1906, 1 1/2 x 3 1/8" **800**

Bottle, "Christmas Coke" marked "Pat'd Dec. 25, 1923" **3-8**

Bottle, seltzer, ten-sided, cobalt blue, Bradford, Pennsylvania, 12 1/4" h. **400**

Vintage Coca-Cola Six-Pack Carrier

Bottle carrier, "Season's Greetings - Drink Coca-Cola," cardboard six-pack carrier, red bands w/white wording alternating w/white bands of holly sprigs against white, ca. 1930s, unused, 7 1/4 x 13" (ILLUS.) **121**

Bottle carrier, wooden, closed box base, pointed ends joined by a straight wooden handle, "Drink Coca-Cola" on sides, 1940s **150**

Bottle display rack, for six-bottle cartons, holds 24, "Take home a Carton - Coca-Cola - 6 Bottles - 25¢ - Plus Deposit," 1930s **400**

Coca-Cola Bottle-shaped Opener

Bottle opener, bottle-shaped metal w/ribbing & name on one side & a red fired-on round logo on the other side, some scratches & soiling, 8" l. (ILLUS. of two sides) **61**

Bottle opener, flat brass finish wrench-form, embossed "Drink Coca-Cola in bottles," 1910 .... **75**

Bottle opener, in original box, white plastic front w/picture of Sprite boy & bottle of Coke, metal hardware for mounting, box is marked "The Starr Bottle Opener," 2 3/4" w., 6" h. (soiling & wear to box, opener faded) **28**

Bottle opener, metal, bottle-shaped, Glascock, ca. 1930 .... **100**

Bottle opener, metal, "Key Ring," w/cigar box cutter & nail puller plus square hole, ca. 1905-15 .... **50**

Bottle opener, metal "Shoe Horn," 1930-40 ..... **250**

Bottle topper, figural classic, 100% intact, 1 5/8 x 7 x 7 1/4" **675**

Bottles & carrier, glass bottles & debossed metal carrier w/metal handle, four bottles have embossed lettering & two have decals, 5 x 8", 8" h. (denting & wear to carrier, scratches & soiling to bottles) **44**

Box, 1996, featuring 1962 Santa Claus by Haddon Sundblom, playing with Lionel Santa Fe train set while drinking a Coke, w/24 cans inside, price for box **25**

Can, large white diamond design, 1960 .... **175**

Can, red & white diamond design, 1960s........... **25**

Cans, 1996 Coca-Cola 24-pack, each can pictures a reproduction of 1962 Haddon Sundblom scene of Santa playing w/Lionel Santa Fe train set while drinking a Coke, price for each can................ **5**

Car key, metal, on key ring, ca. 1959 .... **50**

Carton insert, "Serve Coca-Cola - Stock up for the Holidays," die-cut cardboard w/a colorful image of Santa Claus holding a bottle of Coke in front of the round logo & above a white card & a six-pack of Coca-Cola, dated 1952, unused, 12 1/2 x 21 1/2" **55**

Chair, metal, folding-type w/"Drink Coca-Cola" on back, ca. 1960................ **175**

Cigar bands, bottle on one & glass on other, 1930s, each **175**

Cigarette box, oblong, frosted glass, 1936, "50th Anniversary - Coca-Cola - 1886 - 1936" **700**

Cigarette lighter, bottle-shaped, opens at center, tin cap w/"Coca-Cola" logo, 1950s, 2 1/2" h. **25**

Cigarette lighter, red & white diamond design, 1960s **30**

Cigarette lighters, figural bottle, pull-apart type w/original box, 2 1/2" h., set of 10 .... **350**

Cigarette lighters, musical, Bluebird model, by Hadson w/original presentation box, works, 2 1/4" h. **200**

Clicker, tin, marked w/logo, 1940s................ **125**

Cooler, Glascock ice chest-type, double case model, "Drink Coca-Cola" on side panels, 1929-32, 24 x 67" **1,000**

Cooler, metal, painted silver w/metal handle & embossed lettering reading "Drink Coca-Cola" on front, inside tray, 9 1/2 x 19", 18" h. (denting, scratching & soiling) **149**

Cooler, metal w/galvanized interior & tray, chest-type w/handle, in original box, 17 x 12", 19" h. (very minor scratches & soiling to cooler, wear to box)................ **418**

Cooler, metal, single case, junior size, red chest on brown frame legs, sides of chest read "Drink Coca-Cola," 1929, 17 1/2 x 17 1/2" sq., 27 1/2" h. (casters missing, edge wear, rust spotting, scratches, soiling & paint chips to frame & signs)................ **852**

Counter display bottle, "Christmas Coke" style marked "Pat'd Dec. 25, 1923," clear, 20" h. **375**

Coupon, w/magazine ad illustrating Lillian Nordica, 1905, 6 1/2 x 9 3/4" **275**

Coupon, cardboard, entitles customer to one free Coca-Cola, central lettering flanked by two bottles of Coke, reverse side reads "Millions Drink Coca Cola - 7,000,000 Sold a Day," 1929, 2 3/8 x 3 5/8" **30-60**

Cuff links, 10k (yellow gold), figural bottle, 3/4" l., pr. **50**

Cuff links, celluloid, round, red w/white logo, 1920s, pr. **75**

Dart board, center marked "Drink Coca-Cola," 1940s-50s **125**

Dispenser, wooden barrel w/two tin Coca-Cola signs, one Nesbitt's Root Beer sign & one Nesbitt decal, complete, 25 1/2" h. **650**

Buddy Lee Doll

Doll, plastic, Buddy Lee dressed in white striped uniform & cap, black visor, bow tie, belt & shoes, emblem on hat & shirt w/"Drink Coca Cola," ca. 1950s, 12" h. (ILLUS.)................ **1,000**

Doll, Santa Claus standing holding bottle of Coca-Cola, cloth stuffed body, white boots, ca. 1950-60................ **100**

Coca-Cola Doll

Doll, stuffed cloth, painted smiling face, blue & white striped outfit, blue socks & white shoes, red & white striped stocking hat, band marked "Coca-Cola," 1969, 14" h. (ILLUS.)... 100
Door knob, brass, ca. 1913-1915 400
Door push plate, aluminum, marked "Ice Cold Coca-Cola in Bottles," 1950s................. 425
Door push plate, porcelain, red & white, "Ice Cold Coca-Cola in Bottles," 1950s, 4 x 30"... 400
Earrings, sterling silver, figural bottle, screw-on, ca. 1960s, pr. 35
Fan, cardboard, fold-out type, front w/bouquet of flowers in vase, reverse w/"Drink Coca-Cola - Delicious and Refreshing," ca. 1950s..................................... 65

Coca-Cola Fan

Fan, cardboard, front shows the Sprite boy peeking around bottle w/"Have a Coke" & reverse is marked "Compliments of your local Coca-Cola Bottling Co.," minor discoloration, 9 x 9 1/2 (ILLUS.) 88
Fan, cardboard, "Quality Carries On - Drink Coca-Cola," illustrates hand holding Coca-Cola bottle, 1950s................................... 60
Fan, wicker, heart-shaped w/"Drink Coca-Cola in Bottles," ca. 1950s 65

Coca-Cola Festoon

Festoon, cardboard, "Chinese Lanterns," center w/young woman wearing hat & glasses & holding glass, 1920s (ILLUS. above) 5,000
Festoon, cardboard, "Swans," four swans swimming among lily pads & flowers, late 1930s... 1,000
Festoon, cut-out cardboard, band of colorful maple leaves, girl holding bottle at center, 1927... 4,000

Rare Coca-Cola Fish Festoon

Festoon, end pieces of stamped tin w/wood end logos, six fish are detachable stamped tin, center is stamped tin over wood backing, logo is cut-out wood, canvas straps & rope connectors, ca. 1937, Kay Displays, rare (ILLUS. above) 3,600
Game, board-type, Chinese Checkers, 1940s.. 125
Game, cribbage board, wooden, w/pegs, 1940s.. 65
Game, Dominos, in original box, 1940s.............. 60

Tick-Tac-Toe Game

Game, Tick-Tac-Toe, wood w/figural bottle pieces, 1940s-1950s, Milton Bradley (ILLUS.)... 185
Golf ball, marked w/logo, ca. 1950s 20
Hatpin, cloisonné, oval w/logo, ca. 1930s, 1 1/2 x 2".. 350
Hats, paper, in original box, lot of 90 130

Ice bucket, cov., brass finish, barrel-shaped, two-handled, 1950s, 10" h. 400
Ice tongs, aluminum, 1940s, 9" l. 250
Knife, pocket-type, stainless steel, one blade & nail file, various logo designs & manufacturers, 1950-1970 35-50
Letter w/envelope, letterhead stationery & envelope w/logo & advertising, signed by Asa G. Chandler, dated 1892 (edge wear on envelope)..................... 1,200
License plate holder, metal, red w/white lettering "Drink Coca-Cola," 1960s-70s........... 40

License plate holder, metal, w/"Drink Coca-Cola in Bottles," Dura Products Mfg. Co., Canton, Ohio, 1940s-1950s (ILLUS.)............................ 425
Lighter, gold-plated, metal & plastic in original bag w/lettering "Gold Plated Lighter Reg. $1.00 Value Only $.49 When you buy a carton of Coca-Cola King Size," 2 1/2" h. (lettering on bag faded)..................... 94

Rare Coca-Cola Lunch Box

Lunch box, tin, rectangular, red w/white lettering & handle, marked "Drink Coca-Cola - Trade Mark Regd - Comeonin Coke," 1970s, rare (ILLUS.) 200
Marbles, glass swirls in plastic bag, "Free with every carton! - Drink Coca-Cola in Bottles - Delicious & Refreshing," 1950s 50
Matchbook, white w/green oval showing girl holding bottle, ca. 1914 750

1901 Coca-Cola Menu

Menu, 1901, featuring Hilda Clark on front marked "What shall we Drink?" & back w/floral spray & red circle marked "Drink Coca-Cola 5¢," some light stains, minor wear, light edge wear, 4 x 11 3/4" unfolded (ILLUS.) 1,485
Menu board, die-cut wood w/metal half bottle in original menu insert, Kay Display, early 1940s, all original, 16 1/2 x 34 1/2"... 1,875
Menu board, plastic, rectangular w/clock on left side, 1960s................................ 200
Menu board, tin, Art Deco style, "Drink Coca-Cola" & "Specials To-Day" at top, 1929................................. 600
Menu board, wood & Masonite, Art Deco style, "Drink Coca-Cola" & the silhouette of a girl at the bottom of the frame, 1939...... 650
Menu board, wall-type, tin, Coca-Cola logo at top, 1960s, 20" w., 28" h. (scratches, soiling & dent to chalkboard) 93
Message board, die-cut tin oval top w/"Drink Coca-Cola - Be refreshed" self-framed w/"Have a Coke!" at bottom, 17 3/4" w., 26" h. (soiling & stains on edges, small hole at bottom, minor scratches & paint chips) 110

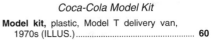

Coca-Cola Model Kit

Model kit, plastic, Model T delivery van, 1970s (ILLUS.)..................................... 60

Cooler Music Box

Music box, doll on round disk marked "Have Plenty on Hand for Family and Friends," above figural cooler marked "Drink Coca-Cola - Ice Cold," 1950s, rare (ILLUS. of one version) **2,000**

Coca Cola Needle Case

Needle case, cardboard, pictures pretty girl holding glass on front, bottle & filled glass on table w/flowers in background on the back, ca. 1924, 2 x 3" (ILLUS.) **88**

Note pad, celluloid, shows Hilda Clark holding glass, top marked "Compliments of The Coca-Cola Company" & marked at bottom "Atlanta - Philadephia, Chicago, Los Angeles, Dallas, New York, Boston, Baltimore," 1903, 2 1/2 x 5" **600**

Paper dolls, "The Coke Crowd," cut-out book, four male & four female figures w/various outfits, printed by Merrill Co., Publishers, Chicago, Illinois, 1946 .... **185**

Pencils, in original sleeves, ca. 1940s, box of six dozen **187**

Pillow, cloth, bottle-shaped, 1950 .... **125**

Pin, brass, routeman's, figural bottle, Indianapolis Bottling Co., ca. 1930, 2 1/2" h. **150**

Safe Driving Award Pin

Pin, deliveryman's ten year "Safe Driving Award," gold, winged tire below enameled white cross in green enameled oval w/"Universal Safety" in border, red enameled banner at top w/"Coca-Cola" (ILLUS.) **350**

Anniversary Plaque

Plaque, pressed metal, round, marked "50th Anniversary - Coca-Cola - 1886-1936," red, gold & white w/chain hanger, 1936, 16" d. (ILLUS.) **1,250**

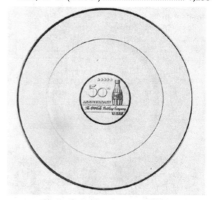

Coca-Cola Anniversary Plate

Plate, ceramic, circle in center w/"50th Anniversary - the Coca-Cola Company" below five stars, bottle on the side, Lenox China, 1950s, 10 1/2" d. (ILLUS.) **475**

Plate, china, shows bottle & glass & "Drink Coca-Cola - Refresh Yourself " around rim, American Chinaware Corp., 1931, 7 3/8" d. **425**

"Drink Coca-Cola" Plate

Plate, 7 1/2" d., china w/lettering reading "Drink Coca-Cola," bottle & glass in green, yellow, red, brown, & cream w/red, black & yellow lettering, marked "Vitreous/Edwin M. Knowles China Co./31-2-1," crazing (ILLUS.)............ **385**

Playing cards, shows bottle being handed to young woman putting on ice skates, 1956, full deck in original box **85**

Playing cards, girl holding bottle & glass on each,1939, complete deck **475**

Playing cards, girl wearing cowboy hat & drinking from a bottle of Coca-Cola, 1951, complete deck **85**

Early Coca-Cola Girl Postcard

Postcard, pictures a pretty girl & "The Coca-Cola Girl" in the bottom left-hand corner & "Drink Delicious Coca-Cola" in the bottom right corner, Hamilton King artwork, 1910 (ILLUS.).................................... **700**

Coca-Cola Framed Poster

Poster, colorful cardboard litho in green wooden frame, depicts a smiling girl standing behind table laden w/cookies & bottles of Coke, reads "Come Over For Coke," Forbes-Boston Litho, 1947 The Coca-Cola Co., 36 1/2" l., 20 3/4" h., minor scratches, some creases & hole in middle (ILLUS.) **253**

Poster, cardboard, colorful scene of bottle of Coca-Cola floating in Arctic waters, "Have a Coke," 1944, framed, 20 x 36" **500**

Coca-Cola Pretzel Dish

Pretzel dish, aluminum, round bowl supported by three bottle-shaped legs, ca. 1930s (ILLUS.)... **225**

Radiator Plate Sign

Radiator plate, chrome, "Coca-Cola In Bottles" in script, 1920s, 17" (ILLUS.).......... **585**

Coca-Cola Radio

Radio, carrying case-style, "Coca-Cola refreshes you best," 1950s (ILLUS.)................ **950**

Radio, figural cooler marked "Drink Coca-Cola - Ice Cold," 1950s, 7 x 9 1/2 x 12" **750**

Radio, vending machine-shaped, 1970s.......... **135**

Riding toy, plastic, "Kiddy-Car," figural can on wheels, 1970s... **85**

Rocking horse, wood, giveaway item from the Salem New Hampshire Coca-Cola Bottling Co. & Rockingham Park racetrack, 1960s.. **200**

Salesman's sample, counter dispenser w/three spigots, all plastic w/heavy canvas padded carrying case, ca. 1960s, 12 x 16 1/2"... **2,500**

Salt & pepper shakers, can-shaped, 1970s, pr. **15**

Sandwich toaster, electric, used in soda fountains, embossed "Coca-Cola" on sandwich (no cord) **1,000**

Salesman of the Month Award

Service award, "Salesman of the Month," cast metal, figure of driver standing on bottle cap, ca. 1930, 6 1/2" h. (ILLUS.) **675**

continues into bottom tabs, dated 1954, new unused condition, colorful, 12 x 20" (ILLUS.) **44**

Classic Coca-Cola Santa Sign

Sign, die-cut cardboard, a tall colorful scene of Santa Claus seated among toys above the head of a sleeping boy in bed, "Season's Greetings" in red & white across the end of the bed, dated 1962, light overall edge wear, light crease at left edge, minor wear w/scattered spotting, 31 1/2 x 49" (ILLUS.) **440**

Coca-Cola Santa Display Insert Sign

Sign, cardboard display insert-type, a color full-figure image of smiling Santa Claus against a gold background, w/hanging tree ornaments, one in red printed in white "Serve Coca-Cola in Bottles," dark blue wording reads "Good taste for all - Take enough home," figure of Santa

Coca-Cola Santa Die-Cut Sign

Sign, die-cut counter-top cardboard style, a standing figure of Santa Claus holding a bottle of Coke in one hand & reading a letter, a big sack of letters in front w/a large red dot Coca-Cola logo button over a gold banner reading "Greetings," dated 1945, few scuffs, 8 1/2 x 14" (ILLUS.) **413**

Scarce Coca-Cola Arrow Sign

Sign, die-cut double-sided tin arrow, shaft in white w/large Coca-Cola logo in white, black tail & tip w/white wording reading "Ice Cold - Sold Here," dated 1929, nicks, scratches & overall flecks, 7 11/16 x 29 7/8" (ILLUS.) **1,045**

Large Framed Coca-Cola Sign

Sign, double-sided porcelain in original iron frame w/hooks, rectangular w/a green band w/gold wording at top reading "Fountain Service" above red ground section w/white wording reading "Drink Coca-Cola - Delicious and Refreshing," ca. 1930s, some light scratches & small chips, one hanger pulled away, 42 x 60 1/4" (ILLUS.) **2,530**

Hanging Coca-Cola Two-sided Sign

Sign, double-sided porcelain, square w/rounded corners & original factory hanging hooks at the top, color image of a large red, white & steel grey stairstep-shaped soda dispenser, dated 1939, minor edge chips, small hole at bottom center, few tiny edge chips & scattered scratches, 25 1/4 x 26 1/4" (ILLUS.).......... **1,430**

Embossed Tin Coca-Cola Script Sign

Sign, embossed tin, narrow rectangular form, a dark green border band & thin yellow band around a dark red ground w/white wording reading "Drink Coca-Cola," very minor scattered nicks & scratches, few bends at top, 5 3/4 x 17 3/4" (ILLUS.) **358**

Sign, round embossed tin, narrow green & yellow border bands around the red ground printed in large yellow & white wording "Ice Cold - Coca-Cola - Sold Here," dated 1933, 19 5/8" d. (two light creases at bottom, small chip & few tiny nicks) **440**

Sign, "the gift for thirst," a color poster w/a large bust portrait of Santa Claus at the left holding a bottle of Coke, children w/Christmas gifts on the right below the Coca-Cola logo all on a dark background, dated 1952, 10 1/2 x 23" **44**

Coca-Cola Syrup Bottle

Syrup bottle w/original metal top, marked w/"Drink Coca-Cola" surrounded by wreath w/bow, ca. 1910 (ILLUS.).................. **500**

Tie bar, silver plate, delivery driver, ca. 1930, 7/8 x 1 3/4"... **50**

Coca-Cola Toy "Cobot"

Toy, "Cobot," can-shaped w/logo, in original box (ILLUS.) **150**
Toy, yo-yo, shaped like bottle cap, red & white plastic, "Drink Coca-Cola," 1960s.......... **12**
Toy, cardboard cut-outs of "Toy Town," 1927, 10 x 15 .... **125**
Toy, cardboard cut-outs, "Uncle Remus Story," 1931, 10 x 15" **325**

1950s Coca-Cola Delivery Truck

Toy truck, battery-operated, route delivery-type, yellow & white w/red lettering, 1950s, Sanyo, w/original box (ILLUS.)....... **1,265**
Toy truck, metal, delivery-type, ca. 1960, Matchbox... **55**

1950s GMC Coca-Cola Truck

Toy truck, route delivery type, green & yellow, GMC, ca. 1950s, 5 1/2" (ILLUS.) **1,000**

1932 Coca-Cola Truck

Toy truck, route delivery type, red w/yellow bottle holder in truck bed, marked "Every Bottle Coca-Cola Sterilized," No. 171 Metalcraft w/rubber wheels, 1931 (ILLUS.)... **975**

Coca-Cola Route Truck

Toy truck, route delivery-type, battery-operated, white & yellow metal w/red hood, "Drink Coca-Cola" on side panels, Allen Haddock Co., 1950s-60s, w/original box, 12 1/2" l. (ILLUS.)... **330**
Toy truck, metal cab & frame w/wood bed containing fourteen wood block Coca-Cola cases, Smitty Toys, Smith-Miller, California, 13 1/2" l. (scratches & soiling, chips to sides of truck bed) **715**
Toy wagon, wood & metal, 1960 .... **125**

Coca-Cola Trolley Sign

Trolley sign, cardboard, girl w/glass peeking over top of lacy open fan marked "Drink Coca-Cola," shaded pink background marked "Delicious - Refreshing," 1914, 11 x 20 1/2" (ILLUS.) **6,000**
Tumbler, bell-shaped glass, marked "Coca-Cola" w/trademark in tail of first C, 1929-1940 .... **40**
Tumbler, bell-shaped, pewter, ca. 1930s, w/leather pouch... **550**
Tumbler, flared clear glass w/syrup line, marked "Coca-Cola," 1904.............................. **450**
Tumbler, soda fountain-type, clear glass, straight sides, marked w/"Coca-Cola" logo near top, syrup line all around the base, ca. 1900-04... **1,000**

Umbrella, six panels, alternating white marked "Drink Coca-Cola" & red w/bottle, 1920s **900**

Urn, cov., ceramic, 1970s reproduction miniature used for display purposes, white w/red lettering & gold design (ILLUS. left) **132**

Large & Small Reproduction Urns

Urn, cov., ceramic, 1970s reproduction used for display purposes (1896 originals were syrup dispensers) white w/red lettering & gold design, approximately 18" h. (ILLUS. right) **935**

Restored Model 72 Vending Machine

Vending machine, Model 72 upright machine, tall w/rounded top corners, dark red w/white wording across the top & colored pictures of a hand holding a bottle on each side, double-chute type, dime

operation, meticulously restored, 16 x 25", 58" h. (ILLUS.) **1,045**

Model 81A Coke Vending Machine

Vending machine, Model 81A machine, tall upright form w/rounded top, dark red w/small white wording across the top, long narrow dispensing door on the left side, dime operation, slot mechanism on the right, professionally restored, works, 18 x 27 1/4", 58 1/2" h. (ILLUS.) **3,471**

Vending machine, Model No. 44, restored & working, 58" h. **2,300**

Vienna Art plate, tin, topless girl pictured, issued by Western Reserve, original ornate giltwood frame, ca. 1908 .... **1,800**

Window display, cardboard cut-out log-shaped planter containing various flower plants, 1924, 11 x 24" **375**

Coca-Cola Window Display

Window display, folding cardboard, three-fold theatre stage design, lithographed in deep blue, greens & red, the center stage section w/a cameo illustration of a pretty lady w/glass, flanked by theatre curtain side panels each printed w/"Drink Coca-Cola" in an oval, 1913, some stains, minor edge wear & separated at folds (ILLUS.) **7,000**

Chapter 6
Display Cabinets

Apothecary, "Humphreys'," hardwood w/tin front, marked "Humphreys' Specifics (two side-by-side lists) Humphreys' Witch Hazel Oil, The Pile Ointment" in yellow lettering on blue background, hinged door on reverse opens to 36 individual dovetailed drawers, 21 3/4" w., 9 1/2" deep., 27 3/4" h. (missing eight drawers, some discoloration to front tin).. **$633**

Bean display counter, oak, double section store-type, six drawers, 24 x 34", 32" h. **700-1,000**

Bread, "Crescent Bread Company," top oak & glass, w/etched glass front panel, 24" h. **600-750**

Bread, "Ward's Bread," oak w/acid etched lettering, sliding back doors, 32" h. **500**

Clothing & accessories, "Brighton Silk Garters," wood & glass, rectangular, eight-drawer w/simulated stained glass front, stenciled wood on other three sides & marked "Brighton Silk Garters for 25 cents," 14" w., 10 1/2" deep, 19" h................. **575**

Diamond Dyes "Presentation" Dye Cabinet

Dyes, "Diamond Dyes," birch w/tin lithographed front panel showing "Baby," known as the "Presentation" cabinet, Wells & Hope Co., 912-922 Vine St., Philadelphia, Penn., ca. 1887, VG, 9 1/2 x 16 1/2", 20" h. (ILLUS.)........ **1,400-1,600**

DeLaval Cream Separator Parts Cabinet

Cream separator parts, "DeLaval," oak w/tin litho panel in door "The World's Standard," interior has drawers for parts, early version, ca. 1900, 10 1/2 x 17 1/2", 23 1/2" h. (ILLUS.) **950-1,150**

Diamond Dyes Cabinets with Children

Dyes, "Diamond Dyes," oak w/tin front, depicts children skipping rope near a large garden staircase in front of mansion, includes numerous pieces of product, 16" w., 8 1/2" deep, 25" h. (ILLUS.)............ **1,925**

Dyes, "Peerless," roll-front style, 18" x 32"
(ILLUS.) **375-600**

Putnam "Fadeless" Dyes Cabinet

Dyes, "Putnam Dyes," lower left corner
w/scene of Colonel Putnam on horseback chased by Redcoats, red & blue lettering reading "Putnam Fadeless Dyes -
Tints - To Dye Use Boiling Water - To Tint
Dip in Warm Water," ca. 1910, 9 x 21",
10" h. (ILLUS.) **175-250**

Dyes, "Rainbow Dyes," rectangular
w/arched top, wood w/paper decals,
w/original contents, marked on top,
"Rainbow (over colored rainbow) - Beau-
tifully Brilliant" & written below "One Dye
For All Fabrics - No Fading - No Poison -
No Ripping - No Odor - No Crocking - No
Acid - Easiest - Simplest - Cleanest -
Most Economical For Home Use - 10¢ a
Package," 6" w., 12 1/2" l., 16 3/4" h.
(edge wear, scratches, soiling, staining,
front edge of base missing) **825**

Dyes, "Rit Dye," tin, "New Improved Rit -
Guaranteed to Fast Dye or Tint - Washes
as it Dyes" on side, area in front w/slot for
message to be inserted, three drawers in
rear each w/three compartments, other
product information on top & side,
11 1/4 x 14", 8 1/4" h. (minor denting,
soiling & staining) **88**

Diamond Dyes Cabinet

Dyes, "Diamond Dyes," wood w/lithograph
of woman standing at a table dying article
of clothing, other clothes hanging on line
behind her, marked "It's Easy to Dye
With Diamond Dyes," includes some
products & three-page color card & distributor label from Sacramento, Califor-
nia, 10 x 22 x 29 3/4" (ILLUS.) **1,320**

Dyes, "Diamond Dyes," wooden front opening w/embossed tin lithograph front
showing children playing w/balloon, tin
lithographed rear door, 24 1/2" h. (minor
repair) **1,200**

Dyes, "Dy-O-La Dye," oak w/tin facing on
front door, full insert & instructions on inside front door, wood facing on back,
13 3/4" w., 8 1/2" deep, 17" h. **202**

Dyes, "Magic Dyes," wood, rear opening
w/tin lithograph front, 36 3/4" h. (stains &
scratches) **2,400**

"Peerless" Dyes Cabinet

Shot Cabinet

Gun shot, ash, rectangular glass windows
w/iron lever releases for eight different
sizes of shot, ca. 1890, 10 x 25",
12 1/2" h. (ILLUS.) **700-800**

Octagonal Hardware Cabinet

Hardware, ash & soft maple, octagonal revolving-type, 72 pie-shaped drawers w/wood pulls, The American Bolt & Screw Case, Dayton, Ohio, Pat. Apr. 27 '80-May 12 '03, 21 1/2" x 33" (ILLUS.) **2,000-2,400**

Hanford's Counter Display Cabinet

front, by Economy Sign Co., N.E. Or. Broad & Race, Phila., 17" w., 8" l., 23 3/4" h. (edge wear, rust spotting, scratches, soiling & staining) **990**

Musical instruments, "Hohner Harmonica," wood, tiered tri-fold design w/paper marquee depicting people from around the world playing Hohner harmonicas, includes nine lithographed harmonica tin boxes, 18 cardboard boxes w/graphics including 13 original harmonicas, 5 1/2" w., 10 1/2" h. **920**

Hunt's Pen Cabinet

Pens, "Hunt's," oak, applied gold lettering, ca. 1920, 15"x 22", 6" h. (ILLUS.) **325-400**

"Eli Lilly Co." Medical Display Cabinet

Medicine, "Eli Lilly Co.," oak, hanging-type, double door, w/engraved company name across top panel, approximately 7 x 32", 35" h. (ILLUS.) **900-1,200**
Medicine, "Hanford's Balsam of Myrrh," oak w/glass door on front, ca. 1890, 9 3/4 x 14 1/2", 24" h. (ILLUS.) **450-525**
Medicine, "Munyon's Homeopathic Remedies," wood w/tin front & back w/original product contents, lists products & cost on

"Spencerian Steel Pens" Display Cabinet

Pens, "Spencerian Steel Pens," oak, small, 12 x 16", 7" h. (ILLUS.) **325-400**

Ribbon Cabinet

Ribbon, oak, 12 tip-out drawers w/glass fronts, six slide-out end racks, three over three, A.N. Russell & Sons, Ilion, N.Y. USA, ca. 1910, 27 x 28", 38" h. (ILLUS.) **1,300-1,600**

Sewing adjuncts, "Belding Brothers & Company," oak, 13 spool drawers on each side, bottom marked "Spool" on one side & "Silk" on other, 34" w., 18 1/2" deep, 35 1/2" h. **1,438**

Sewing adjuncts, "James Needles," wood w/reverse painting on glass labels, two dovetailed drawers, 15 1/2" h. (cracks & flaking) **450**

Rare Belding Spool Cabinet

Spool cabinet, "Belding Silk," walnut, wording on ornate crestrail centered by a clock dial, thirty drawers w/curved glass fronts on upper drawers, mirrors center door at top, ca. 1890, 17 x 34", 45" h. (ILLUS.) **2,400-2,800**

Spool cabinet, "Brainard Armstrong," walnut, incised side plaques, slanted front, 24 glass front drawers, four lower

wood drawers w/incised wood, 36" l., 32" h. **1,000-2,500**

Spool cabinet, "Brooks," ornate oak front, paneled sides, solid panel back, 25" h. (slight checking) **725**

Spool cabinet, "Clark's O N T Embroidery," wood, five-drawer **375-450**

"Clark's Thread" Thread Cabinet

Spool cabinet, "Clark's Thread," oak, w/tambour roll-up side doors, 17" sq., 23" h. (ILLUS.) **975-1,600**

Spool cabinet, "Corticelli Silk," oak w/eight drawers, good condition, approximately 19 x 23", 30" h. **875-1,250**

J. & P. Coats Spool Cabinet

Spool cabinet, "J. & P. Coats," ash, six-drawer, J. P. Co. brass anchor pulls, black lettering on tin inserts, ca. 1890, 18 x 25", 21" h. (ILLUS.) **900-1,500**

"J & P Coats" Thread Cabinet

Spool cabinet, "J & P Coats," oak, two-drawer, tin fronts, for handwork & machines, original pulls, 14 x 20", 7" h. (ILLUS.) **225-325**

Kloster Spool Cabinet

Spool cabinet, "Kloster," circular, stained poplar wood, ca. 1910, 12 x 14" (ILLUS.) **900-1400**

Spool cabinet, "Merricks," round, revolving, w/two curved glass panels w/lettering, 12 1/2" h. **1,400-2,000**

Tobacco, "Sweet Cuba," lithographed tin, square store bin w/slanted lid marked "Sweet Cuba Fine Cut" & front marked "5¢" w/product package shown, 8 x 8 x 10" (minor dings & scrapes) **182**

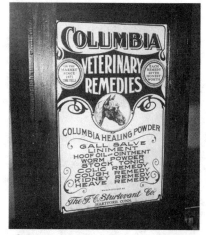

Columbia Veterinary Remedies Cabinet

Veterinary medicine, "Columbia," birch w/walnut finish, tin lithograph in door, The F.C. Sturtevant Co., Hartford, Conn., ca. 1915, 9 x 18", 24" h. (ILLUS.) **950-1,200**

Dr. LeSure's Famous Remedies Veterinary Medicine Display Cabinet

Veterinary medicine, "Dr. LeSure's Famous Remedies," ash, tin lithograph of horse head in front, ca. 1910, 6 3/4 x 20 1/2", 27" h. (ILLUS.) **3,800-4,500**

Dr. Daniels' Medicine Cabinet

Veterinary products, "Dr. Daniels' Warranted Veterinary Medicines," wood, front-opening w/embossed tin lithographed front panel showing the doctor & various remedies w/list of prices at bottom (ILLUS.) **6,710**

Veterinary products, "Humphreys' Specifics," wood, blue background w/two-sided two-faced listings of 35 veterinary products, 22" w., 9" deep, 28" h. (minor soiling) .. **1,265**

Veterinary products, "Humphreys' Veterinary Specifics," walnut, front-opening w/heavily embossed composition panel w/a profile of a horse, scarce version reading "Humphreys' Veterinary Homeopathic Specifics," dated 12/14/87, 10 x 21", 34" h. **5,000-6,000**

Watches, "Elgin Watches," wooden front opening w/reverse-painting on glass front, small drawers on inside (several missing), image of Father Time, 37 3/4" h. (some scratches) **900**

Chapter 7
Display Cases

Automotive products, "Rusco Fan Belts," upright rectangular metal case w/three open shelves at the back, w/a slant-front printed w/a black ground & "Rusco Fan Belts" in white above a small red parrot saying in red "Carry a spare in your tool box," lower front panel reads "A Rusco Product...," top & sides in maroon, wood base, w/two belts, 12 1/2 x 22", 16 3/4" h. (some denting, spotting, scratches & soiling) **$193**

Cake, "Freihofer's Cakes," tin w/glass front & front portion of sides, three metal shelves w/wood frame, sign on top reads "Freihofer's Quality Cakes" w/"Freihofer's Quality Cakes - A cake for every taste - Pound - Sponge - Fruit" on side, minor denting, rust spotting, scratches & soiling, 24 3/4" w., 17" l., 27 1/2" h. (ILLUS. below) **660-1,100**

Chewing gum, "Colgan's Gum," wood frame, base & top w/glass sides & shelves, acid etching highlighting six different flavors, 8 x 9 x 18" (new shelves, pin supports, finish & hinges) **660-1,100**

Chewing gum, "Primley's Gum," wood frame & base, curved glass front & glass sides, goldleaf lettering on front, 12 x 18" (some wear to wood)........................... **550-1,100**

Chewing gum, "Wrigley's," metal w/nickel plating, revolving-type **175-275**

Chewing gum, "Wrigley's," tin, five compartments (ILLUS.) **250-325**

Wrigley's Counter Display Case

San Felice Cigars Humidor Showcase

Cigars, "San Felice Cigars," floor model, birch w/cherry stain, ca. 1920, 24 x 71", 42" h. (ILLUS.) **750-900**

Curved-front Display Case

Counter-top showcase, curved glass front, German silver frame, ca. 1900, 21" sq., 12" h. (ILLUS.) **375**

Counter-top showcase, curved glass front, nickel trim w/mirrored door, 22 x 30"..... **273-375**

Freihofer's Cakes Display Case

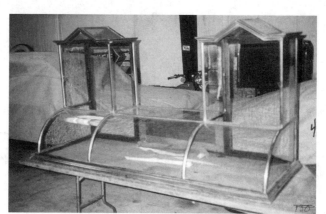

Double Steeple Countertop Showcase

Countertop-type showcase, oak, double steeple-style, German silver trim, w/curved glass front, original condition, 38 x 74" to top of steeple (ILLUS.).. **4,500-5,000**

Eisenstadt's Pen Case

Fountain pens, "Eisenstadt's Incomparable," floor model, cherry-stained maple w/reverse-etched front glass, rare, ca. 1915, 16 x 17", 42" h. (ILLUS.).............. **375-450**

Ideal Fountain Pen Case

Fountain pens, "Ideal," oak & glass, holds two trays of pens, applied transfer lettering inside door, ca. 1910, 8 1/2 x 17 3/4", 7 1/2" h. (ILLUS.) **375-425**

Medicine, "Feen-a-mint," tin w/oval mirror top center w/"Feen-a-mint" above woman pictured holding a tablet w/"The Chewing Laxative - Chew it Like Gum" above a picture of the product in a box, wooden base, one shelf in back for product storage, 5 1/2 x 7 1/2", 16 1/4" h. (scratches & minor paint chips & dents) **501**

Sewing adjuncts, "Crowley's Needles," wood, wide drawers across top & bottom w/two center rows of five small drawers, all w/original porcelain knobs, decal letters "Crowley's" across top drawer & "Needles" across bottom drawer, 9 5/8 x 18 3/4", 9 1/2" h. (soiling, staining, six small drawers new) **253**

Arrow Counter Display Case

Shirt collars, "Arrow," oak frame w/glass on four sides, reserve transfer lettering on front, three columns of collars, ca. 1910, 7 x 19", 26" h. (ILLUS.).......................... **775-900**

Shirt collars, "E & W Collar," glass & wood case contains 14 collars, 25" h. (minor scratch to decal) **550**

Chapter 8
Display Figures & Displays

Bosch Battery Counter Display

Automotive products, "Bosch Battery," chalkware, figural gas station attendant holding battery, 7 x 7 1/2", 25" h. (ILLUS.) **$660**

Automotive products, "Buss Auto Fuses," metal, depicts motorist in front of stationary vehicle & package of Buss Auto Fuses, yellow lettering & decoration on black background, 8 1/2" w., 3" deep. 7 1/2" h. **154**

Automotive products, "Trico Wiper Blades & Rods," tin lithograph w/paper lithograph label on back, depicts woman at top, orange, black & cream, 2 1/2 x 9 1/2 x 14" **242**

Batteries, "Burgess Batteries," painted metal, hinged top has zebra holding battery & advertising & slot w/original business reply card, "Here are Burgess Batteries to fit Every Size Flashlight" in white letters at top, "New Burgess Batteries" at bottom & "Advertising Metal Display Co. Chgo & NY - Made in U.S.A." on back, 10 3/4 x 11 3/4", 14 3/4" h. (chips w/minor rust on bottom section, some soiling, scratches & paint loss) **33**

Bud Light Spuds McKensie

Brewing company, molded plastic model of a dog, Bud Light "Spuds McKensie," March 10, 1988 stamped on bottom, 1986 Anheuser Busch Inc. embossed on back leg, white paint on feet, soiling, 15 3/8" h. (ILLUS.) **165**

Brewing company, "Blatz" painted aluminum figure of man w/keg torso w/logo, holding mug of beer & standing next to sign w/"Milwaukee's Finest Beer," & "Blatz on draft" on base, some minor paint loss, 15 1/2" h. **35**

Candy, "Wanna Pop," cast plaster model of small seated Pug dog on a square base, brand name in black on front of base, cast overall w/holes for inserting the lollipops, retains most of its paint, 5 1/4 x 6 3/4", 7" h. (a few dings & abrasions) **226**

Western Super-X Shells Sign

Cartridges, "Western Super-X Shells," die-cut cardboard, stand-up type, shows cut-away shell near box of shells, birds, cloudy sky & hunters in background, marked "15 to 20 Yards More Range - New Seal-tite Wads - Progressive Burning Powder," 11 x 21" (ILLUS.) **644**

Full Hickman's Silver Birch Gum Box

Beech-Nut Counter Display

Chewing gum, "Beech-Nut," tin litho, for mints, fruits & chewing gum, ca. 1920, 9 1/2 x 17", 13 1/2" h. (ILLUS.) **750-900**

Chewing gum, "Hickman's Silver Birch Chewing Gum - 5¢," counter display box full & complete w/20 packges, original slip cover top w/wording in green & red against a white birch bark ground, a blue-bird in one corner, near mint, 4 1/2 x 6 1/2" (ILLUS.) **688**

Chewing gum, "Sen Sen Chewing Gum," cardboard display box, fine overall condition, includes some original packages, 3 x 3 1/2", 4" h. **44**

Chewing gum, "Walla-Walla Peppermint Chewing Gum," cardboard box printed in red & pale green on cream, low rectangular form, 4 x 6" (minor scuffs) **55**

Chewing gum, "Wrigley's Spearmint Gum," cardboard, looks like oversized pack of gum, ca. 1950s, 8 1/2 x 10 x 36" **175**

Florida Chewing Gum Display

Chewing gum, "Florida Chewing Gum," counter box w/scene of woman reclining on lounge w/packs of gum around her, marked "Florida Chewing Gum - 3 Flavors - 5¢" w/"This Box Contains 20 Packages" on bottom edge of box, along w/20 unopened packages of gum (ILLUS.) **2,530**

American Field Counter Sign

Clothing & accessories, "American Field Hunting Garments," die-cut cardboard w/jump-out model of mallard, hunter in background, ca. 1940-50, 14 x 16" (ILLUS.) **138**

Hills Bros. Coffee Store Figure

Coffee, "Hills Bros. Coffee," painted plaster, ca. 1930, 19" h. (ILLUS.).... **1,000-1,300**

Film, "Kodak Film," metal, painted yellow w/"don't forget . . . Kodak Film" in black & red letters above lithograph of Ed Sullivan saying "Hold it! Got film" & "See the Ed Sullivan Show - Buy 2 and have enough!," plastic cover above film slots, "Made in U.S.A." on back, 7 1/2 x 12 1/2", 15" h. (soiling, minor fading, chips & scratches, surface rust inside back)............ **55**

Food, "Beech-Nut Gum," metal w/double tier, 15" w., 9 1/2" h. **21**

Black Cross Teas Countertop Sign

Food, "Black Cross Teas," embossed cardboard, stand-up type, figure of young girl wearing large pink bonnet holding sign reading "'Oh You Black Cross - The Widlar Co.'" & showing box marked "Black Cross Pure Selected Teas," few minor scrapes, 7 1/4 x 16" (ILLUS.)........................ **204**

Food, "National Biscuit," oak w/stylized decal, curved kickplate, 68" h. **825**

Food, "Simple Simon Nuts," metal, dark green w/gold lettering, reads "Simple Simon Salted Nuts 5¢," upright stand w/round black base, holds individual sacks of nuts, made by "American Nut Co. Indianapolis Ind." (scratches & some paint loss)........................ **121**

Early Kessler Football Display Figure

Football, "Kessler," rubber composition standing figure of an early football player holding a ball & wearing a green, red, gold & white uniform, original paint, 11 x 18", 46" h. (ILLUS.)........................ **385**

Gunpowder, "Curry & Metzgar, Pittsburgh, Pa. Gunpowder," tin, roll-top style, black background paint w/gold, white & red lettering & decoration, ca. 1870-1880, minor denting & chipping, 13 1/4" w., 15 1/2" deep, 19 1/2" h. **253**

Hair accessories & supplies, "Gainsborough Hair Net," wood, lower front & marquee depict lady w/mirror admiring hair w/hair net, contains 18 original Gainsborough Hair Net envelopes, 15" w., 17 1/2" deep, 17 1/2" h. **230**

Hair accessories & supplies, "West Electric Hair Curler Company," tin, triangular w/"West Hair Nets - West Electric Hair Curlers - Softex Shampoo" on different sides, round rotating pedestal, ca. 1922, 10 x 8 1/2 x 18" **460**

Locks, "Master Padlock," wood w/12 hangers for displaying locks, embossed lion head w/Master logo in mouth top right corner, one padlock sample, marked "Master Lock Co., Milwaukee, Wisconsin, U.S.A.," 11 5/8" w., 23 1/4" h. (wood soiled & metal holders have some rust, soiling & scratches, one hook missing & one loose) 325

Medicine, "Dr. Morse's Indian Root Pills," die-cut cardboard, three-section, colorful scene depicts river in background w/tents & Native American sitting near campfire & marked "Dr. Morse's Indian Root Pills - Favored for 50 Years - for Constipation and Biliousness," John Igelstoem Co., Masillon, Ohio, 41 1/2" l., 27" h. (edge wear & soiling) 605

Medicine, "Dr. Morse's Indian Root Pills," multicolored lithographs on a board, includes tri-fold display, paper banner & four individual countertop displays contained in original cardboard folder, all depict various scenes of Native Americans, ca. 1915-1925 358

Medicine, "Gowan's Preparation For Pneumonia For Croup," counter display box made of cardboard w/hanging string, white & black depicting a box of the product, printing on all four sides, ca. 1900-1910, 6 x 9 1/2" 99

Medicine, "Smith Brothers'," pressed steel & black enamel marked "Smith Brothers' S.B. Cough Drops" on top above graphic of product box & "5¢," 3 3/4 x 4 1/4 x 9 3/4" 413

Peanuts, "Planters Peanuts" four-sided red pyramid display for bags of peanuts, several white Mr. Peanut figures on sides & top w/"Planters Salted Nuts" in white letters at top, ca. 1950s, 15" h. (light soiling, few bends) 1,760

GE Man Jointed Display Figure

Radios, "General Electric," large jointed wood figure of the GE Man in a band major uniform, painted in red, white, gold, black & pink, early 20th c., 19" h. (ILLUS.)... 880

Alaska Refrigerator Counter Display

Refrigerator, "Alaska Refrigerator," cardboard die-cut standup, lithograph of seal & Eskimo child in furry white suit w/hood, holding green sign w/snow on top, marked "Alaska Refrigerator," child's

Potato Chip Display

Potato chips, wood & glass, w/vending display case, approximately 12" sq., 17" h. (ILLUS.)... 200-350

hood marked "Alaska" & "The Seal of Perfection" on side of brown seal, litho by Edwards & Deutsch, Chicago, Illinois, minor scrapes & creases w/tape, small tack hole, 12 1/2 x 16 1/4 (ILLUS.)....................... **187**

Howard Johnson Pie Man Display

Restaurant, "Howard Johnson," plaster composition figure of pie man walking toward the fair carrying a stack of pies, good old repaint, 6 x 27", 42" h. (ILLUS.) **358**

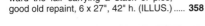

Rush Park Seed Counter Display Box

Seeds, "Rush Park Seed Co.," "Unrivaled Garden Seed," paper litho inside lid & front of box, ca. 1890, 13 x 24", 6 1/2" h. (ILLUS.) **250-325**

Shoes, "Poll-Parrot Shoes," metal cage, post & shoe holders w/green, yellow & red plastic parrot in center, wooden sign base & red oval sign on top w/"Poll-Parrot," separate motor unit, metal case & cardboard cover attaches to metal housing unit to make parrot & shoes spin, 20" w., 33" h. (paint chips to post, soiling & small paint chips to cage, shoe holders & parrot) **160**
Shoes, "Red Goose Shoes," model of goose drops egg & toys, 1950s-60s **300**

Robin Hood Shoes Display Figure

Shoes, "Robin Hood Shoes," painted plaster, ca. 1920, 15" h. (ILLUS.).......... **375-450**
Thread, "Clarks Thread" spool holder w/suffragette theme **1,430**
Tobacco, "Model Smoking Tobacco," die-cut cardboard w/"Model Man," as a cigar store Indian, ca. 1940s, 12" h........................ **65**
Varnish, "Ohio Varnish Co.," cardboard, marked "Floor Enamel for any surface - Interior or Exterior - Chi-Namel Product," w/interior & exterior scene of person using the product, color samples attached, ca. 1920-30s, 12 x 18" (few minor scuffs) **66**
Veterinary products, "Clayton's Dog Remedies," figural bulldog, embossed "Clayton's Dog Remedies" on both sides, includes "Dr. Clayton's Treatise on all Breeds of Dogs" booklet, 27" l., 19 1/2" h.. **1,725**

Chapter 9
Display Jars & Containers

Apothecary bottle, cylindrical, "Acidum Tannic" on label-under-glass, smooth lip, smooth base, original tin lid, France, ca. 1875-1885, turquoise, 10 1/4" h. **$143**

Apothecary bottle, cylindrical, "Benzine Rect:" on label-under-glass, tooled lip, smooth base, original ground glass stopper, ca. 1865-1890, 8" h. **121**

Large Apothecary Bottle

Apothecary bottle, cylindrical, "Creta C: Camph:" on label-under-glass, applied mouth, polished pontil, original ground glass stopper, England, ca. 1875-1890, pink amethyst, 11 5/8" h. (ILLUS.) **633**

Apothecary bottle, cylindrical, embossed "Liq. Potas Arsenit" in oval, tooled lip, "Phila Whitall Tatum & Co New York" on smooth base, original ground glass stopper, ca. 1890-1910, cobalt blue, 4 1/4" h. **770**

Apothecary bottle, cylindrical, "Ferri Sub-carb." on label-under-glass, flared lip, "W.N. Walton Patd Sept 23d 1862" on smooth base, ca. 1865-1875, cobalt blue, 11 1/8" h. **242**

Apothecary bottle, cylindrical, "Syr. Sa-rasp. Co." on label-under-glass, tooled mouth, "Pat Apr 2 1883 W.T. & Co." on smooth base, period clear notched stopper, ca. 1883-1890, cobalt blue, 8 7/8" h. **143**

Apothecary bottle, cylindrical, "Tr. Can-nab. Ind." on label-under-glass, tooled mouth, "W.T. & Co." on smooth base, original ground glass stopper, ca. 1880-1900, cobalt blue, 7 3/4" h. **330**

Apothecary bottle, cylindrical w/ribbed neck, footed pedestal smooth base, label reading "1378 Anise 'Anis' Pimpinella anisum L. Umbelliferae," original ribbed ground glass stopper, filled w/anise, ca. 1900-1920, clear, 13 " h. **303**

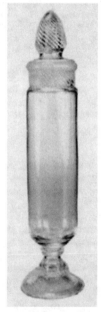

Counter Display Apothecary Jar

Apothecary bottle, cylindrical w/ribbed neck, footed pedestal smooth base, original ribbed ground glass stopper, ca. 1900-1920, clear, 5 5/8" h. to top of lid (ILLUS.) **1,650**

Apothecary bottle, rectanglar w/beveled edging, embossed "Benjamin Green Apothecary Portsmouth, N.H.," tooled lip w/long ringed neck, "W.T. & Co. U.S.A." on smooth base, ca. 1885-1900, cobalt blue, 7 1/4" h. **165**

Apothecary bottle, square, "Silver Nitrate 5%" on label-under-glass, wide tooled lip, smooth base, original notched glass stopper & "Poison" label, ca. 1890-1910, amber, 4 5/8" h. **44**

Apothecary Jar Set

Apothecary jars, labels-under-glass w/letters "D-E-P-E-N-D-A-B-L-E-S-E-R-V-I-C-E," tooled lips, "Wt. & Co. U.S.A." on smooth bases, all w/original ground glass stoppers & in original shipping boxes, ca. 1890-1910, 8 3/4" h., set of 18 (ILLUS.) **715**

Apothecary Globe

Apothecary globe, cylindrical stained glass leaded globe tapering to point, open-top w/metal edging & three-chain attached hanger, cast-iron eagle flange, one cracked square in globe, globe 21" l., eagle 19" l. (ILLUS.) **2,300**

Apothecary jar, cylindrical, impressed "J. Milhau Druggist, 183 Broadway N-Y," dark brown glazed stoneware, ca. 1820-1830, 6 1/2" h. **207**

Apothecary jar, flared lip w/short cylindrical neck, bulbous body tapering to bottom ring, applied stem & foot, original round tapering stopper w/bottom ring, light powder blue milk glass, ca. 1870-1890, 13" h. **495**

Old Milk Glass Show Jar

Apothecary show jar w/original stopper, blown glass, tall ovoid body raised on a slender pedestal & round foot, the tall cylindrical neck w/a flared rim, tall bulbous ovoid stopper, milk glass, 19th c., 11 3/4" h. (ILLUS.) **121**

English Apothecary Jar

Apothecary jar w/original ball stopper, blown glass, spherical body w/tall tapering neck & rolled lip, deep purple w/original painted white & black round label w/"5," ground pontil, probably England, ca.   1850-70,   11 1/2" h. (ILLUS.) **275**

Three-Piece Drugstore Show Jar

Apothecary show jar w/original stopper,
three-piece, mold-blown glass, a bulbous
ovoid body above a round stepped foot,
a tall cylindrical neck w/a tooled rim, the
stopper formed as a miniature jar form
w/another small teardrop green glass
stopper, two lower tiers in clear,
American-made, early 20th c., 11 1/2" h.
(ILLUS.) **165**

Dakota Globe Candy Jar

Candy jar, cov., "Dakota Globe," w/ground
lid, 16" (ILLUS.)..................................... **525-650**
Candy jar, cov., "Zatek Chocolate Billets,"
embossed clear glass, 16 1/2" h. (rim
chips to lid) **300**
Candy jar, six piece, stacking-type,
20" h. **375-375**

Century Candy Jar

Candy jar, cov., "Century," 26" h.
(ILLUS.) **700-875**

Peters Popular Cartridge Box

Cartridges, "Peters Cartridge Co.," display
box w/pointer-type hunting dog on front
flanked by "25 Load - 10 Ga. 230"
w/"Popular Cartridge" above & "The Pe-
ters Cartridge Co." below (ILLUS.) **2,173**

Dakota Candy Jar

Candy jar, cov., "Dakota," cylinder,
w/ground stopper, 30" (ILLUS.) **1,600-2,000**

Adams Display Tin

Chewing gum, "Adams Spearmint," tin, lithographed on four sides & top, lift lid-type, ca. 1920, 4 3/4 x 6 3/4", 6" h. (ILLUS.) **500-600**

Adams Chewing Gum Display Box

Chewing gum, "Adams Tutti Frutti Chewing Gum," counter display box of cardboard printed in color w/a large rectangular bust image of Lillian Russell, advertising in white on red around the edges, intact w/glass inside, minor scuffs & edge tear, 4 1/4 x 10", 1 1/4" deep (ILLUS.) **242**

Chewing gum, "Chiclets Gum," cylindrical tin counter-top holder for loose packages of Chiclets gum, color stripes around the outside show different flavors of the gum including "Charcoal" **127**

Colgan's Counter Display Jar

Chewing gum, "Colgan's Taffy Tolu Gum," figural jar top w/lettering on jar, ca. 1910, 5 1/4 x 5", 11" h. (ILLUS.) **325-425**

Brother Jonathan Store Bin

Chewing tobacco, "Brother Jonathan Chewing Tobacco," metal store size bin depicting caricature of Brother Jonathan seated in a tobacco field (ILLUS.) **6,050**

Drug bottle, "A. B. Stewart Druggist, Seattle W.T." (below monogram), rectangular w/rounded shoulders & tooled lip, clear, ca. 1880-90 .... **385**

Drug bottle, brown slip stoneware w/slightly formed pour spout, debossed "R.H. Lackey Pharmacies Philda," ca. 1845-1860, 7 1/2" h. **165**

Drug bottle, "C.W. Snow & Co., Druggists (design of eagle w/shield & mortar & pestle), Syracuse, N.Y.," square w/tooled lip, ca. 1885-95, deep cobalt blue, 8 1/4" h. **468**

Drug bottle, "Citrate of Magnesia - H.B. Wakelee - Druggist," cylindrical w/applied mouth & smooth base, cobalt blue, 7 5/8" h. (lightly cleaned) **143**

Drug bottle, cylindrical, embossed "G.W. Merchant Chemist Lockport N.Y.," applied sloping collar mouth, iron pontil, ca. 1845-1855, medium Lockport green, 7 1/2" h. **330**

Drug bottle, cylindrical, embossed "J & C Maguire Chemists And Druggists St. Louis. Mo.," applied double collar mouth, smooth base, ca. 1855-1865, medium cobalt blue, 7 1/2" h. **330**

Drug bottle, cylindrical, embossed "Strong, Cobb & Co. Wholesale Druggists Cleveland, O.," applied mouth, smooth base, ca. 1875-1885, cobalt blue, 6 1/4" h. **110**

Drug bottle, cylindrical, embossed "Strong, Cobb & Co Wholesale Druggists Cleveland," applied mouth, marked "C & I" on smooth base, ca. 1875-1885, cobalt blue, 10 3/8" h. **121**

Drug bottle, "D. Vollmer, Druggist, Ft. Wayne, Ind.," base marked "B.F.G. Co.," square w/beveled corners, ca. 1875-85, medium electric cobalt blue, 7 1/2" h. **550**

Drug bottle, "G.W. Merchant - Chemist - Lockport - N.Y.," cylindrical w/applied sloping collar, deep emerald green, ca. 1855-65, 7 1/4" h. 198

Drug bottle, "J.D. Morgan - Druggist - Pittsburgh," rectangular w/rolled lip, ca. 1845-55, deep bluish aqua, 5 1/4" h. 121

Drug bottle, "Jacob's Pharmacy (motif of eagle on mortar & pestle) Atlanta GA," tooled mouth,"W.T. Co. U.S.A." on smooth base, 70% original label for "Strychnine Sulphate," ca. 1885-1910, amber, 2 1/2" h. 77

Drug bottle, "Maguire Druggist, St. Louis Mo.," rectangular w/paneled sides & applied sloping collar, light apple green, ca. 1845-55, 5 3/4" h. (lightly cleaned, small flake at base) 633

Drug bottle, rectangular w/beveled edges, embossed "We Never Sleep Muegge The Druggist Baker Ore. - Muegge's" tooled lip, smooth base, ca. 1885-1900, rich yellowish green, 8 1/4" h. (ILLUS.)......... 143

Drug bottle, rectangular w/sloping shoulder, embossed "Jozeau" & "Pharmacien" on opposite ends, rolled lip, pontil-scarred base, ca. 1840-1855, deep olive green, 4 1/2" h. 165

Drug bottle, "The Owl Drug Co. (design of owl on mortar & pestle) Trade Mark," rectangular w/tooled lip, clear sun-colored amethyst, ca. 1900, 10" h. 143

Hair lotion bottle, "St. Clairs Hair Lotion," rectangular w/paneled sides & tooled lip, cobalt blue, ca. 1900, 7 1/4" h. (lightly cleaned) 66

Rare Druggist Bottle

Drug bottle, rectangular, embossed "J & C Maguire Chemists And Druggists St. Louis. Mo.," applied double collar mouth, iron pontil, ca. 1845-1855, cobalt blue, 7 7/8" h. (ILLUS.) 2,145

Leech Jar

Leech jar, white porcelain w/black transfer reading "Sangsues," base marked "J. Mourier & Cie. 15. rue Pastourelle, Paris, Depose, Gandois Successeur," includes jar, insert & lid, France, ca. 1890-1910, 12 3/4" h. (ILLUS.)...................................... 3,960

Short Horlick's Glass Display Jar

Malted milk, cov., "Horlick's," cylindrical clear glass w/low domed cover, printed in dark blue "Horlick's - The Original Malted Milk," on both sides, 4 1/2" d., 5 3/4" h. (ILLUS.).. 75

Muegge's Druggist Bottle

Rare Early Horlick's Jar

Malted milk, cov., "Horlick's Malted Milk...," clear glass, tall squared footed w/a fitted ground-rimmed domed cover w/thumb-print border, label under glass in white w/dark blue & red printing & gold border, bottom embossed "Patent Applied 1889," 9 1/4" h. (ILLUS.) **295**

Peanuts, cov., clear glass flattened football shape on raised base, two sides embossed "Planters Salted Peanuts," clear glass lid w/peanut finial **425**

Planters "Fish Bowl" Jar

Peanuts, cov., "Fish Globe Planters Peanuts," clear glass fish bowl jar w/tin lid, fish-shaped white label on front (ILLUS.)...... **375**

Peanuts, cov., "Planters Brand Peanuts," clear glass fish bowl jar w/clear glass lid w/peanut handle, yellow rectangular label w/black & red lettering **450**

Peanuts, cov., "Planters Peanuts," clear glass barrel jar w/clear glass lid w/peanut handle **550**

Peanuts, cov., "Planters Peanuts," clear glass four-sided jar w/large molded pea-

nut on each corner, "Planters" vertically embossed between peanuts, peanut finial **525**

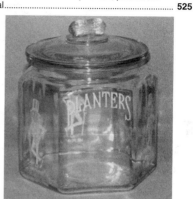

Planters Hexagonal Display Jar

Peanuts, cov., "Planters Peanuts," clear glass hexagonal jar and clear glass lid w/peanut handle, yellow lettering reads "Planters," yellow Mr. Peanut figure (ILLUS.) **155**

Peanuts, cov., "Planters Peanuts," glass, octagonal, highly embossed on all eight sides w/"Mr. Peanut" on four panels, peanut finial on lid, 13" to top of finial **230**

Peanuts, cov., "Planters Peanuts," glass, oval w/rectangular base, embossed "Planters Salted Peanuts" on front & back, peanut finial on lid, 9" h. (very small chip in lid) **288**

Peanuts, cov., "Planters Peanuts," clear glass square jar & clear glass lid w/peanut handle **110-185**

Peanuts, cov., "Planters Peanuts," w/"Please Keep Jar Always Covered," clear glass slant jar w/tin lid, lid embossed w/Mr. Peanut & black, gold & white lettering **175**

Tom's Toasted Peanuts Jar

Peanuts, "Enjoy Tom's Toasted Peanuts - Delicious," cylindrical clear glass w/inset domed cover, red knob & blue wording on sides, appears unused, 7 x 10 1/2" (ILLUS.) **55**

Planters Counter Display Box

Peanuts, "Planters Salted Peanuts," 24-count cardboard box, w/"For a Victorious America, Buy U.S. War Bonds and Stamps" across the top in white lettering, Mr. Peanut & unshelled peanuts in blue ink, depending on condition & die-cut (ILLUS.)... **150-900**

Peanuts, "Squirrel Brand Salted Peanuts," clear glass squared jar w/metal lid printed in brown, tan & red w/a center picture of a squirrel, 5 1/2" sq., 9" h. (ILLUS. right).. **77**

Pickles, "Heinz Pickles," clear glass display bottle w/ground stopper, 11" h. (rim chips & soiling to label) **300**

Soap, "Fairbanks Fairy Soap," wooden shipping container w/paper label on inside cover, center design of large red rose supporting a winged woman in white, marked "Fairbanks - The Soap of the Century - Pure - White - Floats - For the Toilet, Bath & Fine Laundry Use," 8 x 15 x 16" **358**

Squirrel Brand Peanut Jar

Soup, "Campbell's Soup," display box featuring Tomato Soup can on two sides & the Campbell Kids on each end, red & white, front reads "Campbell's Soups - Tomato Juice - Pork and Beans - Franco American Spaghetti," ca. 1920s-30s, 17 x 27 x 27" (light insect damage & minor wear & soiling)...................................... **253**

Vinegar, "Heinz Cider Vinegar," on base, frosted & clear embossed glass bottle w/"Heinz" etched in pickle cork stopper, spigot at bottom, 14 1/2" h. (edge wear to labels, rim chips, hairline on base) **450**

Chapter 10
Match Holders & Safes

Early Cast-iron Figural Match Holder

Cigar dealer, "Compliments of Wm. A. Weber Wholesale Cigar Dealer," cast-iron model of a turtle opening to hold matches, fine original finish, slight traces of surface rust, 3 1/4 x 5 1/4" (ILLUS.) **451**

Blatz Beer Match Safe

Beer, "Blatz Beer," brass, rectangular, embossed floral decoration at corners, center marked "Blatz Brewing Co. - Milwaukee - U.S.A.," ca. 1910, 1 1/2 x 2 3/4" (ILLUS.) **$150-225**

Rosa de Valle Cigars Match Safe

Cigars, "Rosa de Valle Cigars," flat rectangular safe w/celluloid portrait insert in tiger stripe-plated safe, fine colors, appears unused, 1 5/8 x 2 1/2" (ILLUS.) **165**

Early Brewery Match Safe

Brewing company, "Scheidt (Adam) Brewing Co.," silver plated brass, flattened rectangular form w/rounded corners & hinged lid, stamped scroll border, inscribed "Adam Scheidt Brewing Co. (w/logo) Norristown, Pa.," worn plating around edges, some dents, early 1900s (ILLUS.) **36**

DeLaval Figural Match Safe

Cream separator, "DeLaval Cream Separator," plated & painted metal miniature cream separator in black & silver, unused in original cardboard box w/a picture of a lady using the separator on the front, dated 1908, box 4 x 6 3/4" (ILLUS.) **918**

Two Sharples Match Holders

Cream separator, "Sharples Separator Co.," hanging holder, color-printed metal, long rectangular form w/arched scalloped top & bottom, color scene of cows in pasture above a woman seated at the cream separator, holder reads "Tubular Cream Separator - The Sharples Separator Co. - West Chester, Pa...." (ILLUS. left) **230**

Cream separator, "Sharples Separator Co.," hanging holder, color-printed metal, long rectangular form w/arched scalloped top & bottom, color scene of cows in pasture above a mother & young daughter operating the separator, reads "The Pet of the Dairy - Tubular Cream Separators - The Sharples Separator Co. - West Chester, Pa...." (ILLUS. right) **260**

Ceresota Flour Tin Match Box Holder

Flour, "Ceresota Flour," hanging holder, die-cut embossed lithographed tin, a color image at the top of a young boy cutting a large loaf of bread, a rectangular compartment for a box of

matches at the bottom, printed w/the company logo & "Ceresota Prize Bread Flour of the World," overall bright color w/some tiny scrapes, near mint, 2 1/4 x 5 1/2" (ILLUS.) **440**

B.P.O.E. Match Safe

Fraternal order, "B.P.O.E." (Benevolent & Protective Order of Elks), brass w/silver plate, rectangular, embossed fraternal symbols & marked "Cervus Alles," ca. 1910, 1 1/2 x 2 3/4" (ILLUS.) **125-175**

Beach Wickham Grain Co. Match Safe

Grain, "Beach Wickham Grain," metal & celluloid, rectangular, lithograph of horse head above "At Your Service," reverse marked "Compliments of Beach Wickham Grain Co. - Board of Trade - Chicago," three match heads shown in upper right corner, litho by Whitehead & Hoag, ca. 1900, 1 3/8 x 2 1/4" (ILLUS. of both sides) **150-200**

World Automatic Injector Match Safe

Injector, "World Automatic Injector," metal & celluloid, rectangular, lithograph depicts injector on cover, American Injector Company, Detroit, Michigan, litho by Whitehead & Hoag, ca. 1905, 1 3/8 x 2 1/2" (ILLUS.) **125-200**

Liquor dealer, metal w/paper, rectangular, novelty-type, reads "You Can't Find A Match For - John B. Gahn - Dealer in Wines, Liquors & Cigars," ca. 1910, made in Austria, 1 3/8 x 2 1/2" **85-125**

Motor oil, "Purol Tiolene," hanging holder, metal, red & yellow w/black lettering, reads "Purol Tiolene (motif of arrow & circle target) Gasoline Motor Oil," standard size (paint chips) **94**

Harley Davidson/Merkel Motorcycle Match Safe

Motorcycle, "Harley-Davidson - Merkle Motorcycle," metal, rectangular, paper insert reads "There's No Match - to the - Harley-Davidson - or - Merkel Motor Cycles - Sold by South Side Cycle Co., St. Louis, MO.," holds book matches, ca. 1930's, 1 1/2 x 2 1/2" (ILLUS.) **75-125**

Soft drink, "Coca-Cola," rectangular, celluloid, for stick matches, marked "Drink Coca-Cola in Bottles - Springfield Coca-Cola Bottling Co.," 1930s **350**

Soft drink, "Coca-Cola," Westinghouse vending machine container, can hold twelve packs of matches **160**

Soft drink, "Dr. Pepper," hanging holder, metal, light green, 3 1/8 x 3 1/4 x 6" **80-250**

World's Fair Souvenir Match Safe

Souvenir, brass, rectangular, depicts The Electricity Building at St. Louis World's Fair in 1904, 1 1/2 x 2 5/8" (ILLUS.) **75-125**

Stewart Stoves Match Safe

Stoves, "Stewart Stoves & Ranges," silver metal & celluloid, rectangular, front w/logo in center marked "Stewart Stoves & Ranges," w/"The Fuller-Warren Co. Milwaukee, Wis." marked below, reverse w/color lithographed image of Eros & Psyche, Litho by Whitehead & Hoag, ca. 1905, 1 1/2 x 2 7/8" (ILLUS. of both sides) **175-250**

Keen Kutter Match Safe

Tools, "Keen Kutter," aluminum, flip-out-type, Simmon's Hardware, St. Louis, Missouri, ca. 1893, 1 1/4 x 1 1/2" (ILLUS.) **75-125**

Rare Rockford Watch Match Holder

Watches, "Rockford Watch," hanging holder, color-printed metal, an upright rectangular form w/scalloped top w/hanging hole, red ground printed at the top w/a small steam train above a large hand holding a watch, white & black wording, reads at top "The Incomparable Rockford Watch" (ILLUS.) **1,400**

Chapter 11
Paperweights

Glass

Palmer House Cigars Paperweight

Cigar, "Palmer House Key West Cigars," round w/a colorful label centered by a red & gold crown, slight foxing on upper edges, 3" d. (ILLUS.) **$55**

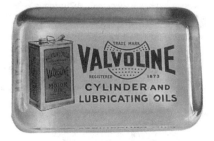

Valvoline Oil Paperweight

Motor oil, "Valvoline Cylinder and Lubricating Oils," rectangular thick glass backed by paper advertising w/a black, white & green sketch of a can on the left w/black wording on the right, ca. 1920, very minor scratches, 2 5/8 x 4" (ILLUS.)................. **121**
Safety glasses, "Violet Ray Lens," cornflower colored glass w/figure of baby on base imprinted w/"Safety First" & "Use Violet Ray Lens," 3 1/8" h. plus base (some soiling & dirt in engraved areas) **110**

Feronia Cigars Paperweight

Cigars, "Feronia Cigars," rectangular clear glass w/rounded corners, paper label glued to bottom w/gold & red wording on white, shows brand name & "James F. Martin, Inc. - Peekskill, N.Y. - Phone 88," mirrored back, 2 1/2 x 4 1/4" (ILLUS.)............. **44**
Corn flakes, "Kellogg Toasted Corn Flakes," milk white glass, flat, depicts trademark image of little girl in wicker basket, 3 1/4" w., 5" l...................................... **109**
Grain elevator, "State Milling & Elevator Co., Cache Junction, Utah," rectangular, depicts image of three different flour sacks on milk glass back, 7/8 x 2 3/4 x 4 1/4" **149**

Telephone Company Paperweight

Telephone company, "Bell System," blue glass, bell-shaped w/white lettering "Bell System - New York Telephone Company" on one side & "Local and Long Distance Telephone" on reverse, 3 1/4" w., 3" h. (ILLUS.) **209**

Metal

Automobile, "Chalmers Motor Company," rectangular, brass, "Chalmers" embossed top center flanked by embossed automobiles, center embossed scene of factory w/"The Home Of The - Chalmers Motor Company - Detroit, Mich." embossed at bottom flanked by logos, 3 1/2" w., 2 1/4" h. **132**

Automobile, "Chevrolet," embossed bow tie logo, 1 1/2 x 3 1/2", 2" h. **88**

Automobile, "Packard," brass, flat squared form w/rounded top, slanted sides & notched lower corners, embossed scene of people riding in an open car below the wording "Ask the Man Who Owns One," back marked "Packard Motor Car Co. Detroit, Mich.," early 20th c., 3 1/2" x 3 1/2" (minor tarnish) **358**

Bank, "Nassau Bank," figural turtle, brass w/metal oval button reading "The Nassau Bank Safe Solid Sound Safe Deposit Vaults," marked "Whitehead & Hoag Co. Newark, Pat. May 3, 1904," 2 1/2" w., 4 1/4" l., 1" h. (some scratches & soiling) **88**

Richfield Paperweight - Pen Holder

Gasoline, "Richfield," a bronzed metal square platform w/beveled edges & the brand name at the front supporting a pen holder & a standing figure of an early airplane pilot, 7" h. (ILLUS.) **160**

Rare Cupid Cigars Paperweight

Cigars, "Cupid Cigars," cast metal w/a seated figural Cupid on the top resting on a tapering rectangular base w/embossed wording including "Jno. W. Loves 'Cupid' Cigars," minute edge crack at base, 2 1/2 x 4", 4" h. (ILLUS.) **259**

Havana Plantation Cigars Paperweight

Cigars, "Havana Plantation" cigars, cast metal oval form cast in relief w/a long cigar, embossed wording reads "Havana Plantation - A.A. Arnold. Mfr.," 1 1/2 x 4" (ILLUS.) **83**

St. Louis Pumps Paperweight

Gasoline pump, "St. Louis Pumps," cast-iron model of an early slender gas pump w/copper hose & nozzle, painted red w/white globe at the top & black lettering down the side, repainted, some chipping, 7 3/4" h. (ILLUS.) 550

Motor oil, "Husky," metal, figural husky dog on rectangular platform, embossed "Western Oil & Fuel Company" on front of base, 4 1/2" w., 3 3/4" h. 193

Lion Oil Company Paperweight

Motor oil, "Lion Oil Company," brass, figural lion on rectangular base, minor wear to base, 1 1/2 x 2 3/4 x 3 3/4" (ILLUS.) 77

Husky Refining Company Paperweight

Oil refining company, "Husky Refining Company," heavy cast-metal w/bronzed finish, a model of a standing husky on a flaring rectangular platform base w/advertising across the front, original felt on base, minor wear, 2 3/8 x 3 7/8", 4 3/8" h. (ILLUS.) 55

Peanuts, "Planters Peanuts," figural pot metal Mr. Peanut **775-800**

Other

White Eagle Advertising Paperweight

Oil refining company, "White Eagle Refining Company," molded plaster model of a perched white eagle on a thick oblong base, well-detailed, dated 1924, light to moderate overall wear, 6 1/8" h. (ILLUS.) **209**

Chapter 12
Pinback Buttons

Polarine & Red Crown Gas Pinback

Miller High Life Pinback Button

DuPont Smokeless Powder Button

Remember the Belle Pinback Button

Chapter 13
Pocket Mirrors

Scott-Wilkerson Ambulance Service Pocket Mirror

Ambulance service, "Scott-Wilkerson Ambulance Service," round, celluloid, scene of antique vehicle w/trees in background, marked at bottom "Scott-Wilkerson Superior Ambulance Service - Memphis, Tenn.," ca. 1915, 3 1/2" d. (ILLUS.) **$125-175**

Automotive, "Excelsior Gasoline," round, celluloid on metal back, celluloid printed across the upper border w/white stars on a blue ground & around the lower border w/red & white stripes, a large gilt scroll-bordered white center reserve printed in red & blue "EXCELSIOR - Motor Oils & Grease - GASOLINE - Lubricating Oils - For All Purposes," the lower border overprinted in black "C. E. Mills Oil Co., Syracuse, N.Y.," 2" d. (scratches on mirror, soiling & scratches on back) **83**

Kern Barber Supply Co. Pocket Mirror

Barber supplies, "August Kern Barber Supply Company," round, celluloid, center w/image of barber chair marked "America" & border w/"August Kern Barber Supply Co. - Saint Louis, MO.," ca. 1910, 2" d. (ILLUS.) **125-175**

Studebaker Pocket Mirror

Automotive, "Studebaker," oval, celluloid, lithograph scene of automobile production plant by Bastian Bros., marked "Studebaker Vehicle Works - Largest in the World - South Bend, Ind. U.S.A.," ca. 1900, 1 3/4 x 2 3/4" (ILLUS.) **200-250**

Victory Bicycles Pocket Mirror

Bicycles, "Victory Bicycles," oval, celluloid, black w/gold trim, centered by large V & "Victory" on red band, "Chicago" above w/"Bicycles - Tires - New York" below & "Edwards & Christ Co. - Detroit - Cleveland - Philadelphia - Newark" around edge, Parisian Novelty Co., ca. 1900, 1 3/4 x 2 3/4" (ILLUS.) **150-200**

Cracker Jack Pocket Mirror

Candy, "Cracker Jack," round, celluloid, dark blue w/white, red & blue package in center below "The More You Eat - The More You Want." w/"Look At The Cracker Jack On The Other Side - Rueckheim Bros. & Eckstein, Chicago" at the bottom, ca. 1897, 2" d. (ILLUS.).............. **175-225**

Parry Carriage Mfg. Co. Pocket Mirror

Carriage, "Parry Manufacturing Company," colored lithograph scene of factory by Bastian Bros., marked "Parry Manufacturing Company - The Largest Carriage Factory In The World - Indianapolis, Ind." above & "Our Goods Are Sold By - John Theroff, Donnellson, Iowa," ca. 1910, 1 3/4 x 2 3/4" (ILLUS.) **175-225**

Bee Hive Overalls Pocket Mirror

Clothing, "Bee Hive Overalls," pocket-type, oval celluloid by Whitehead & Hoag, Newark, NJ, shows woman wearing overalls & marked "Bee Hive Overalls Best Maid - Made by Bittner, Hunsicker & Co., Allentown, PA," ca. 1910, mirror broken, 1 3/4 x 2 3/4" (ILLUS.)............................ **286**

Old Reliable Coffee Pocket Mirror

Coffee, "Old Reliable Coffee," round, celluloid, colorful lithograph of man wearing red jacket & brown hat, one elbow resting on can, marked "Old Reliable Coffee - Always Good," litho by Bastian Bros., ca. 1910, 2" d. (ILLUS.)................................... **75-125**

H.S. & B. Company Pocket Mirror

Cutlery, "H.S. & B Co.," oval, celluloid, white w/blue circular band marked "Cutlery - & Tools," center blue band centered by dark blue shield form flanked by gold scrolls, center marked "O - V - B" in white letters under gold letters reading "Our Very Best," below banner marked "H.S. & B. Co.," Cruver Mfg. Co., Chicago, Illinois, ca. 1910, 1 3/4 x 2 3/4" (ILLUS.)... **125-175**

J.I. Case Company Pocket Mirror

Farm machinery, "J. I. Case," oval, celluloid, white w/image of eagle atop a world globe marked "J. I. Case Threshing Machine Company Incorporated - Racine,

Wis. - U.S.A.," ca. 1900, 1 3/4 x 2 3/4"
(ILLUS.) **225-300**
Flour, "Big Joe Flour," round **40**
Flour, "Kansas Expansion Flour," round **45**
Ice cream, "Thompson's Ice Cream," round,
depicts colorful bust of Andy Gump
w/"Thompson's Unexcelled Ice Cream"
around edge & "Andy Gump - for Presi-
dent" flanking the figure **231**

*Travelers Insurance Company
Pocket Mirror*

Insurance, "Travelers Insurance
Company," oval, celluloid, depicts
approaching train engine w/skyline in
background, "The Travelers Insurance
Company - Hartford, Conn." in red letters
above & "The Railroad Men's Reliance"
in red lettering below, ca. 1900,
1 5/8 x 2 3/8" (ILLUS.) **125-175**

Cascarets Pocket Mirror

Laxative, "Cascarets," round, celluloid, image of cupid on chamber pot above "Cascarets - Did It - They Work While You
Sleep" & "All Going Out - Nothing Coming In," Sterling Remedy Company, Chi-
cago, Illinois, ca. 1910, 2" d. (ILLUS.) **95-135**

Horlick's Pocket Mirror w/Gold Border

Malted milk, "Horlick's Malted Milk," round,
celluloid, a round central scene of a
young dairy maid holding a can of the
product & standing beside Jersey cow
printed w/"Ask for Horlick's at all Druggists," the gold outer border band printed
in blue w/"The Diet for Infants Invalids
and Nursing Mothers - The Original Malted Milk - Ask For Horlick's - Avoid Substitutes," litho by Bastian Bros., ca. 1900,
2" d. (ILLUS.) **125-200**

Horlick's Malted Milk Pocket Mirror

Malted milk, "Horlick's Malted Milk," round,
celluloid, colorful lithograph of young girl
in long dress & white apron standing next
to brown cow, white border marked "The
Diet For Infants, Invalids And Nursing
Mothers - The Original Malted Milk - Ask
For Horlick's - Avoid Substitutes," litho by
Whitehead & Hoag, ca. 1900, 2" d.
(ILLUS.) **100-175**

Angelus Marshmallows Pocket Mirror

Marshmallows, "Angelus Marshmallows,"
oval, celluloid, cupid standing on square
base marked "Angelus Marshmallows"
playing horn & holding box also marked
"Angelus Marshmallows," Rueckheim
Bros. & Eckstein, Chicago, Illinois, ca.
1900, 1 3/4 x 2 3/4" (ILLUS.) **125-175**

Angelus Marshmallows Pocket Mirror

Marshmallows, "Angelus Marshmallows," oval, celluloid, scene of a dark-haired & a blond cupid leaning on box marked "Angelus Marshmallows," Rueckheim Bros. & Eckstein, Chicago, Illinois, ca. 1900, 1 5/8 x 2 3/8" (ILLUS.) **95-150**

Ohio Match Company Pocket Mirror

Matches, "Ohio Blue Tip Matches," round, celluloid, dark blue border w/white letters reading "Ohio Blue Tip Matches - The Ohio Match Co." & "J.C. Orrick & Son Co. - Cumberland, MD. Distributors" above scene of factory w/white & blue product package below, Ohio Match Company, Wadsworth, Ohio, ca. 1900, 3 1/2" d. (ILLUS.) **175-225**

Victor Victrola Pocket Mirror

Phonograph, "Victor Victrola," rectangular w/rounded corners, celluloid, lithograph by Parisian Novelty shows logo in upper left corner opposite "Have You A Victrola In Your Home," image of phonograph center right opposite "This is a Victrola XI - $100 - Mahogany or Oak - Other Sytles $15 to $200 - We Will Demonstrate It and Play Any Music You Wish to Hear," dealer information at bottom, ca. 1910, 1 5/8 x 2 3/4" (ILLUS.) **175-225**

Checkers Popcorn Pocket Mirror

Popcorn, "Checkers Popcorn," round, celluloid, an image of a red & white checkered box marked "Checkers" w/"Eat - Eat - Eat" above & "A Nice Prize in Each Package - Shotwell Mfg. Co. Chicago" below, ca. 1910, 2 1/4" d. (ILLUS.) **125-175**

Razor, "Gillette," round, marked "Shave Yourself - Gillette Safety Razor - No Stropping - No Honing" **110**

Morton's Salt Pocket Mirror

Salt, "Morton's Salt," round, celluloid, white w/blue & white product package depicted filling salt shaker, reads "An Every Meal Nessessity - Morton's Salt - Makes Food Taste Better," litho by Parisian Novelty, ca. 1900, 2" d. (ILLUS.) **125-175**

Queen Quality Shoes Pocket Mirror

Shoes, "Queen Quality Shoes," oval, celluloid, brown w/image of woman w/long brown curls, brown bonnet w/filmy tie under chin, marked at bottom "Queen Quality - Shoes," A.M. Farwell & Company, Franklinville, New York, ca. 1900, 1 3/4 x 2 3/4" (ILLUS.) **100-175**

New King Snuff Pocket Mirror

Snuff, "New King Snuff," rectangular w/rounded corners, celluloid, ivory w/center image of brown jar w/tan & yellow label below reading "The New King Snuff," Weyman-Bruton Company, Nashville, Tennessee, litho by Pilgrim Spec. Co., Malden, Massachusetts, ca. 1915, 1 3/4 x 2 3/4" (ILLUS.) **75-125**

Soft drink, "Coca-Cola," die-cut cardboard cat's head, opens to reveal mirror & advertisement, ca. 1920s, Germany, 2 1/2" **600**

Stove, "Buckwalter Stove Co.," pocket-type, oval celluloid w/graphic of black & silver cooking stove on green ground & marked "An Enameled Range Beautifies and Modernizes Your Kitchen," distributor's name at bottom, few minor scratches, 1 3/4 x 2 3/4" **99**

Garland Stoves Pocket Mirror

Stove, "Garland Stoves," oval, celluloid, colorful lithograph by Whitehead & Hoag depicts the production plant below logo marked at top "Largest Makers of Stoves and Ranges in the World" w/"Where They - Are Made" flanking logo w/"Garland Stoves and Ranges," ca. 1910, 1 3/4 x 2 3/4" (ILLUS.) **175-225**

Peninsular Stove Company Pocket Mirror

Stove, "Peninsular Stove Company," oval, celluloid, lithograph scene of factory by Bastian Bros., Peninsular Stove Company, Detroit, Michigan, ca. 1910, 1 3/4 x 2 3/4" (ILLUS.) **225-275**

Mennen's Talcum Powder Pocket Mirror

Talcum powder, "Mennen's Talcum Powder," oval, celluloid, depicts container decorated w/pink & gold florals, marked "Mennen's Flesh Tint Talcum" in gold & flanked w/pink & gold floral decoration, gold top, gold lettering at bottom reads "A Pink Powder Not A Rouge," Gerhard Mennen Co., Newark, New Jersey, ca. 1910, 1 3/4 x 2 3/4" (ILLUS.) **125-175**

Remington Typewriter Pocket Mirror

Typewriter, "Remington Typewriters," round, celluloid, red w/white sawtooth border, lithographed image of typewriter in center w/white lettering above reading "To Save Time is to Lengthen Life - Standard" & "Remington Typewriter," below, litho by Parisian Novelty Company, ca. 1915, 3 1/2" d. (ILLUS.) **150-200**

Mennen's Talcum Powder Pocket Mirror

Talcum powder, "Mennen's Toilet Powder," oval, celluloid, decorated w/bouquet of purple violets & green leaves w/image of man w/mustache on lower leaf, marked at bottom "Use Mennen's Violet Talcum Toilet Powder," Gerhard Mennen Co., Newark, New Jersey, ca. 1910, 1 3/4 x 2 3/4" (ILLUS.) **125-175**

Typewriter, "Oliver Typewriter," oval celluloid w/photo of young girl & typewriter, image by Photo Jewelry, Chicago, Illinois, 2 x 2 3/4" (minor scratches)................. **44**

Berry Bros. Celluloid Pocket Mirror

Varnish, "Berry Bros. Varnishes," pocket-type, oval celluloid by J.B. Carroll, Chicago, colorful scene of young boy wearing overalls & straw hat pulling a wooden wagon w/red wheels holding a dog, 1 3/4 x 2 3/4" (ILLUS.) **154**

Chapter 14
Signs & Signboards

Cardboard

Ammunition, "Shoot - 'Dominion' Ammunition," counter-top type w/easel back, a color image of a young hunter running across a snowy field holding his rifle & a dead rabbit, his dog running beside it, based on artwork by Tom Hall, 21 x 25 1/2".. **$77**

Antacid, "Alka-Seltzer," die-cut, easel-back, features "Speedy" holding glass & stick, minor soiling & overall wear, area behind stick reinforced, light creases at top areas, edge wear, 21 3/4 x 39 3/4" (ILLUS.).. **132**

Cities Service Anti-Freeze Sign

Anti-Freeze, "Cities Service," double-sided, die-cut, string-hung type, both sides display comical image of penguin dressed in winter clothing holding thermometer, marked at bottom "Use Cities Service Koldpruf Anti-Freeze," tiny nicks & flecks, 11 1/2 x 18" (ILLUS.)...................................... **231**

Alka-Seltzer Die-cut Sign

Mica Axle Grease Sign

Axle grease, "Mica Axle Grease," (Standard Oil), rectangular, blue, yellow & green, image of hand holding magnifying glass over grease gun, can at bottom pops back to allow the display of a one pound can, marked "Mica Axle Grease - The Mica fills the Pores - Wheels Turn Easier," some warping, minor edge wear, missing top right corner, 14 x 17" (ILLUS.)................................ **171**

Beer, "Kingsbury Pale Beer," color-printed & self-framed w/border of crossed logs surrounding a color picture of two birds, titled at top "Bobwhite Quail," marked at bottom edge "Kingsbury Pale Beer," 1950s, 17 x 20" (very minor creases)............. **38**

Beer, "McGovern Pilsener Beer," color-printed, large image of a kicking mule, framed, 1940s, 10 x 13" (slight yellowing & a few stains)... **22**

Pabst Blue Ribbon Beer Sign

Beer, "Pabst Blue Ribbon Beer," rectangular, scene of African-American in waiter's uniform, one hand holding a tray of bottles & glasses, reads "Quality - Yes - Suh-h," ca. 1938, Pabst Brewing Company, Milwaukee, Wisconsin, 24 x 34" (ILLUS.) **300-375**

Woodward's Candy Sign

Candy, "Woodward's Peanut Butter Sticks," die-cut cardboard w/easel back, scene of a young boy in brown uniform & hat holding a box of candy & offering a piece to the young girl wearing a blue dress & white cap seated next to him, sign at bottom bordered by peanut shells & marked "Woodward's Peanut Butter Filled Stick Candy - John G. Woodward & Co. 'The Candy Men' - Council Bluffs, Iowa," wood frame, ca. 1900, 15 x 21" (ILLUS.).... **1,400-1,800**

Pabst Blue Ribbon Beer Sign

Beer, "Pabst Blue Ribbon Beer," rectangular, smiling elderly gentleman pouring beer from a bottle into a glass, reads "Pabst Blue Ribbon - The Beer of Quality," ca. 1933, Pabst Brewing Company, Milwaukee, Wisconsin, 20 x 25 1/2" (ILLUS.)................................ **300-375**

Camera, "Kodak Camera" window display w/scene of a couple in a canoe.................. **1,650**

Baum's Polish Sign

Car polish, "Baum's Polish," rectangular, die-cut cardboard, yellow w/image of early red auto w/woman at wheel, red & black letters reading "Baum's Wonderful Polish - Shines Like Magic - Never Injures - Will Not Scratch the Finest Surfaces," cut-outs at center to display a product bottle, 9 1/4 x 10 3/8" (ILLUS.)................ **187**

Western Lubaloy Counter Sign

Cartridges, "Western Lubaloy Rifle and Pistol Cartridges," color-printed cardboard counter display sign, blue rectangle in center w/red, white & gold wording, border picture of an autumn landscape w/packages of the product at bottom, unused, 13 1/2 x 14 1/2" (ILLUS.) 242

Catsup, "Snider's Catsup," embossed die-cut, dark red border w/white center reserve printed in color w/a large bottle of the product w/tomato plants & a black & white center banner w/"Snider's," ca. 1930s, 11 x 17" (edge wear, some light rubbing & medium wear at top, few light bends).. 523

Kis-Me Gum Die-cut Framed Sign

Chewing gum, "Kis-Me Chewing Gum," die-cut cardboard in wood frame, beautiful woman in lace-trimmed pink dress, stockings & shoes, curly blonde hair w/rose-trimmed pink hat, marked at bottom "'Kis-Me' - Kis-Me Gum Co., Louisville, KY," ca. 1900, 14 x 26 1/2" (ILLUS.)... **1,300-1,700**

Kis-Me Gum Sign

Chewing gum, "Kis-Me Chewing Gum," die-cut cardboard in wood frame, scene of two young girls under a yellow umbrella, one dressed in long blue dress, the other in pink, marked at bottom "'Kis-Me' - Kis-Me Gum Co., Louisville, KY," ca. 1900, 11 x 13" (ILLUS.) **550-700**

Framed Kis-Me Gum Die-cut Sign

Chewing gum, "Kis-Me Gum," die-cut, lithographed in color, profile of a young woman w/dark hair fashioned in a bun, lacy ruffled collar over red dress w/a border of arching pink & red roses, advertising above & below portrait, framed (ILLUS.) **2,000**

Wrigley's Gum Trolley Sign

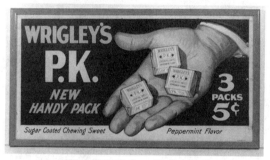

Wrigley's P.K. Gum Trolley Sign

Kis-Me Gum Sign

Chewing gum, "Kis-Me Gum," die-cut, lithographed in color w/a beautiful young woman wearing a low-cut pink gown leaning against a background of arching pink & red roses, advertising above her head, matted & framed, 9 1/2 x 15 1/2" (ILLUS.) **2,805**

Chewing gum, "Wrigley's Gum," rectangular, trolley-type, yellow w/"Help Yourself! - Wrigley's" in black & red letters & "Good For You" in white letters on green arrow pointing to product displays, "On Every Dealer's Counter" in yellow letters at bot-

tom, wood frame, ca. 1927, 12 1/4 x 22" (ILLUS., top) **750-850**

Chewing gum, "Wrigley's P.K. Gum," rectangular trolley-type, black background w/hand open & holding three packages of gum, yellow, white & black lettering reading "Wrigley's P.K. New Handy Pack - 3 Packs 5¢ - Sugar Coated Chewing Sweet Peppermint Flavor," wood frame, ca. 1928, 11 3/4 x 22" (ILLUS., second from top).................................. **650-750**

Shaw & Truesdell Feed Sign

Chicken feed, "Shaw & Truesdell Co's Scratch & Chick Foods," color scene of pretty young lady in large pink hat & blue dress feeding black & white chickens & yellow chicks, white wording at top reads "You will get eggs and have healthy sturdy chicks if you use...," slight upper left moisture damage, early 20th c., 21 x 31" (ILLUS.) **1,018**

Cigars, "Free Lance Cigars," w/string hanger, embossed cigar label insert, marked "Smoke a 5¢ Free Lance Cigar and be Convinced," 9 1/2 x 11" **55**

Hoffmanettes Cigars Sign

Cigars, "Hoffmanettes Cigars," rectangular, scene of two men leaning out of a window to see a man standing below & smoking a ciragette, reads "'It's up to you' - Smoke - Hoffmanettes 5¢ Cigar - The Hilson Co. Makers - New York," wood frame, ca. 1900, 15 1/2 x 21 1/2" (ILLUS.) **350-425**

Clothing, "Finck's Overalls," stand up-type, die-cut, painted, w/easel back, pig shape w/"Finck's - Detroit-Special - Overalls - 'Wear Like a Pig's Nose.'" w/"For Sale Here" & "Union Made" on base, 34 3/4" w., 14 1/2" h. (creases, edge wear, scratches, soiling & warped) **198**

Clothing & accessories, "Shirley President Suspenders," lithographed, w/scenes of six women engaged in various sports, under glass in wood frame, 52 1/2" l. (tearing) **1,900**

Early Pyrene Fire Extinguisher Sign

Fire extinguisher, "Pyrene," die-cut color lithographed w/a nighttime scene w/an open early auto hood w/the engine ablaze standing out from background to form 3-D effect, a young father using a fire extinguisher on the fire w/his wife & baby standing behind him, oval in upper corner contains wording "Pyrene Kills Auto Fires," ca. 1920s, soiling, creases, 21" w., 32 1/2" h. (ILLUS.) **825**

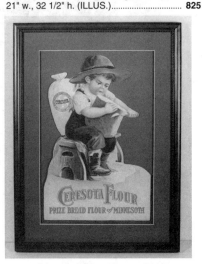

Cerosota Flour Die-cut Sign

Flour, "Ceresota Flour," die-cut cardboard in wood frame, small boy wearing boots & large hat sitting on stool & slicing a loaf of bread, flour sack behind him, marked "Cerestoa Flour - Prize Bread Flour of Minnesota," by Edward Deutsch & Co., Chicago, Illinois, ca. 1900, 13 x 17 1/2" (ILLUS.) **1,300-1,600**

Flour, "Ellison's Flour," color-printed, counter top easel-style, dark blue ground w/center design of swimming white swan flanked by packages of the product, reads at bottom "Assures Good Color & Fine Texture," unused, 13 x 24" **143**

Standard Gasoline Sign w/Mickey Mouse

Gasoline, "Standard Gasoline," rectangular, coated cardboard, Disney theme showing Mickey Mouse on skis, his muffler marked "Unsurpassed," minor edge & field wear w/a few creases, 14 x 17" (ILLUS.) **1,100**

Gunpowder, "Infallible Smokeless Shotgun Powder in Loaded Shells - Hercules Powder Co.," rectangular display-type w/easel back & string hanger, dark gold ground w/a color image of a young female hunter dressed in dark blue carrying her rifle w/her black & white hunting dog beside her, traces of small water marks, few scrapes, 10 x 15"........................ **275**

Nestle Permanent Waving Sign

Hair care, "Nestle Permanent Waving," die-cut & dimensional display sign, shaded tan w/gold highlights, woman's head at top w/"Nestle Permanent Waving - Licensed Nestle Shop," original paper tag on back, by Kay Display Signs, rests on wooden feet, easily detached for moving, slight fading & wear to gold, light soiling, 15 x 18" (ILLUS.) **1,265**

Wildroot Hair Cream-Oil Sign

Hair cream-oil, "Wildroot Hair Cream-Oil," die-cut, easel-back display shows illustration of Al Capp Dick Tracy character Fearless Fosdick w/smoking gun & removing his hat, saying "Fearless Fosdick Says - Get Wildroot Cream-Oil Charlie!,"

letters above gun read "Grooms the Hair - Relieves Dryness - Removes Loose Dandruff," center of sign flanked by die-cut red, white & blue striped barber poles, letters on globes reading "Time For A Haircut" & "Best Haircut in Town" & dated "1954" at bottom left, minor edge & surface wear, 30 x 30 1/4" (ILLUS.) **248**

Lucky Tiger Hair Oil Sign

Hair oil, "Lucky Tiger," rectangular, easel-back, center w/image of blonde woman & head of tiger & bottle containing green liquid in lower right corner, top reading "Lucky Tiger - For Hair and Scalp - With Oil or Without," minor wear, 22 x 33 1/2" (ILLUS.) **550**

Foster Hose Supporters Sign

Hose supporters, "Foster Hose Supporters," rectangular, porcelain over cardboard, image of corset & hose supporters & woman wearing red skirt & green blouse, reads "The Foster Hose Supporters - 'The Name is on the buckles'," litho by F.F. Pulver Co., Rochester, New York, ca. 1890, 9 x 17" (ILLUS.)......... **900-1,300**

Hettrick Hunting Garments Sign

Hunting garments, "Hettrick American Field Hunting Garments," colorful die-cut counter top style w/easel back & a die-cut projecting running rabbit appearing to jump off edge of sign, hunter in fall landscape taking aim in the distance, 1940-50, 14 x 16" (ILLUS.).. **88**

Pearl Oil Kerosene Sign

Kerosene, "Pearl Oil Kerosene," rectangular, string-hung, center w/kerosene can, label reads "Pearl Oil Kerosene for Oil Heaters, Cook Stoves &

Lamps," household images at bottom, also marked "We Sell Heat and Light - Refined by Standard Oil Company California," minor soiling & warping & wear, 10 3/8 x 14" (ILLUS.) **303**

Witter's Laundry Sign

Laundry, "Witter's Laundry," embossed die-cut of a cute baby seated in a cloth sling tied at the top w/blue ribbon, decorated w/blue flowers at top & around baby who holds a card which reads "My Clothes are at Witter's Laundry - Are Yours?," image 4 3/4 x 11 3/4 in 13 x 17" period frame (ILLUS.).. **583**

Laundry supplies, "Fairbank's Gold Dust Washing Powder," die-cut cardboard, two-sided, depicts black children at each end holding box of Fairbank's Gold Dust Washing Powder, a box under each "Gold Dust" letter, each pc., 7 1/2 x 15 1/2" **7,475**

Motor Oil, "Monogram Motor Oil," rectangular w/wood lathe board backing, depicts a long line of soldiers in grey & white uniforms w/large black hats, the lineup disappearing into the distance, white top w/red letters reading "Monogram Motor Oil," the lower section shaded yellow, green & gold w/black letters reading "Stands Up!," glossy slick finish, crazing & cracking to finish, scattered nail holes at borders, 11 1/4 x 35 1/2" (ILLUS.)............ **248**

Monogram Motor Oil Sign

Nesbitt's Orange Drink Sign

Orange drink, "Nesbitt's Orange Drink," rectangular, colorful scene of girl in white bathing suit relaxing near swimming pool, orange trees in background, a table nearby w/bowl of oranges & bottle, the chair's blue tented cover marked in white & orange letters reading "Drink Nesbitt's California Orange," original Nesbitt frame, ca. 1955, 28 1/2 x 39" (ILLUS.).. **350-450**

OshKosh Overalls Sign

Overalls, "OshKosh Overalls," rectangular, top w/wide red band marked in white & yellow "OshKosh B'gosh - Union Made - The World's Best Overall," center section light background w/four men of different sizes pictured wearing overalls indicated for "Fat - or Thin - Short - or Tall" the men in middle holding yellow sign marked "OshKosh B'Gosh Fits 'Em All," bottom marked "Always Buy Your Correct Size," ca. 1930, 13 1/2 x 14 1/2" (ILLUS.) **175-250**

Oysters, "Oysters R in Season - Shelder Island Oyster Co.," embossed rectangular form, green & red lettering on yellow ground, ca. 1930s, 7 x 11" **23**

Peanuts, "Squirrel Brand Salt Peanuts," die-cut counter display sign, a seated grey squirrel on top with the sign in red w/white & gold wording & a gold picture of the product, unused, 11 x 12" (ILLUS.)..... **143**

Squirrel Brand Peanuts Sign

Pickles, "Heinz's Preserved Sweet Mixed Pickles - Keystone Brand," embossed rectangular form w/a gold border band, dark blue inner ground w/white wording & red, white & blue banners at the center right & a red ring-formed logo w/a white keystone design on the left, appears unused, 4 x 11".. **187**

Early Popsicle Cardboard Sign

Popsicle, "Popsicle - The Frozen Drink On A Stick," rectangular, a black background w/a large word in light yellow above the color image of a red-haired cartoon girl holding a huge popsicle w/a balloon in yellow & red w/"5¢," grey band at the bottom w/blue wording, dated 1932, appears to have been cropped, very minor surface wear, 9 3/4 x 12" (ILLUS.)................. **176**

Wise Potato Chip Sign

Potato chips, "Wise Potato Chips," die-cut stand-up cardboard, lithographed figure of owl perched on log, "Wise Potato Chips" in white lettering on breast & bag of chips near wing, copyright Wise Delicatessen Co. Litho in U.S.A., tape repair to edges, corner on back & to vertical crease at end of log, ears w/bent tips, piece of cardboard added for support on easel, 20" w., 29 1/2" h. (ILLUS.)................... **715**

Ithaca Featherlight Repeaters Sign

Rifles, "Ithaca Featherlight Repeaters," die-cut wall hanger, a large flying Canada

Goose above a birch branch all in color, ca. 1940-50, 15 x 17" (ILLUS.)........... **303**

Salt, "Diamond Crystal Shaker Salt," easel-backed color lithographed, rectangular, an orange background w/two hands holding a container of the product & filling a salt shaker, black wording reads "Ask For Diamond Crystal - Diamond Crystal Shaker Salt," reverse dated "4/22," rounded corner, 10 1/4 x 15" **303**

Carborundum Scythe Stones Sign

Scythe stones, "Carborundum Scythe Stones," long rectangular lithographed design w/a narrow black border around a red ground w/a round color logo of a Native American chief's head, large wording in white, string-hung, early 20th c., 3 1/2 x 12" (ILLUS.)...................................... **149**

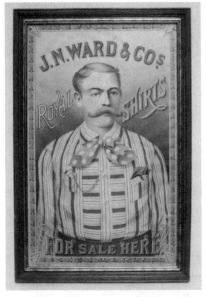

J.N. Ward & Co. Shirt Sign

Shirts, "J.N. Ward & Co. Shirts," rectangular, lithographed paper on cardboard, depicts man wearing blue & white striped shirt, blue & white polka dot tie, red & white letters read "J.N. Ward & Cos. Royal Shirts - For Sale Here," wood frame, litho by J.W. Frank & Sons, Peoria, Illinois, ca. 1880, 14 x 21" (ILLUS.) **475-650**

Shoes, "Paul Bunyan Loggers," easel-back countertop type, showing the logger w/an axe & his bull Babe & marked "Hand Made - Union Made - Bone Dry Shoe Mfg. Co.," 12 3/4 x 21 1/2" **121**

Shoes, "Red Goose Shoes," die-cut stand-up type, three dimensional, 23" l. **2,000**

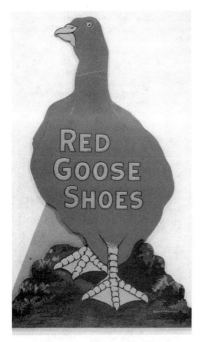

Winchester Shotgun Shell Sign

Red Goose Shoes Die-cut Sign

Shoes, "Red Goose Shoes," embossed die-cut figural red goose w/yellow beak, eye & feet, easel-back, marked "Red Goose Shoes," ca. 1910, Friedman-Shelby Shoes, 9 x 14" (ILLUS.) **650-800**

Shotgun shells, "Winchester," lithographed color scene of a flock of grouse in tall grass, reads "Winchester - Factory Loaded Shotgun Shells - The Hunter's Choice - We Carry A Full Stock" (ILLUS.) **2,255**

Winchester Shell Sign

Shotgun shells, "Winchester," case insert string-hung paper on cardboard litho-graph w/colorful graphic of pheasant w/wings & tail feathers spread against a blue background & product container w/"Winchester Repeater Paper Shot Shells - Smokeless Powder" on top & "24 Winchester 12 Ga. Repeater Paper Shot Shells.... " w/large W superimposed on front above two shells, by American Litho Co., New York, 9 1/4 x 13 3/4" (ILLUS.) **2,530**

Colorful "Baco-Curo" Cardboard Sign

Smoking cure, "Baco-Curo," colorfully printed die-cut gold sunburst form w/a round smiling man's face smoking a ci-gar, brand name at top w/"Cures Tobac-co Habit" on lower face, early 20th c., 9 1/2" d. (ILLUS.) **468**

Andrew Jergens & Co. Soap Sign

Soap, "Andrew Jergens Toilet Soap," rectangular, die-cut cardboard in wood frame, depicts two young girls in long dresses w/a large white & brown dog, marked at lower left corner "Andres Jergens & Co. Fine Toilet Soaps - Always Pure," ca. 1880, rare, 20 x 22 1/2" (ILLUS.)...................... **1,500-1,800**

Soap, "Lifebuoy Soap" trolley-type w/scene of teacher & pupils, "Teachers and Mothers know that LIFEBUOY Health Soap Protects Health," wood frame, 12 1/4 x 22 1/4" **132**

Soft drink, "Clicquot Club Ginger Ale," die-cut string-hung type, color image of a pretty young blonde woman holding the Clicquot Club eskimo child who holds a large bottle of the product, a pale blue square at center right reads "Full Quart 10¢," 7 1/4 x 9 5/8" (overall wear, soiling spots)... **121**

Soft drink, "Coca-Cola," cut-out, easel-back, young blonde girl wearing white dress w/blue ribbon trim at neck, white stockings & blue slippers, sitting on crate marked "5 cents - Delicious! - Refreshing! - Coca Cola - at the Soda Fountain," ca. 1890s, Wolf & Co., Philadelphia, Pennsylvania, rare 5 1/2 x 8 1/2" (ILLUS.).......................... **5,000**

Soft drink, "Coca-Cola," "Airplane Hangers," lithograph prints of WW II era planes w/original folder, created by William Heaslip, 12 x 14", set of 20.................... **730**

Colorful Coca-Cola Framed Sign

Soft drink, "Coca-Cola," color image in the original narrow stainless steel frame, large full color image of a gas station attendant placing a case of Coca-Cola in the trunk of a car for young pretty young blonde-haired woman, gas station in background, green band below w/large yellow wording reading "Let us put a case in your car," minor surface wear, light bend in one corner, two tiny nail holes at top, 12 x 15 1/4" (ILLUS.)................................ **825**

Coca-Cola 1890s Display Sign

Coca-Cola Christmas Sign

Soft drink, "Coca-Cola," decorated Christmas tree below ribbon banner reading "Host for the Holidays," Santa shown at top holding bottle, 1952, 8 x 17 1/2" (ILLUS.).. **350**

Coca-Cola 1949 Cut-out Sign

Soft drink, "Coca-Cola," cut-out of woman w/bouquet of daisies, daisies in her hair, holding glass, 1949, 14 x 18" (ILLUS.).......... **750**

Soft drink, "Coca-Cola," singer Ricky Nelson, light pink shirt & red cardigan, holding bottle, "Got A Long Thirst? - Get A Long King! - says Ricky Nelson - Coca-Cola - Refreshes You Best!" & at the bottom "Tune in the Ozzie & Harriet Show Wednesday Evenings 8:30 P.M.," ca. 1959-60, 14 x 18 1/2" **600**

Soft drink, "Coca-Cola," cut-out, easel-back, figure of Eddie Fisher holding bottle w/"Have a Coke," 1954, 19" h. **1,200**

1954 Coca-Cola Santa Sign

Soft drink, "Coca-Cola," cut-out, stand-up type, Santa holding a bottle & standing next to grandfather clock, bells & bow in foreground w/"Good taste for all - Drink Coca-Cola in Bottles," 1954, 10 1/2 x 19" (ILLUS.).. **300**

Soft drink, "Coca-Cola," cut-out of large platter of snacks centered by a container of ice & bottles, floral bouquet at top corner near sign marked "Good with Food", bottle at lower corner, 1950s, 20 x 21 1/2".. **185**

Soft drink, "Coca-Cola," cut-out of large glass resting in snow, bottom of sign marked "Served Here - Ice Cold," 1937, 19 x 25 1/2".. **500**

Coca-Cola Snowman Sign

Soft drink, "Coca-Cola," depicts snowman w/scarf, bottle cap hat & earmuffs on a toboggan w/large bottle, sign in snow reads "Drink Coca Cola" w/"Bring home the Coke" below, gold wood frame, 1957, 16 x 27" (ILLUS.).. **450**

1956 Coca-Cola Sign

Soft drink, "Coca-Cola," Western scene of saddle on rail fence near two bottles, mountain in background, "Sign of Good Taste" at top, lithograph by Edwards & Deutsch, Chicago, Illinois, 1956, unused condition, 16 x 27" (ILLUS.) **501**

Girl on the Calendar Sign

Soft drink, "Coca-Cola," lettering in center reads "The Girl on the Calendar-Through the Years" w/small round Coca-Cola logo underneath, surrounded by 12 different pictures of ladies from previous calendars on a blue background, gold metal frame, 1939, 56" w., 27 1/2" h. (ILLUS.) **500-1,000**

Girl With Horse Sign

Soft drink, "Coca-Cola," shows girl in riding outfit standing near flowers next to horse, holding Coke in right hand, blue & white sky w/round Coca-Cola logo in upper left corner, 1940s, framed, 30" w., 50" h. (ILLUS.) **1,320**

Soft drink, "Coca-Cola," girl sitting on floor w/left arm resting on step & holding bottle, talking on telephone w/"I'll bring the Coke," logo in upper corner, ca. 1946, 27 x 56" **450**

Framed Coca-Cola Sign

Soft drink, "Coca-Cola," nearly square mounted in a gilt-metal Kay Displays frame w/white ribbed bands across the top & bottom, color scene w/a black ground & a color bust portrait of a lovely blonde 1940s era glamour girl beside the red Coca-Cola logo button, very minor scattered nicks, scratches & wear, frame repainted, 34 x 35 1/2" (ILLUS.) **660**

Soft drink, "Coca-Cola," girl w/bottle sitting on either side of world globe w/"Drink Coca-Cola - 'Here's to our G.I. Joes'," 1944, 20 x 36" **850**

Soft drink, "Coca-Cola," blonde girl emerging from swimming pool, "Hello Refreshment," framed under glass, 1940s, 20 1/4 x 36 1/4" **1,800**

Coca-Cola Sign with Loretta Young

Soft drink, "Coca-Cola," cut-out, easelback, features Loretta Young holding bottle, marked "Loretta Young - Pause and Refresh Yourself with Ice Cold Coca-Cola," Niagara Litho Co., 1932 (ILLUS.).... **1,300**

Deco girl at right, wording in dark blue & red at the left, reads "Three Star - Jennessy Extra Dry Pale Ginger Ale - full o pep...," Royer Studio, San Francisco, ca. 1930s, 11 x 14" **72**

Kist Beverage Die-cut Sign

Soft drink, "Kist," die-cut dimensional easel-back display, young woman in low-cut black top w/bottle & glass, background of large pink flowers & leaves, reading "Get Kist here - Orange and Other Flavors," edge wear, 5 x 9 x 12" (ILLUS.) **237**

Coca-Cola Sign with Jean Harlow

Soft drink, "Coca-Cola," cut-out figure of Jean Harlow in bathing suit, holding glass, 1932 (ILLUS.) **6,000**
Soft drink, "Coca-Cola," marked "Drink Coca-Cola in Bottles 5¢," score board below, 1920s **575**
Soft drink, "Dr. Pepper," winter scene w/woman & dog & "Smart List," 20 1/2 x 33".. **250**

Soft drink, "Moxie," die-cut, jockey on horse & horse-form Moxiemobile, Moxie written on each side, ca. 1918, excellent condition, 9" l. **1,650**
Soft drink, "Moxie Soda," stand-up w/Ted Williams.. **1,925**
Soft drink, "Nehi," string-hung, features young woman, 15 1/4 x 23", very rare (some damage w/repair) **210**

Green Spot Orange-Ade Sign

Soft drink, "Green Spot Orange-Ade," rectangular, young woman removing a bottle from ice-filled cooler, reads "Thirsty?," cooler marked "Ice Cold - Green Spot - Orange-Ade 5¢," ca. 1920s, 23 x 33" (ILLUS.) **125-175**
Soft drink, "Jennessy Ginger Ale," gold ground printed w/a naked posing Art

Nehi Sign

Soft drink, "Nehi," rectangular w/easel back, outdoor scene of two boys running, reads "Hey Gang! Mom's Treating Us to Nehi - in Your Favorite Flavor," ca. 1930, 26 x 39" (ILLUS.) **550-750**

Soft drink, "Squeeze," die-cut heavy easel-back type, shows father & son in a boat, fishing, 19" h. **175**
Soft drink, "Squirt," double-sided die-cut oval, string hanger, yellow, red & green, depicts two monkeys holding a bottle & marked "Why Monkey? Drink Squirt," dated 1941, 7 1/2 x 9 1/2" **77**

Colorful Spark Plug Sign

Spark plugs, "Auto-Lite Spark Plugs," rectangular printed to resemble a roadside billboard, the sign w/the upper band in light yellow & the lower band in dark blue, the top printed in red "Don't Miss" above lower white wording reading "Auto-Lite Spark Plugs - Ignition Engineered by Ignition Engineers," a large spark plug on a blue band shown at the far right, minor edge & corner wear, 14 x 21 3/4" (ILLUS.)...................................... **138**

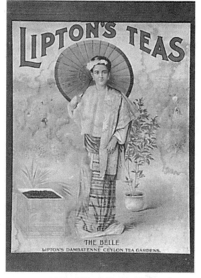

Early Lipton Teas Sign

Tea, "Lipton's Teas," lithographed w/a color-ful scene of a Ceylonese girl w/parasol standing before a tea harvesting scene, titled "The Belle," the reverse w/"Drink And Enjoy Lipton's Teas," some water staining, 16 x 19 1/2" (ILLUS.)........................ **72**

Mennen's Talcum Powder Sign

Talcum powder, "Mennen's Talcum Pow-der," rectangular, die-cut cardboard in wood frame, depicts young child writing in a book w/a quill pen, the page w/black letters reading "Mennen's Borated Tal-cum Toilet Powder - For Infants and Adults - It Cures: Prickly Heat, Nettle Rash, Chafing, Measles, Eczema, Sweaty Feet, Pimples, Etc. - Delightful After Shaving - 25¢ Per Box" & at bottom "Mennen's Sure Corn Killer," ca. 1880, rare, 19 1/2 x 22 1/2" (ILLUS.)......... **1,500-1,800**

Weed Tire Chains Die-cut Sign

Tire chains, "Snow Ahead - Buy Weed Chains," die-cut, color photo image of a pretty standing lady wearing a red cap & jacket & black skirt holding a pair of skis, a tire w/chains to her side, rectangular sign at top in bright yellow w/grey, red & dark blue wording, scattered soiling &

stains, minor warping, minor wear, 26 1/2 x 65" (ILLUS.).. 50

Savage Tires Sign

Tires, "Savage Tires," oil board tullograph, depicts "Little Heap" leaving a roadside sign & offering a peace pipe to a motorist w/poem about the little Indian & the quality of Savage Tires at bottom, framed, surface wear, 23 x 30" (ILLUS.) **1,760**

Tobacco, "Spear Head Tobacco," lithographed, one edge w/a half-length profile portrait of a Native American chief in headdress holding a long pointed spear above his head, large writing to the left reads "Chew Spear Head Tobacco - Save The Tags," in a wooden frame, some minor paint loss, crease in upper right corner, 15 x 21"..................................... **285**

Glass

Harvard Ale Sign

Ale, "Harvard Ale," rectangular, reverse-painting on glass w/cardboard backing, easel-back, cardboard images of bottles & glass on left, right side w/"Harvard Ale ... Has What it Takes" below logo, red band at bottom reads "Export Beer - Ale - Porter," cardboard images appear faded, 13 x 19" (ILLUS.).. **88**

Beer, "Budweiser," round, reverse-painted glass, red w/gold lettering "We feature Budweiser Bottled Beer," logo at top, 10 1/2" d. **149**

Buffalo Lager Sign

Beer, "Buffalo Lager," reverse-painted wrap-around corner type, crackle glass lettering against a view of the brewery w/"Buffalo Lager - Buffalo Brewing Co., Sacramento, Cal.," 9 1/4 x 16 x 25 1/2" (ILLUS.)... **6,050**

Beer, "Burger Beer," lighted reverse-painted glass in tin frame, upright diamond-shaped sign attached to narrow rectangular electric platform, signed w/color crest at top above oval border around "Burger" above "Beer," 1950s, 10" sq. (frame spotted)..................................... **95**

Beer, "Gilt Edge Best Ruhstaller Beer Lager," reverse-painted glass, metal enclosure w/two wall brackets, Achrach & Co., San Francisco, California, 18" d. **550**

Beer, "Old German Premium Lager," rectangular, reverse-painted glass restroom signs, one w/brand name & "For Men" w/cartoon of man, the other w/"For Women" w/cartoon of woman, like new, 1950s, pr. **72**

Feigenspan Quality Brews Sign

Brewery, "Feigenspan Quality Brews," reverse-painting on glass, "P.O.N." (Pride of Newark), in large gold letters, framed, minor wear to reverse detail, some flaking, 13 x 16" (ILLUS.) **88**

La Venga Cigars Sign

Cigars, "La Venga Cigars," rectangular, reverse-painting on glass, black w/logo in center flanked by embossed brass scrolls, "La Venga" above & "Havana Cigars - Celestino Vega & Co. Tampa, Fla." below, wood frame, ca. 1910, 20 1/2 x 26 1/2" (ILLUS.) **235-300**

Dairy, "Driggs Dairy Farms," reverse-painted milk bottle on black on left w/"Driggs Dairy Farms Certified Quality Milk - Cream" in red letters on tan, original metal frame for easel or wall-mounting, by Micro Products, High Point, North Carolina, clean, unused condition, 8 x 16" **385**

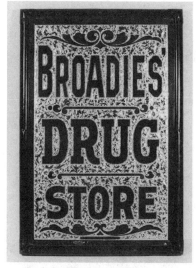

Broadies' Drug Store

Drugstore, "Broadies' Drug Store," rectangular, reverse-painting on glass, gold leaf on glue chip glass, scroll decoration, copper frame, ca. 1890, 17 1/2 x 25 1/2" (ILLUS.) **900-1,300**

Drugstore Sign

Drugstore, beveled glass w/ornate filigree background, reads "Drugs," copper frame, 47 " l., 7 1/2" h. (ILLUS.) **460**

Ice cream, "Storock's Ice Cream," reverse-painted scene depicts stork, wood frame, 21 1/2" l. **325**

City of New York Insurance Company Sign

Insurance, "City of New York Insurance Company," rectangular, reverse-painted glass w/"City of New York - Insurance Company - Fire" above & below oval sepia scene of New York city flanked by embossed brass scrolls, wood frame, ca. 1920's, 21 1/2 x 30" (ILLUS.) **425-500**

Refrigerator, "Mohawk Refrigerator - With The Duozone Unit," reverse-painted glass w/a black ground, the large print brand name in red & gold letters above other wording in white & red below, a color or bust of a Native American chief in the lower left, framed, 9 1/2 x 17 1/2" **55**

Star Brand Shoes Sign

Shoes, "Star Brand Shoes," round, reverse-painted on convex glass, white background w/red & yellow letters reading "Star Brand - Shoes - Are Better," wood frame, ca. 1920s, 22" d. (ILLUS.) **450-600**

Soft drink, "Coca-Cola," reverse-painted glass, shows tilted bottle in center & reading "Pause... Delicious and Refreshing - Drink Coca-Cola in Bottles," foil back, metal frame, 1937, 10 x 12" **4,000**

Standard Distilling Company Sign

Whiskey, "Hanover Pure Rye," round, reverse-painted convex glass front w/ornate openwork gold metal frame, image of brown horse head in center flanked by grain wreath & encircled by dark blue border w/"Standard Distilling Co. - Cincinnati, Ohio" in gold letters, further encircled by wide white border w/gold leaf letters reading "Hanover - Pure Rye," , ca. 1890, 24" d. (ILLUS.) **850-1,100**

Whiskey, "Jas.E.Pepper & Co.," reverse-painted glass w/center scene of the Pepper distillery buildings w/"Jas.E.Pepper & Co. - Pepper Distillery - Lexington, KY." above flanked by shield forms reading "'Pepper' Distillery Hand Made Sour Mash Jas.E.Pepper & Co. Distillers Lexington, KY' & "The Oldest and Best Brand of Whiskey - Made in Kentucky," w/wide ornate frame (ILLUS.) **4,000**

Neon

Beer, "Schaefer Beer," "Schaefer" in script & "Beer" in block letters, mounted on metal framework, 11" h. (soiling, cracks & wear to rubber tips) **170**

Car dealer sign, "Dodge - Plymouth," rectangular neon-type w/stepped lower corners, dark blue ground w/white word "Dodge" in larger letters over "Plymouth" in smaller letters, the narrow white border band set off w/a neon band, lights white, newer transformer, 28 x 60" (repair to neon, water stain & chips to sign) **1,650**

Dairy products, "Borden Company," one-sided, die-cut, on wooden platform w/easel support, yellow & white neon lights, head w/ring of flowers around neck & front paws of Elsie (porcelain chips around edges, corners & along bottom edge, creases, denting, fading, scratches, soiling & staining) **1,870**

Ice cream, "North Pole Real Ice Cream," green neon lettering against a black background, soiling, 7" deep, 12 x 26" **231**

"Jas.E.Pepper" Whiskey Advertising Sign

Neon Optometrist Sign

Optometrist, large bluish white spectacles in the center w/reddish orange wording above & below "Glasses On Credit - Easy Terms," mid-20th c. (ILLUS.) **250**

Radio, "Motorola Auto Radio," glass & metal, pink & yellow neon lighting, 25 1/2" w., 11 1/2" h. **715**

Large Dog N Suds Neon Sign

Restaurant, "Dog N Suds," metal & neon, a large round top section w/the restaurant dog logo outlined in blue, white, red & yellow neon, a lower picket fence border w/the name in orange neon, works, 8' l., 7'6" h. (ILLUS.).. **2,310**

Wareco Neon Sign

Service station, "Wareco," round red composite board backing w/white, black & pink half-figure of a saluting service station attendant above the name in blue neon, a border of orange neon, transformer on the back, newer neon, works, 20" w., 20" h. (ILLUS.) **187**

Shoes, "Buster Brown Shoes," porcelain & neon, nearly square form w/a red, yellow, blue & pink image of Buster Brown & Tige all outlined in yellow or white neon above a bottom red band w/"Buster Brown Shoes" in yellow w/yellow neon, ca. 1950s, 54 x 55" (some later tube repair, some minor surface wear, light stains, small chips, mounted on deep wooden frame) **1,540**

Poll Parrot Shoes Neon Sign

Shoes, "Poll Parrot Shoes," porcelain cutout of a colorful parrot outlined in various colors of neon tubing, all neon is newer, 16" w., 48" h. (ILLUS.) **2,146**

Soft drink, "Coca-Cola," reads "Drink Coca-Cola," late 1940s, 18 x 28" **1,800**

Soft drink, "Coca-Cola," w/transformer, blue letters reading "Coca-Cola" on black plastic background w/orange border, 26" w., 14" h. **330**

Truck, "GMC General Motors Trucks," round wall-type, glass & metal, orange, black & white decoration & lettering, 18" d. (new face w/original face included)..... **633**

Paper

Bathtubs, "United States Mfg. Co. Sanitary Bathtubs," color lithograph depicting woman sitting in tub, framed under glass, 23 1/2" h. (creases & repairs) **600**

Eveready Radio Batteries Poster

Batteries, "Eveready Radio Batteries," litho-graphed paper w/archival backing, color-ful outdoor scene of group of young boys in makeshift "Broadcasting Studio" w/box marked "Eveready Radio Batteries," dat-ed "1930" & signed "Jackson," fold marks, creases, scuffs, thumbtack marks at top touched up, 24" w., 32" h. (ILLUS.)................. **242**

Budweiser Poster

Beer, "Budweiser" poster-type, framed litho-graph entitled "Custer's Last Fight," de-picts battle scene w/company logos at each bottom corner w/"Anheuser-Busch, St. Louis Missouri, U.S.A. - World's Larg-est Brewery - Home of Budweiser & Oth-er Anheuser-Busch Fine Beers" (ILLUS.) **300**

Colorful Falstaff Beer Sign

Beer, "Falstaff Beer," lithographed, long rectangular form, dark green ground w/a color scene of seated Falstaff on the right having his tankard of beer refilled by a pretty young lady in a low-cut gown standing behind him, gold & red wording reads "An Old Friend! - Falstaff Beer - The Choicest Product of the Brewer's Art," based on artwork by Irene Patten, glued to mat board, 9 3/4 x 21" (ILLUS.) **77**

Beer, "Minnesota City Brewery Bock Beer," lithographed paper in color w/a scene of a Cavalier blowing a horn while riding on a ram leaping over a beer barrel, light wear & stains, framed, ca. 1900, 25 x 37" **622**

Framed Pabst Blue Ribbon Beer Sign

Beer, "Pabst Blue Ribbon Beer," rectangu-lar color lithograph scene of two bottles w/blue ribbons tied around the necks, a filled glass & a plate of oysters, signed wood frame, ca. 1920s, Pabst Brewing Company, Milwaukee, Wisconsin, 22 x 25 1/2" (ILLUS.)............................... **225-300**

Beer, "Rainier Beer - Bock," printer's mock-up lithograph, design for imprinting on standard lithograph, color design w/a large ram head in center left w/a sand-wich & large foaming mug of beer in the front right, "Rainier Beer" in red at top & "Bock" in large pale green letters at the bottom, one-of-a-kind, framed, 24 x 29" **219**

Beverage, "Kickapoo Joy Juice," litho-graphed, 22 x 28 3/4".................................... **170**

Biscuits, "National Biscuit," colored, pic-tures silent film star of 1920s, Diana Allen, holding a plate of cookies above "National Biscuit Company Does My Baking," newer frame, 20" w., 27" h. (mi-nor tears & wear to edges, fold mark across center) **1,650**

Wonder Bread Howdy Doody Sign

Bread, "Wonder Bread," die-cut heavy pa-per, jointed Howdy Doody character, plaid shirt, jeans & boots, "C Kagran print-ed in U.S.A.," 1" d. top layer paper in hair missing, very minor wear to edges, some fading, 5 1/2" w., 13" h. (ILLUS.) **200-300**

Packard Cable Sign

Cable, "Packard Cable," rectangular, lake scene of young girl dressed in red sitting on post w/attached cable marked "Tie To Packard Cable," wood frame, ca. 1900, 18 1/2 x 25 1/2" (ILLUS.) **350-425**

Cartridges, "Union Metallic Cartridge Co.," showing various shell casings & scene of battleships in background w/smaller boat in waves in foreground & marked "Rim Fire - Central Fire Pistol, Sporting and Military UMC - The Union Metallic Cartridge Co. Bridgeport, Conn. U.S.A.," ca. 1898, framed (ILLUS., below)..................... **4,125**

Cartridges, "Winchester Shells," colorful woodland scene depicting bird, titled "Cock of the Woods," ca. 1905, overall 15 x 25" (top & bottom bands missing, 3" tear mid left at tail feathers to edge, uneven tear on bottom edge) **836**

Wrigley's Spearmint Gum Sign

Chewing gum, "Wrigley's Spearmint Pepsin Gum," rectangular color lithographed picture of the red, white & green gum package against a black ground, gold wording reads "Fine for digestion! - Fine for Teeth!," near mint, 9 x 19" (ILLUS.)......... **149**

Cigarettes, "Mecca Cigarettes," lithographed w/a colorful half-length portrait of a lovely lady wearing a wide-brimmed hat w/her back to the viewer & looking over her shoulder, signed "P. Earl Christy," advertising below "Mecca Cigarettes - Perfect Satisfaction," wide flat wooden frame, some staining in upper corner, 15 1/2 x 23 1/2" **285**

Bloomer Club Cigar Sign

Cigars, "Bloomer Club Cigar," lithographed w/an unusual design of a scene in a ladies' athletic club w/two seated women in the foreground wearing bloomer outfits and smoking cigars, other figures in the background, molded wooden frame, small chip under one chair, 22 x 27" (ILLUS.).. **3,163**

Cigars, "Petoskey Chief 5¢ Cigar," lithographed w/a bust portrait of a Native American chief w/feathered headdress, an expansive landscape in the distance, reads "Try A Petoskey Chief - Our Best 5¢ Cigar," wide flat wood frame, repaired tear in lower corner, overall soiling, 27 1/2 x 36"... **3,795**

Union Metallic Cartridge Co. Cartridge Board Sign

Red Belt Cigar Sign

Cigars, "Red Belt 5¢ Cigar," colorful lithographed image of a pretty young woman wearing a large feathered hat & dark red dress, seated on the lawn tying her shoe, a red umbrella beside her & a signpost behind her, framed, 15 x 20" (ILLUS.)........... **853**

Framed Chase & Sanborn Coffee Sign

Coffee, "Chase & Sanborn Coffee," rectangular, scene of four older men sitting around an old round heating stove, dog lying nearby, the shopkeeper in the background, titled "An Old Fashioned New England Grocery" & "Compliments of Chase & Sanborn," signed mat & wood frame, Chase & Sanborn, Boston, Massachusetts, ca. 1897, 22 1/2 x 24 1/2" (ILLUS.).. **550-700**

Sanita Malt Coffee Poster

Coffee, "Sanita Malt Coffee," rectangular, depicts two young children sitting at a table, marked "Both of us drink only Sanita Malt Coffee," metal bands at top & bottom, framed, 10 x 14 1/2" (ILLUS.)............... **187**
Cream separator, "DeLaval Cream Separator," lithograph shows five different images of farm women w/machines, framed under glass **1,050**
Farm machinery, "Adriance Buckeye Harvesting Machinery," color lithograph shows young woman gathering grain surrounded by four images of various horse-drawn harvesting machines, matted & framed, image 26" h. (creases & minor stains)... **475**
Fertilizer, "Griffith and Boyd," lithograph showing woman playing solitaire, under glass in oak frame, image 21 1/2" h. **625**

Colt Firearms Sign

Firearms, "Colt Firearms," rectangular, lithograph of smiling girl wearing Western hat, brown skirt & belt, white blouse w/striped brown neckerchief, ammunition belt around hips & holding pistol, ca. 1900, wood frame, this version without Colt imprint cost 25¢, 39 1/2 x 37" (ILLUS.)... **1,800-2,500**

Marlin Rifle Poster

Firearms, "Marlin," 1907, rectangular, outdoor scene w/one man in canoe & a second man pushing the canoe away from the river bank, a campsite in the wooded background, w/"Marlin Repeating Rifles and Shotguns - 'The Gun For the Man Who Knows'" (ILLUS.) **2,145**

Ground oats, "'Meckumfat' Regd. Sussex Ground Oats," color lithographed paper on cardboard, rectangular, advertising above & below a colorful farmyard scene showing various types of fowl including ducks, chickens & turkeys, "To Be Obtained From All High Class Shops" across the bottom, 14 1/2 x 18 3/4" **275**

Gunpowder, "Austin Powder Company," w/wooden frame, depicts two pointers in field above "Austin Powder Company," 23" w., 19" h. **518**

Dead Shot Gunpowder Sign

Gunpowder, "Dead Shot Gunpowder," rectangular, bird falling to the ground w/"Dead Shot" above & "American Powder Mills - Boston - Chicago - St. Louis" below, wood frame marked "Gunpowder," ca. 1910, 25 x 31" (ILLUS.) **1,200-1,800**

Comic Hercules Powder Poster

Gunpowder, "Hercules E.C. & Infallible Smokeless Shotgun Powders - L. & R. Orange Extra - Hercules Powder Co.," color poster w/a large comic scene of a black man & boy with hunting dog in a winter landscape, the man reaching into his game bag, titled "I'se done lost de lunch," by artist Frederick Spiegle, bands missing, 1923, 15 1/2 x 24 1/2" (ILLUS.) **908**

Framed Remington Guns Sign

Guns, "Remington Guns," lithographed w/original metal bands at top & bottom, central rectangular scene of a flying duck w/examples of guns & shells above & below, wide flat wood frame, some overall creases, minor chipping & tearing at edges, 25 x 30" (ILLUS.) **2,300**

Wildroot Hair Tonic Poster

Hair tonic, "Wildroot - with oil for the Hair," large poster w/a dark blue ground featuring color bust portrait of a handsome man standing behind a pretty blonde, white & blue wording, narrow black border band, ca. 1940s, 25 x 36" (ILLUS.) **116**

Hand soap, "Everybody's Hand Soap - 'Cleans All Hands'," rectangular color printed design w/a large blue & yellow image of the can in the center w/a crowd of heads at the top & white wording on dark blue at the bottom reading "Best for Everybody," ca. 1920, 28 x 42" **77**

Stetson Hats Lithograph

Hats, "Stetson Hats - naturally- - -," color lithograph of cattle roundup, four cowboys wearing Stetson hats, near mint condition, 17 x 22 (ILLUS.)............................. **77**

Gulf Oil Disney Magazine

Magazine, "Gulf Exclusive Wonderful World of Disney Magazine, 25¢," depicts Donald Duck in lower left corner, 44" w., 33 3/4" h. (ILLUS.)............................. **77**

Magician, "Carter the Great," poster-type mounted on linen, the eight sheets form-ing a full-color image w/a spirit leaving the body of a hanging man w/the man's bust portrait to the right above a crowd of pointing on-lookers, name at the top & white wording across the bottom reads "Carter Condemned to Death for Witch-craft Cheats the Gallows," ca. 1920s, 7 x 9' (few minor wrinkles)............................. **633**

Medicine, "Kickapoo Indian Remedies," depicts Chief Red Spear dressed in full regalia, by lithographer J. Ottmann, 18" w., 24" h. **432**

Motor oil, "Sterling Motor Oil," paper, depicts baseball umpire, catcher & man at bat & reading "Play Safe! Change to Sterling Motor Oil For Summer Driving," Sterling Motor Oil logo on mid-right side, 22" w., 31 3/4" h. (some creases & soiling) **187**

Newspaper magazine, "New York Sunday Journal," 1898, rectangular, scene of sailboat on water featuring the Yellow Kid comic strip character, w/"Around the World with the Yellow Kid - in the Great New York Sunday Journal" w/"The Yellow Kid Sails Jan 17" at the bottom (ILLUS., below) **4,950**

Gilmore Lion Head Pennant Sign

New York Sunday Journal Poster

Oil company, "Gilmore Lion Head Motor Oil," heavy printed paper pennant-form, double-sided, long hanging triangular shape w/creamy yellow ground & wording in orange & dark blue, a lion head logo near the top, 10 x 20 3/4" (ILLUS.) **303**

Houbigant Perfume Sign

Perfume, "Houbigant Parfums," rectangular, paper on cardboard, scene of young woman standing at an open window & holding & smelling blossoms on vine beside the window shutter, mat marked "Parfums Houbigant - Paris," ornate frame, ca. 1920s, 16 1/2 x 20 1/2" (ILLUS.) **250-325**

Petroleum products, "Gulfpride," paper w/linen backing, depicts squirrel on nut & reading "Winter's Ahead, Change to Gulfpride Now!," gold background, marked "Form SS-78 For Posting October 16-31, 1940 All Divisions," ca. 1940, 28" w., 42" h. **143**

Remington UMC Poster

Rifles, "Remington - UMC," poster-style, colorful scene of two men w/rifles on mountaintop, clouds in background, marked "Remington - UMC - Firearms - Ammunition" by H. G. Edwards, lithograph by American Litho Co., NY, minor wrinkles, 18 x 26" (ILLUS.)........................... **1,870**

Salt, "Morton Salt," rectangular, depicts product in center w/potatoes on left & a split baked potato & salt shaker on right, "What's a potato without Morton's?," ca. 1940s-50s, framed under glass, wrinkles, light edge wear, minor marks & stains, 18 x 36" (ILLUS.) **187**

Morton's Salt Poster

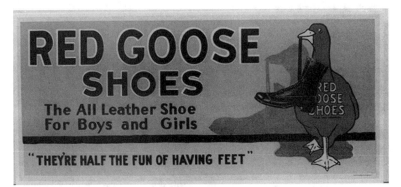

Red Goose Shoes Sign

Red Goose Shoes Sign

Sewing machine, "Illinois Sewing Machine Co.," lithographed, a colorful bust portrait of a Native American chief in a feathered headdress which is printed w/"New Royal is Chief," across the white bottom edging "Illinois Sewing Machine Co.," molded wood frame, 25 1/2 x 32" (minor crease in left border) **1,438**

Shoes, "Red Goose Shoes," rectangular, red goose holding black high-top shoe by the laces in his beak, reads " Red Goose Shoes - The All Leather Shoe For Boys and Girls - 'They're Half the Fun of Having Feet'," green, yellow, red & black, ca. 1910, Friedman-Shelby Shoes, 8 x 18" (ILLUS.) **275-325**

Shoes, "Red Goose Shoes," rectangular, scene of mother examining shoe of crying boy, reads "Don't blame the Boy - Buy him All-Leather Shoes - Red Goose Shoes for Boys for Girls - The Friedman-Shelby 'All-Leather Shoe'," yellow, red & green, ca. 1910, Friedman-Shelby Shoes, 8 x 18" (ILLUS.) **275-325**

Shoes, "Walk-Over Shoes," lithographed w/a tall narrow rectangular color scene of a young cowgirl in leather outfit leaning against a large tree w/"Walk-Over"

carved in the trunk, artist-signed, copyright 1911, in a wide flat wood frame, 18 x 38" **1,150**

Shotgun shells, "Dead Shot," color lithograph w/original metal bands at top & bottom, scene of a large falling mallard drake w/hunter in distance, reads "Smokeless - Black" at the bottom, wide flat frame, 24 x 33" (some minor creasing, minor edge tears) **3,508**

Skin products, "Satin Skin," lithographed paper w/archival backing w/"Satin Skin Powder - 4 Tints, Flesh, White, Pink, Brunet." above a colorful bust portrait of a young lady w/flowers in her upswept dark hair holding a fan which reads "Don't You Want Satin Skin," flanked by two containers & "Satin Skin Cream - Copyright, 1903 by Albert F. Wood. MFR. The Satin Toilet Specialties, Detroit, Mich." below, gold, red, white, & green w/black lettering, 30 3/4" w., 45" h. (very minor soiling) **175-250**

Soap, "Ivory Soap," color lithograph titled "A Busy Day" by Maud Humphrey, artist-signed, gesso frame, 10" w., 22 1/2" h. **259**

Wolverine Soap Chips Sign

Soap, "Wolverine Soap Chips," rectangular, colorful lithographed display of various products surrounding red center marked "Not Kept in Stores - But Sold - Direct to Consumers - By Our Own Canvassing Agents" & marked at bottom "Agents - Wanted," Terriff & Co., Portland, Michigan, litho by Calvert Litho Company, De-

troit, Michigan, wood frame, ca. 1900, 28 1/2 x 34" (ILLUS.) **750-1,100**

Soft drink, "Coca-Cola," rectangular window-type, a black background printed at the far left w/a large yellow "5¢" beside the large red button logo w/"Drink Coca-Cola" beside a large bottle of Coke, a three-quarters portrait of a smiling boy at the far right, dated 1950, w/Kleen-Stick tape points for window attachment, 11 x 24 1/2".................................. **314**

Soft drink, "Orange-Julep," rectangular, black w/yellow lettering outlined in red, "Drink - In Bottles - At Fountains - How's Orange-Julep - The Perfection of Orange Drinks," wood frame, ca. 1915, 12 x 30 1/2" (ILLUS.)............................. **125-175**

Soft drink, "Whistle," heavy lithographed design w/"Giant Family Size," 15 x 35" **30**

Stock feed, "International Stock Food Company," rectangular, scene of pacer horse "Dan Patch" & jockey, information on horse at lower left, marked at bottom "Dan Patch 1:55 - Owned by International Stock Food Co., Minneapolis, Minn.," wood frame, ca. 1910, 20 x 27 1/2" (ILLUS.) **225-325**

Orange-Julep Sign

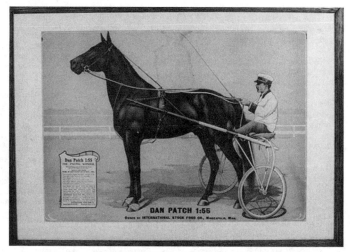

International Stock Food Co. Sign

Early Pennsylvania Tire Sign

Tires, "Pennsylvania Oilproof Vacuum Cup Tires," color lithographed w/a half-length portrait of a lovely young lady wearing a pale green dress & a large straw hat w/green trimmings, portrait titled "Euphemia," advertising in lower section, also printed "Pennsylvania Rubber Company, Jeannette, Pa. U.S.A.," early 20th c., in a narrow oak frame, minor frame wear, 25 1/4 x 35 1/2" (ILLUS.) **440**

Rare Daisy Air Rifles Poster Sign

Toys, "Daisy Air Rifles," color lithograph showing a young boy holding an American flag in one hand & a Daisy rifle in the other, standing on a rock w/"1620" on it w/other boys & a small ship in the background, 1911 (ILLUS.) **4,565**

Mayo's Plug Linen Poster

Tobacco, "Mayo's Plug - Light and Dark," rectangular, linen, yellow w/black lettering & image of rooster w/blue, green & black feathers, standing on brown boxes w/labels, 17 3/4 x 30" (ILLUS.) **770**

Toothpaste, "Euthymol Toothpaste," color lithograph w/young woman, framed under glass, 37 1/4" h. **1,000**

Rare Daisy Air Rifles 1908 Poster

Toys, "Daisy Air Rifles," titled "Two Daisies" by Calvert Litho Co., Detroit, Michigan, shows boy walking arm in arm w/girl & holding rifle on his shoulder, other children at play in background, top & bottom bands w/hanger, reverse pictures No. 1, No. 2, No. 3, No. 30 & the "Little Daisey" w/full descriptions, 15 1/2 x 22 3/4" (ILLUS.) **4,620**

Rare "Buffalo Bill's Wild West" Sign

Traveling show, "Buffalo Bill's Wild West," lithographed poster-type large colorful scene of a Native American warrior on horseback in the foreground, advertising above "Buffalo Bill's Wild West and Congress of Rough Riders of the World," at bottom "The Red Fox 'Red Cloud' Waiting and Watching," w/wide flat oak frame w/beaded rim, minor soiling, 28 x 34 1/2" (ILLUS.) **5,175**

Whiskey, "Pride of Kentucky Whiskey," lithographed w/a colorful scene of a wide landscape w/the distillery in the distance & a lovely lady in riding habit w/a handsome horse in the right foreground beside a large barrel of whiskey, advertising across the top & bottom, copyrighted in 1896, molded giltwood frame, 39 x 51" (some border spotting, staining & soiling) .. **2,875**

M. Hommel Wines Sign

Wine, "M. Hommel Wines," rectangular, lithograph w/center scene of vineyard below medals & bunches of grapes flanked by wine bottles, top marked "M. Hommel - Highest Awards Over All American

Champagnes - At World's Columbian Exposition - 1893," the bottom marked "Sandusky, Ohio - U.S.A.," wood frame, litho by Wittemann Litho Co., New York, ca. 1910, 28 x 34 1/2" (ILLUS.).... **225-300**

Solona White Port Wine Sign

Wine, "Solona White Port Wine," rectangular, scene of woman in green dress w/her arm on the shoulder of a dark-haired man in dark suit, white shirt & bow tie, the couple seated at a table trimmed w/pink flowers, two glasses & wine bottle, wood frame, ca. 1900, 16 x 18" (ILLUS.) **175-225**

Carrollton Woolen Mills Advertisement

Woolen mill, "Carrollton Woolen Mills," lithographed w/bust portrait of pretty young blonde girl wearing a ruffled red & white bonnet tied under her chin, reading "Compliments of Carrollton Woolen Mills - Our Brands of Jeans - 'Eagle Valley' - 'Garlands' - 'Port William'" & "Jeans and Jeans Pants - Double Seamed - Patent Machine Tacked   and Warranted to Stand the Storm - Brands of Pants - Carrollton Eagle Valley No. 10," framed (ILLUS.).. **45**

Porcelain

Nash Service Sign

Auto service, "Nash," shield-shaped, double-sided, shades of blue & white, marked "Authorized - Nash - Service," chips at mounting hole, edge & field, 22 x 36" (ILLUS.) **2,640**

Auto service, "Pontiac," rectangular, black & white, reads "Oakland - Sales - Service - Pontiac," 23 3/4 x 35 1/2" (minor edge wear, scratches & small chips) **633**

Automobile, "Buick," one-sided, round, dark blue outer ring w/"Authorized Service" in white surrounding inner "Buick" logo in blue & white, ca. 1930s, 42" d. (one edge chip w/a few other small rim chips) **660**

Jaguar Dealer Sign

Automobile, "Jaguar Sales & Service," one-sided die-cut rounded shield form, jaguar head logo at top, creamy wording on a maroon ground, good luster, minor chips to mounting holes & edges, 18 3/4 x 19 3/4" (ILLUS.) **1,650**

Automobile club, "National Automobile Club," double-sided, white w/shield form, eagle on globe w/image of United States, stars & stripes w/"National Automobile Club" at top below black letters reading "OFFICIAL," Balto Enamel Mfg. information on lower right corner, 18 x 21" (minor edge & mount hole chips & wear) **292**

Automotive products, "Bowes Seal Fast Auto Products," rectangular, flange-type, white w/black & white lettering, reading "For Smoother Motoring - Bowes Seal Fast - Auto Products," large red seal at bottom, 14 x 19 1/2" (couple small edge & flange chips) **275**

Red Seal Dry Battery Sign

Battery, "Red Seal Dry Battery," curved die-cut, red, white & blue battery-form reading "Guaranteed for all Open Circuit Work - Red Seal Dry Battery - A Battery Suitable For Every Use," chips, scratches & wear, 14 1/2 x 34 1/4" (ILLUS.) **798**

Beer, "Bull's Eye Beer," square, target in red, white & blue w/"Bull's Eye Beer - Golden West Brewing Co's. Oakland, California," 18" (waterstain & edge wear) **352**

Beer, "Heineken," one-sided porcelain pillow-form, red w/center image of figural beer glass waiter carrying two glasses of beer on a tray, "Heineken" in white lettering above, logo below w/"Heineken bier," 16" w., 23 1/2" h. (very minor scratches) **275**

Beer, "Cherry Rail," one-sided porcelain w/rounded sides, depicts early steam engine below "Door County's Premium Lager" & "Cherryland Brewing, Ltd." below, rectangular white panel w/"Cherry Rail" across center, red, white & black w/red lettering 19" w., 14" h. **275**

Bulk oil, "Gargoyle/Mobiloil," "GW" for gears, 8 3/4 x 10 3/4" **1,100**

Bus, "Greyhound Lines," double-sided, 20 1/4 x 36" **725**

Bus depot, "Greyhound Bus Line," double-sided showing bus, 30" h. **2,300**

Trailways Bus Depot Sign

Bus depot, "Trailways," rectangular, double-sided, white w/red letters at top reading "Bus Depot," above black image of
map of the United States w/yellow banner w/red letters reading "Trailways" &
"National - System" in yellow letters,
small chips overall, 18 1/4 x 22" (ILLUS.) 688

Sweet-Orr Overalls Sign

Clothing, "Sweet-Orr," depicts six men in a
tug-of-war w/pair of overalls w/"Sweet-
Orr - Union Made - Overalls" in white letters on blue, fading & scratches to graphic, chips to "w" & edges, cracking,
14 x 20" (ILLUS.) 413

Kodak Film Sign

Camera film, "Kodak Film," rectangular,
double-sided, both sides w/Art Deco
style image of film roll & product box in
yellow w/red letters, dark blue background bordered by two narrow yellow &
a wide black band, white lettering at top
reading "Developing & Printing," minor to
moderate surface wear & scratches,
edge wear & chips, reverse w/lower field
chips, 14 x 20" (ILLUS.)................................. 660

Fry's Cocoa Sign

Cocoa, "Fry's Cocoa," rectangular, large
yellow can of the product w/royal crest &
red & black lettering against a dark blue
ground w/white lettering across the bottom "4 1/2 d. per 1/4 lb Tin 4 1/2 d.," minor edge chips & corner mounting hole,
14 x 21" (ILLUS.) 385

Life Savers Sign

Candy, "Life Savers," black w/red arrow &
package of candy in white & yellow,
marked "Real Life Savers - 'Always good
taste,'" ca. 1920s-30s, some touchup &
repair, clear coated, 27 x 60" (ILLUS.) 1,100
Chewing gum, "Wrigley's," shows both
Spearmint & Doublemint packages, 36" l. .. 1,900
City limits, "City of Ardmore," one-sided
oval, dark green ground w/outer band
printed in black on white "City of Ardmore" w/stars, a central oval w/scenic vignettes in brown, white & green showing
a steer, oil rigs & a motor boat,
10 1/2 x 16" (chips at grommet holes).......... 303
Cleanser, "Sunbrite," curved corner mount-
style w/sun & cloud graphics,
15 x 17 3/4".. 525

Dale Brothers Coffee Sign

Coffee, "Dale Brothers Coffee," rectangular,
white w/red letters reading "Dale Bros.
Coffee," image of friar holding coffee cup
on left side, minor edge chips, corner
bends, surface scratches & wear,
14 x 42" (ILLUS.) 358

"Piley's Cream Station" Sign

Cream station, "Piley's Cream Station," two-sided, rectangular, dark blue ground w/white lettering reading "Piley's Cream Station," two holes at top, 17 x 22" (ILLUS.) **165**

Credit card, "American Amoco Gas - Courtesy Cards Honored Here," double-sided, rectangular, white ground w/oval red, black & white logo at top above other wording in black, 15 x 24" (minor edge, field & mount hole chips & flecks) **110**

Credit card, "Gulf," double-sided, 30" d. **400**

Rare "Keen Kutter" Sign

Cutlery/tools, "Keen Kutter," flat two-sided sign reading "E. C. Simmons - KEEN KUTTER - Cutlery and Tools," white letters on red ground, several edge & hole chips, 11 x 14" (ILLUS.) **440**

Shamrock Dairy Sign

Dairy, "Shamrock Dairy," depicts leprechaun surrounded by shamrocks, marked "Shamrock Dairy - Guernsey - America's Table Milk," ca. 1940s-50s, light wear, marks, chips & nicks, 22 x 56" (ILLUS.) **1,100**

Rose Exterminator Co. Die-cut Sign

Exterminator, "Rose Exterminator Co.," die-cut, black, white & flesh-tone figural "spraying man," minor edge chips, 10 3/4" h. (ILLUS.) **358**

Exterminator, "Rose Exterminator Co.," oval, die-cut, white w/owl logo bottom center & red & blue letters reading "Rose - Exterminator Co. - Since 1860 - Wise Protection," 11 1/4 x 18 3/4" **149**

Large John Deere Implements Sign

Farm implements, "John Deere Farm Implements," long rectangular one-sided style, black ground w/large gold & red lettering centered by an squared center reserve in red & gold showing the three-legged leaping deer company logo, overall edge wear, bent top right corner, 24 x 72" (ILLUS.) **2,200**

Farm lubricant, "Texaco," single-sided, dated "10-8-48," 22 x 30" **500**

Farm supplies, "Big Dutchman Automatic Feeders," 24 x 35" **360**

Fertilizer, "Swift's Red Steer Brand," die-cut, 20 x 30" **1,200**

King Arthur Flour Sign

Flour, "King Arthur Flour," rectangular w/white lettering on blue ground, central round logo w/"King Arthur Flour - Sands, Taylor & Wood Co." above & below, chipping, ragged edges, 36 x 40" (ILLUS.) **204**

Flour, "Pied Piper Flour" (Aunt Jemima Mills), curved corner mount-style, by Burdick of Beaver Falls, Pennsylvania, 18 x 22", rare **1,500**

Fruit grower, "Sunkist Grower," rectangular, a light green border band around a dark green ground w/the top word in large white letters outlined in orange & the lower word in dark orange outlined in white, 11 1/2 x 19 1/2" (some scattered edge chips & wear)......................... **149**

Gasoline, "Calso Supreme Gasoline," pump sign, a large round disk in red w/white wording above the blue, white & red Chevron logo, 11 x 13 3/4" (tiny scratches & edge flecks, missing top left grommet)..................... **468**

Gasoline, "Conoco Gasoline," double-sided, round, a yellow background w/narrow blue border band, dark blue & red words at top & bottom centered by a colored picture of a standing Minute Man, 30" d. (four mount holes added, small bullet hole in center, reverse w/filled chips & restoration)..................... **2,420**

Conoco Gasoline Sign

Gasoline, "Conoco Gasoline," round, double-sided, yellow w/"Minute Man" in center, top marked "Conoco" in black letters, "Gasoline" in red letters at bottom, crazing, chips, wear & overall scratches, 25 1/4" d. (ILLUS.)..................... **880**

Gasoline, "El Paso," die-cut pump sign, a red & blue flaming torch behind a narrow rectangular bar w/the brand name in red on white, near mint, 10 1/4" w., 11 1/4" h. (ILLUS.)..................... **990**

Gasoline, "Humble," oval w/white ground & large red letters spelling the brand name, 7 x 14" (slightly crude factory edges, subtle, small scratches) **242**

Gasoline, "Indian Gasoline," one-sided, painted in green, orange, navy blue, yellow & white Indian design, 10 1/4" w., 18" h. **303**

Rare Indian Gasoline Pump Sign

Gasoline, "Indian Gasoline," pump sign, tall rectangular form w/a dramatic turquoise blue upper background w/red, black, white & yellow Native American beaded designs above a dark blue lower panel w/the brand name in white & turquoise blue letters, dated 1940, tiny surface scratches & edge flecks, chip at top left grommet, 12 x 18" (ILLUS.) **688**

Rare El Paso Gasoline Sign

Mobil Gasoline Flange-type Sign

Calendars

1904 DuPont Powder
Company calendar $3,080
Courtesy of Past Tyme Pleasures,
San Ramon, California.

1894 Union Metallic Cartridge Company
calendar. $5,005
Courtesy of Past Tyme Pleasures,
San Ramon, California.

Rare 1909 Coca-Cola calendar
with World's Fair scene $16,100
Courtesy of James D. Julia, Fairfield, Maine.

1931 Coca-Cola calendar with
artwork by Norman Rockwell. . . $1,000
Courtesy of Allan Petretti, Hackensack,
New Jersey.

Calendars & Match Holders

1891 Simmons Hardware
Company calendar with
gilt frame, 13 x 16½" ...... $225-$325
Courtesy of Richard Penn, Waterloo, Iowa.

Rare 1913 Selby Smelting &
Lead Company gunpowder
calendar, 21 x 27½" $4,455
Courtesy of Past Tyme Pleasures,
San Ramon, California.

Hanging metal match holders.
Left: Sharples Separator Company
with scene of a lady operating a
cream separator $230
Right: Sharples Separator Company
with scene of a young mother & her
daughter operating a cream separator .. $260
Courtesy of Gene Harris Antique Auction Center,
Marshalltown, Iowa.

Rockford Watch lithographed
metal hanging matchbox
holder $1,400
Courtesy of Gene Harris Antique Auction
Center, Marshalltown, Iowa.

Match Safes & Door Push Plates

From Left: World Automatic Injector match safe, ca. 1905 . . . . $125-200
Early Harley-Davidson - Merkle Motorcycle match safe, ca. 1930s $75-125
Aluminum Keen Kutter flip-out match safe, ca. 1893 . . . . $75-125
Blatz Beer brass match safe, ca. 1910 . . . . $150-225
All courtesy of Richard Penn, Waterloo, Iowa.

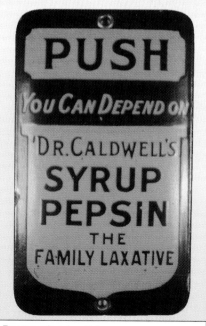

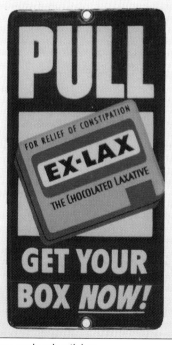

Door push advertising
Dr. Caldwell's Syrup Pepsin
laxative, ca. 1920s $150-200
Courtesy of Richard Penn, Waterloo, Iowa.

Door push advertising
Ex-Lax, ca. 1920s $150-225
Courtesy of Richard Penn, Waterloo, Iowa.

Coca-Cola Items

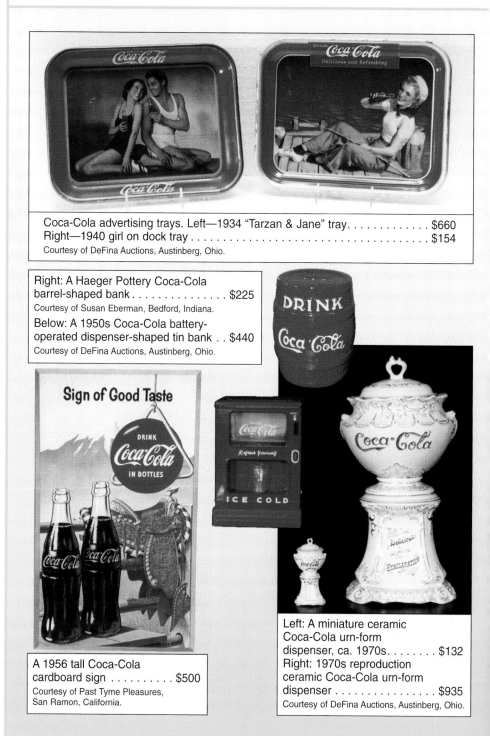

Coca-Cola advertising trays. Left—1934 "Tarzan & Jane" tray. $660
Right—1940 girl on dock tray $154
Courtesy of DeFina Auctions, Austinberg, Ohio.

Right: A Haeger Pottery Coca-Cola
barrel-shaped bank $225
Courtesy of Susan Eberman, Bedford, Indiana.
Below: A 1950s Coca-Cola battery-
operated dispenser-shaped tin bank . . $440
Courtesy of DeFina Auctions, Austinberg, Ohio.

A 1956 tall Coca-Cola
cardboard sign $500
Courtesy of Past Tyme Pleasures,
San Ramon, California.

Left: A miniature ceramic
Coca-Cola urn-form
dispenser, ca. 1970s $132
Right: 1970s reproduction
ceramic Coca-Cola urn-form
dispenser $935
Courtesy of DeFina Auctions, Austinberg, Ohio.

Display Cabinets

Left: Belding Silk 36-drawer spool cabinet with clock $2,400-2,800
Right: Diamond Dyes spool cabinet with "Court Jester" color scene . . $2,800-3,600
Both courtesy of Richard Penn, Waterloo, Iowa.

Left to right: Humphreys' Veterinary Homeopathic Specifics cabinet . . $5,000-6,000
Octagonal revolving 72-drawer hardware cabinet. $2,000-2,400
Both courtesy of Richard Penn, Waterloo, Iowa.
Diamond Dyes display cabinet with color scene of children jumping rope. . . $1,925
Courtesy of Past Tyme Pleasures, San Ramon, California.

Signs & Signboards

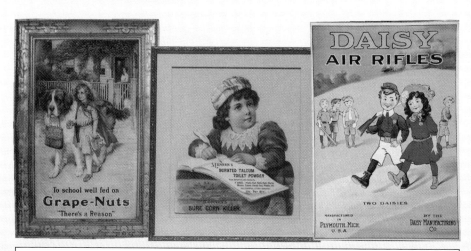

From Left: Grape-Nuts cereal embossed metal self-framed sign with
girl & St. Bernard, ca. 1900, 20 x 30" $1,100-1,900
Mennen's Talcum Powder die-cut cardboard sign
mounted in a frame, ca. 1880, 19½ x 22½" $1,500-1,800
Both courtesy of Richard Penn,Waterloo, Iowa.
Daisy Air Rifles color lithographed poster sign, ca. 1908 . . . . $4,620
Courtesy of Past Tyme Pleasures, San Ramon, California.

From Left: Packard Cable paper sign with a colorful scene
of a bathing beauty, ca. 1900, 18½ x 25½" $350-425
Ceresota Flour die-cut cardboard sign mounted in a frame,
ca. 1900, 13 x 17½" . . . . $1,300-$1,600
Both courtesy of Richard Penn, Waterloo, Iowa.
Red Belt 5¢ Cigar lithographed paper framed sign, 15 x 20" $853
Courtesy of Past Tyme Pleasures, San Ramon, California.

Signs & Signboards

John Deere medallion-form
dealer sign, ca. 1937 . . . . $825
Courtesy of Jackson's Auctioneers, Cedar Falls, Iowa.

Baco-Curo embossed
cardboard sunburst sign
with comic face, 9½" d. $468
Courtesy of Past Tyme Pleasures,
San Ramon, California.

Very rare Campbell's Soups
'American flag' tin sign,
27½ x 39½" $28,750
Courtesy of James D. Julia, Fairfield, Maine.

Cherry Blush metal over
cardboard sign, ca. 1900,
6¼ x 9" $650-800
Courtesy of Richard Penn, Waterloo, Iowa.

Hires Root Beer metal
flange-type sign, ca. 1940s,
12 x 14" $225-300
Courtesy of Richard Penn, Waterloo, Iowa.

Winchester Repeating Arms Co.
"Double W" design lithographed
board sign, 40 x 58", ca. 1902 . . . . . $4,600
Courtesy of Past Tyme Pleasures,
San Ramon, California.

Signs & Signboards

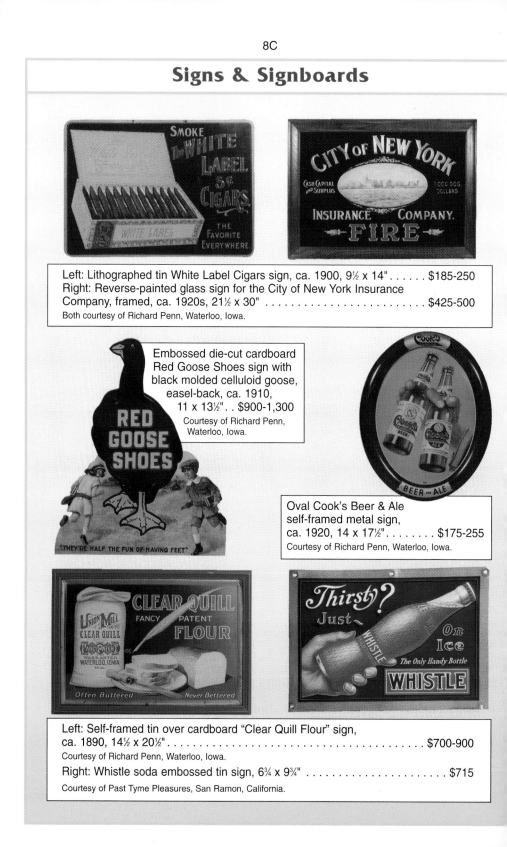

Left: Lithographed tin White Label Cigars sign, ca. 1900, 9½ x 14"...... $185-250
Right: Reverse-painted glass sign for the City of New York Insurance
Company, framed, ca. 1920s, 21½ x 30" $425-500
Both courtesy of Richard Penn, Waterloo, Iowa.

Embossed die-cut cardboard
Red Goose Shoes sign with
black molded celluloid goose,
easel-back, ca. 1910,
11 x 13½".. $900-1,300
Courtesy of Richard Penn,
Waterloo, Iowa.

Oval Cook's Beer & Ale
self-framed metal sign,
ca. 1920, 14 x 17½"........ $175-255
Courtesy of Richard Penn, Waterloo, Iowa.

Left: Self-framed tin over cardboard "Clear Quill Flour" sign,
ca. 1890, 14½ x 20½"..................................... $700-900
Courtesy of Richard Penn, Waterloo, Iowa.
Right: Whistle soda embossed tin sign, 6¾ x 9¾" $715
Courtesy of Past Tyme Pleasures, San Ramon, California.

Pocket Mirrors

Left to right: Mennen's Toilet Powder oval celluloid pocket mirror,
1¾ x 2¾", ca. 1910. . . . . $125-175
Angelus Marshmallow oval celluloid pocket mirror, ca. 1900, 1¾ x 2¾" . . . $125-175
Old Reliable Coffee round celluloid pocket mirror, ca. 1910, 2" d. $75-125
All courtesy of Richard Penn, Waterloo, Iowa.

Cascarets laxatives celluloid round
pocket mirror, ca. 1910, 2" d. $95-135
Courtesy of Richard Penn, Waterloo, Iowa.

Scott-Wilkerson Ambulance
Service pocket mirror,
ca. 1915, 3½" d. $125-175
Courtesy of Richard Penn, Waterloo, Iowa.

Ohio Blue Tip Matches
celluloid pocket mirror,
ca. 1900, 3½" d. $175-225
Courtesy of Richard Penn, Waterloo, Iowa.

Thermometers

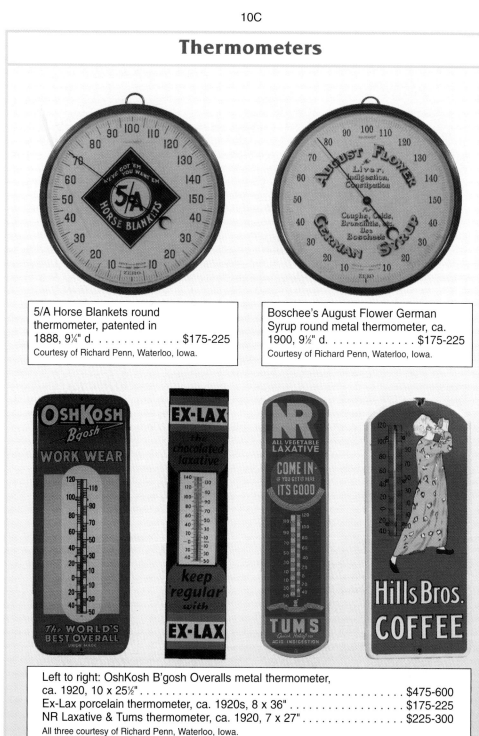

5/A Horse Blankets round
thermometer, patented in
1888, 9¼" d. $175-225
Courtesy of Richard Penn, Waterloo, Iowa.

Boschee's August Flower German
Syrup round metal thermometer, ca.
1900, 9½" d. $175-225
Courtesy of Richard Penn, Waterloo, Iowa.

Left to right: OshKosh B'gosh Overalls metal thermometer,
ca. 1920, 10 x 25½". $475-600
Ex-Lax porcelain thermometer, ca. 1920s, 8 x 36". $175-225
NR Laxative & Tums thermometer, ca. 1920, 7 x 27". $225-300
All three courtesy of Richard Penn, Waterloo, Iowa.
Hills Bros. Coffee porcelain thermometer, dated 1915, 8¾" x 21". $908
Courtesy of Past Tyme Pleasures, San Ramon, California.

Tins

Left to right: Fort Pitt Coffee tin with fort scene, 4¼" d., 5½" h. $470
Roaster to Customer 2½ lb. coffee tin, 5½ x 7¼" $578
Both courtesy of Past Tyme Pleasures, San Ramon, California.
Rare The Planters Mother's Brand Salted Peanuts 10 lb. tin $12,430
Courtesy of William Morford Auctions, Cazenovia, New York.

Left to right: League Brand Tomatoes tin $440
Turkey Brand Coffee 3 lb. tin, 5½ x 10¾" $1,650
Galt House Blend Coffee 1 lb. tin, 4¼ x 5". $495
All courtesy of Past Tyme Pleasures, San Ramon, California.

Trays

DeLaval Cream Separators change
tray, ca. 1906, 4¼" d. $275-325
Courtesy of Richard Penn, Waterloo, Iowa.

Lehnert's Beer change tray with stag
head, ca. 1910, 4¼" d. $125-175
Courtesy of Richard Penn, Waterloo, Iowa.

Globe-Wernicke Bookcases change
tray, ca. 1915, 4½" d. $125-175
Courtesy of Richard Penn, Waterloo, Iowa.

National Cigar Stands Co. change tray
with portrait, ca. 1910, 6" d. . . . $75-125
Courtesy of Richard Penn, Waterloo, Iowa.

Frost Wire Fence Co. change tray,
ca. 1910, 4¼" d. $125-175
Courtesy of Richard Penn, Waterloo, Iowa.

Gypsy Hosiery change tray with gypsy
girl portrait, ca. 1910, 6" d. . . . $75-125
Courtesy of Richard Penn, Waterloo, Iowa.

Trays

Quick Meal Ranges change
tray with scene of chicks,
ca. 1900, 3¼ x 4¼"......... $150-200
Courtesy of Richard Penn, Waterloo, Iowa.

Monticello Whiskey change
tray, ca. 1915, 4⅜ x 6⅛"..... $225-275
Courtesy of Richard Penn, Waterloo, Iowa.

Sears, Roebuck & Co. change
tray, ca. 1920, 4⅜ x 6".... $125-175
Courtesy of Richard Penn, Waterloo, Iowa.

Stollwerck Chocolate & Cocoa
change tray, ca. 1910, 5" d.... $75-125
Courtesy of Richard Penn, Waterloo, Iowa.

White Rock Table Water round change
tray, ca. 1900, 4⅜" d....... $225-300
Courtesy of Richard Penn, Waterloo, Iowa.

Rockford Watches change
tray, ca, 1900, 3¼ x 5"..... $125-175
Courtesy of Richard Penn, Waterloo, Iowa.

Trays

White Rock Table Water rectangular change tray, ca. 1910, 4⅛ x 6⅛"......... $225-275
Courtesy of Richard Penn, Waterloo, Iowa.

King's Pure Malt oval change tray, ca. 1915, 4¼ x 6"...... $100-175
Courtesy of Richard Penn, Waterloo, Iowa.

Lily Beer rectangular change tray, ca. 1915, 4½ x 6½"..... $175-275
Courtesy of Richard Penn, Waterloo, Iowa.

Miller High Life Beer rectangular change tray, ca. 1960s, 4½ x 6½"................. $35-65
Courtesy of Richard Penn, Waterloo, Iowa.

Left to right: Fairy Soap round change tray, ca. 1910, 4½" d. $100-175
Carnation Chewing Gum round change tray, ca. 1900, 4¼" d. $200-275
The Davenport Co. round change tray, ca. 1903, 4¼" d................ $75-125
All courtesy of Richard Penn, Waterloo, Iowa.

Miscellaneous

Budweiser ceramic mugs. Left to right: New Hampshire $46
Pick A Pair of 6 Paks $52
Bud Man Hero No. 1 . . . . $50
Brew House $33
Courtesy of Peter J. Kroll, Sun Prairie, Wisconsin.

Left to right: Newer ceramic "Horlick's" pitcher marked "Churchill,
England," 4½" h. $27
Courtesy of Susan N. Cox, El Cajon, California.

General Electric Radio GE Man made of jointed wood,
one arm loose, 19" h. $880
Courtesy of International Toy Collectors Association Auction, Springfield, Illinois.

Rare early die-cut cardboard Aunt Jemima Pancake Flour climbing toy $7,590
Courtesy of William Morford Auctions, Cazenovia, New York.

John Deere watch fob in black enamel & silver, original leather strap $880
Courtesy of Jackson's Auctioneers, Cedar Falls, Iowa.

Miscellaneous

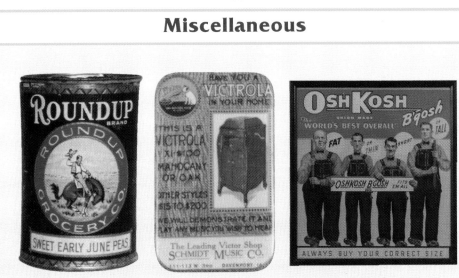

Left to right: Roundup Grocery Co. Peas tin $305
Courtesy of Past Tyme Pleasures, San Ramon, California.
Advertising pocket mirror of "Victor Victrola," ca. 1910, 1⅝ x 2¾" $175-225
OshKosh B'gosh Overalls cardboard sign, ca. 1930, 13½ x 14½" $175-250
Both courtesy of Richard Penn, Waterloo, Iowa.

Left to right: John Deere Plow Co. celluloid cricket clicker with deer logo $743
Courtesy of Jackson's Auctioneers, Cedar Falls, Iowa.
"Fan-Taz" rare baseball-shaped syrup dispenser, ca. 1900, 16" h. . . . . $8,000+
Remington Typewriters round celluloid pocket mirror, ca. 1915, 3½" d. $150-200
Both courtesy of Richard Penn, Waterloo, Iowa.

Gasoline, "Mobil Gasoline," flange-type, two-sided, a die-cut figure of the red Pegasus logo mounted in an angled iron bracket w/scrolling ends, touch-up to overall chips, some fading, water stain, soiling & scratches, 32 1/2 x 40 1/2" (ILLUS.) **1,760**

Gasoline, "Mobilgas Gasoline," die-cut pump sign, shield-shaped w/a white ground & large red Pegasus logo above the wording in black & red, 11 1/2 x 12" (minor edge & mount hole chips, minor surface wear, factory crazing) **451**

Gasoline, "Phillips 66," two-sided shield-shaped, red lettering on black at top & black & red below, "SPS 57" at bottom, 29 1/2" w., 29 1/2" h. (chip to numeral each side, minor edge chipping) **495**

Gasoline, "Red Crown Gasoline," round two-sided, white ground w/an outer ring w/the wording in red, the center circle w/a large red, white & blue crown symbol, 42" d. (slight touch-up to ground, minor scratches & soiling) **715**

Gasoline, "Shamrock Cloud Master Premium," pump sign, rectangular, a white background w/a large green shamrock w/white lettering above a blue oval w/a white cloud w/black lettering, 10 1/2 x 12 1/2" (minor surface wear & scratches, few scattered edge flecks & chips) **176**

Gasoline, "Shell Gasoline," two-sided die-cut shell-shaped, orange w/red lettering, 24 1/2" w., 24 1/2" h. (minor chips, scratches, soiling) **660**

Gasoline, "Texaco," cylindrical, reads "Texaco" above star logo on white background, marked "Made in U.S.A./3-5-61," (scratches & small chips to edges) **825**

Gasoline, "Texaco," round w/a white background & a large red star centered by a large green "T," the brand name above, 8" d. (couple of tiny rim flecks) **231**

Piggly Wiggly Sign

Grocery store, "Piggly Wiggly," round blue sign w/yellow head of pig wearing butcher's hat marked "Piggly Wiggly," ca. 1940s, 42" d. (ILLUS.) **1,045**

Red Cross Field Director Sign

Health services, "Red Cross," flange-type, red, white & blue reading "Field Director of The American Red Cross" w/Red Cross logo, minor scratches, some minor edge chips, 11 x 14" (ILLUS.) **160**

Heating oil, "Standard," die-cut, 15 3/4 x 20" (probably used on delivery trucks) **525**

Ice cream, "Eskimo Pie," rectangular, white w/blue letters, 6 1/2 x 36" (minor edge chips, soiling & wear) **215**

Gollam's Ice Cream Sign

Ice cream, "Gollam's," two-sided, heavy, depicts small boy holding very large ice cream cone, marked "We Serve Gollam's Lebanon Ice Cream," ca. 1941, minor dents at edge, scratches & paint chips, slightly ambered (ILLUS.) **550**

Insurance, "American Eagle Fire Insurance," black & white ground w/a large spread-winged eagle at top above wording "American Eagle Fire Insurance Company - New York," ca. 1930s, 14 1/2 x 15" (small corner chip & few small edge chips, minor warping) **88**

Niagara Fire Insurance Sign

Insurance, "Niagara Fire Insurance," fired-on ink scene of the falls, marked "Safety Fund Policies - Niagara Fire Insurance Company - New York," ca. 1910-15, 11 x 21" (ILLUS.) **2,970**

Kerosene, "Esso Elephant Kerosene," one-sided, elephant depicted in center, 12" w., 24" h. (minor edge chips) **688**

Lubricant, "Texaco Marine Lubricants," dated "10/2/59," 15 x 30", rare **2,600**

Milk, "Arden Milk," die-cut double-sided w/scene of boy & large creamer bottle, 28 x 33" **575**

Carnation Milk Truck Sign

Milk, "Carnation fresh Milk," die-cut shield-shaped truck sign, green border band around red & white background w/wording in white & green w/a cream-colored bottle of milk, very minor surface scratch-es, minor edge & mount hole chips, 22 x 23" (ILLUS.) **385**

Kerr-View's Milk Sign

Milk, "Kerr-View's Milk," two-sided die-cut, bottle-shaped, marked "From Our Own Herd - Use Kerr-View's Raw & Pasteurized Milk and All Other Dairy Products," ca. 1920s-30s, minor edge chips & nicks, 19 x 48" (ILLUS.) **1,760**

Milk, "Quaker Maid Milk," die-cut, red w/pretty milkmaid & blue banner reading "First in Quality" in center, wear, edge & mount hole chips, 24 x 41" (ILLUS.) **633**

Motor oil, "Ace High," double-sided, 17 1/4 x 23 1/4", very rare **3,400**

Quaker Maid Milk Sign

Aeroshell Sign

Motor oil, "Aeroshell," one-sided die-cut, reads "Aeroshell Lubricating Oil Stocked Here" below seashell w/wings, minor chipping to edges, 38" w., 10 3/4" h. (ILLUS.) **3,850**

Golden Shell Motor Oil Rack Sign

Motor oil, "Golden Shell Motor Oil," die-cut rack sign, in the shape of shell in dark gold w/red wording, three mount tabs on the back, tiny edge flecks & subtle surface scratches, 12 x 12 1/4" (ILLUS.) **3,520**

Motor oil, "Mobiloil," marked "Gargoyle (motif of gargoyle), Mobiloil, 'A,' Vacuum Oil Company Ltd" in orange & navy blue on white background, 11 1/4" w., 9" h. **403**

Motor oil, "Mobiloil," standing curb-type, the sign w/a rounded upper portion w/the red flying Pegasus logo on white, the lower narrow rectangular portion w/"Mobiloil" in white on a black ground, raised on a slender iron post w/a round foot, 30 1/2" w.,

64" h. (minor touch-up, scratches & water stain, hole at bottom where sign meets post) **770**

Motor oil, "Mother Pen," double-sided, by Reliance Adv. Co., Chicago, Illinois, 13 x 20" **750**

Mother Penn Motor Oil Sign

Motor oil, "Mother Penn," two-sided, painted in red, white & blue, depicts elderly woman in circle above, "1879 Mother Penn 1879, All Pennsylvania, Motor Oil, Dryer Clark & Dryer Oil Co." in rectangle below, scratches, 8 1/2" w., 5 3/4" h. (ILLUS.) **523**

Motor oil, "Pennzoil, Outboard Motor Oil, 100% Pure Pennsylvania, Safe Lubrication," the sign above cast-iron lollipop base, curb-type, marked "Ingram Ricardson, Beaver Falls, PA.," 32" w., 46 1/2" h. (repainted base, minor chips & scratches) **358**

Motor oil, "Royal Triton 76," single-sided rack sign, round w/a white ground, a blue & yellow can at the top w/printing in white center by the orange Union 76 logo, blue wording at bottom reads "America's Finest Motor Oil!," 14" d. (tiny edge flecks) **375**

Die-cut Shell Motor Oil Sign

Motor oil, "Shell Motor Oil," two-sided die-cut, in the shape of an upright rectangular can, grey top, side in black w/yellow-outlined red lettering & large shell logo in the center, "Shell-Mex Ltd." & London address at the bottom, minor chips on graphic & edges, ragged edges & part of one grommet hole missing, 15 3/4 x 20" (ILLUS.) **660**

Motor oil, "Sunoco Motor Oil," one-sided, marked "Mercury Made, Sunoco, Motor Oil" in black lettering on painted yellow background, 10" w., 12" h. **495**

Goodyear Motorcycle Tires Sign

Motorcycle tires, "Good Year," flange-type, rectangular base in blue & red w/"Good (logo) Year" in yellow, "Made in USA" at base of flange, black & white die-cut image of rider on motorcycle at top, same image on both sides, minor edge & flange chips & wear, 19 x 24" (ILLUS.) **8,250**

Simple Notary Public Sign

Notary public, "Notary Public," narrow long rectangle, large wording in blue block letters, red sunburst in center, early 20th c., 3 x 15" (ILLUS.) **44**

Texaco Oil Distributor Sign

Oil distributor, "Texaco - Larson Oil Co. - Distributor," truck door keyhole-shaped sign, white ground w/round red & green Texaco logo above a rectangular section w/the distributor's name, dated 1956, very minor edge wear, missing two bottom grommets, 10 5/8" w., 12 1/2" h. (ILLUS.) **550**

Overalls, "Duckhead Overalls" (O'Bryan Brothers), Ingram Richardson, 12 x 16" **325**

Rare Phoenix Pure Paint Sign

Paint, "Phoenix Pure Paint," curved corner-type, large central color scene of a young

Native American brave dancing while holding mirror & applying war paint from a can of the product in the foreground, a teepee shown to the left, a desert landscape in the background, grey background w/red wording "Easily Applied and Durable - Phoenix Pure Paint - W.P. Fuller & Co., Portland - Seattle - Tacoma - Spokane," very minor edge wear, fleck chips, some mount holes, small chip at left corner, 12 3/4 x 20 1/4" (ILLUS.) **12,650**

Chicken Producers Reward Sign

Poultry producers, "Member - Poultry Producers of Central California," rectangular w/dark gold ground, black border & wording, lower half reads "$250 Reward For Felony Conviction of Anyone Stealing Poultry From This Ranch - Nulaid," minor rust on edges, 14 x 20" (ILLUS.) **110**

Sherwin-Williams Paint Sign

Paint, "Sherwin-Williams," convex, colorful design of a yellow & red paint can marked "SWP" pouring red paint over a green globe w/white wording "Cover The Earth," ca. 1940-60, light wear, 18 x 34" (ILLUS.) **550**

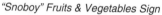

"Snoboy" Fruits & Vegetables Sign

Produce, "Snoboy," round w/central logo of snowman wearing red mittens & earmuffs & "Snoboy - 'Picked for flavor' - Fresh Fruits and Vegetables" in yellow & white letters, ca. 1940s, bright colors & luster finish, several small chips, 20" d. (ILLUS.) **168**

Sunray D-X Petroleum Products Sign

Petroleum products, "Sunray D-X Petroleum Products," octagonal, yellow sunrays on orange w/D-X logo near bottom, white letters on black at bottom reading "Petroleum Products," missing top grommet, 9 x 9" (ILLUS.) **1,320**

Foreign Railroad Sign

Railroad, embossed self-framed porcelain w/black silhouetted engine on a yellow ground, foreign-made, one-sided, Neuhas Paris, Vitracier Japy, rust spotting, scratches & soiling, triangular, 37" w., 36 1/2" h. (ILLUS.) **149**

Gillette Razor Blades Sign

Razor blades, "Gillette," two-sided die-cut flange-type, relief-molded safety razor depicted next to box of blades & marked "Gillette," trademark appears in French in small print, made in Europe, possibly Canadian in origin, ca. 1920-30, light edge wear, chips & cracks, 19 x 22" (ILLUS.) **3,080**

Refrigerator, "Dry-Kold Refrigerator Company," rectangular, white w/black oval in center bordered by icicles & w/white lettering w/icicle decoration reading "The 'Dry-Kold' - Refrigerator Company - Niles - Michigan," 11 3/4 x 22" (minor scratches, bottom edge cut down from larger unknown size)...................................... **138**

Carey-ized Salt Sign

Salt, "Carey-ized Salt," die-cut w/silhouetted salt products above a wide diamond, printed in red w/white & blue lettering, overall chips, fading, scratches, 49 x 50" (ILLUS.) **716**

Scales, "Fairbanks-Morse," black w/white letters reading "Fairbanks-Morse Scales," by Burdick, Chicago, Illinois, bright luster finish, 9 x 50" **77**

Seeds, "Aggeler & Mussler," reads "Plant Seeds in Confidence," 20 x 30".................... **575**

Soap, "Hudson's Soap," clock-style w/"We Close At........Today," 10 1/2 x 18"................ **725**

Soap, "World Soap," flange-type w/"Groceries, Teas & Coffees" by Ingram Richardson, ca. teens, 12 x 18" **1,100**

Soft drink, "Canada Dry Beverages," door kick plate, 10 x 30" **50**

Soft drink, "Coca-Cola," round, one-sided, painted dark blue, reading "Drink Coca Cola Ice Cold," allegedly foreign fridge sign, 14" d. (minor fading) **357**

Coca-Cola Die-Cut Sign

Soft drink, "Coca-Cola," die-cut in the shape of a Coca-Cola bottle, brown, gray, green, red & white, 5" w., 16 1/2" h., minor scratches, some chipping at edges (ILLUS.)............................ **200-250**

Soft drink, "Coca-Cola," button-form w/red lettering on gold, French, 18" d. **525**

Soft drink, "Coca-Cola," flange-type, reading "Coca-Cola" in white lettering & "Iced Here" in yellow on red background, 1949, 17 3/4" w., 19" h. (scratches, fading & chips to edges)... **550**

Soft drink, "Coca-Cola," double-sided shield form w/"Fountain Service - Drink Coca-Cola," ca. 1930s, 26" h. **2,200**

Soft drink, "Coca-Cola," rectangular, left side light green background w/dark green lettering reads "Fountain Service," w/words separated by white wavy lines, right side red background w/white lettering reads "Drink Coca-Cola," 1950s, 12 x 28" (chips to edges & creases, scratches) **231**

Soft drink, "Coca-Cola," rectangular, green & red w/tan lettering reading "Fountain Service" & white lettering reading "Drink Coca-Cola Delicious and Refreshing," 45 1/2 x 60" (chips to raised border) **2,420**

Soft drink, "Coca-Cola," two-sided, "lollipop" school zone pedestal base w/"Drink Coca-Cola," one side shows silhouette of young girl w/pigtails, running w/books & marked "School - Slow," the reverse w/"Drink Coca-Cola in Bottles," 30" d., 5' h. **750**

Soft drink, "Nesbitt's Orange," 3/8" reverse lip at edges, 10 x 19"..................................... **305**

Early Campbell's Soup Sign

Soup, "Campbell's Tomato Soup," cut-out can shape printed in red, white, gold & black w/familiar label, curved, top edge ragged, chips to edges & mounting holes, rust on back, 12 1/2 x 22" (ILLUS.) **468**

Tea, "Horniman's Pure Tea," by Patent Enamel Co., Ltd, 24 x 30" **800**

Salada Tea Curb Sign

Tea, "Salada," die-cut, two-sided curb-type w/cast-iron base, model of a stylized teapot in orange w/black wording "'Salada' Tea Served Here," minor edge chips, 42" w., 29 1/2" h. (ILLUS.) **793**

Fine King Cole Tea & Coffee Sign

Tea & coffee, "King Cole Tea and Coffee," one-sided, top oval reserve w/a color bust portrait of a jolly King Cole holding cup & saucer, rectangle below w/wording "King Cole Tea and Coffee," corner tip missing at bottom, scratches, minor fading, 9 x 15" (ILLUS.) **1,500-1,700**

Telephone, "Bell Telephone," rectangular two-sided flange-type, dark blue ground w/"Telephone" above round white & blue Bell logo w/"The Bell Telephone Company of Canada," ca. 1940-60 (large chip at top of flange) **220**

Telephone, "Telephone," flange-type, telephone pay station w/independent shield logo, 8 x 18" **400**

Fisk Tires & Auto Supplies Sign

Tires, "Fisk Tires," flange-type, rectangular, red & black w/white letters reading "Gasoline - Fisk Tires - Auto Supplies," early Ingram-Richardson sign w/volcano-style mount holes, scattered edge chips & field scratches, 18 x 24 1/4" (ILLUS.) **1,018**

Early Goodyear Tires Flange Sign

Tires, "Goodyear," flange-type, rounded view of a large grey & black tire printed at the center w/a black band w/the name in large yellow letters over a red winged sandal logo, overall edge wear, small chips, muddy colors on reverse, scattered soiling, ca. 1920s, 21 3/4 x 34" (ILLUS.).. **361**

Tires, "Goodyear Tires," one-sided, die-cut model of hot air blimp w/"Good Year #1 in Tires," few edge chips & scratches, manufacturer's defect to color blue, probably a prototype, 40" w., 18 1/2" h. (ILLUS.) **3,300**

Tires, "Michelin," one-sided, rectangle tapering to point at bottom, green center circle depicts "Michelin Man" on tractor, reads "Michelin" in black lettering at top, yellow background, marked "Email, Koek, TP 8141.99.65," 18 1/4" w., 24 1/4" h. **330**

Tires, "Michelin," one-sided, rectangular w/pointed bottom edge, dark blue ground w/yellow name at the top & running white Michelin man w/black tire, 27 x 31 1/2" (ILLUS.).. **330**

Tobacco, "Model Smoking Tobacco," rectangular w/white lettering on a red ground, depicts bald gentleman w/large mustache holding a smoking pipe w/"Yes, I said 10¢ MODEL Smoking Tobacco," chipping near hanging holes (ILLUS.).. **160**

Tractor, "Fordson Tractors" two-piece, black w/white lettering reading "Service Fordson" w/"Tractors" on a smaller sign suspended by chains (ILLUS.) **375**

Michelin Tire Sign

Fordson Tractors Sign

Goodyear Tires Sign

Model Smoking Tobacco Sign

Truck dealer, "GMC Trucks," two-sided, long rectangular form w/rounded lower corners, light & dark green w/"GMC" in a small circle above "Trucks" in large letters, 24 x 48" (minor scratches & edge chips) 572

Early Munsing Wear Sign

Underwear, "Munsing Wear," a black background w/white lettering & the figure of a young man opening his red robe to show his white long underwear, reads "Beyond Compare - Munsing Wear - Always Perfect Fitting - The fit won't wash out" (ILLUS.) **10,000**

Varnish, "Sherwin-Williams Varnish," flange-type, rectangular, a black ground w/white & red wording, a large white & black globe surrounded by red rays being painted by a large hand & brush, a can of the product at the center top, reads "Sherwin-Williams Varnish - Brightens the Earth - Sold Here," early crude rolled iron construction, 16 x 22" (minor edge chips, flecks & surface scratches) 605

Tin

U.S. Ammunition Self-framed Sign

Ammunition, "U.S. Ammunition," self-framed large rectangular color scene w/soldiers from around the world standing around an American rifleman in the center, titled "Championship of the World," won by the American Rifle Team in England in 1908, the frame in black w/the brand in gold at the top & gold wording along the bottom edge "Demonstrated Standard of the World," great colors, only minor dings & scrapes, 22 1/4 x 28 1/4" (ILLUS.) **2,035**

Auto service, "Ford," rectangular, thick tacker-style, blue top w/white letters reading "Service Station - Ford - Sales Agency," white arrow at bottom w/blue letters reading "Schenck Manufacturing & Supply Co. - Parkers Landing, PA.," minor bends at some corners, scratches, 11 5/8 x 35 1/2" **798**

Automobile, "Rambler," two-sided, round w/red wide border ring & crossbar printed in white "Rambler - Parts - Service," 1950s, 42" d. **523**

Willys-Overland Whippet Sign

Automobile, "Whippet Automobile," red w/embossed gold letters reading "Dollar for Dollar Value - Whippet - Product of - Willys-Overland Company," by M.C.A. Sign Company, Massillon, Ohio, wood frame, ca. 1920's, 15 x 25" (ILLUS.) **125-150**

National Refining Company Sign

Automotive, "National Refining Co.," two-sided lithographed metal, curb-type on signed iron base, figure of boy wearing black & white checked knee pants & red stockings holding rectangular black sign w/red border & yellow border w/black letters reading "En-Ar-Co Motor Oil - En-Ar-Co Gear Compound - White Rose Gasoline - National Light Kerosene," litho by Mathews Indus. Inc., Detroit, Michigan, ca. 1917, 27 3/4 x 45" (ILLUS.) **2,500-3,500**

Baby formula, "Malt Nutrine," rectangular, self-framed tin w/cardboard back, depicts a stork carrying in his beak two bottles tied together & flying over a man w/a raised whip in a carriage pulled by a racing white horse, titled "A Hurry Call," frame marked "Malt Nutrine," Anheser-Busch Brewing Company, St. Louis, Missouri, ca. 1915, 7 1/2 x 12 1/2" (ILLUS.)... **250-350**

Baby formula, "Malt Nutrine," rectangular, self-framed tin w/cardboard back, scene of a doctor dressed in black, carrying his bag & an umbrella up the lane towards a house in the distance, his shadow cast in the form of a stork, titled "Coming Events....," Anheuser-Busch Brewing

Company, St. Louis, Missouri, ca. 1915, 7 1/2 x 12 1/2" (ILLUS.) **250-350**

Exide Battery Sign

Battery, "Exide Batteries," flange-type, die-cut battery-form, black & red, marked "Exide" on front & side, date coded 5-53, rust, wear & paint flakes on outer edge, bend w/paint flake on upper terminal, 19 1/2 x 26" (ILLUS.)..................................... **358**

Anheuser-Busch Malt Nutrine Sign

Malt Nutrine Sign "Coming Events... "

Majestic Batteries Sign

Battery, "Majestic Batteries," rectangular, embossed tin, dark blue w/logo at center in yellow & red w/"Majestic" in white, "Sales and Service" above & "Batteries" below, minor surface scratches & edge wear, 19 1/2 x 26" (ILLUS.) **440**

Hamm's Preferred Stock Beer Sign

Beer, "Hamm's Preferred Stock Beer - Fully Aged," color-printed & embossed, rectangular, in red, white, blue, black & yellow, few small rust spots & light scuffs, 17 3/4 x 23 3/4" (ILLUS.) **435**

Berghoff Beer Sign

Beer, "Berghoff Beer," rectangular, cardboard backing, string-hung, snowy scene w/two hunting dogs, one brown & white, the other black & white, soiling & wear, minor subtle bends, 13 x 21" (ILLUS.) **72**
Beer, "Blatz Beer," rectangular, white ground printed in color w/a banner reading "Take Home" above "draft-brewed Blatz - Milaukee's Finest Beer," 1950s, 8 1/4 x 14" (some paint chips at edges, screw holes, few scratches) **105**
Beer, "Champagne Velvet Beer," tin lithographed over cardboard, colorful scene of fisherman standing in stream, two other men sitting on bank near woods, oval at side reads "Champagne Velvet Beer" bottom marked "The Beer With The Million Dollar Flavor" & signed "Hg. Hintermeister," Terre Haute Brewing Co., Inc. Terre Haute, Indiana, 14 1/2 x 19 1/2" (scratches & soiling) **176**
Beer, "Chief Osh-Kosh." die-cut flange-type showing Native American Indian in top hat & tuxedo, 13 1/2 x 18" **975**
Beer, "Gold Crown Beer," color-printed tin over cardboard, rectangular, gold lettering on a black ground at the right, a narrow red band w/black logo on the left, 1940s, 7 x 14 3/4" (some scratches & scuffs, sticker residue) **47**

Hudepohl Beer Tin Sign

Beer, "Hudepohl Beer," color-printed tin over cardboard, rectangular, a mottled pale yellow ground printed w/"Ask For Good Old Hudepohl Beer - Cincinnati, Ohio" in silver, black & red, a color image of the bottle at the center, only minor scuffs, 1930s, 9 x 13" (ILLUS.) **460**
Beer, "M.K. Goetz Brewing Co.," oval rolled self-framed tin, a half-length portrait of a poor African-American man smiling & holding a large glass of beer, titled "Jerry's Smile," advertising for the company on the wood-grained frame border, copyrighted in 1903, 22 1/2 x 28 1/2" (some frame wear, minor background chipping) .. **7,475**
Beer, "Steinhaus Beers," color printed tin over cardboard, rectangular, brown woodgrain background printed in silver, red & black "Steinhaus Beers - For Fine Flavor - Pilsener and Lager," 1930s, 9 x 13" (few scratches) **201**

Ziegler's Beer Sign

Beer, "Ziegler's Beer," rectangular, metal w/cardboard back, black w/bottle on right, white & white outlined w/red lettering reading "Drink Ziegler's Beer - Beaver Dam, Wisconsin," ca. 1920s, 8 1/4 x 11 1/2" (ILLUS.) **175-225**

Fort Pitt Beer Sign

Beer, "Fort Pitt Beer," painted metal, embossed colorful scene of couple seated at table w/a bottle of beer & filled glasses, "Thanks to Our Courageous President and Sound Thinking Members of Congress and U.S. Senators" above, "for this Delicious - Fort Pitt Beer - Pittsburgh, Pennsylvania -- Sharpsburg, Suburb" below, denting around edges, touch up to rust spotting & nail holes overall, 26" w., 22 3/4" h. (ILLUS.).. **990**

Cook's Beer & Ale Sign

Beer & ale, "Cook's Beer and Ale," oval blue center w/hand holding a bottle of beer & a bottle of ale, self-framed brown border marked at the top "Cook's Goldblume" & at the bottom "Beer and Ale," F. W. Cook Company, Evansville, Indiana, ca. 1920, 14 x 17 1/2" (ILLUS.)............................. **175-225**
Beverage, "Silver Springs Beverages," self-framed, 11 x 35" (some damage) **55**

White Rock Lithia Water Sign

Beverage, "White Rock Lithia Water," oval, embossed self-edge tin w/beautiful lithograph scene of fairy kneeling on rock at water's edge, by Chas. W. Shonk Co., wear on self-edge, minor scratches & dings, 16 1/2 x 19 3/4" (ILLUS.) **1,210**

White Rock Sign

Beverage, "White Rock Sparkling Beverages," embossed scene depicting fairy crouching on large rock near water, ca. 1950s, shallow dent, heavy scratch on raised border, light wear, 33 x 57" (ILLUS.) **550**
Beverage, "Budweiser," tin over cardboard, Prohibition era non-alcoholic drink, shows bottle on wooden case, 7 x 17"......... **750**
Boat, "Starcraft Boats," rectangular embossed tin, yellow, blue & red, image of boat on water, blue & red letters read "Starcraft - Metal Boats of Distinction - Authorized Dealer," 17 3/8 x 23 3/8" (grainy paint, flecks & wear) **121**
Bread, "American Bread," lithographed w/image of a child, self-framed, 17" h. (slight scratches) **425**
Bread, "Merita Bread," embossed tall rectangular form, a red ground w/a color embossed loaf of bread flanked by the word-

ing "Buy Enriched Merita Bread - Always Fresh!," wording in red, yellow & white, 1940-50, 18 x 54" (some mild discoloration, light edge wear) **633**

Lone Ranger "Merita Bread" Sign

Bread, "Merita Bread," embossed tall rectangular form, the top half w/a color image of the Lone Ranger riding Silver w/blue skies & mountains in the background, the lower half w/a large color image of a loaf of bread against a pale yellow ground w/blue & red wording reading "It's Enriched - Buy Merita Bread," dated 1954, 24 x 36" (ILLUS.) **4,000-5,000**
Bread, "Sunbeam Bread," embossed long narrow rectangular form w/narrow dark green border band w/a half-length color portrait of the Sunbeam girl in a blue dress at the left, red background w/yellow & white wording to the right "Reach For... Sunbeam - Energy-Packed Bread," 1950s, 19 x 55" (some tiny dark spots, near perfect) **688**
Bread, "Sunbeam Bread," embossed & self-framed w/large image of Miss Sunbeam, dated 4/62, 11 3/4 x 29 3/4" **375**

Early Anheuser-Busch Tin Sign

Brewing company, "Anheuser-Busch," rectangular self-framed type w/wide mottled green border w/brand in red at the top & "Budweiser Girl" in red at the bottom, colorful center scene shows a pretty girl in German costume seated by a leafy lattice holding up a bottle & a glass of beer, early 20th c., some minor fading & scratches mostly on edges, 25 1/2 x 37 1/2" (ILLUS.) **1,815**

Bit-O-Honey Sign

Candy, "Bit-O-Honey," embossed, left side of sign w/green plant, the product package & several almonds w/"Bit-O-Honey Candy with roasted almonds," 9 x 20" (ILLUS.) **220**
Car radio, "Motorola Car Radio," rectangular, double-sided, both sides white & blue w/red & white letters reading "Motorola - Car Radio - Installation Station," 20 x 28" (nicks, scratches & soiling) **110**

Grape-Nuts Sign

Cereal, "Grape-Nuts," embossed metal, self-framed, lithograph of young girl walking to school w/St. Bernard dog, house in background w/her mother standing at front gate, reading at the bottom "To school well fed on Grape-Nuts - 'There's a Reason'," ca. 1900, 20 x 30" (ILLUS.) **1,100-1,900**

Fleers Gum Sign

Chewing gum, "Fleers Bubble Gum," lithographed red w/black & white package marked "Fleers Dubble Bubble Gum - 1¢," in center w/"Thanks! - Call again for ---" above & "Fleers Dubble Bubble Gum" below, few dents & scratches around edges, 3 3/4 x 6 7/8" (ILLUS.) **143**

Honey-Fruit Gum Sign

Chewing Gum, "Honey-Fruit Gum," tin over cardboard, rectangular, black ground printed w/white package of gum, white wording "Nothing Like It - Delightful Flavor" (ILLUS.) **2,750**

Chewing gum, "Oh Boy Gum," narrow vertical rectangle, black ground w/a color half-length image of a smiling boy w/an elf whispering in his ear, the boy holds four large, colorful packages of the gum, printed in yellow at the bottom "1¢ - It's Pure!," 1930s, framed w/no glass, 7 1/2 x 16" (light wear & edge bends) **688**

Wrigley's Gum Sign

Chewing Gum, "Wrigley's Gum," rectangular, metal w/cardboard easel-back, colorful lithograph by American Can Company shows packages of four different gum flavors on black background, marked "Wrigleys" in red letters & "Delicious Lasting Flavors" in white letters, ca. 1920's, 6 7/8 x 11" (ILLUS.) **325-400**

Cigars, "A.K. Walch's Cigars," rectangular, lithographed, red w/white lettering reading "Smoke A.K. Walch's 'Good Company' 3¢ Cigars - 4 for 19 cts. - Have No Equal - Have You Tried The Silver Quarter 5¢ Cigar? - If Not, Why Not! - A.K. Walch, Phila, Pa.," 7 1/2 x 13 3/4" **204**

Ben-Hur Cigars Framed Sign

Cigars, "Ben-Hur 5¢ Cigars," rectangular lithographed design w/a dark brown wood-grained background centered by a large oblong gilt scroll-trimmed color reserve showing a chariot racer pulled by four white horses, wording in red above & below the reserve, in a gilt gesso ornate shadowbox period frame, very minor dings & surface wear, few subtle edge bends, 24 1/2 x 32 1/4" (ILLUS.) **660**

Colonial Club Cigars Flange Sign

Cigars, "Colonial Club 5¢ Cigars," long rectangular flange-type double-sided style, a dark blue background w/large white lettering w/thin red outlines above smaller red lettering w/thin white outlines, 8 3/4 x 18 3/4" (ILLUS.) **198**

Devlish Good Cigar Sign

Cigars, "Devlish Good Cigars," rectangular, chain-hung embossed display, blue w/center image of box of cigars, lid depicts three babies smoking cigars, reading "The Devlish Good - Cigar - None Better - 5 Cents," red flames above large black letters, wear, flecks & soiling, light bend at top center, 10 x 13 3/4" (ILLUS.) **171**

Cigars, "Diamond Bell," lithographed w/"Organized Labor ask for 'Diamond Bell' & 'Full Jewel' 5¢ Cigars - Made by Your Own Craft - A.K. Walch, Phila PA," red & white, 7 3/4 x 13 3/4" (minor scratches & fade) **176**

Missing Miss Cigar Sign

Cigars, "Missing Miss," octagonal w/rolled edge, entitled "Viola," lithographed bust portrait of beautiful young woman w/long brown hair, wearing a low-cut dress w/red scarf draped over shoulder, reading "Missing Miss" at the top w/"5¢" on each side & "Cigar - Tony Bennauer Mfr., Mendota, Ill.," dated 1908, by Meek Co., minor flaking & surface rust, 14 1/2" (ILLUS.) **661**

Optimo Cigars Sign

Cigars, "Optimo Cigars," rectangular w/center oval depicting bust of man w/mustache wearing hat, tie & coat wcolorful tropical scene in background, reads "Optimo - Mild - Aromatic - Sweet," wood frame, ca. 1910, 23 x 27" (ILLUS.) **475-550**

San Felice Cigars Sign

Cigars, "San Felice Cigars," rectangular, embossed tin, yellow w/center black circle w/box of cigars, black & red lettering reads "San Felice Cigars - 'For Gentlemen of Good Taste'" & "5¢" on each side, wear & scratches, 11 1/2 x 17 1/2" (ILLUS.) **182**

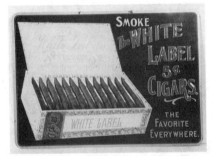

White Label Cigars Sign

Cigars, "White Label Cigars," rectangular, black w/lithographed image of white box containing cigars on the left, right side marked in yellow "Smoke - The Favorite Everywhere," green embossed letters outlined in yellow read "The White Label 5¢ Cigars," litho by Sentenne & Green, New York, ca. 1900, 9 1/2 x 14" (ILLUS.) **185-250**

Cleanser, "Old Dutch," tin over cardboard, figure of Dutch girl on left w/"For Healthful Cleanliness There's nothing like Old Dutch," ca. 1930s-40s, light paper marking from original paper, corner nicks, shallow dent, 9 x 18" (ILLUS., below) **935**

Clothing, "Duxbak," mounted over cardboard, shows birds in air over water, marked "Duxbak Serviceable Clothes For Life in The Open - 'Sheds water like a Duck's Back'," 15 x 18 1/2" (minor rust bottom edge) **330**

Clothing, "Hub Clothing," scene of a black boy holding sign, 53" h. **2,100**

Cocoa, "Walter Baker & Co.," lithographed scene shows 18th c. maid serving cup of cocoa, framed, 13 x 19" **1,450**

Old Reliable Coffee Sign

Old Dutch Cleanser Sign

Coffee, "Old Reliable Coffee," shows man in coat & hat w/product package nearby, marked "Always Good - Old Reliable Coffee," ca. 1920s-30s, 6 1/2 x 9 1/2" (ILLUS.) **660**

White House Coffee Flange Sign

Coffee, "White House Coffee," flange-type, a large hand holding up a large can reading "White House Coffee - 1 lb. - Net - Dwinell-Wright Co. - Boston Chicago," printed above hand "None Better at any Price," early 20th c. (ILLUS.) **4,300**

De Laval Cream Separators Sign

Cream separator, "DeLaval Cream Separator," rectangular, lithographed tin on wood, center oval reserve depicting milk maid & cow flanked by four colorful farm scene vignettes featuring the separator, red background w/yellow letters reading "De Laval Cream Separators - Save $10 to $15 Per Cow Every Year of Use - 1,750,000 in Use" & marked below center image "The De Laval Separator Com-

pany" w/several locations listed at bottom, ornate gold Victorian-style frame w/"De Laval" tag on bottom edge, ca. 1910, 29 1/2 x 40 1/2" (ILLUS.) **2,800-3,800**

Near Mint Wyandotte Detergent Sign

Detergent, "Wyandotte," self-framed, wide false-grained frame around color scene of standing Native American warrior shooting arrow, a round company logo in each corner, brand name on frame & top w/"J.B. Ford Company - Wyandotte, Michigan U.S.A." on frame at bottom, near mint, 28 x 39" (ILLUS.) **4,950**

Dog food, "Friskies For Your Dog," flange-type, large red circle w/a narrow white border & flange, black, white & red image of the Friskies dog logo above the wording in white & black, 17 1/2 x 18" (very minor wear & paint flecks) **450-500**

Ken-L-Ration Dog Food Sign

Dog food, "Ken-L-Ration Dog Food," rectangular blue base w/white & yellow letters reading "Feed Your Dog the Best - Ken-L-Ration - Ken-L-Biskit - Ken-L-Meal," top w/die-cut dog head logo in yellow w/black nose & eyes, red tongue, minor scratches, 14 x 21" (ILLUS.) **330**

Drugstore, "Rexall," rectangular w/rounded ends, painted "The Rexall Store" in green, red & blue enamel, ca. 1915-1930, 38 3/4" l., 8" h. (some minor chipping to edges)... **242**

Dye, "Diamond Dyes," tin lithograph over cardboard w/"A Busy Day in Dollville," 17" l.. **2,900**

Winchester Western Round Sign

Firearms, "Winchester Western," round double-sided printed in color w/a Pony Express rider w/rifle above red wording all on a black ground w/white & red border bands, w/original hanging bracket & factory box, ca. 1960s, 38" d. (ILLUS.)........ **380**

Flour, "Clear Quill Flour," self-framed, w/cardboard back, blue w/image of white quill pen over table holding loaf of bread & slices on plate w/white flour sack at left marked w/red letters "Union Mill Company - Clear Quill - Fancy Patent - Warranted Waterloo, Iowa - 49 lbs.," red & white letters read "Clear Quill Fancy Patent Flour - Often Buttered - Never Bettered," ca. 1890, 14 1/2 x 20 1/2" (ILLUS.) **700-900**

Flour, "Polar Bear Flour," long rectangular, a large color image at the left of a polar bear on an iceberg in blue seas w/a wide colorful rainbow or Northern Lights in distance, red & blue wording on white at right reads "Polar Bear Flour - Try it today," overall paint wear at edges, some bends, scattered nicks, scratches & surface wear, 13 3/4 x 35 1/4" (ILLUS.) **578**

Clear Quill Flour Sign

Polar Bear Flour Sign

Fine Sleepy Eye Flour Sign

Flour, "Sleepy Eye Milling Co.," self-framed, large colorful oval central reserve w/bust portrait of Chief Sleepy Eye marked "Trade Mark - Old Sleepy Eye," the edges w/various Native American vignette scenes & symbols, banner across the bottom w/"'Sleepy Eye' The Meritorious Flour," 20 x 24" (ILLUS.)............... **8,050**

Garage door holders, "Stanley Garage Door Holders," rectangular, lithographed image of garage w/double doors open, right side w/blue letters on yellow background reading "Stanley Garage Door Holders" w/red letters near bottom reading "Hold Your Garage Doors Open!," by H.D. Beach, ca. late 1900 - 1920s, slots at bottom held brackets that displayed the product, minor bends, wrinkles, dings, dents & scratches, 26 1/4 x 34" (ILLUS.) **853**

Stanley Garage Door Holders Sign

Gasoline, "Bruinoil - Bruin Gasoline," double-sided flange-type, a large oval w/a pale greyish yellow ground featuring large arched red wording above & below a large image of a charging, growling brown bear, logo & "The Bear of Them All" flank the bear, black flange, some wear on flange & key hole areas, few tiny nicks & scraches, rare, 13 1/2 x 17 3/4" (ILLUS., below) **7,150**

Gasoline, "Pure Oil Company," flange-type, one-sided, round, blue w/white letters reading "Energee - True Gasoline - The Pure Oil Co." 17 1/2 x 20" **330**

Gasoline, "Shell Gasoline," two-sided die-cut painted orange shell-shaped, flange-type, 21 1/2" w., 17 1/2" h. (minor scratches to both sides)............................... **1,595**

Gasoline, "White Rose Motor Gasoline," rectangular, lithographed tin, green & black, rose blossom & bud shown in upper right corner, reads "White Rose Motor Gasoline and National Carbonless Motor Oil," 9 3/4 x 13 3/4" (edge wear, soiling & wrinkles)............................. **743**

Rare Bruinoil-Bruin Gasoline Sign

Dupont "Generations" Tin Sign

Gun powder, "Dupont," self-framed, a large color central scene of a young boy w/his grandfather getting ready to fire rifle, hunting dogs in foreground, "Dupont" logo in upper left, printed in small black words across the bottom "Generations Have Used duPont Powders," based on artwork by Edmund H. Osthaus, 23 x 33" (ILLUS.).. **1,870**

E.D. Pinaud's Hair Dressing Sign

Hair dressing, "E.D. Pinaud's Eau de Quinine," rectangular, bottle in center flanked by embossed florals, w/"Use Only The Genuine - E.D. Pinaud's" above & "Eau de Quinine - An Ideal Hairdressing" below, wood frame, ca. 1900, 17 1/2 x 23" (ILLUS.).............................. **225-275**

Van Camp Hardware Sign

Hardware, "Van Camp Hardware," round die-cut, flange-type, blue & white w/center image of windmill under large red letters reading "Van Camp - Trade Mark" & white letters around border reading "Highest Grade - Van Camp Hardware & Iron Co. Indianapolis, Ind." & blue letters on flange reading "Goods Bearing This Trade-Mark Are Of The Highest Quality," litho by New York Metal Sign Works, New York, ca. 1890, 13 1/2 x 18" (ILLUS.).... **650-750**

Hot dogs, "Armour Franks - Plump, Juicy, Tender! - Served Exclusively," embossed, w/blue & yellow wording & a comical portrait of a young boy eating a big hot dog, 12 x 15" **259**

Ice cream, "Borden's Ice Cream," painted flange-type, nearly square w/rounded corners, bust portrait of Elsie the Cow w/wording "Borden's Ice Cream - If It's Borden's It's Got To Be Good," in red, white, blue & yellow, scratches, small spot of paint loss, 15 x 16" **550**

Ice cream, "Darigold Ice Cream," embossed image of a carton of ice cream in blue w/gold & white bands w/red wording, a dish of vanilla ice cream w/chocolate topping, 24 x 33" (minor nicks, scratches & wear).. **88**

Hood's Ice Cream Sign

Ice cream, "Hood's Ice Cream," two-sided circular flange type, painted metal w/trademark cow in center, red border w/white lettering, some surface paint missing, rust & waterstain on flange, 19" d. (ILLUS.) **1,320**

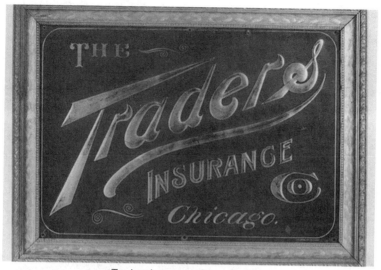

Traders Insurance Company Sign

Mission Orange Juice Sign

Ink, "Sanford's Inks," embossed, rectangular, a large central display of various ink products below the wording "Faultless: Sanford's Inks and Mucilage," wooden frame w/stamped brass corner trim, some in-painting, overall scratching & chipping, 19 1/2 x 26".............................. **2,990**

Invincible Motor Insurance Sign

Insurance, "Invincible Motor Insurance," rectangular, lithographed tin, green w/image of battleship & touring car, marked "Invincible - Motor Insurance by Instalments - Invincible Policies Limited," British origin, minor edge wear, 9 1/2 x 20" (ILLUS.).. **242**

Insurance, "Traders Insurance Company," rectangular, lithograph by Charles Shonk, black w/gold lettering reading "The Traders Insurance Co. Chicago," wood frame, ca. 1910, 17 x 23" (ILLUS.) **325-425**

Juice, "Mission Orange Juice," rectangular, black w/yellow sun & sunrays, embossed red letters outlined in white & white letters reading "Drink Mission Orange - It's Real Juice, wood frame, ca. 1920s, 13 x 31" (ILLUS.) **125-175**

Rare Majestic Range Tin Sign

Kitchen range, "The Great Majestic Range," embossed w/a colorful scene of a young maid working at a large Majestic kitchen range, wording above reads "The Great Majestic Range," wording at bottom reads "Charcoal Iron Bodies Malleable Iron Frames," wide flat oak frame, some in-painting, overall soiling, 20 1/2 x 25 1/2" (ILLUS.) **3,738**

Milk, "Arden Protected Milk - 27 Protections," long rectangular form w/a dark red background & large yellow wording above white script wording, the uniformed milk delivery boy company logo in the lower right, 15 x 41 1/2" (scattered small nail holes, stains at top, scattered wear, beds at edges, few small field neck & scratches) **578**

Mineral water, "Sheboygan Natural Mineral Water," upright rectangular design, a central color image of a seated, smiling Native American chief at a table holding a glass w/a bottle in his other hand, two African American waiters holding up trays stand behind him, pale yellow wording across top reads "Chief of Them All," black & pale green wording under image reads "Sheboygan Natural Mineral Water - Better Than Imported," narrow black border

band, dated 1904, 10 1/2 x 14 1/2" (small dings at bottom, added frame) **798**

Motor oil, "Invader Motor Oil," rectangular, yellow w/black, white & red image of knight on horseback on the right flanked by black letters reading "Lasts Longer - Serves Better," large black letters on left read "Use Invader Motor Oil" above red seal marked "100% Pure Pennsylvania Oil," touch-up repair lower left corner, wear, light bends, 9 x 26" (ILLUS., below) **440**

Ring-Free Motor Oil Sign

Motor Oil, "Macmillan Ring-Free Motor Oil," die-cut embossed tin, the rectangular blue base w/image of a hand holding the die-cut can in red, white & blue, marked "Ring-Free - Motor Oil," white letters on bottom of sign reading "Raise Your Car's Standard of Living," minor edge & surface wear, 27 1/4 x 34" (ILLUS.) **281**

Motor oil, "Pennfield Motor Oil," rectangular, embossed tin, image of oil derrick & red letters on yellow read "Pennfield" w/yellow lettering on black reading "Motor Oils - Finest from Pennsylvania Fields," 13 3/4 x 19 5/8" (discoloration at left side, few small wrinkles & scratches) **330**

Invader Motor Oil Sign

Rajah Motor Oil Sign

Motor oil, "Rajah Motor Oil," die-cut, top w/head of man wearing turban & marked "100% Pure Pennsylvania," the rectangular base w/rounded bottom reads "Double Mileage - Rajah Motor Oil - A Penn-O-Tex Product," yellow & blue, three mount holes at center, scratches & wear, small minor bend at top left edge, 10 x 28" (ILLUS.) **468**

Motor oil, "Richlube Motor Oil," rectangular, double-sided rack-type, red w/yellow & white letters reading "Richlube - All-Weather Motor Oil - 30¢ Per Quart - 100% Pure Pennsylvania," date coded 7-38, 12 x 16" (minor edge wear, light surface scratches **523**

Motor oil, "Sinclair Opaline Motor Oil," embossed tacker-type, rectangular w/narrow red border band & pale green background w/dark green wording & a green sketch of an oil can at the left side, 11 7/8 x 19 1/2" (few tiny wrinkles, paint rub at bottom) **495**

Motor oil, "Texaco 'New' Motor Oil," heavy, double-sided, dated "2-37," 11 1/4 x 21 1/2" **450**

Motor oil, "Use Penn-Drake Motor Oil," embossed, long rectangular form, black ground w/a white, orange & black company logo on the left & large white & orange wording on the right, 9 11/16 x 27 7/8" (very minor edge wear & scattered wrinkles)........................... **209**

Motor oil, "Wolf's Head Oil," embossed & self-framed, 13 3/4 x 19 3/4" **400**

Coles Nerve Tonic Sign

Nerve/blood tonic, "Coles Peruvian Bark and Wild Cherry Bitters," porcelain on metal, blue w/white letters reading "No More Malaria - Coles Peruvian Bark and Wild Cherry Bitters Will Cure You - The Best Nerver and Blood Tonic" & in upper left corner "Cure Debility " & lower right corner "Cure Dyspepsia," framed, ca. 1880, 7 1/2 x 17 1/2" (ILLUS.) **700-900**

Nuts, "Tom's Nuts/Snacks," embossed & self-framed, dated 9/58, 19 1/2 x 28" **355**

Outboard motors, "Evinrude and Elto," embossed, rectangular reading "Evinrude and Elto Outboard Motors - Hooded Power - Floated in Rubber - Bruce L. Pierce, Lake Tippecanoe, Leesburg, Ind.," orange, black & white, 11 3/4 x 23 3/4"... **479**

Lee Union Overalls Sign

Overalls, "Lee," embossed scene of workman in overalls in lower left corner, logo at right & "Lee - Union-Alls -Overalls - Whizits - Union Made," ca. 1930s-40s, minor bends, edge wear, chips & nicks & light scratches, 13 x 27" (ILLUS.) **413**

Overalls, "Smith's Overalls," narrow rectangular form, yellow ground w/dark blue & white wording "Smith's Overalls - Trademark," 1930s, 2 1/2 x 7" **248**

John Deere Medallion Dealer Sign

Plows, "John Deere," dealer sign composed of two copper-color large medallions, one w/a bust of John Deere marked "He Gave to the World the Steel Plow - John Deere," other reading "John Deere Centennial - 1837-1937" around plow (ILLUS.)... **825**

Raytheon Radio Tubes Sign

Radio tubes, "Ratheon Radio Tubes," flange-type, rectangular, red, white & blue lettering reading "Radio Service - We use and recommend Raytheon Radio Tubes - For Better Reception," tube & box pictured on left, 1934 date on tube box, background yellow/tan from paper staining, some paper marks visible, nicks & scratches, paint loss at flange edge area, 14 x 18" (ILLUS.) 270

Shoes, "Hurd Shoes," tin over cardboard, string-hung, rectangular, a dark wood-grained background design w/red, white & tan wording reading "Hurd Shoes - Are Good Shoes," 6 x 13 1/2" (minor to moderate surface wear & scratches) 33

Shotgun shells, "Remington/UMC," embossed rectangle featuring "Nitro Club Shotshell" box & reads "Arms & Ammunition - Complete Stocks - High Quality - Low Prices - Soo Hdw. Co. 300-302 Ashmun St. - Sault Sainte Marie, Mich.," lithograph by American Art Works, Coshocton, Ohio, 9 5/8 x 27 1/2" 380

Soap, "White King Washing Soap," lithographed scene depicting the product box on a red ground w/"Granulated" in white letters in upper corner, "White King Washing Machine Soap" on box w/logo & "It Takes So Little And It Goes So Far," 10 x 14" (few minor dings in outside border) 259

Soft drink, "Barq's," embossed bottle & "It's Good" & "Barq's," by Donaldson Art Sign Co., 11 3/4 x 29 3/4"....................................... 220

Soft drink, "Drink Bubble Up - 5¢," long narrow embossed rectangular form, a red ground centered by a cluster of large white bubbles, yellow lettering over red & red letters outlined in yellow over the bubbles, dated 1939, 3 x 12 1/2" (fine surface scratches) 138

Soft drink, "Canada Dry," embossed lithographed palm press-type, 3 x 9" 110

Fine Captain Kidd Beverages Sign

Soft drink, "Captain Kidd Beverages," rectangular w/black border & narrow orange border around center lithographed scene of pirate on shore & galleon offshore printed in black, orange & white, banner across top w/brand & further wording below (ILLUS.)... 1,650

Cherry Blush Sign

Soft drink, "Cherry Blush," rectangular, metal w/cardboard back, black w/bunch of cherries & leaves & "Cherry Blush" in white outlined in red in center, red lettering above w/"Drink" & green lettering at bottom reading "Cherries Only Rival," ca. 1900, 6 1/4 x 9" (ILLUS.) 650-800

Cleo Cola Sign

Soft drink, "Cleo Cola," embossed rectangular, green & black w/tiled effect border, image of Cleopatra on right & reading "Genuine Cleo Cola - 12 ounces for 5 cents," soiling, nicks & scratches, 12 1/2 x 27 3/8" (ILLUS.)............................... 358

Soft drink, "Clicquot Club Beverages," embossed self-framed style, long rectangular form, dark red ground w/embossed white wording above & below a round logo of the Eskimo child w/a bottle, 17 3/4 x 47 3/4" (moderate to minor edge wear, minor scattered scratches).................. 231

Coca-Cola Die-cut Tin Sign

Soft drink, "Coca-Cola," die-cut depicting 12-pack of bottles, 1955, 13 x 20" (ILLUS.) **3,150**

Soft drink, "Coca-Cola," flange-type, rectangular, reading "Drink Coca-Cola," picture of bottle of Coke w/yellow background underneath rectangle, 1940s, 24" w., 20 1/2" h. (scratches, touch-up under "C" in "Coca" on one side) **605**

Soft drink, "Coca-Cola," one-sided, self-framed, painted yellow, depicting Sprite boy pointing to a bottle of Coke resting on a small red Coca-Cola sign, made in USA & used for exporting, 1947, 13" d. **1,430**

Very Rare Hilda Clark Sign

Soft drink, "Coca-Cola," oval, self-framed, featuring picture of Hilda Clark, popular Victorian beauty, surrounded w/floral border & "Coca-Cola" written on bottom of border, very rare, 1903 (ILLUS.) **83,375**

Soft drink, "Coca-Cola," painted white w/green border, top half w/red logo reading "Drink Coca-Cola - Sign of Good Taste," bottom half showing a bottle of Coke, 1963, 17 1/2" w., 53 1/2" h. (scratches to edges) **300**

Soft drink, "Coca-Cola," rectangular, white w/logo at top & six-pack of bottles pictured, red & gold highlights, marked "Take home a carton - Big King Size," 1961, 20 x 28" (light wear, few very shallow dents, few light scratches) **1,210**

Soft drink, "Crescent Cola," embossed lithographed w/image of a woman **230**

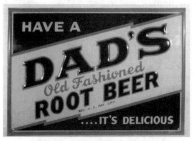

Dad's Root Beer Sign

Soft drink, "Dad's Root Beer," rectangular, black & yellow wembossed lettering in black outlined in red, "Have A Dad's Old Fashioned   Root   Beer   ....It's Delicious," ca. 1950s, 19 x 27" (ILLUS.) **225-300**

Soft drink, "Dad's - The Old Fashioned Root Beer," embossed die-cut colorful design w/a large round image of the bottle cap in blue, yellow & red above a yellow rectangular panel w/dark blue & red wording, 20 x 28" (very minor nicks, scratches & wear) **303**

Gold-en Girl Cola Sign

Soft drink, "Gold-en Girl Cola," flange-type, showing cup & saucer marked "Gold-en Girl Cola - Sun-drop - Refreshing as a Cup of Coffee," ca. 1940s-50s, 15 x 21" (ILLUS.) **358**

Soft drink, "Grapette Soda," oval, embossed, 28 x 47 1/2" **210**

Soft drink, "Hire's Ginger Ale," embossed tacker-type w/"None   So   Good," 9 3/4 x 13 3/4" (some minor damage) **135**

Hires Root Beer Sign

Soft drink, "Hires Root Beer," rectangular, flange-type, green w/yellow & black lettering reading "Hires - Made with Roots - Barks - Herbs - So Refreshing," ca. 1940s, 12 x 14" (ILLUS.) **225-300**

Howel's Root Beer Figural Sign

Soft drink, "Howel's Root Beer," embossed die-cut bottle shape, minor soiling & wear, 8 3/8 x 29 1/2" (ILLUS.) **413**
Soft drink, "Mit-Che Cola," embossed, 15 1/2 x 23 1/2" (some wear & rust) **85**
Soft drink, "Orange Crush," embossed & self-framed baseball scoreboard, dated 10/39, by Scioto Signs, 18 x 54" (some nicks & creases **600**

Early Bottle-shaped Pepsi-Cola Sign

Soft drink, "Pepsi-Cola," die-cut bottle-shaped sign in realistic colors w/the red, white & blue labels featuring the early logo, minor to moderate edge wear, rust bubble under paint, minor rubs, scratches & dings, 12 x 44 1/2" (ILLUS.)................. **990**

R-Pep Soda Tin Sign

Soft drink, "Drink R-Pep 5¢," long embossed rectangular form, dark red ground w/large white wording & smaller yellow & white words, a yellow rising sun at the center bottom, a colored bottle of the soda at the right side, very minor nicks & wear, 17 5/8 x 35 3/4" (ILLUS.) **495**
Soft drink, "Rock Creek Ginger Ale," lithographed convex form, 12" h. **160**
Soft drink, "7Up," embossed long rectangular vertical form, a large green pop bottle against a white ground w/"Fresh up' with" at the top in red & black, 1962, 18 x 48" (light edge wear & scratches, small chip upper right) **418**

Pepsi-Cola Sign

Soft drink, "Pepsi-Cola," die-cut bottle cap-shaped sign w/red, white & blue double dot logo, minor surface scratches, 13 1/4 x 13 7/8" (ILLUS.) **385**

7Up Bottle Sign

Soft drink, "7Up," embossed tin bottle-form, dated 7-62 at bottom, minor edge wear, 13 x 44 1/2" (ILLUS.)......................... **413**

Early 7Up Flange Sign

Soft drink, "7Up," flange-type, a stylized arm & hand holding a round tray w/a bottle of 7Up & a red & white logo box reading "We Proudly Serve 7Up," early 20th c. (ILLUS.)... **2,300**

Smile Orange Beverage Sign

Soft drink, "Drink Smile," die-cut, double-sided flange-type, round, black & orange w/logo at bottom, both sides w/same display, minor scratches, 10 x 12 3/8" (ILLUS.)... **385**

Color "Squeeze" Tin Sign

Soft drink, "Drink Squeeze," long narrow rectangular form printed in bright yellow & red w/black & white, cartoon of two children hugging under a full moon on the left, reads "Drink Squeeze - 'That Distinctive' - Carbonated Beverage," few minor wrinkles at edges, 10 x 28" (ILLUS.)............ **259**

Soft drink, "Squirt," embossed, dated 1958, 9 1/2 x 27 1/2"... **135**

Squirt Sign

Soft drink, "Squirt," rectangular, flange-type, double-sided, both sides yellow & display waving blue flag reading "Drink Squirt - It's Tart-Sweet," dated 1941 at bottom, minor wear & scratches (ILLUS.)..... **385**

Soft drink, "Vernor's Ginger Ale," lithographed convex form, 29 1/2" l. **200**

Soft drink, "Ward's Orange Crush," embossed   tacker-type,   rare, 14 1/2 x 27 1/2"... **425**

Whistle Arrow-shaped Tin Sign

Soft drink, "Whistle," die-cut arrow-shape, black ground w/orange border band, long orange rectangle w/the brand in large black letters, left-facing, very minor soiling & wear, ca. 1920s, 6 7/8 x 26 1/2" (ILLUS.)... **440**

Soft drink, "Whistle," embossed, rectangular, narrow yellow border around a dark blue ground w/a large angled orange bottle of pop w/white wording "thisty? - just - (Whistle) - Demand the Genuine," orange & blue Whistle logo in lower right, 1930s, 6 1/2 x 9 1/2" (very light edge wear, minor paint chipping)............................ **660**

Soft drink, "Whistle," embossed tacker-type w/"Thirsty - 5 cents," dated 1939, 3 x 12 3/8".. **150**

Soup, "Campbell's Soups," lithographed & stamped, long rectangular form designed w/a large American flag composed of red white & blue soup cans below a red banner reading "Campbell's Soups - 21 Kinds - 10¢," in white across the bottom "Just Add a Can of Hot Water and Serve," 27 1/2 x 39 1/2" (ILLUS.) **28,750**

Campbell's Soups Sign

Soup, "Campbell's Soups," rectangular, red top w/white & yellow letters reading "Campbell's Soups - M'm! M'm! Good!," white center w/various soups listed & image of Campbell Kid on left, yellow band at bottom w/red letters reading "Ready in a Jiffy," light wear, scratches & rubs, 11 1/2 x 17 1/2" (ILLUS.) **165**

A.C. Spark Plugs Sign

Spark plugs, "A.C. Spark Plugs," embossed, self-framed rectangular, blue & yellow w/large red circle in center w/spark plug flanked by the letters "A - C," tan band at bottom w/black letters reading "Spark Plugs" & dated 11-41 at bottom left, nicks & scratches, factory flaw at right side top to bottom in blue to tan, 9 x 18" (ILLUS.).................................... **275**

Spark plugs, "Champion Spark Plugs," rectangular embossed tin, a bright yellow ground w/the Champion logo centered by a large spark plug on blue band across the center, small black type at top reads "Double Ribbed," black wording below logo reads "Spark Plugs," 13 3/4 x 29 5/8".................................... **300-400**

Spark plugs, "Champion Spark Plugs," rectangular, flange-type, black, red & white, white & black letters reading "Dependable - Champion - Spark Plug Service," ca. 1950-60s, 23 3/4 x 35 1/2" (light nicks & scratches)................................ **149**

Small Lithographed Rev-O-Noc Sign

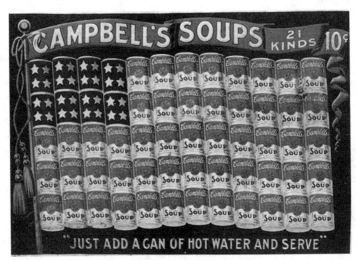

Very Rare Campbell's Soups Sign

Sporting goods, "Rev-O-Noc Sporting Goods," rectangular, lithographed over cardboard w/scenes of baseball, golf, fishing & hunting, marked in upper left corner "H.S.B. & Co. Rev-O-Noc" & upper right corner "Fire Arms - Sporting Goods - Fishing Tackle" (ILLUS.) **2,970**

Store sign, "Red Owl," porcelain, double-sided, shows large red owl, 56" h. **1,700**

Stove, "Enterprise Stove," flange-type, double-sided, flat surface, 18" l. (minor flaking) **350**

Garland Stoves Sign

Stove, "Garland Stoves," square, curved corner-type, porcelain on tin, white w/black logo printed "Garland Stoves and Ranges" w/banner at bottom marked "'The World's Best'," B. S. Co., State St., Chicago, Illinois, 24 x 24" (ILLUS.) **1,300-1,750**

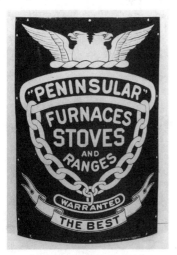

Peninsular Stoves Sign

Stove, "Peninsular," rectangular, curved corner-type, porcelain on tin, black w/white image of double eagle heads & wings over shield-shape formed w/bars & chain links reading "'Peninsular' - Furnaces - Stoves and Ranges" w/'Warranted - The Best' on banner at the bottom, made by B.S. Co., State St., Chicago, Illinois, ca. 1890, 18 x 24" (ILLUS.) **1,300-1,750**

Peninsular Stoves Flange-type Sign

Stove, "'Peninsular Stoves'," rectangular, flange-type, porcelain on tin, black, white & red, marked on ribbon at top "A Guarantee Bond - With Every Stove" & "'Peninsular' - Furnaces - Stoves and Ranges" w/"Warranted - The Best," ca. 1890, 15 1/2 x 23 1/2" (ILLUS.) **1,800-2,500**

Tea company, "McCormick's Tea," orange, black & yellow, dated "1936" w/lithograph scene of a house on one side, front w/teapot & marked "Banquet - McCormick's Orange Pekoe Tea," 1 lb., 3 3/4 x 6" **44**

Tires, "Corduroy Tires," rectangular, embossed self-framed tin, red & black w/white letters reading "Replace With Corduroy - Factory Fresh Tires - Extra Quality Since 1919," 15 1/4 x 60" (soiling, scratches & wear, minor denting at edges).. **413**

Tires, "Goodyear," die-cut molded flange-type, a large narrow white & blue tire w/name imprinted under a dark blue bar w/"Goodyear" in gold over the red winged sandal logo, made in Germany, ca. 1930s, 22 x 34" (some light stains & edge chipping w/light wear & surface marks, small tip bend)................................. **1,485**

Tobacco, "Edgeworth Smoking Tobacco," rectangular tin over cardboard, color image of large open tin of tobacco beside a pocket tin of tobacco behind a pipe in an ashtray, red rectangular bar at top w/white wording reads "Edgeworth Smoking Tobacco - Extra High Grade," ca. 1930-50, 9 x 11" (dent in upper left, few minor crimps, light overall wear, small paint chips & nicks).................... **248**

Edgeworth Smoking Tobacco Sign

Tobacco, "Edgeworth Smoking Tobacco," rectangular, yellow w/red & black letters reading "Edgeworth - Extra High grade - Smoking tobacco - Ready-Rubbed or Plug Slice," the lower corners depicting a laughing balding man, overall light wear, scratches, rust pitting & flecks, two nail holes added at top, 11 1/4 x 27 1/4" (ILLUS.) **369**

Five Brothers Plug Tobacco Sign

Tobacco, "Five Brothers Plug - Toothsome as Honey," lithographed tin over cardboard, featuring adorable black bear cubs on red background w/yellow lettering (ILLUS.) **6,050**

Tobacco, "Hi-Plane Tobacco," embossed rectangular, green w/red & white vest pocket tin w/airplane on left & reading "Hi-Plane Tobacco - for Pipe and Cigarettes - 10¢" in black & white letters, 11 3/4 x 35 1/4" (minor high point wear & scratches) **215**

Underwear, "Wright's Union Suits," color lithographed, two pieces attach at center, depicts man standing in union suit, wood frame, 72" h. (some flaking & stains) **1,050**

Veterinary Medicines Sign

Veterinary medicine, "Dr. A.C. Daniels' Horse Cat Dog Medicines," rectangular embossed design, black ground w/bold white wording "Use Dr. A.C. Daniels' Horse Cat Dog - Medicines - For Home Treatment," unused, early 20th c., 17 1/2 x 28" (ILLUS.) **231**

Veterinary medicine, "Kow-Kare," two-sided flange depicting packages of Kow-Kare, Bag Balm Dilators & Bag Balm, cow logo, 12 1/2" w., 9 1/2" h. **288**

Hickman-Ebbert Company Sign

Wagon, "Hickman-Ebbert Co.," rectangular, self-framed colorful lithographed scene depicting girl picking apples & a boy loading them onto a horse-drawn green wagon w/red wheels, titled "In The Shade Of The Old Apple Tree," upper left corner reads "Best at the Price - The Ebbert - Owensboro, KY - Always the Same," litho by Charles W. Shonk, frame marked "The Hickman-Ebbert Co. - Owensboro, Kentucky," ca. 1906, 25 1/2 x 37 1/2" (ILLUS.) **1,200-1,800**

Watch, "Hamilton Watch," lithographed over cardboard, raised center image, 19" h. **1,200**

Whiskey, "Buffalo Club Rye Whiskey," lithographed w/buffalo, in oak frame, by Chas. W. Shonk Co. Litho, Chicago, Illinois, 29 x 38" **900**

Rare "Fern Glen Rye" Tin Sign

Whiskey, "Fern Glen Rye," self-framed, a landscape scene of a standing elderly African-American man in a roadway, a chicken under one arm, a watermelon under the other & looking down at a bottle of the product which has fallen from a wagon onto the road, caption reads "I'se in a perdickermunt," large sign in back reads "Fern Glen Rye," further advertising on lower frame plaque, small scratch, minor paint loss, 23 x 33" (ILLUS.) **5,175**

Whiskey, "Paul Jones Rye," self-framed color lithograph, shows old man pouring a drink, 28 1/2" h. **1,400**

Whiskey, "Westminister Rye," self-framed, color lithograph of early motoring scene, 25 x 38" **2,300**

Oshkosh Work Clothes Sign

Work clothing, "OshKosh Work Clothes," red & yellow w/embossed white & yellow letters reading "OshKosh B'gosh - Union Made - Work Clothes," ca. 1930s, 9 1/4 x 13 1/2" (ILLUS.) **100-150**

Trade

Bootmaker, carved & painted model of a high-top boot, white repaint w/black detail of straps & lacing over earlier gilding, on a modern steel stand, late 19th c., 25 1/2" h. (age cracks) **385**

Bootmaker, carved wood large model of a high-top boot, tin weather cap, old gold repaint w/red & blue, from Ohio shoe store, 27 3/4" h. (age cracks, weathering, glued repair) **2,200**

Cast Zinc Bootmaker Trade Sign

Bootmaker, cast zinc model of a large man's boot, suspended from a wrought-iron angled bracket, boot painted golden brown, impressed "570," paint loss, 19th c., 22 1/2" h. (ILLUS.) **1,380**

Chiseled Brass Butcher's Sign

Butcher, "J.W. Goatcher - Butcher," chiseled black wording on a rectangular brass ground, ca. 1900, 4 1/2 x 16" (ILLUS.) **77**

Butcher, painted cast iron, full-bodied model of a standing bull, overall worn gold paint, late 19th - early 20th c., 11 1/2" h. **4,830**

Figural Pacific Butcher's Supply Co. Sign

Butcher's supply company, "Pacific Butcher's Supply Co., San Francisco, CAL," cast-iron dimensional sign w/figural saw, cleaver & knife supporting a figural steer, front plate marked "Gloekler's Patent June 25, 1889," original old paint, 12 lbs., 20 x 24 1/2" (ILLUS.) **1,210**

Early Iron Hatter's Sign

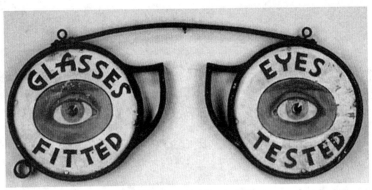

Early Optometrist Trade Sign

Hatter's, painted iron, full-figure model of a tall top hat w/a cockcade at the upper rim, 19th c., paint wear, corrosion, 12" h. (ILLUS.) **1,150**

Locks, "Independent Lock Co., Fitchburg, Mass.," cast metal, large hanging figural key, 20 lbs., 1 x 1 1/2 x 28" **371**

Optometrist, painted cast iron & zinc, double-sided large molded spectacles w/colored eyes in center, black wording on white "Glasses Fitted - Eyes Tested," late 19th c., wear, old paint retouches, 26 1/4" l., 11 1/2" h. (ILLUS.) **4,313**

Optometrist, polychrome & gilt-decorated zinc, double-sided model of large spectacles w/an arched banner below w/worn lettering reading "C.F. Hussey Optometrist," late 19th c., 41" l., 12 1/2" h. (imperfections) **2,645**

Shoe shop, large wooden model of a lady's high-heeled slipper, laminated construction w/worn & weathered yellow, blue & salmon paint, early 20th c., 25" l. **2,365**

winged eagle & stars w/the word "Independence" in red, New England, ca. 1800, 31 x 41 1/2" (ILLUS.) **17,250**

Tavern, painted pine, plank construction w/border molding & an inner rectangular panel w/molded frame, the back painted "Royalton House - 1845," the front w/a spread-winged American eagle w/banner in its beak in the central panel w/"1845" above & "J.M. Currier" below, signed "S. Dodge, painter, Enfield, NH," black ground w/white lettering & dark red & white eagle, suspended on wrought-iron hinges, 34 1/4 x 42 1/2" **9,755**

Pocket Watch Trade Sign

Early New England Tavern Sign

Tavern, "Independence," painted & gilt wood, a black-painted frame of turned posts enclosing molded panels, both sides painted dark green w/a gilt spread-

Watchmaker, carved & painted wood & metal, flattened silhouetted pocket watch form painted on both sides w/white face & black Roman numerals, gold rim, suspended between two brackets, late 19th c., 27" h., 18" w. (ILLUS.) **3,450**

Watchmaker, painted wood, model of a large pocket watch w/top stem & loop, dial w/Arabic numerals marked "J. Fiske Boston," painted in gold, white & black, 19th c., 24" h. **440**

Other

Ale, "Drewrys Old Stock Ale," color-printed composition, rectangular w/rounded corners, brown wood-grained ground printed in pale yellow & red, white oval surrounding a color image of a bottle in the center, printed across the bottom "For those who appreciate The Finest Ale," 1940s, 10 1/2 x 16 1/2" (minor edge dings & soiling, small chips at top of bottle) **95**

Electric Chevrolet Sign

Automobile, "Chevrolet," metal & fiberboard, electric, figure of shaded tan owl sitting on blue & gold Chevrolet logo w/"for Economical Transportation" below, eyes blink & center lights up w/"Wise To Choose A Six," ca. 1920, 22 x 34" (ILLUS.).. **1,700-2,500**

Automobile, "New 1956 Chevrolet Task Force Trucks On Display!," cloth banner, red & black lettering on yellow background, right side depicts black truck on white background, 91" w., 33 1/4" h. (soiling & white paint spots) **77**

Beer, "Betz Beer - Ale - Porter," round, electric light-up type, metal & reverse painted glass, 17" d. (soiling, flaking paint, metal back pitted & rust).................................... **165**

Beer, "Budweiser Beer," electric, model of a large man's pocket watch, gold-colored watch frame w/white dial w/Arabic numerals, printed in red in the center "Budweiser" over small yellow wording "King of Beers," 1950s, 19" d. (some wear & scuffs on gold).. **82**

Beer, "Champagne Velvet Beer," rectangular plastic in color, shows hands forming letters "C-V" above "Signal For CV - Champagne Velvet...," embossed amber bottle on the right edge, 1950s, 9 3/4 x 12 1/4" (some soiling, a few scuffs) **105**

Beer, "Falls City Beer," plastic, rectangular, assorted blocks around the border showing various sporting scenes printed in white on a yellow, green on blue ground, red, white & black central oval w/"Falls City Beer" w/a yellow block at the bottom center printed in black "Year 'Round Favorite!," 1960s, unused, 15 x 21"................... **50**

Beer, "Happy-Peppy Beer," rounded starburst wood sign composed of wedges of wood glued together & printed in red, white & black w/advertising & cartoon figure of walking 1930s man in tuxedo (some wood splits, some discolored spots).. **225**

Beer, "Redtop Beer," vacuum-formed plastic printed in color, rectangular, name in top reserve above lower reverse w/"Bright - Refreshing - Flavor - bottles....cans," 1950s **50**

Kynoch's Cartridges Board Sign

Cartridges, "Kynoch's Sporting & Military Cartridges," color lithographed on board, printed in red, white & black in a diamond shape & mounted w/real cartridges arranged in the central circle, 1897, framed, 18 1/2 x 27" (ILLUS.)....................... **963**

Large Winchester Cartridge Sign

Cartridges, "Winchester Repeating Arms Co.," lithographed on board, a color "Double W" design w/printed arrangements of various cartridges, in a flat oak frame, 1902, 40 x 58" (ILLUS.).................. **4,600**

Yellow Kid Sign

Chewing gum, "Yellow Kid Bubble Chewing Gum," celluloid, yellow, blue & red, center depicts figure marked "YK" bordered by "There is only one - Yellow Kid - Big Bubble Chewing Gum," promoting popular early comic character, Bastian Bros., slight scratch, 8" d. (ILLUS.)................. **43**

Cigars, "Admiration Cigars," embossed & colored chalkware, rectangular, a large boldly embossed man in the moon w/a cigar in his mouth at the center flanked by brown cigars & tobacco leaf, black ground w/white wording at top & bottom "Admiration Cigars - Mild and Mellow to the Last Inch," ca. 1930s, 11 x 15" (light soiling, very few nicks & wear) **633**

Woolrich Outdoorwear Sign

Clothing, "Woolrich Rugged Outdoorwear," genuine birchbark canoe w/hanger, 2 1/2 x 4 1/2 x 18" (ILLUS.)........................... **605**

Foster Hose Supporters Sign

Clothing & accessories, "The Foster Hose Supporters," celluloid w/string hanger, litho by E.F. Pulver Co., Rochester, New York, depicts a corset w/hose supporters w/figure of a woman superimposed, black background (ILLUS.) **550**

Owl Drug Wall Advertisment

Drugstore, "Owl Drug Co.," round, wall-type, plaster, painted orange w/high-relief decoration of flowers around owl & "The Owl Drug Co." at bottom, 12 3/4" d. (ILLUS.)... **358**

Firearms, "Remington," cloth banner, depicts vintage flintlock w/powder horn hanging from firearm, "Remington Since 1816 America's Oldest Gunmakers Sporting Firearms Ammunition," fringed bottom, 29" L., 20" h. **29**

Flour, "Gold Medal Flour," painted wood in wooden frame, 66" l. (stains & scratches)..... **450**

Flour, "Pillsbury's," copper self-framed lithographed metal, leafy-scroll embossed flanged self-frame around a rectangular color sign w/a large spread-winged eagle w/banner in its beak atop a large flour barrel w/a busy port in the background & above a vignette factory scene, reads "Chas. A. Pillsbury & Co. - Merchant Millers - America's Finest - Pillsbury's Best, Minneapolis, Minn. (on barrel) - For Sale Here," minor water spotting in corner, 24 x 30" **4,675**

Arden Ice Cream Sign

Ice cream, "Arden Ice Cream," bevel-edged masonite w/original yellowed surface varnish, center oval w/milkman logo at top w/banner reading "We Serve Delicious," red oval center w/"Arden - Fine - Ice Cream - for Vital Energy" & banner at bottom marked "A Nutritional Vital Energy Food," minor edge & surface wear, 7 1/4 x 12" (ILLUS.)................................. **176**

Cetacolor Sign

Laundry product, "Cetacolor," rectangular, lithographed fabric in wood frame, oval on left side depicts a woman wearing a red & white striped blouse, one side faded flanked by black letters reading "Result Without Using Cetacolor," the other side bright w/"Result With Using Cetacolor," white & green lettering on right side reading "Not a Soap - Cetacolor - Prevents Wash Goods from Fading. - 10¢ Package.," by Acme Sign Printing Co., Dayton, Ohio, ca. 1890, 25 x 37" (ILLUS.) **375-450**

Atlantic Motor Oil Banner

Motor oil, "Atlantic (motif of plane) Motor Oil (motif of car) Aviation Tested," cloth banner, red, navy blue, gold & white, marked "Sweeny Litho Co. Inc. Belleville, N.J. Litho in U.S.A.," some minor fading, 53 1/2" w., 28 5/8" h (ILLUS.) **550**

Motor supplies, "Bure Power Carburetor Center," plastic & metal, electric, rectangular w/yellow, red & black on white background, 2 1/2 x 24 1/4", 11 3/4" h. **242**

OshKosh Overalls Sign

Overalls, "OshKosh Overalls," die-cut composition, stand-up type, figure of small boy wearing overalls standing next to figure of Uncle Sam w/red & white striped shirt & hat & overalls holding a yellow sign reading "OshKosh B'gosh," red band at bottom w/white letters reading "Work Clothes - Union Made," ca. 1920, 6 1/2 x 13 1/2" (ILLUS.) **550-650**

Peanuts, "Planters Peanuts," 3-D hand carved wood Mr. Peanut, green & yellow, approximately 24 x 33" **500-525**

Brass Sign for a Private Club

Private club, "Victoria Legal Friendly Society," heavy brass w/chiseled wording, rectangular, reads "Liverpool - Victoria - Legal - Friendly Society - Established 1848 - Branch Office," 19th c., 8 x 13" (ILLUS.) **66**

Railroad, "Chicago & Alton Railroad," rectangular, paper & cardboard w/hand-colored photographs, the center shows an engine & freight car w/"Chicago & Alton R.R. - 'The Only Way'," in white letters below & w/a photograph on the left of a passenger car interior & on the right an interior photograph of the dining car, wood frame, ca. 1910, 15 x 39" (ILLUS., bottom of page) **635-775**

Grand Trunk Pacific Railway Photograph

Railroad, "Grand Trunk Pacific Railway," duo-tone photograph titled "Moose Lake British Columbia," signed mat & frame, ca. 1900, 28 1/2 x 35" (ILLUS.).. **650-750**

Shaving cream, "Burma-Shave," rectangular painted wood roadside sign, bright red ground w/brand in bold white letters,

18 x 40" (soiling, overall wear, top corners damaged) **275**

Buster Brown Shoes Sign

Shoes, "Buster Brown Shoes," silkscreened cloth, cushioned & mounted on die-cut wood, "Buster Brown" & "Tige" the dog, two separate pieces added together for 3D effect, green, red & brown, edge wear, tips have fabric wear, 24" w., 20" h. (ILLUS.) **385**

Shoes, "Peters Weatherbird Shoes," double-sided, painted wood sidewalk sign, 43 1/2" h. **1,500**

Red Goose Embossed Celluloid Sign

Shoes, "Red Goose Shoes," embossed die-cut w/molded celluloid goose body, easel-back, marked "Red Goose Shoes," flanked by running schoolgirl & schoolboy w/books, marked at the bottom "They're Half the Fun of Having Feet," ca. 1910, Friedman-Shelby Shoes, 11 x 13 1/2" (ILLUS.) **900-1,300**

Chicago & Alton Railroad Sign

World's largest seller

A & W Root Beer Banner

Soft drink, "A & W Root Beer," long rectangular canvas banner, a yellow background w/the round black, orange & white logo at the top above a white quote panel reading "My Root Beer's Here!" above a color cartoon picture of Dennis the Menace holding a mug of the root beer, black wording at the bottom reads "World's largest seller," top & bottom edges cut off & a little rough, was rolled up, 36 1/2 x 91 1/2" (ILLUS.) **220**

Soft drink, "Coca-Cola," plastic & tin, light-up type, lantern shape w/"Better with Coke" on one side & "Have Coke Here" on the reverse, 1960s **135**

Soft drink, "Coca-Cola," rectangular light-up type w/clock, "Drink Coca-Cola - Please Pay When Served," 20" l. **650**

Hires Sign

Soft drink, "Hires," celluloid, bust portrait of young woman w/short brown curly hair, green dress, marked "Drink Hires" (ILLUS.) **770**

Lime Cola Sign

Soft drink, "Lime Cola," round, celluloid over cardboard, string-hung, tan w/bottle in center & reading "Drink - Lime Cola - Trade-Mark Registered," 9" d. (ILLUS.) **413**

Soft drink, "Pennsylvania Dutch 'Birch Beer,'" string-hung celluloid, shows Amish man drinking, "Ju-C Orange of America" at bottom left, copyright 1955, 9 1/4 x 14 3/4" **30**

Soft drink, "Pepsi-Cola," oval celluloid over tin w/cardboard backing, a black & cream-colored photo of an attractive young African-American woman standing talking on the phone & holding a bottle of Pepsi, the Pepsi-Cola bottle cap logo in the lower right, circa 1950s, 8 x 12" (faded, overall scratches & wear, easel-back missing) **220**

Soft drink, "Squirt," double-sided masonite w/"Open" & "Closed" 1955, 12 x 16" **170**

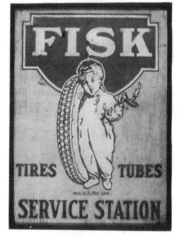

Fisk Tires Sign

Tires, "Fisk Tires," two-sided wood sign & frame, logo of small child w/tire & candle in center & "Tires - Tubes - Service Station" at bottom, image sanded, cracking of wood, soiling & fading of graphic on both sides, 30 1/2" w., 41 1/2" h. (ILLUS.) **825**

OK Tires Die-Cut Sign

Tires, "O K Tires," die-cut masonite, figural logo of boy saluting, chest marked "O K," red, white & black, minor wear, thin paint & soiling, 16 x 25 1/4" (ILLUS.) **121**

Bagley's Smoking Tobacco Sign

Tobacco, "Bagley's Smoking Tobacco," figural wood covered w/paper, window motion display-type w/arms that move, figure of a man wearing long red trousers, long-tailed grey jacket, yellow vest & red

bow tie, the black top hat marked "Bagley's Long Tom Smokin Tobacco," ca. 1890, 36" h. (ILLUS.) **1,100-1,500**

Mayo's Tobacco Large Canvas Sign

Tobacco, "Mayo's Plug Smoking Tobacco," colorfully printed on large canvas, gold ground w/dark blue wording & a crowing black & red rooster at the right, minor soiling at bottom, 24 x 60" (ILLUS.) **171**

Mohawk Tool Works Sign

Tool works, "Mohawk Tool Works," cast brass w/raised detailed logo in center w/"Arrowsharp Axes & Knives - Est. 1893 - Troy, N.Y.," leather-look background, 10 x 16" (ILLUS.) **853**

Whiskey, "Claymore Scotch Whiskey," copper spittoon, marked "J.R. Grant & Son Ltd, London," nice patina, 3 x 4" **77**

Wiper blades, "Trico Wiper Blades," circular, aluminum, flange-type, black & yellow w/white, black & yellow letters reading "Replace Your - Trico Wiper Blades - Once A Year," 18 x 19 3/4" (fading & wear)... **165**

Chapter 15
Soda Fountain Collectibles

Bottle carrier, "Pepsi-Cola," wood, six-pack size, original finish **$140**

Bottle carrier, "7Up," aluminum, marked "Fresh Up," six-pack size.................................. **50**

Bottle topper, "Fowler's Cherry Smash," die-cut cardboard, shows boy in Colonial outfit & tricorn hat, 7 1/4 x 11 1/2"................. **$30**

Chalkboard, "Bubble-Up," self-framed tin, 19 5/8 x 30".. **100**

Chalkboard sign, "Whistle," one-sided embossed tin, reads "Thirsty? Just Whistle," decorated w/an elf at each corner of chalkboard, 20" w., 17" h., ca. 1948, U.S.A., minor scratches (ILLUS.).................. **825**

Cone dispenser, glass & metal w/cone holder, 14" h. **525**

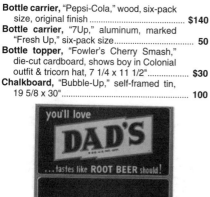

Dad's Root Beer Chalkboard

Chalkboard sign, "Dad's Root Beer," one-sided embossed tin, reads "You'll love Dad's...tastes like Root Beer should!," dents to edge, 19 1/2 w., 27 1/2" h. (ILLUS.).. **220**

Duffy's Pure Malted Milk Container

Counter container, "Duffy's Pure Malted Milk," enameled tin, cylindrical w/a tall tapering domed cover, creamy white ground w/blue wording on the front, some chips on cover, base & edges, some cracking of enameling, a few scuffs & soiling, 6" d., 10" h. (ILLUS.)...................... **138**

Whistle Chalkboard Sign

Pepsi-Cola Mechanical Display Unit

Counter display figure, "Pepsi-Cola," electric mechanical group in plastic & metal, a model of a monkey & a large Pepsi can spin in a circle when plugged in, on a cluster of purple & white flowers on the round platform base w/an oval Pepsi-Cola logo, some scratches, soiling, wear, 26" d., 37" h. (ILLUS.) **1,210**

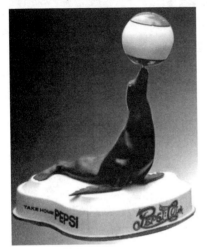

Pepsi Mechanical Display with a Seal

Counter display figure, "Pepsi-Cola," plastic & rubber composite, a white shaped plastic oblong platform base trimmed w/Pepsi-Cola logos supports a heavy rubber composite model of a black seal balancing a red, white & blue ball on its nose, seal moves back & forth when activated, two stress cracks in base, 37 x 40", 39" h. (ILLUS.) **1,843**

Early Moxie Horsemobile Model

Countertop display, "Drink Moxie," molded chalkware model of an early Moxie Horsemobile w/advertising panels at each side, tiny flecks on fender tips, scattered wear on base, early 20th c., 4 x 8", 9 3/4" h. (ILLUS.) **1,540**

Carnation Malted Milk Dispenser

Dispenser, "Carnation Malted Milk," cylindrical porcelain body w/a domed & peaked aluminum lid, red & white background w/white & green wording above & below a cluster of large red, white & green carnations, small chips on reverse bottom, very minor edge chips hidden by lid, 8 1/2" h. (ILLUS.) **413**

Dispenser, "Dixie-Flip," ceramic w/pump, painted on one side, 14" h. (pump not original, scratches & wear) **7,200**

Dispenser, "Thompson's Malted Milk," cylindrical body w/a white ground & red, blue & grey wording on one side, a coat-of-arms style logo on the other side, aluminum peaked lid, 5 5/8" d., 9 1/2" h. (minor surface wear, scattered rim chips, two small base chips) **231**

Borden's Malted Milk Dispensing Jar

Dispensing jar, "Borden's" malted milk powder, label under glass, embossed lid (ILLUS.) **450-600**

Pepsi-Cola Tin Door Handle

Door handle, "Pepsi-Cola," painted tin, squared tab ends w/mounting holes & arched handle, dark blue ground w/wavy white bands on each tab, top reads "Enjoy -Pepsi-Cola" & bottom reads "Bigger - Better" in red & white, very minor surface wear, yellowing to white, 2 3/4 x 12" (ILLUS.) 490

Door push, "Golden Bridge Root Beer," embossed tin, long rectangular form, dark gold ground w/a color image of a large bottle below the word "Remember" in red, 3 3/4 x 11 3/4" (minor scattered wear & scratches) 94

Door push, "Hires Root Beer," tin, long narrow rectangular, dark gold ground w/a large color bottle of the product, red & black wording at top & bottom reads "Finer Flavor because of Real Root Juices - Ice Cold," 3 1/2 x 11 1/2" (very minor bend at bottom, light scratches at bottom center) 187

Door push, "Pepsi-Cola," raised tin, long narrow rectangular form w/a dark blue ground & white wording centered by a wavy white center band w/the old fashioned red Pepsi-Cola logo & "5¢" in a red dot, wording reads "Come In For That Big, Big Bottle of.." & "Buy It By The Carton Too!," 2 3/4 x 10" (minor edge & surface wear, yellowing to the white) 550

Fan, "Dr. Pepper," two-sided cardboard w/wooden handle, pretty girl in yellow dress by Earl Moran, reverse w/bottle & "Drink a Bite to Eat - at 10 - 2 and 4 o'clock," ca. 1930s-40s (light wear on front, back w/soiling on left side & paper tears) 358

Early Pepsi-Cola Hand Fan

Fan, "Pepsi-Cola," die-cut cardboard hand-type, the wide arched blade printed in color on one side w/a wide wavy white center band flanked by dark blue bands, the old fashioned red Pepsi-Cola logo in the center, "Drink" in white at the top w/"12 ounce Bottle - 5¢" w/a small bottle of the soda in the lower band, the reverse w/blue, red & pink comic figures of Pepsi policemen, Pepsi & Peter, pouring a bottle of Pepsi & saying in red "Plenty! - Plenty! - Plenty!" & "Good! - Good! - Good!," white background, dated 1940, w/wooden flat handle, very minor soiling & wear, light creases, 7 3/4 x 12" (ILLUS.) 105

Fan pull, "Dr. Pepper," two-sided cardboard, features Patricia White & autumn leaves, marked "Drink Dr. Pepper - Good For Life!," 8 1/4" l. (ILLUS. left below) 2,640

Dr. Pepper Fan Pulls

Fan pull, "Dr. Pepper," two-sided cardboard, shows a young woman w/large hat & gloves, seated in director's chair & holding bottle, marked "Drink Dr. Pepper - Good For Life!," 8 1/4" l. (ILLUS. right) 1,870

Dr. Pepper Fan Pulls

Fan pull, "Dr. Pepper," two-sided, cardboard w/scene of bathing beauty holding ship's wheel w/clock hands at 10 - 2 - 4, marked "Drink Dr. Pepper - Good For Life - or When You're Hungry, Thirsty or Tired," 7-8" l. (ILLUS. right)......................... **2,200**

Fan pull, two-sided, cardboard figural scarecrow bust w/jack-o-lantern head, white shirt & blue jacket, straw hands, holding bottle, w/"Drink a Bite to Eat at 10 - 2 - 4" across shirt, 7-8" l. (ILLUS. left)...... **1,760**

Old Soda Fountain Stools

Fountain stools, black metal pedestal bases & silvered metal round seat frames w/upholstered seats, ca. 1930s, some overall wear, 12 1/2" d., 19" h., set of 3 (ILLUS.)...................... **66**

Fountain stools, porcelain counter stools w/revolving wooden seats & brass foot rests, 29" h., set of 4....................................... **550**

Soda Fountain Stool

Fountain stools, white wicker seat on porcelain base w/brass foot rest, 38" h., pr. (ILLUS. of one).. **173**

Glass, "Allen's Red Tame Cherry," tall waisted clear glass form w/white wording (ILLUS. second from left with Cascade tumbler).. **25**

Group of Early Soda Fountain Glasses

Glass, "Cascade Ginger Ale," clear cylindrical glass printed in white w/"Cascade Ginger Ale - There's A Toast in Every Glass" (ILLUS. far left)..................... **35**

Glass, "Moxie," clear cylindrical glass w/white wording, reads "Drink Moxie Nerve Food" (ILLUS. second from right)....... **165**

Glass, "Moxie," swelled tapering glass design w/white wording, reads "Drink Moxie" (ILLUS. far right).. **45**

Glass, "Dr. Pepper - King of Beverages".......... **506**

Three Soda Fountain Glasses

Glass, "Orange-Julep," flaring clear glass w/orange printing (ILLUS. left)......................... **44**

Glass, "Peerless - High Grade Soda Water," clear cylindrical glass w/red wording (ILLUS. center)... **25**

Collectible Soda Glass

Glass, Pepsi "Space Mouse" (ILLUS.)................ **55**
Glass, "Rahr's - Beverages - Oshkosh"............ **77**
Glass, "Suncrush Orange," tall slender waisted clear glass w/orange sun face & wording (ILLUS. right w/soda fountain glasses).. **64**

Coca-Cola Attendant's Hat

XXX Cola Fountain Glass

Glass, "XXX Cola," clear flared glass w/orange printing (ILLUS.).. **22**
Glasses, "Orange Crush," syrup line, etched detail, 4 7/8" h., set of 6..................... **650**
Hat, "Coca-Cola," cloth attendant's hat, green w/red strip & logo on both sides, minor wear & soiling, tag inside reads "Made by Bone-Crow Co., Waco, Texas" (ILLUS.).. **61**

Ice Cream Set

Ice cream parlor set, round oak table w/bent wire legs & four bent wire "heart design" chairs, late 19th - early 20th c., table 30" d., the set (ILLUS.) **413**
Ice cream scoop, Gilchrist No. 31 w/wooden handle **35**
Ice cream scoop, heart-shaped, wooden handle, in original box, 11" l. (ILLUS.)...... **15,400**

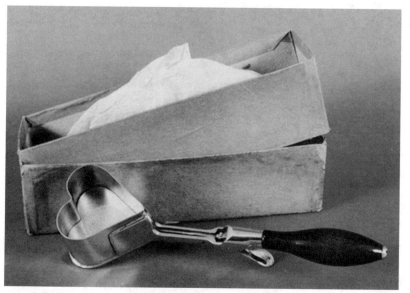

Heart-shaped Ice Cream Scoop

Ice crusher, Dazey, red plastic & metal 60
Malt machine, "Hamilton-Beach," porce-
lain, three-head, fountain-type 250
Malt powder dispenser, Hamilton Beach
Model No. 20D40182B, porcelain base
w/metal frame around cylindrical acrylic
top, Pat. No. 1.965.741, 18 1/2" h. 396

Menu board, "Hendlers Ice Cream," cardboard, chain-hung, top reads "Serving
Hendlers Ice Cream - 'The Velvet Kind',"
flavors listed below on paper inserts,
framed under glass, 10 x 20" (ILLUS.).......... 176
Menu board, "Pepsi-Cola," tin, original
chain, 19 1/2 x 30" (some scratches) 140

Squirt Menu Chalkboard

National Dairy Malted Milk Can

Malted milk can, cov., "National Dairy,"
aluminium, large knobbed finial, painted
advertising on panel reads "National
Dairy - Malted Milk - Extra Rich," denting,
scratches & scuffs, 6" d., 8 1/2" h.
(ILLUS.) 160
Malted milk jar, "Borden's," aluminum 100
Megaphone, "Dr. Pepper," heavy paper
w/metal ring at top, ca. 1950s, unused
(light wear & soiling) 358

Menu board, "Squirt," embossed tin
w/chalkboard, top w/message in circle
reading "Switch to Squirt - Never an Af-
ter-Thirst," flanked by Squirt boy & bottle,
bottom dated 1950, white stains to chalkboard, minor bends & wrinkles,
19 1/2 x 27 1/2" (ILLUS.) 165
Milk shake mixer, "Arnold," w/metal cup,
electric, ca. 1920s... 95
Milk shake mixer, Hamilton Beach green
porcelain, triple head..................................... 500

Hendlers Ice Cream Menu Board

Old Hamilton Beach Shake Mixer

Milk shake mixer, "Hamilton Beach Model 33," electric, single head, light green porcelain base w/chrome top & canister, some soiling & scuffs, 18" h. (ILLUS.)............ **154**

Mug, "Drink Hires Rootbeer," china, depicts trademark boy holding Hires Rootbeer mug, Mettlach, Germany, 4 1/2" h. **403**

Mug, "Hires," glass, boy on front & "Hires" on back, 4" h. **270**

Phonograph record, "Pepsi-Cola," 1943, complete w/mailing folder **55**

Dr. Pepper Pin Trays

Pin tray, "Dr. Pepper," metal, oval, center w/black & white dog against yellow ground, white & light blue border w/scalloped edge w/"Drink Dr. Pepper At All Soda Fountains 5¢" in red letters, light soiling, minor marks, light edge wear, 3 1/4" l. (ILLUS. bottom left) **1,650**

Pin tray, "Dr. Pepper," metal, oval w/white & green scalloped edge, center scene of black boy wearing yellow hat, eating watermelon, blue background w/"Drink Dr. Pepper At All Soda Fountains 5¢" in red letters around edge, light rusting at border near face, pit marks on outer border, 3 1/4" l. (ILLUS. top right)............................ **2,530**

Pin tray, "Dr. Pepper," metal, round, center w/scene of two kittens drinking milk from a bowl, one w/pink ribbon, the other blue, light green background, tan border w/scalloped edge w/"Drink Dr. Pepper At All Soda Fountains 5¢" in red letters, light crazing & edge wear, 2 1/2" d. (ILLUS. top left).. **1,210**

Pin tray, "Dr. Pepper," metal, round, center w/scene of two puppies, light blue background, pink border w/scalloped edge w/"Drink Dr. Pepper At All Soda Fountains 5¢" in red letters, few shallow dents & marks, border wear,2 1/2" d. (ILLUS. bottom right) **1,430**

Playing cards, "Dr. Pepper," black w/logo & pretty girl in red dress holding bottle, complete deck w/calendar card & bridge card, ca. 1946, original box........................... **385**

Radio, "Dr. Pepper," transistor-type, plastic, ca. 1960s, 3 x 7"............................... **297**

Ruler, "Breyer's Ice Cream," brass edge, ca. 1951, 85th anniversary commemorative, 12" l. **5**

Salt & pepper shakers, Coca-Cola Bottle, brown w/silver top, 3 3/4" h., unmarked, pr. **59**

Salt & pepper shakers, Dairy Queen cones, vanilla (salt) & chocolate (pepper) ice cream w/distinctive Dairy Queen curl atop yellow "Safe-T-Cups," 3 3/4" h. pr........... **29**

Service pin, "7Up," enameled gold-filled metal, an oblong frame of gilt laurel leaves surrounding a green, red & gold bottle of 7Up featuring the Bubble girl above a small black square w/a gold "5," for five years of service, 1/2 x 3/4" (very minor wear).. **160**

Sheet music, "Moxie One Step," 1921............. **45**

Sign, "Borden," one-sided tin, shows large ice cream cone, Dairy Products Advertising, Weston-Ontario, scratches, soiling, bent corners, 24" w., 36" h............................ **127**

Sign, "Carnation Ice Cream," one-sided die-cut porcelain, ice cream sundae in footed dish, red, white & green, 22" w., 23" h. (scratches, chips to mounting holes, soiling) **605**

Dairy Made Ice Cream Sign

Sign, "Dairy Made Ice Cream," embossed tin w/wood frame, depicts young child sitting & holding ice cream cone w/"You're sure - It's pure," soiling, edge wear & minor scratches, 26" w., 35" h. (ILLUS.)........... **770**

French Bauer Ice Cream Sign

Sign, "French Bauer Ice Cream," electric, figural milk glass cone mounted in wooden base, wear, ca. 1930s-40s, 17" h. (ILLUS.).. **2,420**

Western Candy Co. Sign

Sign, "Western Candy Co. Denver, Co.," embossed die-cut depicts bright & colorful portrait of beautiful lady w/flowers in her long wavy hair, 10 1/2 x 12" (ILLUS.)..... **303**

Whirla-Whip Sign

Sign, "Whirla-Whip," die-cut masonite, red & white tub filled w/swirled soft-serve ice cream & a red spoon, tub reads "Whirla-Whip Treats - in - a - Tub," minor surface & edge wear, 20 1/2 x 24" (ILLUS.).............. **110**

Dr. Pepper Dispenser

Soda dispenser, "Dr. Pepper," plastic, tombstone-style, two spigots, light green, logo in center, ca. 1960s, wear & pitting, surface scratches, interior soiling, small crack on side below tag (ILLUS.)................... **386**

Soda dispenser, "Fowler's Cherry Smash," ceramic w/pump, printed on both sides, 15" h. (some scratches & wear)................. **1,400**

Soda dispenser, "Fowler's Root Beer," ceramic w/pump, painted on both sides, 14" h. (some scratches & wear)................. **1,900**

Soda dispenser, "Hires," ceramic w/pump, 13" h. **550**

Richardson Root Beer Dispenser

Soda dispenser, "Richardson Root Beer," large wooden keg w/steel bands & double spigots & drip tray at the front, on metal feet, lift-off top, red & white applied sign on side reads "RICHardson - Root Beer - Rich in flavor," ca. 1950s (ILLUS.)..... **425**

Hires Store Sign

Store sign, "Hires," die-cut tin, suspended from hanging chain, colorful figure of smiling child holding a mug marked "Hires" & sign reading "Drink - Hires - It's Pure," 5 x 8" (ILLUS.)................................ **22,000**
Straw dispenser, glass, w/metal bottom & lid, dated 1918... **175-300**

Straw dispenser, glass w/metal lid, 11 1/2" h... **125-250**
Straw dispenser, metal, advertising Hires Root Beer, reads on front "Straws Show Where Hires goes 5¢ a glass" & "5¢ Hires for thirst" on side, metal tabs release straws, 10" l. (ILLUS. bottom)................... **15,125**
Syrup bottle, "Pineapple," label under glass, w/metal top measuring cup **150-250**
Syrup bottle, "Sarsap'lla," label under glass, w/metal top measuring cup **150-250**

Buckeye Root Beer Syrup Dispenser

Syrup dispenser, "Buckeye Root Beer," The Cleveland Fruit Juice Co., Cleveland, Ohio, ca. 1910, 14" h. (ILLUS.) **1,700-2,200**

Hires Root Beer Straw Dispenser

Cherry Chic Syrup Dispenser

Syrup dispenser, "Cherry Chic," ceramic, ca. 1910, 12" h. (ILLUS.).. **4,500-6,500**

Syrup dispenser, "Cherry Smash," ceramic w/original marked pump, cherries & leaves on branch in center, ca. 1920 (surface marks, base chips).......................... **880**

World Record Hires Syrup Dispenser

Syrup dispenser, "Drink Hires It Is Pure" front & back, ceramic, hour-glass shape w/top pump, 11" h. without pump, (hairline crack above "H" on one side)................ **805**

Syrup dispenser, "Drink Hires Root Beer," blue china, multiple images of trademarked boy pointing & holding mug w/"Drink Hires 5 cents" between images, spigot base reads "America's Health Drink Hires Rootbeer" & "Hires Rootbeer is luscious and pure," Mettlach, Germany, 10 1/2" d., 19" h................... **48,300**

Syrup dispenser, "Drink Orange Crush Ice Cold," rectangular, stainless steel w/porcelain advertising on sides, "Crushy" finial on lid, 19" h. to top of finial........................ **748**

Hires Syrup Dispenser

Syrup dispenser, "Drink Hires 5¢" front & back, ceramic, figural barrel, pump marked "Hires" on top, 11 1/2" h. without pump (ILLUS.).. **2,875**

Syrup dispenser, "Drink Hires 5¢," pottery, tall slender waisted pedestal base w/long metal spigot supports bulbous bowl-form top w/domed cover w/pointed knob finial, green banding & black wording w/full-color pictures of the Hires boy around the body, Mettlach pottery, early 20th c., world record, 11" d., 14" h. (ILLUS.)...... **107,250**

Rare Fan-Taz Syrup Dispenser

Syrup dispenser, "Fan-Taz," large ceramic model of a baseball on a round base, orange & black wording w/a tan baseball bat, ca. 1900, 16" h. (ILLUS.)................ **$8,000+**

Cherry Smash Syrup Dispenser

Syrup dispenser, "Fowler's Cherry Smash," glass & chrome, the tapering cylindrical cranberry red glass container printed w/white wording, flat metal cover, base & spigot, bowl 7 1/2 x 9", overall 17" h. (ILLUS.)................................... **633**
Syrup dispenser, "Grape Crush" ceramic, wording below cluster of hanging grapes

front & back, figural barrel w/pump, lavender textured glass, 10 1/2" h. without pump.. **3,163**
Syrup dispenser, salesman's sample Hires Root Beer Munimaker in original carrying case, 12" h. (ILLUS., bottom)................... **77,000**

Orange-Crush Syrup Dispenser

Syrup dispenser, "Ward's Orange-Crush," pottery, large figural orange on rounded green leaf-molded base w/white blossoms, metal cap & pump spigot on top, early 20th c. (ILLUS.)............................ **1,500**

Miniature Syrup Dispenser

Chapter 16
String & Sack Holders

Sunbeam Bread String Holder

Bread, "Sunbeam Bread," painted tin, both sides w/Little Miss Sunbeam eating a slice of bread, string mounted inside on metal rod, red, blue, yellow & white, paint chips & loss w/cracking of paint overall, 90% paint loss on reverse side, 13" w., 16" h. (ILLUS.).............................. **$105**

Hambone Cigars String Holder

Cigars, "J.P. Alley's Hambone Sweets 5¢ - Above All Five Cent Cigars - Finest Quality," embossed die-cut two-sided, colorful decoration centered by a comic pilot flying an airplane & smoking a cigar all on a white ground, 7" d. (ILLUS.)............................ **44**

Coffee, "La Touraine Coffee," nearly square die-cut metal sign w/white & yellow printing on dark blue on both sides, a color picture of a package of the product in the center, each side w/a cut-out post to hold a string cone, reads "La Touraine - Fresh Roasted - Ground To Order - The Perfect Coffee - W.S. Quinby Company - Boston - Chicago," ca. 1910, 20 1/4" w., 17" h. **3,700-4,000**

Flour, "King Midas," die-cut rectangular metal sign w/orange & white wording on dark blue reading "Buy King Midas - The Highest Priced - Flour - In America - Worth All It Costs," arched opening at the bottom holds a tall cone of string, ca. 1910, 20" w., 13 1/2" h. **1,400-1,550**

Horse hames, "U.S. Hame Company," hanging two-sided tin, depicts trademark buffalo standing atop company logo framed by two horses, "U.S. Hame Company" above logo, "USH Co Hames Sold Here" below w/string at bottom, by lithographer Chas. W. Shonk Co., 11 1/2" w., 26" h. **3,450**

Medicine, "Swift's Syphilitic Specific," cast-iron pot w/bail handle, embossed "S.S.S. For The Blood," ca. 1870-1890, 4 3/8" h. (some rust & scratching) **77**

Paint, "Red Seal White Lead," die-cut tin, depicts Dutch Boy painting from scaffolding, 3-dimensional pail holds string, two-sided, 14 1/2" w., 7" h. to bottom of bucket **2,875**

Sack rack w/string holder, "Carey Bro. & Grevenmeyer," quarter-round wood framework w/slots for sacks & ball-shaped pierced iron strong holder at the top, yellow stenciled wording on the side, 8 x 16", 20" h. **350-425**

Shoes, "Red Goose Shoes," tin lithograph, 14" h. **1,300**

Shoes, "Red Goose," die-cut metal in the silhouetted shape of a red goose printed in white w/"Red Goose Shoes," sign suspends a wire frame holding a tall cone of string, two-sided, ca. 1910, 29" h. **2,200 -3,000**

Tea, "Chase & Sanborn's Canister Teas," rectangular lithographed tin sign in white w/dark green lettering, a wire cage string holder fitted at the top center edge, 10 x 13" h. **350-425**

Chapter 17
Thermometers

Winchester Ammunition Thermometer

Ammunition, "Winchester Western - Sporting Ammunition Sold Here," tall rectangular form designed to resemble a large shotgun shell in red w/a dark gold bottom section, the glass thermometer up the center, red wording at top & black wording at the bottom, very minor edge wear, 7 1/2 x 26 3/4" (ILLUS.) **$121**

Antifreeze, "Shellzone Anti-Freeze," metal & wood, oblong, marked "Shellzone Anti-Freeze Permanent Type" above w/Shell logo below, yellow lettering on orange background, 3" w., 17" h. (scratches & soiling, minor rust on back) **176**

Auto dealer, "Oldsmobile - Boise Auto Company - Boise, Idaho," round metal w/domed cover, the Arabic numerals in white on white ground, red arrow & red Oldsmobile logo at top w/the name & address of the dealer in the bottom half, 12" d. (some minor paint flakes at the bottom edge) **495**

Automotive products, "Atlas Perma-Guard," metal tapering oblong, marked "Atlas Perma-Guard Anti-Freeze Coolant" above in white lettering on red, "Year-round Protection" in blue lettering below, red, white & blue sun w/ray design, 8" w., 24" h. (scratches, soiling, paint chips) **83**

Automotive products, "Eyouem," porcelain, rectangular, marked "Eyouem" in white lettering on black background above, depicts spark plug on yellow background below, 12 1/4" w., 38 3/4" h. (chips on edge, scratches) **50**

Automotive products, "Mobil," tin & glass, large round tin disk in white printed w/black numbers around the border, the center w/a grey & red rectangular reserve w/"Mobil" in black letters over a small red Pegasus logo, round glass front, ca. 1957, 12" d. (soiling denting in back, minor paint cracking near top) **440**

Automotive products, "Prestone Anti-Freeze," porcelain, oblong, black background above, "You're Safe...And You Know It" red background below, 9 1/4" w., 36" l. (waterstained & some chipping).. **99**

Automotive supplies, "Signal Products" plastic pole-shaped, 2 1/2 x 7", rare **530**

Barrel Remodeling Co. Thermometer

Barrels, "Barrel Remodeling Company," round, metal w/paper face, black numbers, image of barrel in center over "Barrel Remodeling Co. - Barrels Bought and Sold - Kansas City, Mo.," litho by The American Art Works, Coshocton, Ohio, ca. 1900, 9 1/4" d. (ILLUS.).......... **150-200**

Red Seal Dry Battery Thermometer

Battery, "Red Seal Dry Battery," porcelain, long narrow rectangular form w/rounded ends, dark blue ground w/white border, a large red, white & blue picture of the battery above the black & white thermometer w/glass tube, white wording at the bottom reads "The Guarantee Protects You," ca. 1915, chipping at top mounting hole, touch-up to bottom of thermometer, 7" w., 27" h. (ILLUS.)....................................... **275**

Boots & shoes, "Fin & Feather Boots & Shoes," rectangular embossed tin litho, white w/red lettering, 4 1/2 x 14".................. **110**

Bread, "Sunbeam Bread," metal & glass, "Reach for Sunbeam Bread - Let's Be Friends" above Miss Sunbeam Trademark, copyright Quality Bakers of American Cooperative, Inc., 1957, 12" d. (soiling & surface stain & marks)........................ **413**

Candy, "Clark Bar," rectangular, wood w/glass bulb & metal fasteners, image of Clark bar over a clock w/"4PM - 'Clark Bar O'Clock'" & "Clark Bar - Join The Millions In This Mid-Afternoon Candy Delight," dated Dec. 7, 1920, 5 1/2 x 19" (ILLUS.)..................... **450-650**

Trico Wiper Blades Thermometer

Car wiper blades, "Trico Wiper Blades," glass & metal fan-shaped design w/a white ground, black lettering at the edge & a red arch over red & black wording, soiling, rust & pitting, 15" w., 9" h. (ILLUS.)....................................... **143**

Cigarettes, "Winston," tall rectangular form w/rounded corners, yellow background w/the glass thermometer in the upper right, black wording at upper left reads "How good it is" above a color image of an open cigarette pack, 5 3/4 x 13 1/2" (couple of small nicks)..................... **33**

Coffee, "Golden Sun Coffee," rectangular, porcelain by Beach, Coshocton, white w/black lettering reading "Golden Sun Coffee is Always Good" above graphic of product package & "Buy Coffee of Your Grocer Only" at bottom, ca. 1915, 2 3/4 x 11 1/2" (minor dings at edge)........... **385**

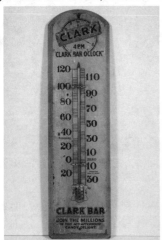

Clark Bar Thermometer

Hills Bros. Coffee Thermometer

Coffee, "Hills Bros. Coffee," porcelain, long rectangular form w/rounded top, dark red ground w/white wording, large image of Arab man in yellow robe drinking from cup, dated 1915, 8 3/4 x 21" (ILLUS.) **908**

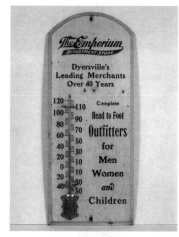

Department Store Thermometer

Department store, "The Emporium Department Store," rectangular wood w/rounded top & slightly curved edges, painted white w/blue lettering reading "The Emporium Department Store - Dyersville's Leading Merchants Over 40 Years - Complete Head to Foot Outfitters for Men - Women - and - Children," ca. 1920, 9 x 21" (ILLUS.) **125-175**

Farm equipment, "Burress Implement Co.," rectangular w/rounded top, aluminum w/red tractor & "McCormick Deering Farm Machinery - International Trucks - Booneville, Miss.," 3 3/4 x 13 1/4" **176**

Flavoring extracts, "Sauer's Flavoring Extracts," wood w/glass tube, "Sauer's Flavoring Extracts" in red above "None Better - 10 and 25¢ - Sixteen Highest Awards and Gold Medals - Purity Strength and Fine Flavor - The G.F. Sauer Co., Richmond, VA" in black letters, 3/4 x 7", 23 1/2" h. (some rust to brackets holding glass, soiling & paint chips, does not work) **193**

Flour, "David Harum Flour," rectangular, wood marked "David Harum Flour - David Harum Feed," dated 1937, 3 x 12" **66**

Flour, "Motley's Big Roller Flour," wood w/rounded top, painted "Motley's Big Roller Flour, Rochester, N.Y., Moseley & Motley Milling Co." in circle above, "High Quality Bread Flour, Buy It Here" on side below, 9" w., 20 1/2" h. **58**

Gasoline, "Shell Gasoline," porcelain, narrow oblong form w/orange printing on dark yellow ground, a shell logo at the top reading "Shell Gasoline," & another at the bottom reading "Shell Motor Oil," w/original tube, patent-dated in 1915, strong luster, 7 1/4" w., 27" h. (chips at mounting holes & edges) **1,980**

Gasoline, "Shell Gasoline - Shell Motor Oil," porcelain, rectangular w/rounded top & bottom, "Pt. Mar. 16, 1915" at bottom, tube intact, 7" w., 27" h. (chips to mounting holes & by 90 degree mark) **1,100**

Gasoline, "Texaco," die-cut embossed tin, pole-type, in original box, 2 5/8 x 6 1/4" **355**

Gasoline/motor oil, "Shell Gasoline, Shell Motor Oil," porcelain, oblong, yellow background w/red trim & lettering, marked "Pat. Mar. 16, 1915.," 7" w., 77" h. **3,750**

Hardware, "Keen Kutter - Simmons Hardware Company," metal on wood, long rectangular form in dark yellow w/black numbers around the front-mounted glass thermometer, Keen Kutter red logo at the top, 1 3/4 x 7 1/4" **176**

5/A Horse Blankets Thermometer

Horse blankets, "5/A Horse Blankets," round, yellow metal w/paper face, black numbers & black diamond shape in center marked "We've Got 'Em - You Want 'Em - 5/A Horse Blankets," & marked along bottom near frame "Standard Thermometer and Electric Company, Peabody, Massachusetts, Pat. May 8, 1888," 9 1/4" d. (ILLUS.) **175-225**

Borden's Ice Cream Thermometer

Ice cream, "Borden's Ice Cream," porcelain, wide oval form w/a white background, a small glass thermometer in the lower left, printed w/large blue letters at the top "Big Boy" above a color image of a strawberry ice cream cone, "Borden's Ice Cream" in blue at the bottom, small chip at top above grommet, 6 x 15" (ILLUS.).................. **798**

Implement company, "Barrows Implement Company," painted aluminum, rounded top, white ground decorated at the top w/a red & black tractor above advertising w/the thermometer below, an International Harvester logo at the bottom, 3 3/4 x 13 1/4" **176**

EX-LAX Thermometer

Laxative, "EX-LAX," porcelain on metal, blue, black w/red & white bands at top & bottom, reads "EX-LAX - the chocolated laxative - keep 'regular' with EX-LAX - Prescriptions - Drugs - Toilet Articles," ca. 1920s, 8 x 36" (ILLUS.) **200-250**

Meat packers, "dpm Flavor Guard Meats - Marysville, California," round lithographed metal, dark yellow ground w/red numbers & wording, ca. 1950s, 12" d. **66**

Medicine, "Abbott's Angostura, Abbott's Angostura Bitters Aid Digestion," wood, oblong, black lettering & decoration, 8 3/4" w., 47 3/4" h. **468**

Boschee's German Syrup Thermometer

Medicine, "Boschee's August Flower German Syrup," round, yellow metal w/paper face, black numbers, center w/yellow lettering outlined in black reading "August Flower for Liver, Indigestion, Constipation - for Coughs, Colds, Bronchitis, etc. - Use Boschee's German Syrup," ca. 1900, 9 1/2" d. (ILLUS.)........................... **175-225**

Medicine, "Lash's Kidney Bitters," rectangular, wood, by American Mfg. Concern, Jamestown, New York, 5 1/4 x 21".............. **523**

Medicine, "Nature's Remedy," rectangular, porcelain, black w/white & red lettering reading "NR To-Night - Tomorrow Alright - Nature's Remedy Tablets" at top & "Come In - If you get it here It's good," edge dings, glass tube broken, 7 x 27"........ **176**

NR & Tums Thermometer

Medicine, "NR (Nature's Remedy) Laxative & Tums," rectangular, porcelain on metal, top marked "NR - All Vegetable Laxative - Come In - If You Get It Here It 's Good" & marked at the bottom "Tums - Quick Relief for Acid Indigestion," black & red w/white lettering, ca. 1920, 7 x 27" (ILLUS.) **225-300**

Medicine, "Tums," aluminum w/glass tube, rectangular w/"Tums for the Tummy" at the top & "Tums Quick Relief for Acid Indigestion - Heartburn" at the bottom, 4 x 9"........ **55**

Motor oil, "Kendall Motor Oil," porcelain, rectangular, orange logo, black lettering on white background, marked "Kendall Refining Company Bradford, PA.," 9" w., 27" h. (soiling) **550**

Valvoline Oil Thermometer

Motor oil, "Valvoline," round metal housing & frame w/glass domed front, dark yellow ground w/dark green numbers along the border w/a large green & white picture of a can of oil w/red & white wording "Ask For The World's First Motor Oil - Valvoline," red gauge, 12" d. (ILLUS.)..................... **220**

Motor oil, "Veedo Motor Oil," porcelain, rectangular, marked "le film de protection" in white lettering above, Veedo logo below, all on red background, (fading, chipping, soiling & loss of luster).................. **176**

OshKosh Overalls Thermometer

Overalls, "OshKosh Overalls," rectangular, metal, red & yellow w/"OshKosh B'gosh - Work Wear" at the top & "The World's Best Overall - Union Made" at the bottom, ca. 1920, 10 x 25 1/2" (ILLUS.)... **475-600**

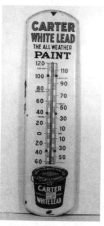

Carter White Lead Paint Thermometer

Paint, "Carter White Lead Paint," porcelain on metal, white, red & black, "Carter White Lead - The All Weather Paint" at the top, paint bucket at bottom marked "Carter White Lead Co. - Chicago &

Omaha - Carter - Strictly Pure - White Lead," dated March 16, 1915, 7 x 27" (ILLUS.)... **235-325**

Peanuts, "Planters Peanuts," Mr. Peanut, tin, 1978, 6 x 7"................................. **65-80**

Razor blades, "Gillette," barometer & thermometer, blue porcelain, reads "Blue Gillette Blades" beneath picture of razor blade at top, thermometer in center & barometer at bottom, reads "Blue Gillette Blades" 6 1/4" w., 27 1/2" h. **1,925**

Shoes, "Peters Weatherbird Shoes," oblong porcelain w/glass tube, bird logo at top over "Peters - Weatherbird," & "Peters - Diamond - Brand - Shoes - Solid Leather Footwear" at the bottom, "Pat. March 16, 1915 Beach, Coshocton, O.," white, black & red, 7" w., 27" h. (soiling & chips to mounting holes & edges)..................... **176**

Shoes, "Red Goose Shoes," porcelain, 27" h. (minor screw hole & edge chip)......... **650**

Soft drink, "Bireley's," lithographed tin, long rectangular form w/rounded corners, a dark gold ground printed in blue, white & orange w/a large orange bottle of the drink & half an orange & leaves & blossoms at the bottom, reads "Got a Minute? Enjoy Bireley's - It's Different - Non-Carbonated," 4 1/2 x 15 3/4" (mercury is separated)..................................... **220**

Soft drink, "Coca-Cola," round, glass front, red banner in center w/"Coca-Cola" in white lettering, black letters above & below read "Drink - Be Really Refreshed," 1960s (minor light scratches on glass, light soiling)..................................... **935**

Figural Bottle Thermometer

Soft drink, "Coca-Cola," tin, figural bottle, 1958, 30" h. (ILLUS.) **150**

Soft drink, "Coca-Cola," embossed metal, bottle-shaped, 17" h. **140**

Soft drink, "Double Cola," rectangular, tin, green w/yellow trim, marked "Drink Double Cola - You'll like it better," 5 x 17" **138**

Soft drink, "Dr. Pepper," circular dial w/"Hot or cold," 18" d. **110**

Soft drink, "Dr. Pepper," die-cut figural classic bottle cap, 11" d................................. **100**

Dr. Pepper Thermometer

Soft drink, "Dr. Pepper," tin & glass, white & red w/aqua highlights, bottle shown opposite thermometer w/clock at top marked "Drink A Bite To Eat At 10 - 2 - 4" & "Dr. Pepper - Good For Life - 5¢" at the bottom, soiling, small edge bend lower right, few marks & light scuffs, ca. 1930s, 4 1/2 x 13" (ILLUS.) **2,310**
Soft drink, "Frostie Root Beer," tin, 3 x 11 5/8" **350**
Soft drink, "Frostie Root Beer," tin, 8 x 36" (some rust & damage) **145**

Hires Root Beer Thermometer

Soft drink, "Hires," painted tin in soda bottle shape, "Hires Since 1876 Root Beer With Roots Barks Herbs," 7 3/4" w., 28 1/2" h. (ILLUS.) **171**

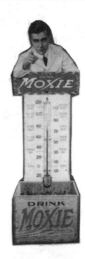

Moxie Outdoor Thermometer

Soft drink, "Moxie Soda," metal over wood, outdoor-type, man at top w/sign reading "Drink Moxie," box at bottom containing miniature bottles also marked "Drink Moxie," 38" h. (ILLUS.) **6,930**
Soft drink, "NuGrape Soda," tin, oblong w/rounded ends, glass tube in center w/"Drink NuGrape Soda" above a row of six bottles & "A Flavor You Can't Forget" below, 6 3/4" w., 16" h. (soiling, denting & paint chips, some white paint drops) **99**
Soft drink, "Orange Crush," porcelain, wide oval shape, white ground printed w/a large bottle on the right, small thermometer on the left, wording in orange at top & bottom reads "From Natural Orange Juice - Naturally it Tastes Better," 6 x 15" (chip in bottom around mounting hole) **132**

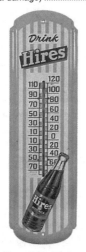

Hires Root Beer Thermometer

Soft drink, "Drink Hires," tin, oblong w/a light blue & white striped background & lettering in yellow & black at the top, a large glass thermometer down the center & a colored bottle of Hires at the bottom, moderate overall nicks, scratches & wear, 8 x 27" (ILLUS.) **154**

Orange Crush Thermometer

Soft drink, "Orange Crush," round metal w/a dark orange background w/white wording & black numbers, 12" d. (ILLUS.) **132**

Large Pepsi-Cola Thermometer

Soft drink, "Drink Pepsi-Cola - Ice-Cold," round metal-framed w/glass lens, large center red, white & blue Pepsi logo w/black numbers around the border, unused condition, ca. 1951, 12" d. (ILLUS.) .. **1,100**

Soft drink, "Pepsi-Cola," metal w/glass lens, "Drink Pepsi-Cola Ice-Cold," red, white & blue, ca. 1951, 12" d. **1,100**

Soft drink, "Royal Crown Cola," tin w/detailed deep embossing **185**

Spark plugs, "Champion Dependable Spark Plugs," wooden, oblong w/upper half spark plug shape, black lettering, 5 1/8" w., 11 1/2" h. **121**

Strawberry Growers Thermometer

Strawberry plant growers, "Waller Bros.," rectangular w/round top, metal, w/bunch of red strawberries & green leaves at top, thermometer on left side & marked "Waller Bros. - Judsonia Ark. The Honest Strawberry Plant Growers," few minor scrapes, 6 x 15" (ILLUS.) **248**

Dominion Royals Tire Thermometer

Tires, "Drive Safely - Ride On Dominion Royals," porcelain, rectangular w/rounded top, small glass thermometer mounted at center right, black & white wording at top & bottom w/large black & white tire in the center all on a dark orange ground, very minor surface & edge wear, chips & flecks, 10 x 30" (ILLUS.) **550-750**

Tobacco Importers Thermometer

Tobacco importers, "Sternemann Bros. & Hayden, Importers of Tobacco - Milwaukee, Wis.," long figural model of a tobacco leaf w/advertising at the top above the mounted glass thermometer, glass tube probably replaced, one metal bracket missing, 5 1/2 x 23 3/4" (ILLUS.) **259**

Varnish, "Valentine's Valspar," rectangular, porcelain w/wooden frame, depicts man & woman above "Valentine's Valspar The Weatherproof Varnish," shows can of varnish below, marked "Beach Coshocton, Pat. Mar. 16, 1915," black, white & mauve, 21 1/2" w., 96" h. (chips overall) **715**

Chapter 18

Tins

Princine Baking Powder Tin

Baker's Delight Baking Powder Pail

Baking powder, "Baker's Delight," round pail w/side handles, lithographed Mammy holding a pan of baked goods, minor rust, soiling & chips to lithograph, 12 1/4" d., 14 1/2" h. (ILLUS.)...................... **$363**

Baking powder, "Princine Baking Powder," 1/2 lb. tin, cylindrical w/side strap handle, red ground w/white & gold wording, round center picture of a smiling lady holding a package of the product, full, unopened, dated 1916, 3 x 3" (ILLUS.).. **88**

Baking powder, "Rough Rider," w/paper label showing man on horse, 2 1/4 x 4 1/2" (minor scrapes & dings)................................... **88**

Baking Powder, "Vision," paper lithographed label depicting angels playing w/fire, 3 x 7" (minor scuffs)............................. **77**

Parrot and Monkey Baking Powder Tin

Baking powder, "Parrot and Monkey," w/paper label in red w/colored scene of a monkey & a parrot on tree branches & marked in white & black letters "Parrot and Monkey Baking Powder" by the "Sea Gull" Specialty Co., Baltimore & New Orleans, full container, unopened, minor paper tears, 2 1/2 x 5" (ILLUS.)...................... **55**

Watkins Baking Powder Trial Size Tin

Baking powder, "Watkins Baking Powder - Purity Guaranteed," trial size, cylindrical w/an orange & red ground w/red & white wording, half-length color image of a 1930s woman holding plate of biscuits, 2 x 3 1/4" (ILLUS.) 59

Biscuit, "Carr's," double decker motor bus model, partial box, 10 1/8" l. (minor dent) .. **1,045**

Biscuit, "Crawford," yellow sedan auto model, excellent, 8 5/8" l. **10,450**

Biscuit, "Crawford's," model of a steamroller, extremely rare w/original box, 7 1/4" l., near mint **6,050**

Biscuit, "Crawford's," model of cruise liner "Berengaria," includes advertisement card, excellent, 14 3/4" l. **3,080**

Biscuit, "Crawford's," model of double decker bus "General," 10 3/4" l. (surface wear to roof) **4,400**

Biscuit, "Crawford's," model of service bus, very good, 11 3/4" l., (minor touchup) **2,420**

Biscuit, "Crawford's," Rolls Royce model, 11 3/8" l., excellent **13,200**

Biscuit, "Crumpsall & Cardif," model of British telephone booth, rare, excellent, 6 1/2" h 880

Biscuit, "Crumpsall & Cardiff," marble game w/the original steel balls, pristine, 4 3/4" x 6 3/4" 352

Biscuit, "Crumpsall & Cardiff," model of CWS sedan w/clockwork mechanism, ca. 1926, excellent, 8 1/4" l. **11,000**

Biscuit, "Crumpsall & Cardiff," model of elephant on wheels, excellent, 6" w., 4 3/4" h. **2,750**

Biscuit, "Crumpsall & Cardiff," model of motorcycle rider w/side car, extremely rare, 7 1/4" l. (minor oxidation) **5,500-6,500**

Biscuit, "Crumpsall & Cardiff," steam crane model, excellent, 7" l., 6 3/4" h. (minor wear to base & roof) **6,600**

Biscuits, "Crumpsall's Cream," delivery van model, ca. 1922, extremely rare, good, 7" l. (some repainting & one wheel replaced) **9,350**

Biscuit, "G&R," Royal Mail delivery van model, excellent, 8" l. 990

Biscuit, "Gray & Dunn's," mailbox-shaped, shows young girl placing letter in mailbox, 5 7/8" h. (minor scuffing & scratches) 330

Biscuit, "Gray & Dunn's," model of city bus, 7 1/2" l. (surface wear & minor scratches) .. **7,150**

Biscuit, "Gray & Dunn's," model of motorcycle w/side car, extremely rare, 7 1/4" l. (minor oxidation) **16,500**

Biscuit, "Gray & Dunn's," model of racing car, 10" l. (minor scratch) **20,900**

Biscuit, "Huntley & Palmer," top w/hunting scene w/numerous dogs & riders, all sides decorated w/rabbits & very nice lithographed lid overhangs the body by 1/2", England, 2 x 8 1/2 x 13 1/4" 230

Biscuit, "Huntley & Palmer," w/fire scenes 235

Biscuit, "Huntley & Palmers," baby carriage model, extremely rare, excellent, 4 3/4" h., 8 1/2" l. **7,150**

Biscuit, "Huntley & Palmers," china cabinet model, excellent , 5 3/4" x 7 1/8" h. (minor denting) **1,100**

Biscuit, "Huntley & Palmers," model of grandfather clock, excellent, 11 1/2" h. **1,100**

Biscuit, "Huntley & Palmers," model of stack of books tied w/strap, bright red w/gold, black & tan trim, 6 1/4" l. 330

Biscuit, "Jacob's," horse on wheels, rare original box, 8" w., 9 1/8" h. **7,700**

Biscuit, "Jacob's," model of locomotive, extremely rare, 9 1/4" l. (crazing to paint) **3,080**

Biscuit, "LMS," trolley model, 9" l. (wear to roof & slight oxidation) 825

Biscuit, model of military ambulance, excellent, 7" l. **1,870**

Biscuit, "Pascall's," penny container, Punch & Judy design, excellent, 2 7/8" h. **605**

Biscuit, "Peek Frean Coconut Shies," w/game set, w/wooden coconut shape pieces, 7 1/2" h. (some staining) **1,045**

Biscuit, "Rowntrees," limousine-shaped, ca. 1926, excellent, 6 1/8" l. **8,250**

Debray French Biscuit Tin

Biscuits, "Debray French Biscuit," two-piece, lithographed hunting scene w/hunters on horseback, dogs & stag, 1 3/8 x 3 1/2 x 7 1/2" (ILLUS.) 110

Biscuits, "John Hill & Son," model of delivery van, excellent, 7 1/8" l. **2,750**

Chewing gum, "Hoadley's" 770

Between the Acts Cigar Tin

Cigars, "Between The Acts Little Cigars," flat rectangular w/the embossed lid printed in red, white & black w/a seated gentleman smoking a cigar in each lower corner, tax stamp dated 1909, bright, 3 x 5 1/2", 1" h. (ILLUS.) 55

Buster Brown Cigar Tin

Orcico Cigar Tin

Cigars, "Buster Brown," round, R. T. Outcault images on both sides of Buster Brown & Tige, including image of cans on table & in Buster's hands, slip lid, small blemishes, rust spots & uniform wear, 5 x 5" (ILLUS.)...................... **1,725-1,795**

Cigars, "Dog-on-Good," paper label **2,310**

Cigars, "Green Turtle," lunch box tin, green & white w/turtle decoration on front, bail handle & latch (ILLUS. bottom right w/tobacco lunch box tins) **287**

Cigars, "Happy," round, front, back & top decorated w/devious bald man winking & smoking cigar, slip lid, 4 x 5 1/4"................... **397**

Cigars, "Home-Run Stogie," round, front & back w/batter & catcher on light blue ground, slip lid, National Can Co., 4 1/4 x 6" **4,600**

Cigars, "Mohawk Chief," bust of Indian chief front & back, 4 x 5 1/2 x 6" (severe fade to front) **173**

Cigars, "Orcico," oblong lift-top tin, decorated w/a colorful image of a Native American chief w/landscapes flanking him, printing in orange & brown, dated 1919, 4 x 6", 5 1/2" h. (ILLUS.)................................... **385**

Cigars, "Orioles," round **375**

Possum Cigar Tin

Cigars, "Possum Cigar," red w/white possum depicted & marked "Possum - Am Good and Sweet," same image on reverse, minor dings & scratches, 5 x 5" (ILLUS.).. **204**

Old Seneca Stogies Tin

Cigars, "Old Seneca Stogies," color image of a Native American chief's face framed by red & white wording against a gold ground, some rim wear, good color, 4 x 5 1/2" (ILLUS.)............................ **264**

Possum Cigars Tin with Gold Ground

Cigars, "Possum Cigars - 3 for 5¢ - 'Am Good and Sweet',," large cylindrical size in dark gold w/brown reserves w/white & red wording around a color image of a white possum, slight wear, 5 x 5" (ILLUS.).. **396**

Acme Coffee Tin

Coffee, "Acme Brand Coffee," 1 lb. tin, front w/a large oval w/the brand name framed by coffee berries & printed in red, blue & gold w/the lower half in white polka dots on red, the reverse w/another oval w/a coffeepot & cup & saucer w/"Home Coffee," 4 x 6" (ILLUS. of two sides) **66**

Possum Cigar Tin with Contents

Cigars, "Possum Cigars - 'Am Good and Sweet'," large cylindrical size in red w/black & white wording around a color image of a white possum, full & w/original insert rim sign reading "Possum - 3 for 10¢ - Extra Mild - Extra Good," strong colors, 5 x 5" (ILLUS.) **421**

Cigars, "Red Dot Junior Cigar," flat rectangular tin, a radiating design of alternating gold & white rays centered by a red dot w/a head of a pretty woman, writing in red on gold, 2 3/4 x 4 3/4" **50**

Cigars, "Sunset Trail," decorated w/scene of riders on horses, blue ground, 4 x 6" **345**

Cigars, "Sunset Trail," scene of riders on horseback on white ground, hinged cover, 4 x 5 1/2 x 6" **230**

Cigars, "Van Bibber," pocket tin........................ **135**

Cigars, "War Eagle Cigars," red w/image of eagle in flight clutching American shield on both sides & marked in white letters "War Eagle - Cigars - 2 for 5¢," 5 x 5" **88**

American Home Brand Coffee Tin

Coffee, "American Home Brand Fresh Roasted Coffee," 1 lb. tin, colorful paper label printed in red, white & blue w/a color scene of large home on one side & a large cup of coffee on the other, very clean, 4 x 6" (ILLUS.) **83**

Yellow Cab Cigar Tin

Cigars, "Yellow Cab," round lid, orange, both sides w/lithographed cigar-smoking passenger driven by cab driver, some non-detracting small dents & light surface scratches, the word dark scratched into lid, 5 1/4 x 5 3/4" (ILLUS.).................... **2,875**

Araban Coffee Tin

Coffee, "Araban Coffee," 1 lb. tin, screw-on lid, red background w/white & gold lettering, a bust profile of an Arab drinking coffee, dated 1929, a few scrapes & dings, 4 1/4 x 6" (ILLUS.) 330

Astor House Coffee Tin

Coffee, "Astor House Coffee," 1 lb. tin w/screw top, black & white w/scene of large building, & marked "Astor House Brand - Coffee," original lustre, 4 x 6 1/4" (ILLUS.) 187
Coffee, "Beech Nut Coffee," key wind sample size by American Can, red w/black & white lettering, 2 1/2 x 3 1/4", 4 oz. 55

Betsy Ross Coffee Tin

Coffee, "Betsy Ross Brand Coffee," 1 lb. tin, colorful label w/a white ground printed w/dark blue & red wording, central diamond-shaped logo, 4 x 6" (ILLUS.) 55

Blanke's Happy Thought Coffee Tin

Coffee, "Blanke's Happy Thought Coffee," figural trunk form, tan w/black lettering, minor scrapes, 4 1/2 x 4 1/2 x 9" (ILLUS.) 77

Buell's Coffee Tin

Coffee, "Buell's," round w/lithographed scene of lady drinking cup of coffee & marked "Buell's Brighton Blend Coffee - Merit - that's all!," George C. Burell & Co., Inc., "Rochester, N.Y. - Established 1846," embossed on lid, "turn to open," minor paint chips & overall soiling, 4 1/2" d., 6" h. (ILLUS.) 176
Coffee, "Bueno Coffee," 1 lb. tin w/slip lid, black & silver w/gold top, marked "Bueno Coffee - Walker-Smith Co., Brownwood Texas," litho by LaCrosse Can, Wisconsin, 4 x 5 1/4" 231
Coffee, "Bunker Hill Coffee," 1 lb. tin, pry-off lid, red ground w/large white wording above & below a central square reserve w/a color image of the Bunker Hill Monument, 4 1/4 x 5 3/4" (slight blemishes & dings, minor fading) 88

Campbell Coffee Four Pound Tin

Coffee, "Campbell Brand Coffee," 4 lb. tin,
lift-off lid, bail handle, dark yellow ground
w/red & brown wording above & below a
vignette of a group of Arabs w/camels, a
few scratches, 7 3/4 x 8" (ILLUS.) **66**

Caswell's Three Pound Coffee Tin

Coffee, "Caswell's Coffee," 3 lb. tin, tall
cylindrical form w/pry-off lid, a center oval
reserve w/a black & white profile portrait
of a lovely long-haired woman, gold on
yellow wording & scrolled reserve around
the portrait against a black & gold spiral
band background, dated 1924, several
small dings & scrapes, 5 1/4 x 9"
(ILLUS.) **154**
Coffee, "Comrade," round w/lithograph of
dog's head & "Comrade Steel Cut Coffee" on one side & "Three pounds net
weight vacuum packed J A Folger & Co.,
Kansas City San Francisco Trade Mark
Reg. U.S. Pat. Off." on reverse, 6 1/8" d.,
7" h. (denting, scratches, soiling, surface
rust & interior staining) **94**
Coffee, "Country Club Coffee," 1 lb. tin,
screw-off lid, a dark blue over black background, gold lettering at the top & light
blue & gold at bottom, a color center reserve showing a country club clubhouse,
few minor scrapes, 4 x 6" **193**
Coffee, "Demi-Tasse Coffee," 1 lb. tin, wide
brown bands at the top & bottom printed
w/large white lettering, a wide central
gold band decorated w/silhouetted figures of walking people & mules, minor
dings & scrapes, hole in top, 4 1/4 x 6" **65**
Coffee, "Dining Room Coffee," 1 lb. tin
w/screw top, litho by Passaic Metalware,
N.J., yellow & black, marked on both
sides "Progress Dining Room Coffee -
Roasted and Packed by American Food
Co., Newark, N.J.," 4 x 6" **165**
Coffee, "Eagle Brand," 1 lb. tin, eagle decoration on front & back, screw-on lid,
4 1/4 x 6" **115**

5th Ave. Brand Coffee Tin

Coffee, "(Fifth) 5th Ave. Brand Coffee," 1 lb.
tin, cylindrical w/pry-off lid, label printed
in gold, dark brown, light brown & cream,
front w/center monogram of The O'Dono-
hue Knight & Gage Company, producers
of the brand, 4 x 6" (ILLUS.) **66**

Fine Fort Pitt Coffee Tin

Coffee, "Fort Pitt Coffee," cylindrical, printed in color w/the brand name around a
vignette of an early fort, in red, white,
black & gold, 4 1/4" d., 5 1/2" h. (ILLUS.) **470**
Coffee, "Franklin," 3 lb. tin, image of Franklin on front & "Sugar" on back, small top,
6 x 9 1/2", some staining **1,898**

Franklin Coffee Tin

Coffee, "Franklin," 3 lb. tin, red & gold
w/lithograph of Ben Franklin (ILLUS.) **1,379**

Galt House Blend One Pound Tin

Coffee, "Galt House Blend Coffee," 1lb. tin,
paper label printed in white, red, gold &
light blue on a dark blue ground, color
scene of the Galt House Hotel in the center, dated 1908, bright colors, 4 1/4" d.,
5" h. (ILLUS.)... **495**
Coffee, "Glendora Brand Coffee," sample
tin, cylindrical w/pry-off lid, dark blue
ground printed w/white & gold w/blue &
gold wording, gold bands around top &
bottom, 2 x 3 1/4".. **47**

Golden West Coffee Tin

Coffee, "Golden West Coffee," 2 lb. key-
wind tin, red w/black band around base,
both sides depict young girl w/necker-
chief & Western-type hat, packed by
Closset & Devers, Portland, OR., dated
1927, 5 x 7" (ILLUS.).............................. **150-175**
Coffee, "Heart's Delight Coffee," 1 lb. tin,
blue w/red heart depicted in center
w/"Heart's Delight" above & "Coffee -
packed by Scoville, Brown & Co., Wells-
ville, N.Y." below, 4 1/4 x 6" **88**
Coffee, "Hoosier Boy," 1 lb. round tin, boy
w/pail of paint by fence on front & back,
paper label, 4 1/4 x 6" **431**

Ideal Brand Coffee Tin

Coffee, "Ideal Brand Coffee," 1 lb. tin
w/screw-on lid, white ground printed
w/red, dark blue & gold wording w/a color
image of a large early percolator on a
round tray w/two cups of coffee, slight
wear, 4 x 6" (ILLUS.)...................................... **143**
Coffee, "Jam-Boy," 1 lb. can, boy w/toast &
jam front & back, screw-on lid, 4 x 6 1/2"
(denting).. **173**
Coffee, "Jersey Coffee," painted salmon
w/stenciled decoration on top   front,
32" h. **850**

Lily of the Valley Coffee Can

Coffee, "Lily of the Valley," 1 lb. tin, shows lily of the valley flowers on front & back, screw-on top, Continental Can Co., 4 x 6" (ILLUS.)... **75**
Coffee, "Log Cabin," 1 lb. tin, key-wind **1,705**

Coffee, "Matchless," 1 lb. tin w/screwtop, green w/gold trim, lithograph w/coffee beans on branch, Continental Can Co., 4 x 6" (minor dings & scrapes) **242**

Matchless Coffee One Pound Tin

Coffee, "Matchless Coffee," 1 lb. tin, fitted flat cover, a dark green ground w/thin gold & red bands at the top & bottom, red & gold & black & gold wording flanks a central image of a long leafy branch of coffee blossoms & beans, minor color fading, several small dents on back, 4 x 6" (ILLUS.)... **215**

Loyl Coffee Tin

Coffee, "Loyl Coffee," 1 lb. tin w/screw top, w/splendid spread-winged eagle & clouds against blue background & marked "Loyl Coffee - Roasted and Packed For (illegible)," litho by Passaic Metal Ware, N.J., same image on reverse, 4 x 6" (ILLUS.) **275**
Coffee, "Luxury Coffee," painted yellow, stenciled top & front w/shipping stencils on ends, 32" h. **1,050**
Coffee, "Mammy's Favorite," 4 lb. pail, black woman holding tray w/steaming coffee in cup, 6 x 11"..................................... **288**

Massasoit Paper Label Coffee Can

Coffee, "Massasoit," round, paper label shows Indian on front & back, slip lid, paper loss to back, 4 1/4 x 5 1/2" (ILLUS.) **150**

Mi-Lady Coffee Deluxe Tin

Coffee, "Mi-lady Coffee Deluxe," cylindrical, lithograph w/a central oval reserve in color showing a pretty woman wearing black from the back & looking at herself in a hand-held mirror, orange background

w/black & white wording w/thin blue top &
base bands, dated 1921, minor dings &
scrapes around the sides, 4 1/4 x 6"
(ILLUS.) 242

Mister Donut Coffee Tin

Coffee, "Mister Donut Exclusive Blend Coffee," 1 lb. tin, key-wind lid, red & black
ground w/black, red & white wording & a
brown & white Mister Donut carton,
3 1/2 x 5" (ILLUS.) 275
Coffee, "Mohican," cylindrical, black, or-
ange & white, marked "The Mohican
Company Distributors, New York,"
4 1/4" w., 5 3/4" h. 121
Coffee, "Parke's Newport Coffee," 1 lb. tin,
color label in red, white & blue w/central
color scene of the factory, 4 1/4 x 6" 303

Parke's Newport Coffee Tin

Coffee, "Parke's Newport Coffee," 3 lb. tin,
color label in red, white & blue w/color
central scene of the factory, 6" d., 8" h.
(ILLUS.) 358
Coffee, "Perfect Coffee," 1 lb. tin w/screw-
on top, white w/black cover, red lettering
above logo w/"A.H. Perfect & Company"
in black letters below, dated 1923, 4 x 6"
(minor scrapes) 77

Coffee, "Planters House Brand Coffee," 1
lb. tin, pry-off lid, red ground w/white
wording & a rose & white scene of a large
hotel, minor dings & rust spots,
4 1/4 x 5 3/4" 275

Rare Roaster To Customer Coffee Tin

Coffee, "Roaster To Customer," 2 1/2 lb. tin,
cylindrical w/paper label, one side w/col-
or image of an early delivery truck, reverse has image of black Mammy &
reads "Blue Ribbon Products Co. Coffee," minor scratches & scuffs,
5 1/4 x 7 1/4" (ILLUS. of front) 578
Coffee, "Rose of Kansas," 1 lb. tin 1,018
Coffee, "Royal Dutch Coffee," 1 lb. tin,
screw-off lid, red & white large wording
w/a background design of a royal shield
& a branch of coffee beans, a band of
pearl-like bead bands at the rim & base,
4 x 6 1/4" (minor fading, few scrapes &
dings) 66

Royal Quality Steel Cut Coffee Tin

Coffee, "Royal Quality Steel Cut Coffee," 1 lb. tin, lithographed design w/a white ground & a red, blue & gold central coat-of-arms, wording in blue, red & gold, 4 x 6" (ILLUS.).. **69**

Coffee, "San Marto Coffee," 1 lb. tin, screw-on lid, gold ground w/bold red wording, the front w/an image of a knight on horse-back, the back w/a shield emblem, 4 x 6" (minor fading) **220**

Coffee, "Sanico," 1 lb. tin, Piggly Wiggly Store brand.. **1,485**

Serv-Us Coffee Tin

Coffee, "Serv-Us Coffee," 1 lb. tin, screw-on lid, red ground w/white & blue wording, blue-trimmed white cup & saucer of coffee at bottom, excellent condition, 4 x 6" (ILLUS.).. **77**

Strong-Heart Coffee Tin

Coffee, "Strong-Heart Brand Coffee," 1 lb. tin, pry-off lid, yellow ground w/black

print, a center oval reserve w/a color bust portrait of a Native American chief, minor scrapes & dings, 4 1/4 x 5 3/4" (ILLUS.)...... **264**

Coffee, "Swansdown," 1 lb. tin, swan pictured on front, snap-on top, Enterprise Stamping Co., 4 1/4 x 6 1/4" (some blemishes) **173**

Coffee, "Swell Blend Chautauqua Brand Coffee," 1 lb. tin, pry-off lid, decorated w/a large dark blue shaped panel enclosing gold & white wording around a center oval reserve showing a steamship, 4 x 6" (minor scuffs & dings) **215**

Coffee, "Table King," 1 lb. tin **963**

Coffee, "Turkey," 1 lb. tin, trademark turkey on both sides, screw-on lid, 4 x 6" (dents)..... **460**

Rare Large Turkey Coffee Tin

Coffee, "Turkey Brand Coffee," 3 lb. tin, tall cylindrical form w/red wording on tan ground w/central brown & red picture of a large turkey, minor dents & scuffs, 5 1/2 x 10 3/4" (ILLUS.) **1,650**

Coffee, "Twin Ports Steel Cut Coffee," 1 lb. tin, screw-on lid, white label w/a large oval reserve w/the brand name in blue above a color scene of a large steamship, other wording in red & blue below w/a blue band around the bottom, dated 1923, 4 x 6" (scrapes & dings) **171**

Coffee, "Welcome Guest," 1 lb. tin (missing lid) **1,705**

Coffee, "WGY Coffee," 1 lb. tin w/screw-on top, litho by Continental Can, Passaic, N.J., both sides w/image of table set w/coffeepot & cup & saucer, blue, tan, black & white, 4 x 6" (minor scrapes near bottom) **132**

Motor oil, "Ace Wil-Flo," 1 qt. tin **130**

Motor oil, "Ben Hur," 1 qt. can, red w/white
& black lettering, Ben Hur Oil Co., Los
Angeles - New Orleans, 4" d., 5 1/2" h.
(minor scratches & staining) 165
Motor oil, "Black Bear," 5 gal. tin, depicts
black bear beside "Black Bear Motor Oil,
SHDX 10W-30," black lettering on deep
orange background, 11" d., 16" h. (dents
& scratches) 72

Scarce Blakely Motor Oil Tin

Motor oil, "Blakely Special 10-30 Heavy
Duty Motor Oil," 1 qt. tin, red ground
w/yellow & silver wording, a center color
image of a race car & checkered yellow &
black flag, text on reverse panels, Arizo-
na-based company, full, very light flat
spot on front, few scattered nicks &
dings, scarce (ILLUS.) 468
Motor oil, "Camel Penn," 1 qt. tin (top re-
placed) 798
Motor oil, "Clipper Penn," 1 qt. tin, name in
large red letters w/a dark green four-en-
gine plane flying between the words on a
white ground, "Motor Oil" in green below
name & above wavy green bottom band
w/"100% Pure Pennsylvania...," 5 1/2" h.
(top missing, minor scratches & denting)... 1,100
Motor oil, "Conoco," 1 gal. tin, upright rectangular form, the sides w/the name in
large blue letters above & below the
standing color profile of a Minuteman all
on a cream ground, the rest of the tin in
dark yellow, original caps, 3 x 8",
11 1/4" h. (paint loss, scratches, soiling,
denting) 1,375
Motor oil, "Conoco," 1/2 gal. tin, man in
Revolutionary period clothing next to
"Conoco, Motorine, Medium, The Continental Oil Company" on pale yellow &
light blue striped background, 8" w.,
6 1/4" h. (minor surface rust, paint chip-
ping & scratches) 275
Motor oil, "Deep Rock Prize," 1 qt. tin 55
Motor oil, "Exceloyl Oils," 1 qt. tin 130
Motor oil, "Ford & Sears, Roebuck," 5 gal.
upright square tin w/a rectangular panel

on one side w/an orange background &
black wording & a black & white scene of
two autos in a village, reads "Special -
Automobile Oil - for - Ford Cars - Sears,
Roebuck and Co.," 9 1/4" sq., 14 1/2" h.
(denting, rust spotting, scratches, soiling)..... 578

Rare French Auto Oil One Gallon Tin

Motor oil, "French Auto Oil," 1 gal. tin, upright rectangular form w/two top spouts &
ring handle, one side w/a large rectangular red-bordered yellow panel enclosing a
green- and red-bordered white ring reading "Marshall Oil Co. - Distributers,
U.S.A.," & enclosing a racing scene in
green & black w/an early race car speeding past a grandstand, center overprinted
w/a large red arrow & "French Auto Oil,"
minor scratches & denting, 3 x 8",
10 3/4" h. (ILLUS.) 2,310

Grand Champion Two Gallon Oil Tin

Motor oil, "Grand Champion," 2 gal. tin, upright rectangular form w/top strap handle & screw-on cap on spout, colorful scene of cartoon-style race cars & drivers racing around a track w/a large red banner across the top w/the brand name in large white letters, minor scratches & wear overall, one heavy scratch on back (ILLUS.) **226**

Motor oil, "Hancock ATF Type A," 1 qt. tin, one side lists 1948-51 car models & fill table **350**

Motor oil, "Hudson," 1 qt. tin, features numerous images of cars, airplanes & a tanker.. **525**

Motor oil, "Husky Hi-Lub," 1 qt. tin **235**

Jay-Bee Motor Oil Underseat Tin

Motor oil, "Jay-Bee Motor Oil," 1 qt. rectangular underseat-style tin, loop bail handle at center of flat top w/straight & angled spouts w/screw-on caps, orange background w/white wording centering the company logo, manufacturer's name in small black wording at the bottom, handsoldered, very minor nicks, scratches & rubs, 2 3/4 x 5 3/4", 4 3/4" h. (ILLUS.) **358**

Motor oil, "Mobiloil," 1 qt. tin, white label w/"Gargoyle" (motif of gargoyle) above "Mobiloil 'B' Extra Heavy," made by Vacuum Oil Company, New York, U.S.A., 3 1/2" d., 7 1/2" h. (scratches, soiling & denting) **154**

Rare Husky Motor Oil Tin

Motor oil, "Husky Motor Oil," 1 qt. tin, color scene of a brown & black Husky in a snowy landscape w/Northern Lights behind him, product name in gold on blue around the top, very minor scratches (ILLUS.) **770**

Motor oil, "Indian," 1 gal. tin, upright rectangular form w/top strap handle & spout w/cap, dark green ground w/a red, black & white profile of Native American in a circle over "Indian Oil" in large red letters above "100% Pure Pennsylvania - Especially Made by the Valvoline Oil Company - New York U.S.A. - for the - Indian Motocycle Company - Springfield, Mass." in small white & black lettering, 3 x 8", 11 1/4" h. (very minor scratches, denting & soiling) **2,090**

Motor oil, "Indian," 1/2 pt. tin, two cycle, red & white, 2 1/2" d., 3 1/2" h. (minor denting & spotting to lid).. **220**

Unusual Mobiloil Conical Tin

Motor oil, "Mobiloil," tall slender conical 2 1/2 gal. tin, small spout at top, white ground w/thin red border bands, black wording & a red gargoyle logo, foreignmade, probably pre-1931, overall soiling & scuffs, rusting & dents, 11" d., 21" h. (ILLUS.)... **226**

Motor oil, "Mona," 1/2 gal. tin, 6" h. **235**

Motor oil, "Oilzum Motor Oil," 1 qt. tin, white ground w/triangular orange company logo w/man's head, blue band w/white wording near base, small blue

wording at bottom reads "Choice of
Champions" (minor dents, nicks &
dings, yellowing).. 83
Motor oil, "Opaline," 1 gal. tin, upright rectangular form w/spouts & strap handle on
top, the sides w/a large rectangular reserve in cream bordered w/a thin green
line, a large black, white & green early
race car charging forward above "Opaline - Motor Oil - Sinclair Refining Company - Chicago" in green & blue lettering, 3 x 8", 11" h. (minor paint chips &
soiling).. 1,760
Motor oil, "Penn-Empire," 5 gal. tin, upright
drum-shaped w/loop at bottom to keep
from rolling, spout & loop handle at the
top, the side printed w/a gold ring w/white
wording reading "Penn-Empire Motor Oil"
enclosing a black ring & an inner gold circle printed "Penn - Empire" & small wording, 8 1/2 x 14", 16 1/2" h. (rust spotting,
denting, scratches & soiling)....................... 446
Motor oil, "Pequot Chief Motor Oil," 1/2 gal.
tin, 6 1/4" h.. 220
Motor oil, "Phillips Higrade," 1/2 gal. tin,
long rectangular form, top strap handle &
spout w/screw-on cap, the sides w/round
logo above "Higrade Motor Oil" in red
above "Medium" in black all on a white
ground, 3 1/4 x 8", 6 1/4" h. (denting, rust
spotting, scratches & soiling) 187

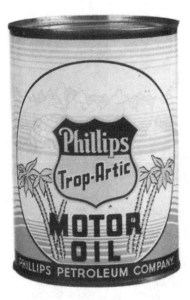

Rare Phillips Trop-Artic Oil Tin

Motor oil, "Phillips Trop-Artic," 1 qt. tin,
shaded striped pale green to orange
ground w/a large center oval reserve
w/an igloo scene above tall palm trees
w/the Phillips shield logo in the center in
green & black above "Motor Oil" in black,
very minor denting & surface rust, soiling
down spine, 5 1/2" h. (ILLUS.)....................... 715

Rare One Gallon Polarine Tin

Motor oil, "Polarine," 1 gal. tin, upright rectangular form w/hand grip, strap handle &
spout w/cap on top, one side w/a large
rectangular panel w/"Polarine - For Motor
Lubrication" in large blue script & white
letters in a blue banner above a pastel
color hilly landscape scene w/a beachside village in the distance & an early
long open roadster in the foreground,
"Standard Oil Company - (New Jersey)"
in blue at the bottom, early 20th c., denting, fading, paint chips,   3 x 7 3/4",
10 3/4" h. (ILLUS.)..................................... 2,090
Motor oil, "Premier Ranger," 1 qt. tin............... 120
Motor oil, "Red Hat," 1 gal. tin, upright rectangular w/top strap handle & spout
w/cap, the sides w/a dark blue ring
around a red Uncle Sam-type top hat w/a
blue hatband w/white stars, blue & white
wording reads "Approved - Red Hat - Motor Oil," further wording in small letters at
the bottom,   3 x 8",   11 1/4" h. (minor
scratches & denting) 2,090
Motor oil, "Ronson," 1 qt. tin......................... 1,375
Motor oil, "Shell Company of California," 1
gal. tin, 11" h. 400
Motor oil, "Shell/Roxana Petroleum Corp.,"
1 gal. tin, 11" h., rare.................................... 600
Motor oil, "Signal Motor Oil/Penn," 1 qt. tin
(top lid missing).. 210
Motor oil, "Sinclair Opaline," 1/2 gal. tin
w/"Enterprise Stamping Co. Pittsburgh,
PA" at bottom edges & "Sinclair Refining
Company Chicago" on side (paint chips
& scratches)... 550
Motor oil, "Speedol," 1 qt. tin, a front-on
view of an airplane above the name in
large red letters all on a white ground, a
wavy blue band at the bottom w/"Motor
Oil," 5 1/2" h. (minor scratches, soiling to
top of rim)... 341

Spinner Motor Oil Tin

Motor oil, "Spinner Motor Oil," cylindrical 1
qt. tin, yellow & red, both sides w/image
of top & marked "Spinner Motor Oil - 35¢
- Top Oil Co. Lubrock, Tex.," punched at
bottom, minor nicks & rubs (ILLUS.) **231**
Motor oil, "Texaco," 1 qt. tin, gold wrap
w/"Texaco, Synthetic Aircraft, Turbine
Oil, 35" & orange & black logo, 4" d.,
5 1/2" h. (denting & scratches) **220**
Motor oil, "Texaco," 1 qt. tin, green w/"Texaco 574 Oil" above Texaco star logo,
made by The Texas Company, Port
Arthur, Texas, minor scratches & dent-
ing, 3 3/4" d., 6 1/4" h. **121**
Motor oil, "Texaco Medium," handi-grip 1/2
gal. tin, 6 1/2" h. **220**

Trop-Artic Auto Oil Tin

Motor oil, "Tro-Artic Auto Oil," 1/2 gal. tin,
lithograph of scene of tropical island
w/car parked near palm tree, Manhattan
Oil Co., minor denting & scratches,
3 x 8", 6" h. (ILLUS.)..................................... **1,210**
Motor oil, "Trop-Artic," 1 gal. upright rectan-
gular tin w/spout & cap & ring handle, one
side w/a large rectangular color panel
showing at the top a mountainous arctic
landscape w/closed touring car & at the

lower half a tropical landscape w/palm
trees & a larger closed touring car, large
red wording curves across the center,
"Manhattan Oil Co." in black across the
bottom, 3 x 8", 10 1/2" h. (minor scratch-
es & soiling) **3,520**
Motor oil, "Veedol," 5 gal. tin in wooden
box, tin w/early touring car on one side,
box marked "Veedol Motor Oil - Tidewa-
ter Oil Co. New York," 8 1/2" h. can, box
11 1/2 x 15" (minor scratches on can,
fading to lettering on box)............................... **314**
Motor oil, "Vulcan," 1 qt. tin............................ **65**
Motor oil, "Wolf's Head Lube," 1 lb. keywind
tin, full **50**

Zephyr Motor Oil Tin

Motor oil, "Zephyr Motor Oil - Guaranteed
100% Paraffine Base," 1 qt. tin, dark orange background w/white angled band
w/brand name in orange, other wording
in dark blue, dark blue base band w/man-
ufacturer's name & address in white, full,
very minor nicks & dings (ILLUS.) **99**

Planters Novola Peanut Oil Tin

Oil, "Planters Peanuts," 5 gal. tin, Novola peanut oil, blue label w/red border (ILLUS.).................................. **225-425**

Ointment, "Petrolina," depicts oil derricks in black & red graphics, 3" w., 3" deep, 4" h. **33**

Peanut butter, "FI-NA-ST Peanut Butter," cov. 1 lb. tin pail, bail handle, image of a man wearing a white coat on both sides by First National Stores, Somerville, Massachusetts, 3 3/8 x 3 3/4"........................ **143**

Peanut butter, "Kamo," 25 lb. store bin, back & front depicts a duck, 9 3/4 x 10 1/2" (professionally restored) **288**

Monadnock Peanut Butter Tin

Peanut butter, "Monadnock Peanut Butter," 1 lb. tin w/bail handle, litho by Canco, red w/gold scrolls flanking white ground w/center oval mountain lake scene & marked "1 Lb. Net Monadnock Brand Peanut Butter - Distributed by The Holbrook Grocery Co. Keene, N.H.," same image on reverse, 3 1/2 x 3 3/4" (ILLUS.) **198**

Peanut butter, "Mosemann's," 1 lb. tin.............. **115**

Peanut butter, "Ontario Brand Peanut Butter" pail, blue design on light greenish blue background, marked "Oswego Candy Works Inc. Oswego, New York," 3 1/2" d., 3 3/4" h. **55**

Planters Peanut Butter Tin

Peanut butter, "Planters," 1 lb. tin (ILLUS.) .. **5,170**

Peanut butter, "Planters," 25 lb. pail w/Mr. Peanut decoration **874**

Peanut butter, "Planters Peanuts," 1 lb. tin pail, Mr. Peanut circus w/lid **775-800**

Red Seal Peanut Butter Pail

Peanut butter, "Red Seal," 10 oz. tin pail w/bail handle & slip lid, decorated w/nursery rhyme scenes around sides, "The Newton Tea & Spice Co. Cincinnati, Ohio" at bottom, rust to lid & handle, scratches & paint chips, 3 x 3 1/2" (ILLUS.)... **121**

Peanut butter, "Sultana," 1 lb. pail.............. **80**

Peanut butter, "Toyland," 1 lb. pail, parade scene, 3 1/2 x 4" (dent & litho chips)............. **127**

Veribest Peanut Butter Tin

Peanut butter, "Veribest," 12 oz. pail w/bail handle, marked in oval "Armour's Veribest Peanut Butter - Armour And Company - General Offices, Chicago," lithographed fairy tale characters shown around sides, product information on lid, Continental Can Co. Chicago, Illinois, minor edge wear rust spotting, scratches & soiling, 3 1/2" d., 3" h. (ILLUS.) **105**

Spice, "A & P Sultana," tall cylindrical form w/fitted cap, pale yellow ground printed in black w/name & a bust portrait of an elderly lady above "Take Grandmother's Advice - Use A. & P Spices," excellent condition, 3 1/4 x 7 1/4"...................................... **33**

Spice, "Amocat Spice," 2 oz. tin, red, both sides w/center oval scene of a house near water, hills in background, marked "Net Weight - 2 Ounces - Amocat Brand - Ginger," West Coast Grocery, Tacoma, Washington, litho by American Can Co., 1 x 2 x 3"... **132**

Spice, "Blue Jewel," 1 1/2 oz. tin, white w/two blue stripes & blue jewel, tin top & bottom, cardboard body, wrap-around paper label, Jewel Food Stores, Inc. **30-65**

Spice, "Busy Biddy Pure Spices - Ground Allspice," upright narrow rectangular form w/the front printed in red, white & black w/a center circle w/a color picture of a native carrying a basket of spices, a hen logo on the side, 2 x 3"............................ **77**

Spice, "Country Club," light green, country club building flying the American flag,The Kroger Grocery & Baking Co. **75-125**

Spice, "Durkee's," 1 1/4 oz. lithographed tin, white & green w/baked turkey on platter, Durkee Famous Foods **20-45**

Spice, "Early Dinner," 2 1/2 oz. tin, dark blue & white, two couples at dinner table w/waiter serving them, dress is early 1900s, Peyton-Palmer Co..................... **100-200**

Spice, "Farmers Pride," 1 1/2 oz. tin, red, white haired man seated in chair wearing straw hat w/arm around shoulders of young girl standing beside him holding a doll, tin top & bottom, cardboard body, wrap-around paper label, Hulman & Co. ... **50-90**

Spice, "French's," 2 oz. round lithographed tin, tan w/French's red flag flying from black staff,The R.T. French Co. **25-55**

Spice, "Gold Bond," 2 oz. tin, red & gold w/"Gold Bond" in white circle, tin top & bottom, cardboard body, wrap-around paper label, Jewett & Sherman Co. **20-45**

Spice, "Golden Drip," 2 oz. lithographed tin, gold w/"Golden Drip" in black, Empire Distributing Co. **30-60**

Spice, "Golden Key," 4 oz. tin, round, yellow, skeleton key & "Golden Key" in white .. **25-55**

Spice, "Grand Prize," 2 oz. lithographed tin, ivory w/four bands of dark blue w/"Grand Prize" on one blue band, red prize ribbon & "spices" written in red, Empire Distributing Company **25-55**

Spice, "H & H," 2 oz. tin, green rectangular label w/Art Deco marking, company name on banner at bottom, The Harnit & Hewitt Co. **30-60**

Spice, "H & K," 1 1/2 oz. tin, red w/four ivory bands, man wearing turban holding tray w/coffee pot, sugar bowl & cup in blue circle, tin top & bottom, cardboard body, wrap-around paper label, Hanley & Kinsella Coffee & Spice Co. **30-65**

Spice, "Happy Hour," 1 3/4 oz. tin, yellow, pink, & blue w/"Happy Hour," written in white, wrap-around paper label, Campbell Holton & Co. **10-35**

Hazel Spice Tin

Spice, "Hazel," tin top & bottom, cardboard body, wrap-around paper label, Geo. Rasmussen Co., 2 oz. (ILLUS.) **75-125**

Spice, "Hoosier Poet," distinguished gentleman w/wire-rimmed glasses, green fields, trees & dirt road, tin top & bottom, cardboard body, pasted-on paper label, M. O'Connor & Co., 1 1/2 oz. **30-60**

Spice, "Hostess," 2 1/2 oz. tin, red, center oval w/four ladies seated at table w/waiter standing by, Paul D. Newton & Co., Inc. **95-225**

Spice, "Hub City," 1 1/2 oz. lithographed tin, black & red w/outline of state of Wisconsin in gold, red circle in center of state w/"Hub City," Hub City Jobbing Co. **30-60**

Spice, "Iris," 1 1/4 oz. lithographed tin, black & white w/purple iris on green stem, Smart & Final Iris Co................................. **10-30**

Pretty Iris Spice Tin

Spice, "Iris Brand Marjoram," 2 oz. tin, flattened upright rectangular form, pry-off lid, dark ground w/a large blue & yellow iris w/green leaves w/wording in gold, white & black, red top & bottom trim bands, 2 1/4 x 3 1/4" (ILLUS.) **121**

Spice, "Jack Sprat," light yellow w/Jack Sprat in green outfit, red bows at knees, light blue knee socks, tan moccasins, black & green hat, carrying plate & silverware in one hand & glass in other, tin top & bottom, cardboard body, wrap-around paper label, Western Grocer Mills, 1 1/2 oz. **35-75**

Spice, "K-W-G," 2 oz. lithographed tin, light yellow & gold w/green wreath & light blue ribbon, "K-W-G" in red lettering across wreath, Kansas Wholesale Grocery Co. ... **30-65**

Little Boy Blue Spice Tin

Spice, "Little Boy Blue," 1 1/2 oz. lithographed tin, Lansing Wholesale Grocery Co. (ILLUS.) **45-70**

Spice, "Maison Royal," 1 oz. lithographed tin, white & red w/bridge spanning river w/outline of city behind, Food Trading Corp. of America **10-45**

Spice, "McCannon's," yellow, green & black w/black person dressed in white wearing red turban leading pack camel, two palm trees & red sun w/sand underfoot, all on yellow background, tin top & bottom, cardboard body, wrap-around paper label, McConnon & Co., 3 1/4 oz. **25-55**

King Crop Spice Tin

Spice, "King Crop," 2 oz. lithographed tin, Lawndale Wholesale Grocery Co. (ILLUS.) **125-225**

Spice, "KO-WE-BA," 1 oz., white w/two men leading camels, red diamond shape at top w/"KO-WE-BA" & butterfly in it, tin top & bottom, cardboard body, wrap-around paper label, Kothe-Wells & Bauer Co. **20-45**

Spice, "L-C-B," 1 1/2 oz. tin, white w/"L-C-B" in red & gold band at top & bottom, head of bulldog in blue circle in center of tin, other lettering is black, Lyle C. Brown Supply Co. **15-35**

Spice, "Leadway," 2 oz. tin, ivory & red w/dark blue arrow pointed down w/band major in full dress, "Leadway" in black letters w/red arrow through letters on ivory stripe, Leadway Foods **35-65**

McCormick Spice Tin

Spice, "McCormick," 7/8 oz. lithographed tin, McCormick & Co., Inc. (ILLUS.) **15-45**

Spice, "Millar," white w/three red flowers, green stems & leaves, tin top & bottom, cardboard body, wrap-around paper label, E.B. Millar & Co., 2 oz. **25-50**

Spice, "Mohican," 2 oz. lithographed tin, red & black, Indian in full headdress within white circle trimmed in light blue & red in center of tin, The Mohican Company **100-150**

Spice, "Monarch," 1 1/2 oz. tin, ivory background w/lion head in center, lettering in black, Reid, Murdoch & Co. **45-80**

Spice, "Monday's," 4 oz. lithographed tin, white, black, light blue & pink, lettering in black w/white & light blue background, The P.C. Monday Tea Co. **25-55**

Spice, "National," 1 1/2 oz. tin, round w/capitol building in center & American flag to right, "National" is red, white & blue, Geo. Rasmussen Co. **55-100**

Spice, "Old Judge," 4 oz., red & yellow background w/brown & yellow owl sitting on green branch in blue circle in center of tin, tin top & bottom, cardboard body, wrap-around paper label, David G. Evans Coffee Co.. **20-45**

Spice, "Old Manor," 2 oz. lithographed tin, red w/manor house in white & green trees on yellow background in center of tin, white lettering, Coffee Industries, Inc. ... **25-55**

Spice, "Our Family," 2 oz., white & dark blue, silhouette of lady's head in dark blue on white background, "Our Family" in white on dark blue background, other lettering in red, tin top & bottom, cardboard body, wrap-around paper label, Nash-Finch Co., 2 oz. **30-65**

Spice, "Red Label," 4 oz. lithographed tin, red w/eagle on top of white bordered shield, lion on each side, S.S. Pierce Co. ... **30-65**

Spice, "Red Plume," 1 1/2 oz. tin, red w/green pasted-on paper label, w/red plume & black lettering, The C. Callahan Co. **15-35**

Spice, "Red Ribbon," 1 1/2 oz. lithographed tin, white w/red ribbon tied in bow in center of tin, "Red Ribbon" in red, other lettering is light blue, J.M. Steiner, Inc. **25-55**

Royal Crown Spice Tin

Spice, "Royal Crown," tin top & bottom, cardboard body, wrap-around paper label, Albert Paper & Products Co., 2 oz. (ILLUS.)... **45-95**

Spice, "Safe Owl," 1 1/4 oz. lithographed tin, white w/red lettering, head of brown owl at bottom of tin, blue center w/celery seed letters in white, Safe Owl Products, Inc. **15-35**

Spice, "Silver Sea," 1 1/2 oz. lithographed tin, dark blue & yellow w/sailing ship in full sail on choppy sea in circle at center of tin, The Koenig Coffee Co. **25-55**

Spice, "Slade's," 3/4 oz. lithographed tin, light blue w/man dressed in white leading brown pack camel & three camels & palm trees in black at bottom of tin, D. & L. Slade Co. **35-60**

Spice, "Stickney & Poor's," 2 oz. lithographed tin, yellow w/sailing ship in full sail on blue sea................................ **25-55**

Spice, "Stuart's Handy," 2 oz. lithographed tin, Stuart Products, Inc. **60-90**

Spice, "Sunny Rose," 3 oz. lithographed tin, red lettering, pure spices in large blue circle & red band at bottom w/company name, Sunny Rose Stores **25-55**

Spice, "Tea Table," 1 1/2 oz. lithographed tin, table w/two chairs on veranda set for tea, including teapot, cups & saucers, sugar bowl, bouquet of red flowers, sea in background, striped awning overhead, Peyton Palmer Co. **100-150**

Pilot Spice Tin

Spice, "Pilot," 1 1/2 oz. tin, General Grocer Co. (ILLUS.)... **50-100**

Spice, "Pine Hills," orange hill w/green pine trees & grass at top w/light yellow sky, black lettering, tin top & bottom, cardboard body, wrap-around paper label, Schultz Brothers Co., 1 oz. **25-50**

Spice, "Quaker," 1 1/2 oz. lithographed tin, red band between white & dark blue bands, Quaker lady in dark dress & hat trimmed in white holding tin in right hand w/left hand on hip, Lee & Cady **15-35**

Spice, "Radio," 1 1/2 oz. tin, yellow w/black band & "Radio" in white, white band at bottom w/company name in red, McKnight-Keaton Grocery Co.......................... **25-55**

Spice, "Telmo," in white lettering on red band across tan circle, tin top & bottom, cardboard body, wrap-around paper label, Franklin MacVeagh & Co., 1 1/2 oz. ... **15-35**

Spice, "Three Crow," 3 oz. lithographed tin, yellow w/red & black lettering, three black crows sitting on wooden fence in circle at center of tin, The Atlantic Spice Co. **35-65**

Spice, "Time O'Day," 2 oz. lithographed tin, clock w/Roman numerals in center of tin, green band at top w/"Time O'Day" in ivory lettering, bottom of tin is ivory w/red & black lettering, Jordan Stevens Co. **30-65**

Spice, "Triangle Club," 1/4 lb., green & white striped background w/red triangle, white lettering across triangle, tin top & bottom, cardboard body, wrap-around paper label, Montgomery Ward & Co. **35-65**

Spice, "Trumpet," 2 oz., red, gold trumpet w/blue cord attached, tin top & bottom, cardboard body, wrap-around paper label, H.P. Coffee Co., 2 oz. **25-55**

Spice, "University," 1 oz. lithographed tin, Eisner Grocery Company (ILLUS.) **35-65**

Spice, "Van Roy," 3 1/2 oz., red & black, half sun w/rays in red background, white lettering in black background, tin top & bottom, cardboard body, wrap-around paper label, The Van Roy Coffee Co., 3 1/2 oz. **45-75**

Spice, "Wards," 3 3/4 oz. lithographed tin, round, palm trees & two sailboats on calm sea, green mountain & white clouds in background, The Ward Co. **15-35**

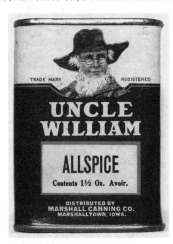

White Villa Spice Tin

Spice, "White Villa," 1 oz. lithographed tin, White Villa Grocers, Inc. (ILLUS.) **25-50**

Tobacco, "American Blend," pocket tin, made for German immigrant market **1,595**

Tobacco, "Bishop's Move Tobacco," horizontal pocket tin, rectangular w/rounded corners, lid printed in red & white on a black ground w/a chess queen & bishop on a checkered board, printed in white across the bottom edge "A Unique Blend of Rare Quality," slight wear, 2 1/4 x 3 1/4" **44**

Tobacco, "Boar's Head," store bin **210**

Tobacco, "Buckingham Bright Cut Plug," trial size, 3/4 x 2 1/4 x 3" (few scrapes)........... **176**

Tobacco, "Buckingham Cut Plug Smoking Tobacco," large cylindrical tin, pry-off cover, brightly printed wording in gold, blue & red on a dark brown ground, 5 x 5" **44**

Tobacco, "Buckingham," pocket tin **95**

Uncle William Spice Tin

Spice, "Uncle William," 1 1/2 oz., tin top & bottom, cardboard body, wrap-around paper label, Marshall Canning Co., 1 1/2 oz. (ILLUS.).. **100-150**

Burley Boy Tobacco Tin

Tobacco, "Burley Boy" (Bagley's), little boxer boy on each side, ring latch & bail han-

University Spice Tin

dle, paint chips & scratches, 5 x 6 1/2", 4" h. (ILLUS.) **1,650**
Tobacco, "Cameron," lithographed gold & black design on red w/green vertical center band, marked "Fine Tobacco Mix," hinged lid, Cameron & Cameron Co., Richmond, VA, 3 1/4" w., 4 1/2" l., 2" h. (very minor paint chips to edges, scratches & soiling) **83**
Tobacco, "Dill's Best Cut Plug," 3 1/4 x 4 1/4" **45**
Tobacco, "Dixie Queen," canister, Southern belle decoration on front & back, knobbed lid, 4 x 6 1/2" **201**
Tobacco, "Dixie Queen," lunch box **127**
Tobacco, "Dixie Queen," Roly Poly Satisfied Customer (ILLUS. top center w/Mayo's Roly Poly tins) **975**
Tobacco, "Donniford," pocket tin **90**

es, rust marks on bottom & lid, 3/4 x 3", 4 1/4" h. (ILLUS.) **385**
Tobacco, "Fountain," round canister, slip lid, image of fountain on both sides, 5 1/4 x 6 1/4" **115**

Game Fine Cut Store Bin

Tobacco, "Game Fine Cut Tobacco," store bin, depicts scene w/quail on both sides, 7 1/4 x 8 x 11 1/2" (ILLUS.) **975-1,200**

1920s Hi-Plane Tobacco Pocket Tin

Tobacco, "Hi-Plane Smooth Cut Tobacco," vertical pocket tin, red ground w/white & blue wording & a flying 1920s airplane, excellent condition, 3 x 4 1/2" (ILLUS.) **132**

Various Lunch Box Tins

Tobacco, "Fashion Cut Plug," 1 lb. lunch box, scene of fasionably dressed couple on side, bail handle (ILLUS. top left) **254**

Forest & Stream Tobacco Tin

Tobacco, "Forest & Stream," two-sided w/hinged lid, illustrated on both sides w/scene of two fishermen & a dog in a canoe, paper label seal on top, by Imperial Tobacco Co. of Canada Limited Factory No. 1 Port 23-D, paint loss & scratch-

Unopened Hi-Plane Tobacco Tin

Tobacco, "Hi-Plane Smooth Cut Tobacco," vertical pocket tin, red ground w/white wordings & image of 1950s airplane, full & unopened, 3 x 4 1/2", 1" deep (ILLUS.)..... **215**

Tobacco, "Hi-Plane" (twin engine), pocket tin.................. **225**

Tobacco, "Himyar Tobacco Tin," scene of man on white horse & marked "Himyar Cigarette Tobacco," intact w/cigarette papers under tax stamp, same image on reverse, 5 1/4 x 6 1/2", 14 oz. **121**

Tobacco, "Hindoo," w/colorful graphic of a snake charmer **1,100**

Tobacco, "Honest Scrap," store bin, slant-top hinged lid, arm gripping hammer shown on each side, front lithograph of outdoor scene w/dog & cat fighting over box marked "Honest Scrap," some paint chips & crazing, hinge separated from lid, 14 1/4 x 18", 12" h. **2,310**

Tobacco, "Honeymoon," depicting a couple cuddling on a crescent moon.......... **852**

Honeymoon Tobacco Pocket Tin

Tobacco, "Honeymoon Rum-Flavored Tobacco," vertical pocket tin, red ground w/gold & white wording, center circle w/a young man seated on a crescent moon looking up at the face of a young woman, 3 x 4 1/2", 1" deep (ILLUS.) **198**

J.J. Bagley Chewing Tobacco Tin

Tobacco, "J.J. Bagley & Co. Chewing Tobacco Fast Mail," w/paper label showing an early train engine (ILLUS.)............ **2,420**

Kim-Bo Vertical Pocket tin

Tobacco, "Kim-Bo Cut Plug," pocket tin, young girl pictured on front, cardboard w/tin top & bottom, Lovell & Buffington Tobacco Co., Covington, Kentucky, complete w/contents, 1910 Revenue Stamp & Union Stamp, 1 x 2 1/4 x 4 1/2" (ILLUS.)........... **385**

Tobacco, "Mayo's," Roly Poly Dutchman (ILLUS. bottom right)..................... **333**

Tobacco, "Mayo's," Roly Poly Inspector (ILLUS. bottom left) **711**

Tobacco, "Mayo's," Roly Poly Mammy (ILLUS. top right) **664**

Tobacco, "Mayo's," Roly Poly Singing Waiter (ILLUS. bottom center)............ **336**

Various Roly Poly Tobacco Tins

Tobacco, "Mayo's," Roly Poly Store Keeper (ILLUS. top left)............... **445**

Niggerhair Smoking Tobacco Tin

Tobacco, "Niggerhair Smoking Tobacco," gold & black w/bail handle, pictures African native w/ear & nose rings on both sides, by Leiderdoft Co., Milwaukee, The American Tobacco Co. Successor, 5 1/2 x 6 1/2" (ILLUS.) 231

Tobacco, "Ojibwa," store bin, cardboard w/tin top & bottom, front & back decorated w/scene of Indian on shore beckoning to Indians in canoe, contains three packs of tobacco, 6 1/2 x 8 x 11" (section of paper missing bottom rear) 173

Tobacco, "Old Colony" (Bagley's), sample tin w/original tax stamp 686

Tobacco, "Pastime," store bin, lithographed scene of man on horse inside lid, 4 x 9 1/4 x 12 1/2" (litho flaking, fading & litho chips to sides) 115

Tobacco, "Peachey," vertical pocket tin 115

Tobacco, "Pedro Cut Plug," rectangular w/dome lid & bail handle, lithographed on top & sides showing corn cob pipe on one end & peace pipe on other w/"John Q. Adam 1910 U.S. Inter Rev." & "Factory No. 2 District of MD... Patent Applied for," part of original seal on side, 5 x 7 3/4", 4 1/2" h. (paint chips, denting, edge wear & soiling) 88

Tobacco, "Pennsylvania Ensign Perfection Cut" 687

Pilot Cigarette Tobacco Tin

Tobacco, "Pilot Cigarette Tobacco," cylindrical w/screw-on lid, decorated w/a small flying plane spelling out the word "Pilot" in white above red wording "Cigarette Tobacco" & a red dot w/the price, all on a light tan ground, 4 1/2 x 4 1/2" (ILLUS.) 55

Plow Boy Store Bin

Tobacco, "Plow Boy," slant-top store bin, sides & front decorated w/scene of man sitting on a plow & smoking (ILLUS.) 1,694

Tobacco, "Poker Club Mixture," square-corner, showing a straight flush, S. F. Hess & Co., 1 1/2 x 3 x 4 1/2" (some fading) 138

Tobacco, "Polar Bear," store bin (damage to one side & back) 455

Tobacco, "Sam's Own Mixture," rectangular w/dog depicted on front, England, 1 x 3 x 4 1/4" 44

Tobacco, "Stag Tobacco," vertical pocket tin w/stag depicted on both sides, 3/4 x 2 5/8 x 3 1/2" 121

Tobacco, "Stanwik," pocket tin 450

Tobacco, "Staple Grain Plug Cut," pocket tin 431

Tobacco, "Sterling Light," store bin, round, logo on front, pack on back, silver & green, 8 x 12" (dents) 230

Sure Shot Chewing Tobacco Tin

Tobacco, "Sure Shot," opens at top w/lithographed scene of Native American w/bow & arrow & marked "Sure Shot - Chewing Tobacco - It Touches The Spot," some denting, edge wear, scratches & soiling, 15 1/2" w., 10 1/4" l., 7" h. (ILLUS.) 440

Tobacco, "Sweet Burley Dark," store bin, round w/square top, pack on back, red, 8 1/2 x 11 1/2" 230

Tobacco, "Sweet Burley," store bin, yellow & red, marked "Light - Sweet Burley - Tobacco," minor dings, 8 1/2 x 10 3/4" 215
Tobacco, "Sweet Cuba," slant-front store bin, green w/bust of woman 155
Tobacco, "Sweet Mist," store bin 333

Tiger "Blue" Store Bin

Tobacco, "Tiger Blue," round store bin, tiger on front & pack on back, 8 1/2 x 11 1/2" (ILLUS.) **1,610**
Tobacco, "Trout-Line," scene of fisherman **707**

Tucketts Orinoco Tobacco Tin

Tobacco, "Tucketts Orinoco," round w/lithographed scene of man sitting & leaning against a tree smoking a pipe, holding a fishing pole, his little dog near his feet, marked "Tucketts Orinoco Cut Coarse" w/"MacDonald Mfg. Co. Limited Toronto" on lid & "Manufactured by the Tuckett Tobacco Co. Limited Hamilton Canada" on bottom, remnants of original seal, paint chips, fading surface rust, scratches, soiling & staining, 4 1/4" d., 3 3/4" h. (ILLUS.) 121
Tobacco, "Union Leader Cut Plug," 1 lb. lunch box, basketweave w/eagle decoration on top (ILLUS. top right w/lunch box tins) 34

Tobacco, "Union Leader," two-sided, "Series of 1910" stamp on top, front w/"Union Leader Redi Cut" above bust portrait of Uncle Sam smoking a pipe w/"Tobacco" below, text on back, (original paper seal w/pieces missing, scratches, soiling & rust at bottom inside) 66
Tobacco, "Von Eicken's Alright" **2,498**
Tobacco, "Whip," vertical pocket tin, 3 1/2" (litho chips) 345
Tobacco, "Winner Cut Plug," 1 lb. lunch box, racing car scene on side, bail handle (ILLUS. bottom left w/lunch box tins) 317

Miscellaneous

Airplane oil, "Texaco," 1 qt. can 775
Auto body polish, "Royal Saxon," front & back scene of man polishing antique car, small screw-on top, 2 x 3 x 7" 81
Axle grease, "Sambo" (Nourse Oil Co.), 1 lb. tin 100
Axle oil, "Mather Thousand Mile Axle Oil" 1 pt. tin, image of buggies on both sides, ca. late 1800s 80

Colgate's Baby Talc Tin

Baby powder, "Colgate's," w/screw top, ivory w/gold top, center oval w/image of baby on both sides, marked "Colgate's Baby Talc," minor surface scratches & small ding, 1 1/4 x 2 1/4 x 6" (ILLUS.) 110
Baking soda, "Calumet," 1 lb. tin 32
Baking soda, "Calumet," sample tin 125
Baking soda, "Gold Label," 6 oz. tin 45
Baking soda, "Royal Baking Soda," 1/8 lb. sample tin, red ground w/white wording & center circle w/color picture of the tin, 1 1/2 x 2 1/2" 33
Baking soda, "Snow King," 5 oz. tin 45
Baking soda, "Staley's," 6 oz. tin 50

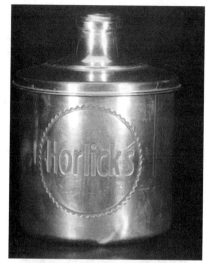

Aluminum Horlick's Canister

Beverage, "Horlick's," cylindrical aluminum container w/low domed fitted cover w/tall central knob, name stamped in circle & highlighted in red, 6" d., 6" h. (ILLUS.)............ **55**

Sanders Candy Tin Pail

Candy, "Sanders," cov. 2 1/2 lb. pail w/bail handle, colorful figures of children around sides, lithograph by Canco, light surface rust on top rim & top, minor scratches, 5 1/2 x 5 1/2" (ILLUS.)................. **330**

Instant Postum Beverage Tin

Beverage, "Instant Postum - A Beverage," sample size, cylindrical w/a printed black & white label w/small red circle in lower half, top w/sketch of a table set for break-fast, 1 1/2 oz., 2 x 3 1/2" (ILLUS.).................... **44**

Blasting caps, "Hercules No. 6," small cy-lindrical form w/pry-off lid, dark gold w/black printing, the flat lid centered by a sketch of Hercules, the side reads "Twenty-five Blasting Caps - No. 6," 1 1/2 x 1 5/8" (minor scrapes)........................ **132**

Buck shot, "Winchester," 1 lb. container, ca. 1939, full box.............................. **30**

New Life Car Polish Tin

Car polish, "New Life," 2 1/2 x 4", 5 3/4" h. (ILLUS.)... **149**

Gibson Girl Cigarettes Tin

Cigarettes, "Gibson Girl," flat rectangular form, dark ground printed w/a color image of a seductive standing Gibson-like girl wearing a long black dress w/pink rose trim & smoking a cigarette, red, black & white logo at top left, slight wear, 3 x 3 1/4" (ILLUS.) 275

Cleaning powder, "Gold Dust Scouring Cleanser," cylindrical w/a dark reddish orange ground w/the black Twins at the top above the wording in white, unopened, 3 x 4 1/2" 55

Ghiaradelli Cocoa Tin

Cocoa, "Ghiaradelli Cocoa," 1lb. tin, tall cylindrical form w/paper label, orange background w/large red wordings surrounding a spread-winged eagle above the company monogram, unopened, 3 1/4 x 6 1/2" (ILLUS.) 77

Cocoa, "Hearthstone," round, paper label showing scene of roaring fire on front, slip top, J.M. McCracken Co., Boston, 6 x 10" 29

Condom, "De-Luxe," shepherd dog decoration 798

Dominion Condom Tin

Condom, "Dominion," depicts young brunette woman (ILLUS.) 1,155

Condom, "Double Tip" 825

Condom, "Gold Pak" 440

Condom, "Nutex" 935

Condom, "Shadows," marked "Shadows (letters reflected as shadow image) As Thin as a Shadow - As Strong as an Ox!," Youngs Rubber Co., 1 5/8 x 2 1/8" 66

Condom, "Sheik - Reservoir End," flat rectangular form, orange ground w/a white vignette of a racing Arab sheik on horseback above wording in dark blue & w/a pale yellow narrow band, full, 1 5/8 x 2 1/8" 33

Condom, "Silver Star" 908

Buffalo Crank Pin Grease Tin

Crank pin grease, "Buffalo Crank Pin Grease," 3 lb. tin w/wire bail handle, pry-off lid, yellow ground w/lid & sides decorated in black w/a vignette of a standing buffalo w/wording above & below, text on reverse, very minor dings, dents & paint wear, 5 1/4" d. (ILLUS.) 402

Cup grease, "MonaMotor," 5 lb. tin, tapering cylindrical form w/fitted flat lid & wire bail handle, blue label printed in black & white "MonaMotor Hard Oil Cup Grease" above a black on blue scene of early car, motorcycle, farm machinery & airplane, 6" d., 6 3/4" h. (denting, rust spotting, scratches, soiling) 55

Engine degreaser, "Triumph," cycle bath, 3" d., 4 3/8" h. (minor denting, fading & scratches) 248

Gasoline, "Powerized Gasoline" (Sunburst Refining), emergency 1 qt. tin, rare 200

Gasoline additive, "Speedoline," flattened upright hand-soldered tin w/a screw-on cap, black & white label, the front w/brand name & advertising centered by a sketch of a speeding early race car, ca. 1920, 2 1/2 x 4", 7" h. 72

Gelatine, "Knox," 1 lb. cardboard container w/contents, "Knox U.S.P. Plain Sparkling" above head of cow flanked by "One - Pound" & "Gelatin - The Highest Quality - Charles B. Knox Gelatine Co., Inc., Johnstown, N.Y., Camden, N.J., U.S.A." below, side shows head of cow flanked by young girls holding plate w/gelatin mold, shrink-wrapped, 2 3/4 x 3 1/2", 5" h. (very minor wear) 110

Grease, "Husky," 25 lb. tin, cylindrical w/clamp-on lid & metal & wooden bail handle, Husky dog logo & "Western Oil & Fuel Co. Minneapolis" on front & back, 12" d., 9 1/2" h. **358**

Gum & lozenges, "Huntley, Boorne & Stevens, Ltd.," Victory-V Grandfather clock model, circa 1922, clock operates, excellent, 5 3/4" x 18" **550**

Gunpowder, "DuPont Schuetzen Smokeless Powder," 1 lb. tin w/paper label, green & gold, man in suit of armor holding gun depicted, 1 1/4 x 4 x 5 3/4" (some discoloration) **67**

Gunpowder, "DuPont Superfine Gunpowder," 1/2 lb. tin, flattened oval upright form, inside thread cap, red tin w/a black & tan paper label w/minor blemishes, early, 1 3/8 x 3 7/8", 4 1/4" h. **44**

Gunpowder, "Hazard Indian Rifle Gunpowder," round 1/4 lb. tin w/colorful lithograph of Native American w/headdress carrying a rifle in wooded scene w/mountain in background w/"Indian Rifle Gunpowder" above & "Hazard Powder Com. N.Y." below, back marked "FFFG," ca. 1890, 1 x 2 1/2 x 2 7/8" (ILLUS.) **660**

Gunpowder, "Hercules Black Sporting Powder," 1/2 lb. flattened ovoid flask-form in orange w/an oval tin lithographed label in blue, orange & white centered by an image of Hercules, belt loop intact, 3 1/4 x 6" **71**

DuPont Gun Powder Tin

Gunpowder, "DuPont Superfine Gunpowder - Wilmington, Delaware," 1 lb. tin, flat-sided w/small top neck w/cap, ca. 1880, 1 1/2 x 4 x 5 3/4" (ILLUS.) **187**

Early Imperial Powder Tin

Gunpowder, "Imperial Power...," large cylindrical form w/a domed top w/a small round threaded neck, dark red ground printed in black, lithographed by B.W. Thayer, Boston, 3" d., 3 3/4" h. (ILLUS.) **187**

Hazard Gunpowder Tin

Indian Rifle Gunpowder Tin

Gunpowder, "Indian Rifle Gunpowder," 1/2 lb., red upright flattened oval form w/small screw cap, the front & back w/colorful paper labels centered by a picture of a Native American hunter stalking game, 1 x 3 3/4", 4 1/4" h. (ILLUS.)............ 204

Gunpowder, "Orange Extra Sporting - Laflin & Rand Powder Co. - New York U.S.A.," 1 lb. tin, flattened upright rectangular form, orange background w/a large circle on the front printed w/a large black & red-striped flag w/gold wording enclosed by a gold wreath, ca. 1900, excellent condition, 4 x 6" (ILLUS.)......................... 94

Nobel's Empire Powder Tin

Gunpowder, "Nobel's Empire Smokeless Sporting Powder - For Shot Guns Only," lithographed tin flat upright rectangular form, label in black & white w/an image of a shotgun shell, 3 1/2 x 6" (ILLUS.)............... 264

Whale Amber Harness Dressing Tin

Harness dressing, "Whale Amber Harness Dressing," shallow round form w/the cover in blue on white, a central scene of a large whale among icebergs, wording around border reads "Blackens - Softens- Waterproofs and Preserves the Leather - Unexcelled For Hoofs," many dents, dirty, 5 1/4" d., 1 1/2" h. (ILLUS.)........ 99

Bradshaw's 3 Bears Honey Tin

Honey, "Bradshaw's 3 Bears Honey," 5 lb. tin, cylindrical w/pry-off lid, cartoon design of Papa, Mama & Baby bear in and around a large white tree w/green leaves against a golden ground, wording

Orange Extra Sporting Powder Tin

in black & white, dated 1949, 5 x 5 3/4"
(ILLUS.) 55
Honey, "Pride of Ontario," pail w/bail handle, shades of red & pink, overall decoration of bees, 4 3/4 x 5" 92

Lard, "Waldock," 50 lb. tin, colorful scene w/geese, slip lid, Heekin Can Co., scattered surface rust specks, 12 x 15" (ILLUS.) 173

Old Faithful Lighter Fluid Tin

Lighter fluid, "Old Faithful Lighter Fluid," flattened upright metal oiler-style tin, lead spout w/plastic cap, red & black graphics show geyser & crowd, 4 oz., 4 3/4" h. (ILLUS.) 143

Pure Canadian Honey Tin

Honey, "Pure Canadian," round w/lid & bail handle, illustration of large beehive w/bees flying nearby, directions to liquefy the honey on back, some rust marks, 6 1/4" d., 6 1/2" h. (ILLUS.) 116
Imitation milk, "SMA Imitation Milk," cylindrical w/pry-off lid, grey ground w/small yellow wording centered by a round color or bust portrait of a pretty blond baby, dated 1929, 4 1/4 x 4 3/4" (few scuffs & scrapes) 66

Pep Boys Lighter Fluid Can

Lighter fluid, "Pep Boys," shows the Pep Boys, Manny, Joe & Jack, Philadelphia, Pennsylvania, scratches, soiling, 2 1/4" w., 1" l., 5" h. (ILLUS.) 132
Lighter fluid, "Shell Lighter Fluid," flattened upright metal oiler-style tin, screw-on cap

Large Waldock Lard Can

w/upright lead spout, orange background w/yellow wording & Shell logo, 3 1/2 oz., 4 7/8" h. (light dent on front, few tiny nicks, some fading) 110

Atlantic Quality Lubricants Tin

Lubricant, "Atlantic Quality Lubricants," 5 gal. tin, wide cylindrical body w/low domed top w/spout & handles, the sides printed in red w/a large red & white square center, printed "Atlantic Quality Lubricants" in red & blue over a large lower-case "a," blue bands down the sides w/small white wording, white bottom band w/red word "Medium," minor soiling & scratches, 11 1/2" d., 16 1/2" h. (ILLUS.) 66

General Petroleum Lubricant Tin

Lubricant, "General Petroleum Corporation," cov. cylindrical metal 5 lb. tin w/bail handle, green w/white letters, front marked "General Lubricants - General Petroleum Corporation - Lubricant - Grade Medium - A Pure Lubricating

Compound," text on reverse, minor overall wear, dings & soiling, partial contents (ILLUS.) 413

Scarce Power-lube Lubricant Tin

Lubricant, "Power-lube Lubricant - The Powerine Company - Denver, Colorado," 1 lb. tin, yellow ground w/rectangular dark blue panel w/yellow wording & yellow & blue stalking tiger, overall heavy wear, scratches & dings, partial contents, 4 1/2" h. (ILLUS.) 578

Lubricant, "Shell Hypoid Gear Lubricant," 1 gal. tin, 11" h. 250

Texaco Home Lubricant Tin

Lubricant, "Texaco," flattened upright metal oiler-style 4 oz. tin, lead spout & cap, green w/white rectangular area at top marked "Texaco Home Lubricant" w/logo below, text on reverse, no contents, soiled overall, fading & push dents on both sides, 4 oz. (ILLUS.) 440

Lubricant, "Texaco Home Lubricant," 4 oz. tin, 5 1/8" h. **350**
Machine oil, "Pfaff," sewing machine oil tin, Germany, 3 x 4", 7" h. (scratches & soiling) **105**
Malted milk, "Borden's," w/metal lid, "Borden's - Reg. U.S. Pat. Office" above triangle w/"Richer Malted Milk" appears three times around can, 6" d., 8 1/2" h. (denting to lid, minor scratches to can & lid) **121**
Malted milk, "Carnation," 25 lb. tin **115**

Horlicks Malted Milk Tins

Malted milk, "Horlick's," 10 lb. round tin, screw-on lid, marked "Horlick's Malted Milk - Fountain Brand - Manufactured by Horlick's Malted Milk Company - Racine, Wisconsin - Net Weight 10 Pounds" tan & black w/black & white lettering, Canco, 7 3/4" d., 9" h. (ILLUS. bottom left) **115**
Malted milk, "Horlick's," 10 lb. round tin w/handle over screw-on lid, scene w/cow, tan & black, 7 1/2" d., 9" h. (ILLUS. top left) **135**
Malted milk, "Horlicks," 25 lb. tin, screw-on lid, red, white & blue, Canco, 9" w., 13 3/4" h. (ILLUS. right) **275**
Marine motor oil, "Texaco," 1 gal. tin, 10 1/4" h. **400**

Blue Bird Marshmallow Tin

Marshmallows, "Blue Bird," triangular, showing winter scene on top, Harry Horne Co., Canada, slight fade to top, 7" l., 3 3/4" h. (ILLUS.) **98**
Oil, "Simoniz Graphite Oil," w/screw-on top, red & yellow litho by Continental Can depicts a witch seated on a large fish, marked "Penetrating Graphite Oil - Stops Squeaks - Lubricates Springs - Dissolves

Rust - The Simoniz Company, Chicago, USA," 2 x 6" **77**
Outboard motor oil, "Oneida," 1 qt. tin, outboard grade, decorated w/Indian graphics **300**

Signal Outboard Motor Oil Tin

Outboard motor oil, "Signal Outboard Motor Oil," 1 qt. tin, wide black & yellow bands printed w/yellow, black & red wording centered by a red & white racing outboard motor, full w/factory seal & full tab on top, reverse w/text & stoplight logo, very minor nicks & dings (ILLUS.) **253**
Outboard motor oil, "Sunoco Outboard," 1 qt. tin w/cone-top **65**
Oysters, "Christy's Oysters," 1 gal. tin, blue & red graphic showing man at ship's wheel & marked "Christy's Choice Quality Oysters," 6 3/4 x 7" **77**
Oysters, "Lady Adams Oysters," w/early paper litho showing a large oyster on the front w/"Lady Adams Oysters - packed expressly for Mebius & Drescher Co., Sacramento, Cal." & directions for use on back, unopened, 2 3/4 x 4 1/4" **88**

Liberty Brand Oyster Tin

Oysters, "Liberty Brand Fresh Oysters," 1 gal. tin, white background printed w/red & black wording, a gold image of The Statue of Liberty w/"Liberty Brand - Fresh Oysters - packed by Ivens and Hudson, Rock Hall, MD," in the lower right in front

of a red disk, minor blemishes & scrapes,
6 1/2 x 7 1/2" (ILLUS.) **215**
Peanut oil, "Planters Italian," 1 gal. tin, decorated w/airplanes, ca. 1930s....................... **963**
Peanuts, "Cream Dove," 10 lb. store bin, round, dove on front, 8 1/4 x 9 3/4" **115**

Peanuts, "The Planters Mother's Brand Salted Peanuts," 10 lb. tin, yellow background w/red & black wording & a central color reserve showing a young mother & child (ILLUS.)... **12,430**

Peanut Tins
Peanuts, "Giant," 10 lb. tin, red, white & blue (ILLUS. right) **236**
Peanuts, "Robinson Crusoe," 10 lb. tin, red, yellow & black (ILLUS. left) **345**

Roundup Grocery Peas Tin
Peas, "Roundup Grocery Company," Spokane, Washington, colorful embossed paper label w/white bowl filled w/peas on one side, scene of cowboy on a bronco on other, marked "Sweet Early June Peas," top cut open, 2 5/8 x 4" (ILLUS.) **303**

Society Brand Peanuts
Peanuts, "Society Brand," 10 lb. tin, scene of man wooing woman w/peanuts (ILLUS.)... **963**
Peanuts, "Superior Peanut Company," 10 lb. tin... **236**

Extremely Rare Large Peanuts Tin

Bomb-Buster Popcorn Tin

Popcorn, "Bomb-Buster," w/paper label showing a pan w/popping kernels of corn, yellow, white & black, 2 1/2 x 5" (ILLUS.) **66**

Popcorn, "Popeye Popcorn," red, white & blue w/image of Popeye on front & marked "Popeye Brand White Hulless Pop Corn" & dated "1949 King Features," American Can Co., 2 x 3 x 4 3/4" **77**

Fairbank's "Gold Dust" Tin

Scouring powder, "Fairbank's Gold Dust," red, white & black, depicts two small black children & marked "Fairbank's Gold Dust Scouring Cleanser" & "Free Sample," dated 1931, 2 x 2 3/4" (ILLUS.) **110**

Seed meal, "Wilbur's Seed Meal," four-sided, painted & stenciled yellow, 36" h. **850**

Shoe polish, "Whittemore's Brown New Era Shoe Polish," flattened round form, the lid printed in white, dark brown & black, center bust portrait of a man, full & unused, 3 1/2" d. **44**

Gordon's Potato Chip Tin

Potato chips, "Gordon's," round, red panel delivery truck above "'Trucks Serving The Best' - Gordon's Fresh Potato Chips - Net Wt. One Pound - Made from Potatoes Cooked in Shortening - Salt Added" & "Mfg. by Gordon Foods Inc. Atlanta, Louisville, Birmingham, Memphis, Nashville, Chattanooga, Cincinnati, Roanoke," minor denting, fading, scratches & soiling, 7 1/2" d., 11 1/2" h. (ILLUS.) **72**

Early Alaska Salmon Tin

Salmon, "Sailor's Brand Alaska Pink Salmon," lithographed color paper label w/the head of a sailor on one side & a large salmon on the other, small tear on shoulder of sailor, other minor tears, early, 3 x 4 1/2" (ILLUS. of both sides) **231**

Selby Air Rifle Shot Container

Shot, "Selby Air Rifle Shot," cardboard tube w/brass cap, twist top to dispense, 3/4 x 3" (ILLUS.) **165**

Soap, "Lindbergh," fine graphics, 1920s **95**

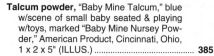

Tip Top Soda Can

Soft drink, "Tip Top Soda," metal, cone top, shows clown, red, white & blue, Madison, Wisconsin (ILLUS.).. 350

Syrup, "Bar-None Brand Imitation Maple Syrup," 5 lb. tin, upright rectangular form, printed w/a rectangular panel w/wording in red & black & a center scene of a cowboy on rearing horse w/mountains in the distance, all on a gold ground, dark brown border, no cap, 3 x 5", 7" h. 88

Syrup, "Dixie Maid," 9 lb. pail, paper label w/child pouring syrup on waffle on front & back, 6 x 7" (dent & minor paper loss) 63

Syrup, "Tole's Wigwam," 1 gal. tin, hotel size, wigwam on front, key-wind, copyright 1921, 6 x 8 1/2 (no lid) 431

Talcum powder, "Baby Mine Talcum," blue w/scene of small baby seated & playing w/toys, marked "Baby Mine Nursey Powder," American Product, Cincinnati, Ohio, 1 x 2 x 5" (ILLUS.) 385

Cute Cadette Talc Tin

Talcum powder, "Cadette Talc," cylindrical tall form w/tall cap printed in color to represent an army cadette in uniform, w/contents, Cadette Products Corp., Rutherford, New Jersey, 2 1/4 x 7 1/4" (ILLUS.)... 154

Talcum powder, "Colgate's Baby Talc," tall slender flattened oval form, white ground w/blue lettering centered by an oval reserve w/a color portrait of a cute baby holding a can of the product, gold shoulder & cap, 2 1/4 x 6" (minor surface scratches & a small ding) 110

"Baby Mine" Talcum Powder

Jess Talcum Powder Tin

Talcum powder, "Jess," embossed scene depicting young woman, flowers at border, by Wm. Brown & Bros., Baltimore, 1 1/2 x 2 1/2 x 4 1/2" (ILLUS.) 358

Talcum powder, "Ward's Talcum Powder," pictures baby on front, by Bullock Ward Co., Chicago, Illinois, 1 1/2 x 2 1/2 x 4" (some scratches) **154**

Egyptian Bouquet Talc Tin

Talcum powder, "Watkins Egyptian Bouquet Talc," upright embossed tapering square form w/small round cap, colorful Egyptian vignettes on each side (ILLUS. of two sides) **204**

Royal Rose Talcum Powder Tin

Talcum powder, "Royal Rose Talcum Powder," tall slender oval form w/round cap, tan ground printed w/pale background stripes of pink & green roses w/a large red rose in the foreground, from Canada, excellent condition, 2 1/4 x 6" (ILLUS.) **143**

Talcum powder, "Winchester After Shave Talc," hunting scene of man & his dog, front & back, by Jolind Dist. Co., New York, 1 x 3 x 4 3/4" **330**

Tea, "Ferndell - Remus," 1 lb. tin, colorful lithographed outdoor scene of Oriental woman on bridge, another woman standing below, many trees in background, marked "Net Weight One-Half Pound - Ferndell - Remus Brand - Tea - Distributed by Sprague, Warner & Co. Chicago, ILL. U.S.A." & "U.S. Trade Mark Reg. No. 116696," 3 1/8" w., 5" h. (soiling & water stain) **28**

Violet Talcum Powder Tin

Talcum powder, "Violet Talcum Powder," black & gold w/portrait of lady w/upswept hair & marked Perfumed Talcum Powder - Violet," top w/same portrait & marked "Violet Talcum Powder," litho by American Stopper Co., Brooklyn, N.Y., 2 x 6" (ILLUS.) **160**

Monarch Tea Bin

Tea, "Monarch," store counter bin, multi-colored litho front & top, ca. 1900, 12 x 13", 15" h. (ILLUS.)... **575-700**

Tire Tube Patch Tin

Tire tube patch, "Favorite," scene of lady driving early automobile w/"Self Vulcanizing - Tube Patch - Sticks and Stays Stuck" (ILLUS.).. **935**

League Brand Tomatoes Tin

Tomatoes, "League Brand," paper lithographed label on opened can, image of tomato on one side, baseball scene on other, California Packing Co., San Francisco, California, minor dings & scrapes, 4 x 4 5/8" (ILLUS.)...................................... **440**

Tooth powder, "Dr. Lyon's," cylindrical w/small screw-on top **52**

Transmission oil, "Iso-Vis," 5 gal. tin, screw-on top, bail handle, front w/"Net Weight Fifty Pounds" at top & "Standard Oil Company Indiana" in circle around logo, "Iso - Vis Lubricant" in outer border, product information on other sides, 12" w., 11 1/2" h., 5 gal. (rest spotting, fading & scratches)...................................... **77**

Old Town Typewriter Ribbon Tin

Typewriter ribbon, "Old Town," shallow round form, the lid w/a color design of an Art Deco lady wearing a long red gown, her arms raised over her head, the sides of her gown swirl up in blue on one side & green on the other all against a black ground, reads around the top "Pure Silk Typewriter Ribbon" & across the bottom "An 'Old Town' Ribbon," new unused condition, 2 1/2" d. (ILLUS.)............................ **55**

Veterinary medicine, "Dr. Roberts Dog Remedy"... **1,595**

Chapter 19

Tobacciana

Ashtray, "Andes Stoves & Ranges," tin, one-sided w/striker, on shield-shaped die-cut cardboard w/illustration of young dark-haired woman wearing a flower-trimmed bonnet w/large bow under chin above "Use ANDES STOVES and RANGES - For Sale By Hessler & Schafer, 512 & 516 N. Salina St., Syracuse, N.Y. - Best in the World - Always Give Satisfaction," 4 5/8" w., 6 1/4" h. (minor fading & water stain, scratches & denting to match strike)... **$171**

Ashtray, cast iron, round dished form w/a high-relief face of a Native American chief at the top rim flanked by tomahawks, center embossed "1750 Fort Ligonier," appears unused, 4 1/2 x 5 1/2" (ILLUS.)... **149**

Ashtray, "Champion Spark Plugs," ceramic, a round black-glazed dish w/two swirled indentations around the top w/two cigarette indentations at the rim, a real "Champion Ford" spark plug standing upright in the center, base stamped "Champion Sill - Manite," 5" d., 3 1/2" h. (scratches, soiling & rust spotting on plug)... **132**

Bartels Brewing Co. Ashtray

Ashtray, "Bartels Brewing Co.," tin, cone-shaped w/removable match holder w/metal striker on top, three cigarette holes around sides w/"Bartels Malt Extract" beneath alternating w/scenes of man holding mug of beer, crazing, fading, scratches & soiling, 4 5/8" d., 4" h. (ILLUS.)... **660**

Fisk Tire Advertising Ashtray

Ashtray, "Fisk Tires," rubber tire-type w/clear glass insert printed under the bottom w/a full-color design of the Fisk tire boy & "Time to Re-tire" - "Get A Fisk" in black all on a yellow ground, soiling, cracking to rubber, some paint loss, 6 1/2" d. (ILLUS.)... **209**

Cast-Iron Ashtray with Indian Chief

Early China Cigar Ashtray

Ashtray, "Foster-Hilson Company - Makers - The Hoffman House Bouquet Cigar - New York," white china w/brown wording & a color picture of a cigar, china mark of the Marx & Gutherz Company of Carlsbad, Austria, ca. 1900, minute age crack, 6" d. (ILLUS.) 259

Ashtray, "Gallagher & Burton, Fine Whiskies, Philadelphia," round, center depicts bottle of Black Label Whiskey, marked "Made by the Chas. W. Shonk Co. Litho Chicago," ca. 1910-1925, 4 1/2" d. 66

Ashtray, "Kelly Tires," rubber tire-type w/glass insert & decal w/"Kelly Tires," 6" d. 20

Ashtray, "Lemp Beer," metal, round, dark maroon w/gold lettering, reads "Extra Pale Famous Old Lemp Beer," 5 1/2" d. (minor ding under "M" on right side) 44

Ashtray, "Michelin Tires," plastic, round black tray w/notched rim, the seated Michelin man in white on one rim, marked "Made in USA," 5 x 51/2", 4 3/4" h. (minor scratches, soiling) 110

Mobil Flying Pegasus Ashtray

Ashtray, "Mobil Gasoline," Art Deco design, a figural cast-metal flying red Pegasus logo rising from one end of the flaring round black glass tray base, some paint wear on Pegasus, 5" d. (ILLUS.) 138

Ashtray, "Phillips 66," rubber tire-type w/clear glass insert printed under the bottom in orange & black w/company logo & name & address of dealer, w/original box, 6 1/2" d. (scratches & wear to box) 132

Ashtray, "Smoke Kools," milk glass, w/penguins trademark 20

Tucker Ashtray

Ashtray, "Tucker," metal, gold colored car on rectangular green base marked "Tucker," brick design under car, cigarette compartment under car, 9" w., 3 1/2" h (ILLUS.) 1,540

Ashtray, "Valencia Cafe & Bar, Cheyenne, Wyo." pottery, model of cowboy hat, cobalt blue w/white trim, ca. 1940-50s, 2 x 4 3/4" 143

Cigar cutter, "Grand Republic 5¢ Cigar," pocket-sized, nickel silver w/gold finish, flat rectangular form w/insert hole for tip & push cutting blade, 1 x 2" 55

"White Owl" Counter-type Cigar Cutter

Cigar cutter, "White Owl" brand cigars, counter-type, w/glass front (ILLUS.) **425-650**

Tenorio Counter-top Cigar Cutter

Cigar cutter & matchbox holder, "Tenorio 5¢ Cigar," nickel-plated metal, countertop design w/oval leaf-embossed base band below ribbed sides around cutter & flanged matchbox holder on one side, finish wear & slight rust on bottom, 3 x 5 x 5" (ILLUS.) 77

Cigar lighter, "White Owl Cigars," pocket-type w/flip-up top, black enameled ground w/a white owl perched on a brown cigar on the sides, excellent condition, 1/2 x 1 1/2" 143

Amoco Motor Oil Cigarette Lighter

Cigarette lighter, "Amoco 300 Motor Oil," metal, can-shaped, printed in red, white & blue on a silver & white ground, w/original blue box, 2" h. (ILLUS.) **77**

Unique Figural Cigar & Match Holder

Cigar & match holder, figural cast metal, the cylindrical holder at the back cast as a cluster of upright cigars, two crossed pipes for holding matches at the front, painted in brown, red, black & white, good original paint, 5" w., 5" h. (ILLUS.) **83**

La Preferendia Cigar Piercer

Cigar piercer, "La Preferencia Cigars," nickel plated metal & celluloid, central celluloid section w/black wording, early 20th c., 3/8 x 2 3/4" (ILLUS.)............................ **83**

Harley Davidson Cigarette Lighter

Cigarette lighter, "Harley Davidson - of Long Beach," silvered metal, Japanese "slimline" design, decorated w/an enameled sketch of a man & woman in tan, red, black & white riding a black motorcyle, wording in red, in original box, very minor wear, design of shop owner's business card on the reverse, 1 7/8 x 2 1/8" (ILLUS.).. **220**

Aluminum Pocket Cigar Case

Cigar pocket case, "Rogert J. - Clear Havana Filler - 5¢ Cigar - 'Are Really Excellent,'" aluminum oblong form molded to hold three cigars, ca. 1930s, 2 1/2 x 5" (ILLUS.) **44**

Cigar pocket pouch, "Bohemian Club - Havana Cigars - Compliments of Dwight J. Russell," red leather w/gold lettering & brass corner trim, unused, 3 x 5" **66**

Mohawk Gasoline Cigarette Lighter

Cigarette lighter, "Mohawk Gasoline," steel rectangular table model by Zippo, red Mohawk logo on the side, on a narrow stepped base, minor overall wear, 3 3/8" h. (ILLUS.) **231**

Texaco-Firestone Cigarette Lighter

Cigarette lighter, "Texaco - Firestone," Japanese 'slimline' style in silvered metal w/white, red & silver advertising on each side, distributor's name & address on each side w/the Texaco logo on one side & the Firestone logo on the other, from Great Falls, Montana, made by Nationwide, 1 7/8 x 2 1/8" (ILLUS.) 176

Cigarette pack, "One-Eleven American Cigarettes," full pack decorated w/a large round bust portrait of a Native American chief in color against a red ground, cream ground on the pack, American Tobacco Company, 2 x 2 3/4" 66

Jose Vila Cigars Counter Pad

Counter felt pad, "Jose Vila Havana Cigars," rectangular cloth in bright gold printed in large red letters & centered by an outline-sketched bust of a 17th c. cavalier, unused, minute moth hole, bright colors, 7 1/4 x 11" (ILLUS.) 55

Dice shaker, "Smoke Banner Cigars," a nickel-plated small metal cylinder holding five miniature bone die & a small round metal token, 3/4 x 1 1/4" 160

Merriam & Co. Bulldog Paperweight

Paperweight, "John W. Merriam & Co. Bulldog Segars," cast hollow spelter model of a standing bulldog w/stamped writing on back, small hole in bottom side, 2 x 3 x 4" (ILLUS. of two views) 110

Admiration Cigars Salt & Pepper

Salt & pepper shakers, "Admiration Cigars," figural porcelain, each molded as the smiling man's rounded face w/a cigar in his mouth, one in white, other in brown, advertising labels on the base, new in the box, 2 1/2 x 2 3/4" (ILLUS. of front & back) 132

Stickpin, "Rosa Cigars," a cast-metal figural cigar embossed w/the word "Rosa" & painted to resemble a lit cigar, on a long pin, appears unused, ca. 1910-15, 1 1/2" l. 77

Saboroso Cigar Store Tape Measure

Tape measure, "Saboroso Cigar Store," round celluloid, decorated on one side w/black wording on cream reading "Compliments Sabaroso Cigar Store - Chestnut & 4th Sts. - Philadelphia," the other side w/a square logo in blue, white gold & red reading "Smoke Vetterlein Bros. Saboroso Philadelphia Cigars," 1/2 x 1 3/4" (ILLUS. of front & back) 44

Chapter 20
Trade Cards

Candy, "Heide's Licorice Pastilles - Mint - and Assorted JuJubes - Are The Best - 5¢ Boxed," a color scene of a cute young boy holding up packages of the candy w/an open crate behind him, printed across the top "Pan American Exposition - This pretty little boy insists that...," w/further advertising down the side & at the bottom, a Sarah Bernhardt testimonial on the reverse, 1901, bright colors, 3 1/2 x 5 1/2" **$77**

Globe Evaporated Milk Trade Card

Evaporated milk, "Globe Evaporated Milk," color image of a young boy dressed as Uncle Sam & standing on a can of the product holding out a white banner, black & red wording, reads at top "I Am the Weather Man - Watch My Flag" above lists of colors & the weather they predict, at center left is "Globe Label Indicates - Highest Quality - Absolute Purity - Perfect Sterilization - Perfection in Canned Milk," further advertising at bottom, 3 1/2 x 6" (ILLUS.) **44**

Coon Skin Cigars Trade Card

Cigars, "I Toot My Horn - For de - Coon Skin Cigars," rectangular, a grotesque color caricature of a black musician playing a long slender horn, ca. 1880s, 1 3/4 x 3 1/2" (ILLUS.) **44**

Beeman's Gum Trade Card

Gum, "Beeman's Pepsin Chewing Gum," color image of a youg girl dressed as an elderly lady w/bonnet & holding knitting seated on a package of gum, titled at bottom "Playing Grandma," 3 1/2 x 5 1/2" (ILLUS.) **33**

Cigar Trade Card with Bathing Beauty

Cigars, "T.R. Keating Cigars," die-cut cardboard, cut to resemble an open seashell w/a colorful bathing beauty in the lower half & advertising in the upper half, 4 1/4 x 6" (ILLUS.) **149**

Colorful Horlick's Trade Card

Malted milk, "Horlick's Malted Milk," die-cut stand-up type w/a full color image of a milkmaid holding a package of the product & standing beside a cow, 4 x 5" (ILLUS.) **77**

Haswell's Studio Trade Card

Photographer, "Haswell's Studio," die-cut cardboard in the shape of an open fan, decorated in the center w/a color portrait bust of a pretty young girl playing a tambourine, advertising to her right, 9 x 15 1/4" (ILLUS.) **66**

Wincroft Ranges & Stoves Trade Card

Ranges & stoves, "Wincroft Ranges and Stoves," color image of a young boy dressed as Uncle Sam & standing on a large crate holding out a white banner, black & red wording, reads at top "I Am the Weather Man - Watch My Flag" above lists of colors & the weather they predict, at center left is "With a Wncroft Range in the Kitchen there is always fair weather in the Dining Room," further advertising on the crate, 3 1/2 x 6" (ILLUS.) **33**

Miller's Crown Dressing Trade Card

Shoe polish, "Frank Miller's Crown Dressing for Ladies & Children's Shoes - Will Not Injure the Finest Leather," die-cut cardboard model of a lady's shoe w/lady & children inside, near mint, 5 x 7 1/2" (ILLUS.) **55**

Babbitts Soap Powder Trade Card

Soap powder, "Babbitts Soap Powder," color scene of Uncle Sam with two bearded men putting bags of gold on a large balance scale w/a large box of the product on the other scale pan, nice landscape background, great color, 4 x 5 1/2" (ILLUS.) **121**

1907 Coca-Cola Trade Card

Soft drink, "Coca-Cola," opens to show young waitress serving drinks to two gentlemen seated at a table, marked "Drink Coca-Cola - When thirsty, tired or headachey, or after a night out try a Coca-Cola High Ball - it hits the spot," closed reads "Appearances are sometimes deceiving but Coca-Cola can always be relied on as nourishing, refreshing and exhilerating" 1907 (ILLUS. open & closed) **850**

Soft drink, "Hires Rootbeer (sic)," rectangular color bust portrait of a pretty blonde late Victorian lady w/a pink rose in her hair & holding a bouquet of pink & red roses all against a pale blue ground, black wording reads "Put Roses in Your Cheeks - Drink Hires Rootbeer," 3 x 5" (minor edge & corner wear, slightly warped) **33**

Tobacco, "Day & Night Tobacco," risque color cartoon of a young woman w/her long dress caught on a rail fence & an elderly farmer on the other side of the fence unhooking the skirt & peeking underneath, advertising on the rails of the fence, 3 1/2 x 5 3/4" **83**

Tobacco, "Lorillard's '49' Cut Plug," a color scene of early gold miners sluicing, produced in San Francisco, bright colors, 3 1/4 x 4 1/2" **253**

Chapter 21
Trade Catalogs

1938 Pontiac Dealer Catalog

Automobile, "1938 Pontiac - New Silver Streak - Sixes & Eights," dealer version w/22 color pages, color image of standing American Indian on the cover w/a red ground & white & gold lettering, unused, 8 1/2 x 11" (ILLUS.) **$55**

1938 Oldsmobile Sale Catalog

Automobile, "Oldsmobile Six and Eight," color cover showing two large stylized autos in red & blue, 28 pages showing all models, 1938, 8 1/2 x 11" (ILLUS.) **55**

1938 DeSoto Auto Catalog

Automobile, "DeSoto - America's Smartest Low-priced Car," 1938 dealer catalog, cover w/dark blue ground & large image of the front of a deep orange car, light blue & gold wording, 20 color pages, 9 x 11 1/2" (ILLUS.) **55**

Colorful Colt Firearms Catalog

Firearms, "Colt," bright red ground w/the name in black & gold, decorated w/a naturally colored hand holding a Colt revolver, all models included, ca. 1950s, 28 pp., 7 1/4 x 10" (ILLUS.) **55**

Miniature Savage Arms 1935 Catalog

Firearms, "Savage Arms," catalog No. 35 miniature size w/the cover picturing a color head portrait of a screaming Native American chief holding up a rifle, 28 pages illustrating all their various firearms, 1935 (ILLUS.) **203**

Rifles, "Savage Rifles," No. 15, rectangular printed in color w/a head portrait of a screaming Native American chief holding up a rifle, 1905, 48 pp., 5 1/2 x 9" **215**

1938 Hudson Auto Catalog

Automobile, "Meet Hudson for 1938 - Hudson Terraplane - Hudson Six - Hudson Eight," yellow & blue wording, color scene w/a red, green & yellow auto, 16 color pages, 6 x 11" (ILLUS.) **44**

Chapter 22
Trays - Serving & Change

to, California," litho by Kaufman & Straus, N.Y., 4 1/2" d. **275**

7-20-4 Cigar Change Tray

Change, "7-20-4 Cigar," lithographed tin in wood-grained brown & gold, rectangular w/rounded corners, good color, 4 1/2 x 6 1/2" (ILLUS.) **$33**

Carnation Chewing Gum Change Tray

Change, "Carnation Chewing Gum," round, metal, yellow & green w/pink carnation flowers & white package in center, red letters read "Dorne's Carnation Chewing Gum" w/black letters at bottom reading "Chew Dorne's Carnation Gum" & "Taste The Smell" in red letters in the top & bottom border, ca. 1900, 4 1/4" d. (ILLUS.)... **200-275**

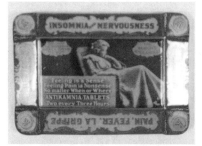

Antikamnia Tablets Change Tray

Change, "Antikamnia Tablets," rectangular, metal, red & gold, image of woman sitting in chair, lettering near her reads "Feeling is a Sense - Feeling Pain is Nonsence - No Matter When or Where - Antikamnia Tablets - Two Every Three Hours," border marked "Insomnia and Nervousness - Pain, Fever, La Grippe," Antikamnia Chemical Company, St. Louis, Missouri, souvenir of 1904 St. Louis World's Fair, by American Can Co., New York & Chicago, Illinois, 3 1/4 x 4 3/4" (ILLUS.) **125-175**

Change, "Bartholomay Beer," round metal, beautiful lady surrounded by clouds, border w/"Beers - Ales & Porter - In Kegs & Bottles," Bartholomay Brewery, Rochester, New York, litho by Chas. Shonk Litho Co., Chicago, Illinois, 4 1/4" d. **237**

Change, "Buffalo Brewing Co.," round, metal, colorful court scene of woman on steps flanked by attendants, border reads "Buffalo Brewing Co. - Sacramen-

City and Suburban Homes Co Change Tray

Change, "City and Suburban Homes Co.," round, metal w/scalloped rim, image of three white horse heads in center, border reads "City and Surburban Homes Co., Ltd. - Real Estate - Loans - Renting

Agents - Fire Insurance - 35 and 37 State St., Detroit," litho by H.D. Beach Co., Coshocton, Ohio, ca. 1910, 4 1/4" d. (ILLUS.) **100-150**

Change, "Clarke's Pure Rye," tin, lithograph of bottle in center w/"Expressly for Family and Medicinal Use Only" on label & flanked by "Bottled - In Bond," red rim trimmed in gold w/gold lettering "Clarke's Pure Rye - The Largest Whiskey in the World," Made in Germany, unused condition, 4 1/4" d. **79**

1916 Coca-Cola Change Tray

Change, "Coca-Cola," 1916, oval, elegantly dressed lady w/large brim hat, decorated wide wood-like rim, lithograph by Passaic Metal Ware Co., New Jersey, 4 1/4 x 6" (ILLUS.) **264**

DeLaval Cream Separators Change Tray

Change, "DeLaval Cream Separators," round, metal, scene of woman in long red dress & white apron at separator, young child near doorway, gold lettering on border reads "DeLaval Cream Separators - The World's Standard," ca. 1906, 4 1/4" d. (ILLUS.) **275-325**

Change, "Eversweet Deodorant," rectangular, tin w/lithograph of dark-haired woman wearing long white dress, arms over her head holding floral spray, border w/geometric designs on sides, marked "Eversweet" at top & "A Toilet Necessity for Refined People" at the bottom, 5" l. (few small spots & light stains, soiling & wear) **495**

Change, "Eye-Fix," tin, round w/raised rim, center colorfully painted w/portrait of classically dressed woman & a cherub holding eye dropper to her eye, blue rim marked "Eye-Fix - The Great Eye Remedy" in red, 4 1/4" d. (minor scratches, some wear to bottom) **358**

Fairy Soap Change Tray

Change, "Fairy Soap," round, lithographed tin, red shading to yellow background w/little girl in red coat & frilly black hat sitting on white oval bar of soap marked "Fairy," black border marked w/yellow letters reading "Fairy Soap - 'Have you a little Fairy in your home?'," N. K. Fairbank Co., Chicago, Illinois, litho by Passaic Metalware Co., Passaic, New Jersey, ca. 1910, 4 1/2" d. (ILLUS.) **100-175**

Change, "Ferro-Phos," round, tin, center of tray reads "Drink" above image of the drink in a glass, flanked by "Non-Narcotic - Non-Alcoholic," all above "Ferro-Phos - The Favorite Beverage - Five Cents," rim reads "Ferro-Phos Co. - Pottstown, PA.," done in brown, black, blue & white, 5" d. (minor scratches) **154**

Fraternal Life Insurance Company Change Tray

Change, "Fraternal Life & Accident Insurance Company," rectangular, metal, center scene of large building, scalloped & ruffled blue border reads at the top "Fraternal Life and Accident Insurance - Reserve Deposited with the State of Iowa" & at the bottom "Home of the Brotherhood of American Yeomen, Des Moines, Iowa," ca. 1920, 3 1/4 x 5" (ILLUS.)........ **65-100**

Frost Wire Fence Co. Change Tray

Change, "Frost Wire Fence Co.," round, metal w/scalloped rim, lithographed metal, center w/three white horse heads, the border marked "Compliments of The Frost Wire Fence Co. - Cleveland, O.," litho by H.D. Beach Co., Coshocton, Ohio, ca. 1910, 4 1/4" d. (ILLUS.).......... **125-175**
Change, "Garcia Grandé Cigar," rectangular, sides read "'Garcia Grandé'" on long sides & "Mild Havanna" & "Cigar" on short sides, center of tray reads "don't be fooled - Ask for by FULL NAME -Garcia Grandé - Cigar - 'Finest Mild Havana Blend'" all to the left of a jester sitting on a mushroom holding a slate chalkboard that reads "2+2=7," 4 1/4 x 6 1/4" (minor paint chips & scratches) **75**

Globe-Wernicke Bookcases Change Tray

Change, "Globe-Wernicke Bookcases," round, lithographed metal, scene of woman seated on a rug & holding a book

near a man standing before a bookcase, the border reading "Globe-Wernicke - Sectional Bookcases - The Orleans Furniture & Undertaking Co. - Licensed Embalmers - Orleans, Ind.," litho by Charles Shonk Co., Chicago, Illinois, ca. 1915, 4 1/2" d. (ILLUS.)..................................... **125-175**
Change, "Gold Medal Beer," round, image of bottle of Gold Medal Beer above "The World's Standard of Perfection," rim reads "Indianapolis Brewing Co. - Lieber's Gold Medal Beer," done in red, blue, yellow, gold & green, 5" d. (minor scratches) **83**

Grain Belt Beer Change Tray

Change, "Grain Belt Beer," round, metal, red & yellow logo in center below "A Barley Malt Product" w/"'The Minneapolis Beer'" below, Grain Belt Brewery, Minneapolis, Minnesota, ca. 1920, 4 1/8" d. (ILLUS.)..................................... **75-125**

Gypsy Hosiery Change Tray

Change, "Gypsy Hosiery," round, lithographed tin, center oval w/gypsy girl in red surrounded by scene of tents & horses, top marked "Gypsy Hosiery" & bottom "E. J. Schroeder, Breese, Illinois," Hargadine-McKittrick Co., litho by H.D. Beach Co., Coshocton, Ohio, ca. 1910, 6" d. (ILLUS.)... **75-125**

Change, "Heptol Splits - for Health's Sake," black border w/gold wording, color center scene of a cowboy riding a bucking bronco, dated 1904, based on artwork by Charles Russell, 4 3/16" d. (scattered stains, overall normal checking, some wear) **200-275**

Hyroler Whiskey Change Tray

Change, "Hyroler Whiskey," lithographed in shades of brown with a center scene of a well-dressed gentleman in top hat & tails, wording around border reads "Hyroler Whiskey - Louis J. Adler & Co.," 4 1/4" d. (ILLUS.) **53**

Ideal Chocolate & Cocoa Change Tray

Change, "Ideal Chocolate & Cocoa," rectangular, tin, scalloped rim, box in center marked "Ideal Cocoa," w/"Once Tried" at top & "Always Used" below & "Ideal Chocolates" on sides, brown & tan, minor scuffs & scratches, 2 1/4 x 3 1/4" (ILLUS.) **100**
Change, "Jenney Aero Gasoline," tin, round w/orange, black & white car decoration & lettering, 4 1/8" d. **149**
Change, "John Hampden Havana Cigar," metal, colorful figure of man in center, black rim w/gold lettering "John Hampden - Havana Cigar," Austria, 4 1/4" d. **97**

King's Pure Malt Change Tray

Change, "King's Pure Malt," oval, center w/black background & image of uniformed maid holding tray w/a glass & bottle, marked in top border "King's" & the bottom w/medals & banner reading "Panama - Pacific - Medal of Award - International Exposition," ca. 1915, 4 1/4 x 6" (ILLUS.) **100-175**

King's Pure Malt Change Tray

Change, "King's Pure Malt," oval, lithographed metal, shows bottle in center marked "Pure Malt," border marked "King's - Strengthening - Healthful - Good For Insomnia," litho by American Art Works, Coshocton, Ohio, ca. 1910, 4 3/8 x 6" (ILLUS.) **125-175**

La Primadora Cigar Glass Change Tray

Change, "La Primadora" cigars, heavy clear glass over a color label w/the bust of a pretty dark-haired woman framed by gold wording & scrolls, 6" d. (ILLUS.) **175**

Lehnert's Beer Change Tray

Change, "Lehnert's Beer," round, lithographed metal, image of stag w/large antlers, border w/"Drink Lehnert's Beer - Made in Catasauqua, PA," litho by American Art Works, Coshocton, Ohio, ca. 1910, 4 1/4" d. (ILLUS.) **125-175**

Lily Beer Change Tray

Change, "Lily Beer," rectangular, metal, table set w/snack food, bottle of beer & full glass below "Lily - A Beverage"

flanked by white calla lily, border reads "Pure As It's Name - In A Class By Itself! - Heathful and Refreshing - Bottled Only By Rock Island Brewing Co. - Rock Island, Illinois," ca. 1915, 4 1/2 x 6 1/2" (ILLUS.) **175-275**

Change, "Maltosia Beer," round, center w/image of spade w/angel astride goose, reads "Bottled At The Brewery" above "Maltosia - Pure Food Beer - Brewed According To The - World-Famed - Maltosia - Process - By The - German American Brewing Co. - Buffalo, N.Y. - U.S.A.," the rim marked "German American Brewing Co. Buffalo, N.Y. - Our Beer is Sterilized - Not Pasteurized," done in gold, white & black, 5" d. (minor scratches) **55**

Miller High Life Beer Change Tray

Change, "Miller High Life Beer," rectangular, metal, center blue w/stars & Miller girl sitting on crescent moon, holding glass, marked "Miller - High Life - The Champagne of Bottle Beer," goldtone border, ca. 1960s, 4 1/2 x 6 1/2" (ILLUS.) **35-65**

Change, "Mokaine Liqueurs," lithographed tin, rectangular w/flanged rim & rounded corners, center color scene of a seated fat man at an outside cafe table looking over at a parrot on perch, titled below "'What Heat' -Try Mokaine and Soda," brown panels w/white wording on each rim flange & small images of the product in each corner, produced in France for the American market, light wear, 3 3/4 x 4" **56**

Monticello Whiskey Change Tray

Change, "Monticello Whiskey," oval, lithographed metal, fox hunt scene w/large building in background, gold border marked "Monticello - It's All Whiskey," litho by Charles Shonk Co., Chicago, Illinois, ca. 1915, 4 3/8 x 6 1/8" (ILLUS.) **225-275**

Change, "Pepsi Cola," oval, tin, reads "Drink Pepsi-Cola Delicious-Healthful 5¢," oval, tin, lithograph w/multicolored scene depicting woman in fancy dress holding glass of Pepsi-Cola at soda fountain, made by "Niagara - Buffalo," ca. 1909, 4 3/8 x 6 1/8" (several pin-size rust spots on right edge) **908**

Quick Meal Ranges Change Tray

National Cigar Stands Co. Change Tray

Change, "National Cigar Stands Co.," round, metal, center w/young girl wearing red sleeveless one-shouldered gown, holding daisies & w/a wreath of daisies in her dark upswept hair, the border designed w/various cigar band seals, marked at the top "Our Brands" & at the bottom "National Cigar Stands Co.," ca. 1910, 6" d. (ILLUS.) **75-125**

Change, "Old Reliable Coffee," round, colorfully painted portrait of young woman in center, reads "Old Reliable Coffee" in gold top & bottom edges, black ground, 4 1/2" d. (crazing to center, wear to edge & bottom) **176**

Change, "Old Scotch Whiskey," porcelain, oval, reads "The 'Antiquary'" above man dressed in 18th c. outfit & "Old Scotch Whiskey," all above "'At Last I Have Found It!'," 4 1/2" w., 6" h. **50**

Change, "Quick Meal Ranges," oval, lithographed metal, scene of young chicks near an empty shell, red border reading "'Quick Meal' Ranges - Made in St. Louis, Mo.," litho by Ohio Art Company, Bryan, Ohio, ca. 1900, 3 1/4 x 4 1/4" (ILLUS.) .. **150-200**

Change, "Red Raven," rectangular metal, red bird, glass & product bottle shown w/"For Headache - For Indigestion" at top corners, "Red Raven" at bottom, Chas. Shonk Litho Co., Cicago, Illinois, 4 1/8 x 6 1/8" (minor crazing) **110**

Change, "Red Raven Splits - Ask the Man," red border band w/gold wording, color center scene w/a large red raven serving another red bird all against a black background, celebrating the 1904 St. Louis World's Fair, appears to be unused, minor rim scuffs, 4" d. **55**

Change, "Red Raven Splits - 'For High Livers' Livers'," center scene of a large red raven beside a small bottle of the product, a dark green border band w/gold lettering, 4 1/4" d. (minor crazing) **58**

Red Raven Splits Change Tray

Olympia Beer Change Tray

Change, "Olympia Beer," round, metal, black & white, image of man dressed as a musketeer holding a bottle, glass on table before him, marked "Olympia Beer - It's the Water," minor crazing, 4 1/4" d. (ILLUS.) **55**

Change, "Red Raven Splits," rectangular w/rounded corners, color center scene of a pretty woman wearing a low-cut black dress, large hat w/red feather & black gloves, one arm around a large red raven, a large bottle of the product to her right, wide green border w/gold rim band, minor edge dings, 4 x 6" (ILLUS.) **44**

Resinol Soap and Ointment Change Tray

Change, "Resinol Soap and Ointment," round, metal, center bust portrait of beautiful woman w/long brown hair, low cut dress w/red flower decoration, red flowers in hair, black border w/gold lettering reading "Resinol Soap and Ointment - For All Skin Diseases - At All Drug Stores," 4 1/4" d. (ILLUS.) **165**

Robert Burns Cigar Change Tray

Change, "Robert Burns Cigars," round, metal, bust portrait of man in center, border w/"Robert Burns - Cigar," ca. 1910, 4" d. (ILLUS.) **75-125**

Rock Island Buggy Co. Change Tray

Change, "Rock Island Buggy Co.," rectangular, metal, ornate scrolled, pleated & scalloped border centering scene of buildings & trees, marked in upper left corner "Compliments of Rock Island Buggy Co., Rock Island, ILL," souvenir of St. Louis World's Fair, ca. 1904, 3 1/4 x 5" (ILLUS.) **125-175**

Rockford Watch Company Change Tray

Change, "Rockford Watches," rectangular, lithographed metal, white, green & pink geometric design border centering an outdoor scene of a young woman in a long green gown sitting on a bench before a tree, at the top "Rockford High Grade Watches" & "For Sale at Dan S. Jones - Independence, IA," litho by H.D. Beach Co., Coshocton, Ohio, ca. 1900, 3 1/4 x 5" (ILLUS.) **125-175**

Sears, Roebuck and Co. Change Tray

Change, "Sears, Roebuck and Co.," oval, metal, scene of factory w/waist-length image of woman holding scales on right, marked at top "Sears, Roebuck and Co. - Chicago" & at the bottom "Originators of the Guarantee that Stands the Test in the Scales of Justice," ca. 1920, 4 3/8 x 6" (ILLUS.) **125-175**

Sen-Sen Aluminum Change Tray

Change, "Sen-Sen Chewing Gum," rectangular, aluminum w/scalloped rim, center w/embossed ribbon-tied package marked "Sen-Sen - 5¢," ca. 1910, 3 1/4 x 4 1/4" (ILLUS.) **65-100**

Tech Beer Change Tray

Slade's Products Change Tray

Change, "Slade's Products," round w/flanged rim, printed in deep orange on white, center reads "Don't Take Chances - All Slade's Products - Are Sure Winners," four border panels each showing a racing horse w/the name of a different food product, appears unused, 4 1/4" d. (ILLUS.) **55**

Change, "Stegmaier Brewing Co.," round, center shows a hand holding four different types of Stegmaier, rim marked "Stegmaier Brewing Co. - Wilkes-Barre, PA.," done in green, yellow, gold, brown & blue, 4 1/4" d. (minor crazing) **121**

Change, "Tech Beer," rectangular w/rounded corners, black ground w/thin red rim band, a large color picture of a bottle of beer in the center, the name in red at the top & "'None Better'," in small white letters under the bottle, dated 1913, few minor edge chips, 4 1/2 x 6 1/2" (ILLUS.) **44**

Change, "Terre Haute Brewing Co.," tin, round w/upturned rim, colorfully painted center scene of a group of people dressed in 18th c. attire standing around table holding their glasses in a toast to four cherubs holding beer bottles, all above "That - Ever Welcome - Beer - Terre Haute Brewing Co. - Terre Haute, Ind.," inside rim reads "Champagne - Velvet - Radium," 4 1/2" d., 1/2" h. (minor scratches & crazing) **170**

Stollwerck Chocolate & Cocoa Change Tray

Change, "Stollwerck Chocolate & Cocoa," round, lithographed metal, gold & red, marked "Stollwerck" in center w/"Gold Brand" above & "Chocolate & Cocoa" below, scrolled border, litho by Kaufmann & Strauss Co., New York, ca. 1910, 5" d. (ILLUS.) **75-125**

The Davenport Co. Change Tray

Change, "The Davenport Company," round, lithographed metal, center w/bust portrait of lady on red background flanked by Art Deco floral designs, brown border w/yellow letters reading "Compliments of The

Davenport Co.," litho by Meek & Co., ca. 1903, 4 1/4" d. (ILLUS.) **75-125**

Welsbach Mantels Change Tray

Change, "Welsbach Mantels," round, lithographed tin, center w/shield form, eagle & banner marked "Welsbach Quality" above red scroll marked in yellow "All mantles are not Welsbachs. See that the mantle you buy has the Shield of Quality on the box.," yellow decorated border, litho by Meek & Beech Co., Coshocton, Ohio, ca. 1900, 4 1/4" d. (ILLUS.) **125-175**

White Rock Table Water Change Tray

Change, "White Rock Table Water," round, lithographed metal, scene w/woman kneeling on rock over water, yellow border w/red & black lettering reads "White Rock - The World's Best Table Water," litho by Charles Shonk Co., Chicago, Ilinois, ca. 1900, 4 3/8" d. (ILLUS.) **225-300**

Change, "Wolverine Toys," lithographed tin, 6 1/2" l. (minor dents & scratches) **77**

Change, "Woodland Whiskey," a colorful design w/a red central panel w/gold wording & a full-length color portrait of a pretty late Victorian lady dressed in blue, green side panels w/color images of the product, 4 1/4" d. (edge scrapes & dings) **358**

Iroquois Beer Change Tray

Change, "Iroquois Beer," lithographed metal, round, gold center w/bust of Indian w/full headdress, red border w/"Iroquois" above & "Buffalo" below, gold rim, Iroquois Beverage Corp., Buffalo, New York, minor edge wear, scratches & soiling, 5 1/4" d. (ILLUS.) **72**

Serving, "A. Gettelman Milwaukee Beer," metal, round, center lithograph of hand holding glass of beer, surrounded by "A. Gettelman - Milwaukee Beer," done in red, yellow, black, green & cream, 13" d. (minor scratches) **28**

Americus Club Whiskey Serving Tray

Serving, "Americus Club Whiskey," rectangular, metal, bottle in center, green background w/"Americus Club Whiskey - Henry Campe & Co., Inc." w/"San Francisco, Ca." at bottom, rim w/scroll & floral decoration on gold, lithograph by Chas. Shonk, Chicago, Illinois, minor crazing & surface rust on back only, 10 1/2 x 13 3/4" (ILLUS.) **231**

Serving, "Anheuser-Busch," metal, oval, colorful lithograph of classically dressed woman holding Anheuser-Busch logo surrounded by cherubs & beer bottle, all below "Anheuser-Busch - Brewing Assn. - St. Louis, Mo. - U.S.A.," 10 1/2 x 13" (chips & wear overall) **143**

Serving, "Anheuser-Busch," oval, brewery scene showing various trains & horse-drawn vechicles, "Anheuser Busch Brewing Ass'n.," Standard Adv. Co., 15 1/2 x 18 1/2" (some minor crazing & chipping).. **2,588**

Serving, "Arrow Beer," lithographed tin, 13 1/4" d. **44**

Serving, "Beverwyck Brewing Co.," rectangular w/rounded corners, large central color scene of a large, fancy brewery building in reds, browns & yellow w/name above factory "Beverwyck Brewing Co., Albany, N.Y.," dark green border band w/yellow wording "Beverwyck Famous Lager," 1910s, 12 1/4 x 17 1/4" (many small chips, overall spots & wear)................ **557**

Blatz Old Heidelberg Brew Serving Tray

Serving, "Blatz Old Heidelberg Brew," lithographed tin, rectangular w/rounded corners, center w/color scene of a bottle & glass of beer w/a dish of food against a black ground, wording in white & blue w/a red band, slight wear, 10 1/2 x 13" (ILLUS.).. **66**

Serving, "Bucyrus Brewing Co.," pre-Prohibition, rectangular w/rounded corners, wood-grained ground, the center w/a color printed standing portrait of a Dutch girl holding a tray of beer, blue apron & red bodice w/white bonnet, gold letters in border read "Ehrenpreis - Bucyrus Brewing Co. - "Brownie" - The Quality Brews," 10 x 13" (some spots & rim chips) **150**

Serving, "Budweiser Beer," tin lithographed, titled "St. Louis Levee in Early Seventies" w/"Copyright 1914 Anheuser Busch, Inc. St. Louis - King of Bottled Beer" at the bottom, 12 3/4 x 17 1/2" (soiling & scratches) **99**

Cardinal Beer Tray

Serving, "Cardinal Beer," porcelain pie tin-shaped, white ground printed in red wording "Drink Cardinal Beer - Costs 25% More to Brew, But Worth More - Standard Brewing Co. of Scranton, PA," narrow dark green border band, minor front scratches, some small back chips, slighly yellowed, 1940s, 12" d. (ILLUS.) **195**

Serving, "Clysmic King of Table Waters," rectangular, multicolored lithograph depicting woman sitting at spring w/bottle of Clysmic Water & an elk, marked "The American Art Works Co.," 14 1/4" x 10 3/4" **209**

Coca-Cola 1931 Serving Tray

Serving, "Coca-Cola," 1931, rectangular, smiling young barefoot boy wearing blue shirt, brown trousers, suspenders & straw hat, relaxing under a tree, eating a sandwich & bottle of Coca-Cola, his small black & white dog watching, Norman Rockwell artwork, 10 1/2 x 13 1/4" (ILLUS.).. **1,000**

1934 "Tarzan & Jane" Serving Tray

Serving, "Coca-Cola," 1934, rectangular, Johnny Weismuller & Maureen O'Sullivan (Tarzan & Jane), 10 1/2 x 13 1/4" rectangle (ILLUS.) **660**

Serving, "Coca-Cola," 1936, rectangular, young woman wearing formal white gown w/orchid corsage on left shoulder, holding glass & sitting near low table w/bottles & glass, 10 1/2 x 13 1/4"................ **450**

1940 "Girl Fishing" Coca-Cola Serving Tray

Serving, "Coca-Cola," 1940, "Girl Fishing," 10 1/2 x 13 1/4" rectangle (ILLUS.) **154**

Coca-Cola 1942 Serving Tray

Serving, "Coca-Cola," 1942, rectangular, "Two Girls at Car," features two girls enjoying bottles of Coca-Cola, one standing & leaning on the door of a convertible where the other woman is sitting, unused condition, 10 1/2 x 13 1/4" (ILLUS.) **605**

Coca-Cola "Lois" Serving Tray

Serving, "Coca-Cola," 1953-1960, smiling woman w/arm propped up & chin resting on hand, holding a bottle of Coke in other hand, multicolored litho w/various scenes on sides, handwritten "Lois" on woman's forehead, 10 1/2" w., 13 1/2" l., minor scratches (ILLUS.).. **40-60**

Columbia Ice Cream Serving Tray

Serving, "Columbia Ice Cream," round oval, tin w/lithograph showing a young woman petting her dog, a horse grazing in the background, scratches, stains & dents, 16" l. (ILLUS.).. **130**

Congress Beer Serving Tray

Serving, "Congress Beer," round pie tin-shaped, printed at the interior top w/a small oval reserve w/a picture of the U.S. Capital above "Congress Beer" in gold & red all on a pale blue ground, gold border w/black wording "Haberle - Congress Brewing Co. - Syracuse, N.Y.," several nicks, 1930s, 13" d. (ILLUS.)......................... **181**

D. G. Yuengling & Son Serving Tray

Serving, "D.G. Yuengling & Son, Inc.," Pottsville, Pa. Beer Ale Porter, round, depicts horse's head inside letter "Y," ca. 1900-1925, 11 3/4" d. (ILLUS.) **88**

Serving, "Dawes Black Horse Ale & Porter," porcelain, round, logo above oval that reads "Dawes - Black Horse - Ale and Porter" all above "Dawes Brewery," done in white, yellow & green, 13" d. (minor scratches) **77**

Orange-Julep Serving Tray

Serving, "Drink Orange-Julep," rectangular w/rounded corners, a large color center scene of a 1920s bathing beauty sitting holding an umbrella & holding a glass of the soda, black border band w/orange wording, a few minor white spots, 10 1/2 x 13 1/4" (ILLUS.) **358**

Deer Run Whiskey Serving Tray

Serving, "Deer Run Whiskey," round, metal, lake & mountain scene w/impressive elk in foreground, black border w/gold lettering reading "Deer Run Whiskey - Aug. Baetzhold's Sons, Buffalo, NY," litho by Haeusermann, New York, 12" d. (ILLUS.) **275**

Dutch Club Beer Serving Tray

Serving, "Dutch Club Beer," scene in the center of a blond Dutch boy holding out a tray w/beer steins, pale yellow & blue, dark blue border, 1940s, minor nicks & scratches, 12" d. (ILLUS.) **110**

Derby Cream Ale Serving Tray

Serving, "Derby Cream Ale," round, large center scene of two horse heads, one black & one brown, racing neck & neck, white background, light blue border band printed in red "Derby Cream Ale - Brilliant and Export Ales.," printed in small letters under the horse heads "National Brewing Co., Syracuse, N.Y.," 1930s, overall scratches, rim chips, 12" d. (ILLUS.) **328**

Serving, "Dr. Pepper," rectangular, metal, pretty girl holding bottle in each hand w/"You'll like it too!" in upper corner, red border w/"Dr. Pepper" at top & bottom & "Drink a bite to eat" on each side, ca. 1940s (small shallow dents, light pitting & surface scratches) **605**

E. Robinson's Sons Beer Serving Tray

Serving, "E. Robinson's Sons," round, tin
w/lithograph scene of factory w/train &
wagons in foreground & "E. Robinson's
Sons - Pilsner Bottled Beer" around border & "Haeusermann M.M. Co. Litho, NY.
Chic." at bottom, paint chips & crazing,
13 1/8" d. (ILLUS.) 762
Serving, "Eagle Brewing Co.," square
w/rounded corners, color center half-
length portrait of a pretty turn-of-the-
20th-century lady w/brown hair wearing a
pale blue gown & holding up a glass of
beer against a dark ground, the border
band printed in gold "The Eagle Brewing
Co. - Ales - Lager - Utica, N.Y. - Both
Phones 645," 1910s, 13" w. (overall
chips & scuffs) 293

Stagg Company Whiskey Serving Tray

Serving, "George T. Stagg Co. O.F.C.
Bourbon," round, metal, image of stag
w/trees & sunset in background, red border reading "The George T. Stagg Company - Frankford, KY," edge scuffs & mi-
nor crazing, 12" d. (ILLUS.) 220

Edelweiss Beer Serving Tray

Serving, "Edelweiss Beer," center color
bust portrait of a pretty young red-head-
ed girl wearing a white & red shawl
against a black ground, the border band
w/edelweiss blossoms, dated 1913,
backside repainted, 13" d. (ILLUS.) 154
Serving, "Ehret's (Geo.) Extra," oval, oval
black central reserve printed in red &
gold w/a six-point star w/monogram
above "New York," wide red oval ring
printed in gold & black "Geo. Ehret's Extra - Hell Gate Brewery," black outer border band printed w/clusters of wheat
along each side & w/a small red star at
the top & bottom end, early 1900s,
13 1/2 x 16 1/2" (wear on black, small
overall nicks, rim chips) 155
Serving, "Fort Schuyzer Ales & Lager,"
round, white lettering reads "Fort
Schuyzer - Ales & Lager" on black
ground, 11 1/4" d. (some scratches) 44
Serving, "Fro-Joy Ice Cream," lithographed
tin, 13 3/4" l. (minor scratches) 28
Serving, "Frontenac Breweries Limited,"
round, large central color scene of the
brewery w/"Frontenac - Canada's Best"
in gold, upright border band printed
"Frontenac Breweries Limited - Montre-
al," 1930s, 12" d. (minor overall scratch-
es) 120

Goebel Beer Serving Tray

Serving, "Goebel Beer," round pie tin-
shaped, center color scene of a German
man wearing a red vest & white shirt
seated at a table holding a mug of beer
w/the bottle in front, border printed in
gold & green w/wheat & hop vines, center reads "Goebel Beer - Detroit, U.S.A.,"
overall wear, some scuffs, few small
spots, 1910s, 12" d. (ILLUS.) 372

Golden Drops Lager Beer Serving Tray

Serving, "Golden Drops Lager Beer," pre-
Prohibition, rectangular w/rounded cor-

ners, center color scene of Cavaliers sitting & standing around a tavern table drinking, red arch above scene reads "Decidedly Different," green lettering below scene reads "Two Rivers Beverage Co. - Twin Rivers, Wisconsin," wide light green border band w/white wording "Golden Drops Lager Beer," minor nicks, few small dings, 10 x 13" (ILLUS.) **165**

Serving, "Grand Complete Horse Furnishers," tin, entitled "Good Morning," depicts stable scene w/dogs coming to visit a mare & her colt, ca. 1909, artist-signed, Henry Stoll American Art Works, 13 x 13" (some overall crazing, pitting, scratching & surface rust) **230**

Haines-CeBrook Ice Cream Serving Tray

Serving, "Haines-CeBrook Ice Cream - 'The Better Kind'," rectangular w/rounded corners, red border band w/gold trim, half-length portrait of a smiling young woman eating ice cream, wearing a red tam hat & black dress fading into the black background, minor scrapes & blemishes, 10 1/2 x 15 1/4" (ILLUS.) **182**

Serving, "Hanley's Ale," center w/black ground, printed w/a large black & white bulldog reclining above gold & red word "Hanley's" above "Peerless Ale" in red, white & black," location of brewery in small white letters at the bottom, narrow red border band w/gold wording, 1930s, 12" d. (minor spots & marks) **67**

Hershey's Serving Tray

Serving, "Hershey's Milk Chocolate," depicts a child holding a bar of chocolate hatching from a cocoa shell, 8 3/4 x 12" (ILLUS.) **86**

Hires Serving Tray with Pretty Girls

Serving, "Hires Root Beer," oval lithographed metal, center color scene w/bust portraits of two pretty young women drinking from large glass w/straws, border band printed w/repeating word "Hires," the center scene includes "Drink Hires" at the right end, based on artwork by Harry Morse Meyers, ca. 1915, professionally restored, 19 1/2 x 23 1/2" (ILLUS.) **1,100**

detail

Early Hires Serving Tray with Hires Boy

Serving, "Hires Root Beer," oval lithographed tin, wide wood-grained border band around a center color image of the Hires boy holding a mug of root beer & laughing & pointing, white wording reads "Say Hires," some professional paint-in, ca. 1907, 20 x 24" (ILLUS.) **1,540**

Serving, "Hires," round, metal w/lithograph depicting Josh Slinger, Hires soda jerk, in white suit, red tie, holding glass, "Hires

5¢" in red near center, Josh Slinger signature near bottom, red border w/"Things
is getting higher but - Hires are still a
nickel a trickle," 1915, 13" d. (heavy
scratches, light chipping & wear) **138**
Serving, "Hoffman's Ice Cream," litho-
graphed tin, 15 1/4" h. (flaking & scratch-
es) **77**
Serving, "Horse Head Beer & Ale," round,
central large brown horse head on a pale
yellow ground titled "Champion Don
Juan," dark green border band w/yellow
wording, 1940s, 12" d. **162**

Howertown Sanitary Dairy Serving Tray

Serving "Howertown Sanitary Dairy," metal,
square, "Howertown Sanitary Dairy -
Clarified and Pasteurized Milk and
Cream" above milk bottle w/image of
baby & a circle reading "Mothers Darling
Fine as Silk - Because She Uses Our
Milk" & flanked by "Grade A Guernsey
Butter & Cottage Cheese" on right side &
"Phone 644 - Northampton, PA. - R.F.D.
No. 1" on the left, Wm. H. Kleppinger
Prop, Northampton, Pa., paint chips to
edges, minor denting, edge wear,
scratches & soiling, 13 1/4" sq. (ILLUS.) **72**
Serving, "Iroquois Beer & Ale," round, cen-
ter reads "Iroquois - Indian Head" above
image of Indian chief head, all above
"Beer & Ale - Buffalo, N.Y.," done in red,
blue, yellow & green, 12" d. **94**
Serving, "Jacob Ruppert Beer Ale," oval
lithographed metal, black & yellow border
bands around a green board background
w/the wording in yellow above two hands
holding up large mugs of beer, ca. 1939,
10 3/4 x 14 1/2" (overall scuffs & soiling) **39**
Serving, "Jno. T. Barbee Whiskey," tin,
oval, lithograph scene of people near log
cabin taste testing some Old Barbee
Whiskey w/"H. D. Beach Co. Coshocton,
O." at bottom, Jno. T. Barbee & Co., Lou-
isville, Ky., 13 1/2 x 16 1/2" **110**
Serving, "Kaier's Beer," oval, colorful large
central image of large cut roses in red,
pink & white w/green & yellow leaves,
border band of hop vines, printed in small
black letters in the center bottom "Kaier's
- Beer, Ale & Porter. - Bottled and Pasteurized at Brewery," early 1900s,

13 1/2 x 16 1/2" (wear, rim chips, few
scratches, light dent in rim) **222**
Serving, "Labatt's Ale Beer," porcelain,
round, red lettering "Ale, Lager - Ane
Stout - Labatt's - London Canada - Established Over 100 Years" above Union
tradmark, all on white ground, 13" d. (mi-
nor chips & scratches) **88**

Lykens Brewing Company Serving Tray

Serving, "Lykens Brewing Company," oval,
tin, depicts beautiful woman & horse,
"Lykens Brewing Company - The Home
of 'Cream Top' Lager Beer," ca. 1905,
Chas. Ehlen, some minor chipping & light
staining, 13 1/2 x 16 1/2" (ILLUS.) **403**

McAvoys Malt Marrow Beer Tray

Serving, "McAvoys Malt Marrow Beer,"
round, tin w/lithograph showing small boy
w/white shirt, blue knee pants, one brown
shoe, the other foot bare, curly hair
w/large cap, holding bottle & horn, brown
& white dog behind him w/red script
lettering "Malt-Marrow" in center,
"McAvoy Beats 'Em All" around border,
"Chas. W. Shonk Co. Litho Chicago" at
bottom, crazing, paint chips & soiling,
12" d. (ILLUS.) **242**

Serving, "Monarch Ale," pre-Prohibition, round, overall dark woodgrain background w/a large printed bottle of the product in the center in color, 12" d. (few scattered chips).. 257

Serving, "National Brewery - St. Louis, Mo.," rectangular w/rounded corners, color lithographed metal w/large brewery scene & picture of a bottle, 10 x 13 3/4", ca. 1900 (few small nicks & spots).. 330

Serving, "National Brewing Co.," round, center w/pale yellow ground centered by a large blue dot under a large red star overprinted in white script "National Brewing Co.," maroon border printed in yellow "Brilliant Ale - Porter and India Pale," 1930s, 12" d. (light overall scratches) 251

Nugrape Serving Tray

Serving, "Nugrape," rectangular, metal, center oval depicts hand holding bottle, black border w/yellow lettering at top & bottom reading "A Flavor You Can't Forget," litho by American Art Works, Coshocton, Ohio, rim chips & minor scratches, 10 1/2 x 13" (ILLUS.) 99

NuGrape Soda Serving Tray

Serving, "NuGrape Soda," rectangular w/rounded corners, beautiful young woman holding bottle, the top & bottom borders reading "A Flavor You Can't Forget," light wear & scratches, 10 1/2 x 13 1/4" (ILLUS.).............................. 121

Serving, "Old Reading Beer," round, colorful center scene of a cartoon-style barkeeper holding a mug of beer high above a begging brown & white dog, red, yellow & white wording on a dark blue ground, dark red border band w/yellow wording "Reading Brewery Inc. - Reading, PA," 1930s, 13" d. (few rim scuffs) 122

Serving, "Oneida Brewing Co.," porcelain pie tin-shaped, round w/center standing black & white portrait of "Chief Shenandoah," black band w/white wording "Oneida Brewing Co. - Ales & Porter - Utica, N.Y.," 1930s, 12" d. (few chips) **466**

Serving, "Pacific Beer," pre-Prohibition, round, a color scene of Mt. Rainier w/a lakeside landscape in the foreground, wide pale yellow border printed in brown "Pacific Beer - Best East or West - Pacific Brewing & Malting Co. - Tacoma," brown border band, back packing slip dated 1912, 12" d. (few rim chips, some light web crackling overall) 140

Serving, "Rainier Pale Beer," ceramic glazed base w/tin plate surround, open D-form side handles, snowy scene w/evergreens & mountain in background, top marked "Compliments - Of - The - Season," light surface scratches, one handle loose, 9 1/4" d. plus handles........................... 99

Serving, "Red Raven," round metal, lithograph scene of small nude boy w/one foot on a box & reaching up onto a cabinet for a bottle, large red bird on box next to him, border reads "Red Raven - Ask the Man," ca. 1910 (light scratches, overall wear, minor dents).................................... **1,265**

Robinson's Sons Brewery Serving Tray

Serving, "Robinson's (E.) Sons Brewery," round pie tin-shaped, large color center scene of a large brewery in red, yellow, green, etc., red border band printed in gold "E. Robinson's Sons - Pilsener

Bottled Beer," 1910s, wear & rim chips, few chips on inside rim, 13" d. (ILLUS.)........ **401**

Ruhstaller Brewery Serving Tray

Serving, "Ruhstaller Brewery," oval tin, lithograph showing man w/beard smoking pipe & sitting in arm chair near table, decorated border w/"Ruhstaller Brewery - Sacramento Cal." & "Ruhstaller Lager & Gilt Edge Steam Beer" upper center, minor scuff marks, surface rust on back, 13 1/2 x 16 1/2" (ILLUS.)................................ **330**

Serving, "Ruhstaller Gilt Edge Lager," lithographed metal, round, center scene of brewery w/"Ruhstaller Gilt Edge Lager & Steam" in gold lettering at top, by American Art Works, Coshocton, Ohio, 13" d. (minor scrapes & edge dings)........................ **440**

Serving, "Seipp's Extra Pale Beer," pre-Prohibition, round, colorful center scene of two pretty young women seated next to each other in a garden surrounded by yellow roses w/a bottle & glass of the beer in the left foreground, wording around the border, 12" d. (overall nicked & spotted)... **196**

Star Brewery Serving Tray

Serving, "Star Brewery," round, metal w/center image of three white horse heads, gold lettering reads "Star Brewery - Brewers of the Famous Hop-Gold," Star Brewery, Vancouver, Washington, few minor scrapes, 12" d. (ILLUS.) **523**

Serving, "Stegmaier's Beer - Ale Porter," round pie tin-shaped, central scene of a red brewery building scene below the

large red wording all on a pale yellow ground, small black wording along lower inner rim "Stegmaier Brewing Co. - Wilkes-Barre, PA," outer border of wheat & hops printed in black on yellow, red border bands, 1910s, 12 1/2" d. (some rust & wear spots).. **213**

Sunrise Beer Serving Tray

Serving, "Sunrise Beer," round, large center scene w/a large rising sun over a lake w/a green & yellow field w/scattered green fields in the foreground, bottle of the product in the front right, printed in red "Sunrise Beer - Brightens Every Day," red border band, 1930s, few minor scratches & chips, 12" d. (ILLUS.) **182**

Serving, "Utica-Club Beer," round w/upturned rim, outside of center reads "Utica-Club - West End Brewery Co. Utica Co.," in the center is a graphic of the brewery below "The Famous Utica Beer," inside of rim reads "Pilsner Lager Beer - XXX Cream le" painted red, yellow, blue, green & black, 12" d. (minor scratches)......... **18**

Wieland's Beer Serving Tray

Serving, "Wieland's Beer," rectangular, tin, depicts beautiful lady reading a letter in a garden, American Art Works, ca. 1909, some overall crazing & chipping to rim, 10 1/2 x 13 1/2" (ILLUS.)............................... **173**

Serving, "Wright & Taylor Old Charter Distillery," round, tin lithographed w/scene of distillery in background & girls wading in pond in foreground, circular insert w/bottle on right side, "Distillery, Louisville, Ky." at top center, border w/"Wright & Taylor - Old Charter Distillery," 12" d. (minor scratches, soiling & staining) **363**

Chapter 23
Watch Fobs

Ft. Worth, Texas bank on the back, original leather strap, fob 1 1/2" w. (ILLUS. of both sides)...................................... **110**
"Coca-Cola," metal, oval w/bulldog on front, "Drink Coca-Cola Delicious and Refreshing 5¢" on back, 1 1/4" w., 1 1/4" h. **150**

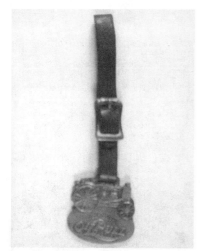

Advance Rumley Oil Pull Watch Fob

"Advance Rumley Oil Pull," metal, embossed tractor, marked on oval base "Oil Pull," leather strap, Advance Rumley, LaPorte, Indiana, by F. H. Noble & Co., ca. 1910, 1 5/8 x 1 1/2" (ILLUS.)... **$225-275**

Saddle-shaped Watch Fob

"Hamley & Co.," stamped brass model of a saddle on a leather strap, marked "The Roundup," from Pendleton, Oregon, 1 1/2 x 3" (ILLUS.)... **110**

Sterling Silver Bank Watch Fob

Bank, "Western National Bank," marked sterling silver, scroll-trimmed medallion-form w/a profile bust of a Native American chief on the front & the advertising for the

John Deere Watch Fob

"John Deere," oval, enameled metal w/brown running deer logo against blue ground, leather strap, ca. 1910, 1 1/2 x 1 3/4" (ILLUS.) **175-225**

Old Dutch Cleanser Watch Fob

"Old Dutch Cleanser," round enameled metal w/Dutch girl image in blue & white on yellow background, braided leather strap, Cudahy Packing Company, by Green Duck Co., Chicago, Illinois, ca. 1910, 1 1/4 x 1 3/4" (ILLUS.)................ **125-175**

Rare John Deere Watch Fob

"John Deere," oval metal medallion w/a black enamel ground & a silvered metal leaping deer & plow logo, on original leather strap (ILLUS.)........................ **880**

Motor oil, "Magnolia Gasoline/Motor Oil," round, cloisonné, blue center w/green petaled flower & "Motor Oil" & reading around border "Magnolia Gasoline," by Robbins Co., 1 5/8" d. (professional repair in border).. **242**

Combination Watch Fob - Cigar Cutter

"Woodward's Pool Parlor," combination fob & cigar cutter, oblong nickel plate over brass w/an embossed image of horse head & bridle on one side & wording on the other, well detailed, 1 1/2 x 1 3/4" (ILLUS. of both sides)............ **160**

Oakland Automobiles Watch Fob

"Oakland Automobiles," enameled green & red acorn shape on leather strap, image of an antique auto & marked "Oakland," by Whitehead & Hoag, Newark, New Jersey, ca. 1910, 1 1/4 x 5" (ILLUS.)...................................... **275-350**

Y-B Cigars Watch Fob - Pen Knife

"Y-B Cigars," key-shaped simulated mother-of-pearl celluloid frame w/single fold-out knife blade, white w/blue lettering, appears unused, 7/8 x 2" (ILLUS.)................ **66**

Chapter 24
Miscellaneous Items

Nabisco Building Logo Sign

Architectural building sign, "Nabisco," die-cut porcelain w/reverse lip, company logo, red & white, removed from a corporate building, bends & chips at "antenna," 33 1/4 x 48", unusual & scarce item (ILLUS.) **$385**

Silhouette Pattern Railroad Ashtray

Ashtray, "Chesapeake & Ohio Railway," china, Silhouette patt. (ILLUS.) **100**

Badge, "Gilmore Lionhead," embossed tin in scroll shape, reads "Gilmore (motif of lion head) Lionhead" above, "Pennsylvania Oil" emblem & "Purest Pennsylvania Motor Oil" w/signature slot below, 2 3/4" w., 1 1/4" h. **385**

Badge, "Shell Oil," metal cloisonné design, seashell-shaped w/"Shell" in red lettering on gold background, 1 1/2" w., 1 1/2" h. **110**

Badge, "Union Pacific Railroad" guard, ca. 1900 .... **135**

Bag rack, "Whistle," tin w/silk screen detail w/elves different from the norm, 16 1/2 x 37" (some rust & wear) **625**

Bag sorter, counter-type, decorated poplar, upright sides w/quarter-round front w/open slots for various bags, the lower sides stenciled in black w/stylized scrolls, leaves & blossoms, old original varnish, red trim, late 19th c., 16" h. (some damage & repair) **550**

Ballpoint Pen

Ballpoint pen, "Planters Peanuts," advertising type, by Cross, blue & yellow, ca. 1970s (ILLUS.) **18**

Bank, "Big Boy," rubber, ca. 1977, 4 x 5 1/4", 9 3/8" h. **17**

Bank, "Boscul Coffee," tin, round, orangish red, reads "Boscul Coffee" in gold & black lettering on cream background label, depicts waiter serving coffee in diamond label, marked "Wm. S. Scull Co. N.J., N.Y., Ohio," 2 1/2" d., 2 1/4" h. **44**

Bank, "Esso," glass w/embossed lettering, reads "Watch Your Savings Grow With Esso," 4 3/4" w., 3 1/4" d., 4 3/4" h. **105**

Esso Bank

Bank, "Esso," molded plastic, service attendant in blue uniform w/Esso logo on shirt, missing trap on back, crackling to logo, 3 1/4" w., 2 1/2" d., 5" h. (ILLUS) **105**

Bank, "Mobilgas," baseball shape w/red Pegasus logo on one side & Indian head on reverse, metal screw cap on bottom w/coin slot, 3" d., 3" h. **77**

Bank, "Phillips 66," square clear glass block, embossed on one side "Phill-up with - Phillips 66 (in logo) - See What You Save," soiling, 3" w., 4 3/4" sq. **149**

Bank, "Phillips 66 Trop-Arctic Motor Oil," tin, oil can-shaped **24**

Plastic Mr. Peanut Bank

Bank, "Planters Peanuts," figural molded plastic, Mr. Peanut found in various colors, coin slot in top of removable hat, pale blue, green, red & peanut tan, 7" h., each (ILLUS.) **15**

Bank, "Sinclair," figural dinosaur, metal w/painted green head, 9 1/4" l., 5 1/4" h. **198**

Bank, "Texaco," plastic, figural gas pump, Texaco logo & "Sky Chief " on front, 1 5/8" w., 4 3/4" h., (top of gas hose broken off, front panel loose) **302**

Bank, "Mission Orange Drink," cylindrical tin, dated 1954, 12 oz. **35**

Bell, brass w/yoke, "Illinois Central Railroad," from steam locomotive, yoke marked "ICRR" **1,750**

Arlington Brand Bill Hook

Bill hook, "Arlington Pickles - Vinegar - Sauerkraut," round celluloid top disk in white, red & gold w/black & white wording, litho by Parisan Novelty Company, Chicago, Illinois, near mint, top 3 1/2" d. (ILLUS.) **99**

Bill hook, "Butter-Nut Coffee," celluloid, blue w/can shown in shades of brown & marked "Ask For Butter-Nut - Coffee Delicious," button 2 x 2 3/4", overall 7" l. **176**

Roberts Turkey Brand Bill Hook

Bill hook, "Roberts Turkey Brand Corned Meats," celluloid top button in white w/a red ring around a large black & red turkey, from a San Francisco dealer, minor scratches, button 2 3/8" d. (ILLUS.) **83**

Bill hook, "Walker Products," hanging-type, oval celluloid button printed in color w/pictures of various canned products, on a long metal hook holder, 2 x 6 1/2" **66**

Blotter, "Dr. Pepper," rectangular, green, shows three tilted bottles wrapped w/ribbon banner reading "Ten - Two - Four" (light mildew & wear)............................... **110**

F.O. Stone Baking Co. Blotter

Blotter, "F.O. Stone Baking Co.," rectangular celluloid giveaway dated 1915, by Whitehead & Hoag, scene of Santa in sleigh pulled by reindeer, Christmas greeting in upper right corner, 3 x 7 3/4" (ILLUS.)... **77**

Blotter, "Pan - Am" logo w/imprint "Keep Pace With Pan - Am Gasoline," illustration of airplane flying over countryside, 6 1/4" w., 3" h. (minor creases, fading & soiling, rounded edges) **176**

Blotter, "Smith Brothers Chewing Gum," rectangular printed in black & white w/bearded logo heads of the brothers & pictures of the products, dated 1913, unused, 4 x 9 1/2" **55**

Sunoco/Sun-Heat Furnace Oil Blotter

Blotter, "Sunoco/Sun-Heat Furnace Oil," rectangular, Disney theme showing Mickey Mouse sleeping in an easy chair near a window showing winter scene, marked "For Winter days, it's hard to beat The Warmth and Comfort of - Sun-Heat Furnace Oil," dealer information at bottom, dated 1939, minor bends, soiling & wear, 3 1/4 x 6" (ILLUS.) **358**

Blotter, "The Aetna Powder Company," long rectangular form w/the company name spelled out in large sticks of dynamite against a white ground, unused, some fly specks, 4 x 9 1/4" **44**

Book, "Post Cereal," titled "A Trip Through Postumville," hard cover, colorful, 1920 .... **45**

Booklet, "Cracker Jack," riddles, ca. 1896 .... **75**

Booklet, "Hercules Powder," 1927 .... **40**

Booklet, "Historic Tours in Socony Land," 1925, very good condition **22**

Booklet, "Pabst Beer, Milwaukee," fine color lithography, ca. 1893 .... **30**

Booklet, "Union Pacific Railroad," discussing Kansas, dated 1890 .... **65**

Bottle, miniature, "Horlick's - The Original Malted Milk - Sweet Chocolate Flavor Lunch Tablets...," cow shown on bottom of paper wrapper, unopened, 1 1/2" d., 3" h. (ILLUS. right) **32**

Horlick's Miniature Bottles

Bottle, miniature, in original wrapping printed w/"Horlick's Sweet Chocolate Flavor Malted Milk...," unopened, 1 1/2" d., 3" h. (ILLUS. left) **32**

Bottle carrying case, "Watkins," wooden, stenciled "Watkins Products" on one side, "Quality for over 70 years" on other,

"Watkins Gold Medal Vanilla" on one end w/"Watkins Coconut Oil Shampoo" on other, includes six Watkins products, five w/Watkins likeness on label, high center handle, 24" l., 8" deep, 10" h. **127**

Bottle opener, metal, folding-type w/corkscrew, marked "Gooderham & Worts Limited, Distillers of Fine Whiskey Since 1832" **125**

Bouillon cup, "Union Pacific Railroad," china, Harriman Blue patt. **35**

Bowl, small, "Missouri Pacific Railroad," china, "The Eagle patt." **75**

Bowl, "Union Pacific Railroad," shallow, china, Harriman Blue patt., 6" d. **25**

Box, "Baby Bunting Oats," cardboard, 1 lb. .. **1,430**

Box, "Mrs. S. A. Allen's World Hair Restorer" cardboard, depicts bust of lady w/full head of hair, 9" l., 4 1/2" deep, 7 1/2" h. (minor soiling & scratching) **316**

Box, "Williams' Root Beer Extract," wooden, paper label depicts comical scene of family in background w/boy spraying baby from bottle w/root beer, foreground depicts couple toasting, "No Other Root Beer Extract Equals Williams' in Strength and Purity" on paper fan, end labels read "The Kind That Suits," 10" l., 5" deep, 7 1/2" h. **230**

Winchester Shotgun Shell Box

Box, "Winchester Ranger Loaded Shot Shells," cardboard, colorful design w/an orange ground w/wording in dark orange & black w/a scene of a hunting dog on point, empty, 2 1/2 x 4", 4" h. (ILLUS.) **61**

Early California Box Label

Box label, "California Poppy Brand Oranges," lithographed paper, colorful design of California poppies on a white ground w/wording in red & blue, ca. 1900, 10 1/2 x 11" (ILLUS.)..................... 578

Box opener, "Wrigley's," wood, paddle-style w/string hanger at end, "Wrigley's Spearmint, Doublemint and Juicy Fruit," 14" l. 52

Bread plate, "Coon Chicken Inn," ceramic, round, white w/a red, pink & black caricature of a black man's face at the top, a dark blue dotted border band, made by Inca Ware, scattered tiny knife nicks, 5 1/2" d. 165

Brochure, "J. I. Case Threshing Machine Company," depicts Case car on front w/red lettering & black background, 36 pages, 5 3/4" w., 8 1/2" h. 33

Broiler, "Quaker Oats," graniteware, speckled black & light greenish aqua, 8" d., 8 1/4" h. 121

Broom holder, "Bond Bread," wooden stand below porcelain sign w/"Fresh Bond Bread," holds six brooms, gold, red & white, 19" w., 40 1/2" h. (wood frame soiled, small pieces missing on base & holes on top, paint loss to base, edge chips to porcelain) 220

Brush, "Chas. P. Shipley Saddlery Co.," premium item, oblong wood handle in yellow w/black prints including two vignettes, red rim band, new & unused in original box, 2 x 7" 33

Bubble gum wrapper, "Mickey Mouse," depicts large Mickey w/smaller images of Mickey, Minnie, Pluto, Clarabell & Horace, matted & framed, 10 x 11" 80-150

Butter pat, "St. Louis & San Francisco Railway," silver plate, by International Silver 100

Butter warmer, "Missouri Pacific Railroad," silver plate, by International Silver............. 50

Early Aviation Celluloid Button

Button, "Aviation Contest - Los Angeles - Jan. 1910," celluloid, large size w/a color panoramic scene of early airplanes, balloons & dirigibles flying above a large crowd of spectators, information on a large white flying banner, easel back stand, 6" d. (ILLUS.)............ 358

Cake box, Schepps tin, embossed on front & top w/artwork by Kaulbach on sides & front, front opening, 13" sq., 14" h. (paint chips, scratches & soiling, minor rust at bottom) 182

Crescent Trailways Bus Pin

Bus driver's pin, "National Trailways Bus System - Crescent Trailways - 186," die-cut painted metal, shield-shaped w/the upper portion in red, white & blue enamel w/the lower portion w/a silvery finish, double screw post mounts, minor overall wear, 2 3/8 x 2 9/16" (ILLUS.) 143

Cane & Umbrella Case

Cane & umbrella case, oak w/glass on four sides & top, Russell & Sons Co., Ilion, N.Y. ca. 1910, 14 x 30", 4" h. (ILLUS.)... 625-700

Cap badge, "Atchison, Topeka & Santa Fe Railway," metal, brakeman 95

Cap badge, "Chesapeake & Ohio Railway," metal, conductor 50

Cap badge, "Minneapolis, St. Paul & Sault Ste. Marie Railway" (Soo Line), metal, brakeman 95

Cap badge, "Missouri, Kansas & Texas Railway," metal, brakeman 60

Cap badge, "Missouri Pacific Railroad," metal, porter 110

Cap badge, "St. Louis & San Francisco Railway" (Frisco Lines), metal, brakeman 70

Carte de visite photo, Pittsburgh Railroad group shot of a work gang, ten men standing beside tracks holding shovels & picks, by B. Dabbs, Pittsburgh (soiling, top stain) 124

Early Locomotive Carte de Visite

Carte de visite photo, Smith, Dawson & Bailey Locomotives, nice shot of an early engine & wood car w/buildings in the background, promotion for Pittsburgh machinists, boiler makers, founders & locomotive makers, side of locomotive marked "B.B. & St. L. RR.," wood car marked on side "Newton," sharp image, corners trimmed, ink doodles at left not on image (ILLUS.) 272

Chair, "Fairbank's Gold Dust Washing Powders," tin insets, slat seat........................ 300

Chalkboard, "Robin's Best - America's Finest Flour," upright rectangular easel-back style, the top section w/a color image of a flour sack & red & yellow wording on a black ground, lower black ground divided by white horizontal lines, wording in top bands reads "Specials Today - Robin's Best Flour...," wording in bottom section in white & yellow reads "and don't forget Robin's Best Flour," 14 x 21 1/4" (very minor surface & edge wear, few small scatches)..................................... 303

Chalkboard w/thermometer, "Nor'Way Antifreeze," rectangular self-framed tin, a tall chalkboard w/a blue thermometer down one side, cartoon mechanic holding a can of the product in the lower left corner, advertising across the bottom in blue & white "Nor'way Reliable Service Anti-Freeze," w/original thermometer tube, 15 1/4 x 22, 14" h. (minor fading, scratches & soiling) 132

Coaster wagon, "Buster Brown Shoes," rectangular red metal bed w/rounded corners, rubber-rimmed red solid metal wheels, black handlebar, white band on sides w/wording in red, original paint & decals, 15 x 36", 15" h. (some scuffs, scratches & paint chips, one hub cap missing) 550

Coat, "Quaker State," beige leather w/sheepskin lining, Quaker State logo on vinyl breast patch, never worn (some fading to sleeves) 61

Coffee grinder, "Elgin National," counter display-type, cast iron, double wheel 400-600

Coffee grinder, "Enterprise," cast iron, floor model, double wheel, w/brass hopper & eagle, restored 1,375-1,800

"Enterprise" Coffee Grinder Counter Display

Coffee grinder, "Enterprise," counter display-type, cast iron, two-wheel, pat'd. 7-12-98 (ILLUS.)..................................... 400-550

Coffeepot, cov., "Chicago & Northwestern Railway," silver plate, International Silver....... 65

Coffeepot, cov., "Monroe-Matic Shock Absorbers," painted metal, footed cylindrical shape w/tab handles, "Is Your Car Safe - We Offer Complete Safety Inspection (Monroe logo) - Let Us Check Your - Shock Absorbers Now," working condition, 12" w., 14 1/2" h. (scratches, soiling & inside staining) 165

Coin, "Planters Peanuts," limited edition Mr. Peanut 75th anniversary, silver, 1 oz. ... 175-200

Comic book, "The Mighty Atom," starring Reddy Kilowatt, 1965............................. 40

Compass, "Dave Cook Sporting Goods Co. - corner 1601 Larimer St., Denver, Colorado," celluloid, lithograph by Parisian Novelty, Chicago, Illinois, working condition, 1 3/4" d. 66

Conductor's lantern, nickel-plated kerosene font w/a clear etched shade w/a foliate wreath centering "G.A. Pierce," marked by Adams & Westlake & patent-dated "64," 10 1/2" h. 460

Cork screw, "Champion," mechanical, cast iron, "Harter's Wild Cherry Bitters" plate attached to wooden bill, ca. 1900-1910, 8 3/4" h. 242

Cork screw, "Sample Dr. Harter's Wild Cherry Bitters The Best on Earth Pat. Apld.," mechanical counter top-style, iron, ca. 1900-1910, 8 5/8" l. 358

Crate, "Dr. Harte's Wild Cherry Bitters Dayton, Ohio, U.S.A. Dr. Harter The Dr. Harter Medicine Co. Dayton, O.," wood

w/black stenciling on all four sides,
13 1/4" w., 9" h. 209

Horlick's Shipping Crates

Crate, "Horlick's Malted Milk - 1/6 Doz. Original - Genuine - Hospital - Beware of Imi-
tations," machine-dovetailed wood, black
lettering & red logo, held packages for
hospital use, early 20th c., 9 x 16", 13" h.
(ILLUS. bottom)... 145
Crate, "Horlick's Malted Milk - Racine,
Wis.," machine-dovetailed wood, black
lettering & red logo, made to hold one
dozen glass flasks, early 20th c. (ILLUS.
upper left).. 80
Crate, "Horlick's Malted Milk Sample Pack-
ages," machine-dovetailed wood w/black
printing & red logo, early 20th c., 7 x 9",
4 1/2" h. (ILLUS. upper right).......................... 55

Mobiloil Crate

Crate, "Mobiloil," wood, contains three glass
quart oil bottles w/metal tops, all w/minor
wear (ILLUS.).. 193
Creamer, "Wabash Railroad," silver plate,
by International Silver 90

Rare John Deere Cricket Clicker

Cricket clicker, "John Deere," celluloid
w/white ground & black wording w/brown
deer leaping over a red-handled plow,
reads "I Chirp For The John Deere Plow
Co. - Omaha, Neb." (ILLUS.)............................ 743
Crock, cov., "Heinz Apple Jelly," stoneware
w/bail handle, 7 3/4" h. 950
Crock, cov., "Heinz Grape Jelly," stoneware
w/bail handle, 9 1/2" h. (tears to label)....... 1,050
Crumb catchers, "Eagle Lye," lithograph by
Chas. Shonk, Chicago, Illinois, semi-cir-
cular form, one w/product container
shown in center & "Use Eagle Lye - Purest & Best" & the other is marked "Send
for Our Book of Valuable Information -
Eagle   Lye   Works   -   Milwaukee
Wis." 1/2 x 6 1/2 x 9 1/4   & 3/8 x 3 x 7",
the pr. 193
Cup, "Baltimore & Ohio Railroad," china,
Centenary patt. 40
Cup & saucer, "Canadian National Rail-
way," demitasse, china, Queen Elizabeth
patt. 50
Cup & Saucer, "Missouri Pacific Railroad,"
china, Bismark patt... 53
Cup & saucer, "Union Pacific Railroad,"
china, Winged Streamliner patt. 20
Cups, "Dickinson's Ace Clover & Pine Tree
Timothy Seed," porcelain over metal,
blue & black lettering over creamy white
background, 2 5/8" d., 2 5/8" h. (some
chipping to porcelain)....................................... 35
Deck chairs, "Piedmont Cigarettes," folding-type, wood w/double sided porcelain
sign back, 31" h., pr. 475
Dice shaker, "Dr. Daniel's Remedies,"
glass, dome paperweight-shaped, depicts Dr. Daniel's on bottom & reads
"Don't Gamble - Use Dr. Daniel's Reme-
dies, Patd. Aug. 18, 1903," five dice, 3" d. 403
Dispenser, "Pulver Chewing Gum," porcelain, three-column tab vendor w/beveled
mirror on front & "Pulver Chewing Gum"
below, 31" h. (some slight chipping)............. 202
Dispenser, "Zeno Gum," oak w/tin lithographed   embossed   front   panel,
16 1/4" h. (some flaking & scratches) 1,100-1,500
Doll, "Malto Rice," cloth, uncut, shown
w/curly dark hair, high neck top, long

sleeves, knee pants & long stockings, instructions to side, "Copyrighted November 1899 By The American Rice Food And Manufacturing Co. Matawan, N.J.," 17 1/2" w., 34 1/2" h. (soiling & fold marks).. 143

Michelin Doll

Doll, "Michelin," plastic, counter top model, marked "1966 Michelin ETCIE-Made in France" on back, 19" h. (ILLUS.) 231

Michelin Man Baby Doll

Doll, "Michelin," rubber, wearing a blue bib embossed "Michelin" & holding a Michelin Man doll, some soil, dirt & paint loss, 4 3/4" w., 7" h. (ILLUS.) 138
Doll, "Miss Flaked Rice," printed stuffed cloth w/hand-made cotton dress in a blue print, early 20th c., 23 1/2" h. (wear, a couple of holes)... 248

Door pane, "Lucky Strike It's Toasted Cigarettes," glass in red, white & black, depicts pack of cigarettes, reverse marked "Thank You - Call Again!," ca. 20th c., 10 1/4" x 14 1/4" 187

Baltimore Enamel Novelty Co. Door Push

Door push, "Baltimore Enamel & Novelty Co.," rectangular, porcelain on metal, green w/black & white letters reading "Please Close Door - The Baltimore Enamel & Novelty Co.," ca. 1910, 2 3/4 x 4" (ILLUS.) **125-175**
Door push, "Bunny Bread," metal w/"Everybody Loves (imprint of bunny head) Bunny Enriched Bread" & "Copyright American Bakers Cooperative, Inc. 4.17.56," 28" w., 3" h. (some soiling & minor paint chips).. 242
Door push, "Butternut Bread," die-cut heavy tin, 8 3/4 x 19 3/4"............................. 300
Door push, "Crescent Flour," rectangular, embossed tin," - Push-And Try A Sack Of (flour bag w/Crescent Flour logo) Crescent Flour Sold Here" in white lettering on black background, 33 3/4" w. 182

Crystal White Soap Door Push

Door push, "Crystal White Soap," rectangular, metal, blue w/white lettering reading

"Come In - Crystal White - The Billion Bubble Soap," minor scrapes, 3 1/2 x 8 3/4" (ILLUS.) **259**

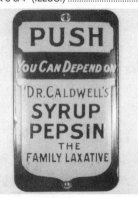

Dr. Caldwell's Syrup Pepsin Door Push

Door push, "Dr. Caldwell's Syrup Pepsin," rectangular, porcelain on metal, black & yellow, reads "Push - You Can Depend on Dr. Caldwell's Syrup Pepsin - The Family Laxative," ca. 1920s, 3 3/4 x 6 3/8" (ILLUS.) **150-200**

Ex-Lax Door Push

Door push, "Ex-Lax," rectangular, porcelain on metal, blue, white, yellow & red, product package in center marked "For Relief of Constipation - Ex-Lax - the Chocolated Laxative," top marked "Pull" & bottom w/"Get Your Box Now!," ca. 1920s, 4 x 8" (ILLUS.) **150-225**

Door push, "Five Roses Flour," porcelain **125**

Door push, "Fleischmann's Yeast," rectangular, lithographed tin by Haeusermann, New York, depicts a bread figure w/apron & chef's hat, marked "Eat Bread" at top & "Made with Fleischmann's Yeast" at bottom, 3 1/4 x 9" **99**

Door push, "Hart Batteries," porcelain, white lettering on black background, 32" w., 3 1/4" h. (scratches) **110**

Door push, "King Cole Tea-Coffee," 3 x 31 1/2" **200**

Pinkerton's Detective Agency Door Push

Door push, "Pinkerton's National Detective Agency," rectangular, porcelain on metal, black w/white letters reading "Member of The Jewelers' Security Alliance - For Protection Against Burglary - Sneak Theft - Holdup - Pinkerton's Nat. Detective Agency - Detective Agents for the Alliance" w/red & white oval image of reclining dog, ca. 1920, 3 3/8 x 7 1/4" (ILLUS.) **325-400**

Pinkertons Detective Agency Door Push

Door push, "Pinkertons Nat. Detective Agency," rectangular, porcelain on metal, blue w/white lettering reading "Member of The Jewelers' Security Alliance for Protection Against Burglary - Pinkertons Nat. Detective Agency - Detective Agents for the Alliance," w/brown & white oval image of reclining dog, ca. 1900, 3 3/8 x 7 1/4" (ILLUS.) **400-500**

Door push, "Savage Stevens Fox," wood, painted "Savage . Stevens . Fox" above w/American Indian logo & "World Famous Rifles & Shotguns" below, 3" w., 20" l. **288**

Door push, "Sunbeam Bread," leaf-shaped, red, white & blue, depicts Miss Sunbeam w/"Sunbeam - Batter Whipped," 9 x 19" **413**

Door push, "Vick's," porcelain, palm press type w/"For Colds," 3 3/4 x 7 3/4" **400**

Door push bar, "Sunbeam Bread," heavy steel, an oblong color image of a loaf of bread in white, blue & red w/a color image of the Sunbeam girl, dark blue mounting strips at the ends, reads "Sunbeam - Batter Whipped," 8 3/4 x 26 1/2" (minor edge wear, scratches & flecks) **248**

Rainbo Bread Door Push & Handle

Door push w/handle, "Rainbo Bread," steel
blue bar w/attached oval sign in blue
w/yellow & red border bands, white letters in center reading "Rainbo is good
Bread," w/vertical blue steel bar & attached metal handle, light scratches,
8 1/2 x 26 1/2" (ILLUS.) **231**
Door transom window, "Mobil Gasoline,"
reverse-painted glass, rectangular long
glass panel w/an early red flying Pegasus logo against a solid black ground
w/a red stripe across the top, set in a
green-painted wood frame, 15 x 37 1/2"
(edge flaking, soiling & some fading) **264**
Doorway arch, "Buster Brown," wood, two-
panel die-cut, depicts "Buster Brown" &
"Tige" playing in trees, each panel 42" w.,
36" h. **58**

Planters Draw-string Pants

Drawstring pants, "Planters Peanuts," Mr.
Peanut pattern on blue background,
lightweight denim, adult sizes, ca. 1960s
(ILLUS.) **50**

George Long Dust Pan

Dust pan, "George Long, Vanderbilt,
Mich.," embossed tin, blue w/gold trim,
bright colorful lithograph center scene of
couple, scalloped top w/floral medallions,
minor scuff marks, 8 3/4 x 9" (ILLUS.) **55**
Engine headlight, "Illinois Central Rail-
way," #2545 .... **2,100**
Envelope, "Winchester Store," 1925................... **40**
Fan, "Bordens Condensed Milk Company,"
cardboard, color illustration of a young
girl on ice skates, ca. 1910.............................. **48**

Rare Kis-Me Gum Paper Fan

Fan, "Kis-Me Gum," folding paper forming a
circle, wooden sticks, wording printed in
black, appears unused, 10" d. open
(ILLUS.).. **523**

Kasco Feed Scale

Feed scale, "Kasco Feeds," metal w/de-
bossed lettering, marked "Milk at Low
Cost (numbered dial) Use the Scales,
Weigh the Milk, Weigh the Feeds," some
tarnish, 4 1/2" w., 16" h. (ILLUS.).................. **143**
Floor display rack, "Blackman's Medicated
Salt Brick," wood w/tin marquee, top marquee depicts horse licking "Salt Brick"
w/"Blackman's Medicated" above & "Every Animal Its Own Doctor" below, manufactured by "Blackman Stock Remedy
Co. of Chattanooga, Tenn.," 16 1/2" w.,
31 1/2" h. **288**
Floor display rack, "Blu-J Brooms," em-
bossed tin, depicts a Blue Jay sitting atop

a broom, advertising front & back, includes four brooms, 23 1/2" w., 35" h. **518**

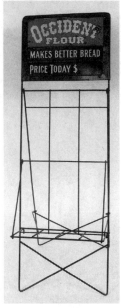

Occident Flour Advertising Floor Stand

Floor stand, "Occident Flour," for bread, tin lithographed advertising panel, 34" h. (ILLUS.) **150-225**
Flour barrel, "Portland Milling Company," wood, end paper label depicts trademark picture of girl wearing large hat, 28" h. **58**

King Midas Flour Scoop

Flour scoop, "King Midas Flour," lithographed tin w/white ground & orange

wording on outside of bowl, slight wear, 1 3/4 x 4" (ILLUS.) **165**
Funnel, "Dr. Van Dyke's Holland Bitters Van Dyke Bitters Co St. Louis," copper w/soldered spout & riveted handle, ca. 1890-1910, 7 3/8" h. **50**

Kanotex Aviation Gasoline Globe

Gas pump globe, "Kanotex Aviation," single lens, airplane image on bottom of lens, tiny surface scratches, 13 1/2" d. (ILLUS.) **2,200**
Glass, juice, "Chesapeake & Ohio Railway" **4**
Glass, juice, "Missouri, Kansas & Texas Railway" **70**
Glass, juice, "Union Pacific Railroad" **12**
Glassine bag, "Planters Pennant Salted Peanuts, The Nickel Lunch," five cent bag, ca. 1940s.. **10**
Globe, "Red Goose Shoes," milk white globe w/debossed red goose on one side & "Friedman-Shelby All Leather Shoes" on reverse, milk white pedestal base, 10" w., 12" h. (repaired & repainted globe)... **288**
Gravy boat, "Missouri, Kansas & Texas Railway," silver plate, by R. Wallace **120**

Rare Pulver's Kola-Pepsin Gum Box

Gum, "Pulver's Kola-Pepsin Chewing Gum," cardboard box, tall red vending machine shown on left, ornate black & pink wording on white ground on right, early 20th c. (ILLUS.)................................... **3,300**

Borden's Products Hat Badge

Hat badge, "Borden's," porcelain, oval, dark blue ground w/white border band & brand name in large white letters, minor wear & scratches, paint chip above one letter, screw posts appear to be replaced, 1 3/4 x 2 3/4" (ILLUS.) **33**

Fina Hat Badge

Hat badge, "Fina," triangular, metal w/porcelain inlay in red, yellow & blue, 1 1/2" w., 1 3/4" h. (ILLUS.) **165**

Hat badge, "National Trailways Bus System," die-cut, from Carolina Scenic Trailways, 2 1/2 x 2 5/8" **425**

Rare Stick of Yellow Kid Chewing Gum

Gum, "Yellow Kid Chewing Gum," wrapper from one stick, in white w/center picture of Yellow Kid dressed in yellow, lettering in black w/red trim, early 20th c. (ILLUS.) .. **1,265**

Gum package, "Sterling Cinnamon Gum," full pack of five sticks of gum, blue & white label, 1/2 x 3/4 x 3" **72**

Hat, brakeman, "Missouri, Kansas & Texas Railway" **120**

Hat, brakeman, "Rock Island Lines" **120**

Hat, conductor, "St. Louis & San Francisco Railway" **190**

Hat, "Harley-Davidson," black cloth & vinyl, Harley-Davidson logo on front, white rope trim, logo stamped in fabric inside hat, size 7 1/4" **160**

Hat, "Kool-Aid," red cloth soda jerk-style, promotes "Junior Aviation Corps" **60**

Yellow Cab Operator's Hat Badge

Hat badge, "Yellow Cab," die-cut metal, squared silvered metal form w/stepped edges, round yellow enameled center w/black wording, outer ring band incised w/"Yellow Cab Co. of Virginia - Operator - 284," double screw post, 1 3/4 x 2 1/4" (ILLUS.) **77**

Yellow Cab Cab Driver's Hat

Hat, "Yellow Cab," yellow nagahyde cap w/black wording, woven vent band & black bill, some embroidery missing, size 7 3/8 (ILLUS.) **110**

B.I. Barlow Ice Pick

Ice pick, "B.I. Barlow - Gold Field, Nev" on four-sided wood handle also reading "Ice and Fuel, Beverage, Flowers and Cereals" & phone number, near mint, rare (ILLUS.) 140

Jar, "Edison," ceramic, white figural battery w/"Edison-Lalande Battery March 20, 1888" on lid, 14" h. 115

Jar, "Roundup Coffee," 1 lb. clear glass jar in wide cylindrical form w/rounded base & shoulder, stippled upper & lower sections w/smooth center band w/a paper label printed in blue, gold, white & red, white metal screw-on lid, made for the Round Up Grocery Company of Spokane, Washington, 4 x 6" 121

Jar, "Horlick's Malted Milk, Racine," clear glass, 1/2 pint 20

Jigsaw puzzle, "Baby Ruth Candy Bar," rectangular cardboard puzzle w/a color scene of a young boy & girl w/their dog, seated on the ground under a large orange umbrella w/each eating a candy bar, a large bar & the label shown in the foreground, professionally framed & matted, puzzle glued down, image 5 1/2 x 7" 77

Key, switch-type, "Atchison, Topeka & Santa Fe Railway" 35

Key, switch-type, "Illinois Central Railroad" 25

Key, switch-type, "St. Louis & San Francisco Railway" 60-65

Key, switch-type, "Texas & Pacific Railroad" 35

Key, switch-type, "Union Pacific Railroad" 75

Key chain, "Planters Peanuts," limited edition Mr. Peanut 75th anniversary coin, silver, rare, 1 oz. 375-400

Key chain, "Planters Peanuts," limited edition Mr. Peanut 75th anniversary coin, brass 100-125

Key chain, "Planters Peanuts," limited edition Mr. Peanut 75th anniversary coin, brass, prototype 100-125

Knife sharpener, "Winchester," on original cardboard 40

Ladle, "St. Louis & San Francisco Railway," silver plate 40

Lamp, "Bosch," plastic figural spark plug w/glass globe, reads "Bosch Germany," 10" d., 21 1/2" h. 231

Lamp, "Poll-Parrot Shoes," electric, metal base w/"Quality speaks for itself" decal label, wood parrot cut-out w/slightly curling decal & perched on an oval sign marked "Poll - Parrot - Shoes," plastic "stained glass" shade w/"Poll - Parrot - Shoes" in oval, 8" d., 19" h. (cord has small nicks) 77

Lantern, "Atchison, Topeka & Santa Fe Railroad," short globe-type, red globe w/raised lettering 140

Lantern, "Baltimore & Ohio Railroad," tall globe-type, clear globe w/raised wording & "Safety First" 120

Lantern, "Boston & Albany Railroad," tall globe-type, red unmarked globe 90

Lantern, "Buffalo, Rochester & Pittsburgh Railroad," tall globe-type, bell-bottom style, clear globe w/raised lettering 160

Lantern, "Burlington Route," tall globe-type, clear globe w/raised lettering 95

Lantern, "Canadian Pacific Railroad," short globe-type, clear globe w/raised lettering, wooden handle 50

Lantern, "Chesapeake & Ohio Railway," short globe-type, clear etched globe 60

Lantern, "Chicago & Eastern Illinois Railroad," short globe-type, clear etched globe also w/"Safety First" 60

Lantern, "Chicago, Milwaukee, St. Paul & Pacific Railroad," short globe-type, clear globe w/raised lettering 50

Lantern, "Chicago, St. Paul, Minneapolis & Omaha Railway," tall globe-type, Dietz barn-style frame, red globe w/raised lettering "C.S.T.P. M. & O." 400

Lantern, "Chicago & Western Indiana Railroad," short globe-type, unmarked red globe 65

Lantern, "Cleveland, Cincinnati, Chicago & St. Louis Railway," tall globe-type, clear globe w/raised wording "Safety First" 80

Lantern, "Colorado Midland," tall globe-type, clear unmarked globe 400

Lantern, "Colorado & Southern Railway," tall globe-type, bell-bottom style, red unmarked globe 200

Lantern, "Delaware, Lackawanna & Western Railroad," tall globe-type, clear globe w/raised wording "Safety First" 90

Lantern, "Denver & Rio Grande Railroad," short globe-type, red etched globe 105

Lantern, "Denver & Rio Grande Railroad," tall globe-type, clear globe w/raised wording "Safety First" 130

Lantern, "Erie Railroad," tall globe-type, clear globe w/raised lettering 90

Lantern, "Florida East Coast Railway," short globe-type, Adlake mark on frame, cobalt blue globe w/MacBeth mark 95

Lantern, "Great Northern Railway," tall globe-type, red globe w/raised lettering 210

Lantern, "Gulf, Colorado & Santa Fe Railway," tall globe-type, bell-bottom style, clear globe w/raised wording "Santa Fe" 210

Lantern, "Gulf, Mobile & Ohio Railroad," tall globe-type, Dietz barn style, unmarked cobalt blue globe 170

Lantern, "Illinois Central Railroad," tall globe-type, clear globe w/raised lettering 135

Lantern, "Minneapolis, St. Paul & Sault Ste. Marie Railway" (Soo Line), short globe-type, cobalt blue etched globe 105

Lantern, "Missouri, Kansas & Texas Railway," tall globe-type, bell-bottom brass top type, clear globe w/raised lettering 625

Lantern, "Missouri Pacific Railroad," tall globe-type, bell-bottom brass top type, clear globe w/raised lettering 625

Lantern, "Missouri Pacific Railroad," tall globe-type, red globe w/raised lettering 160

Lantern, "Nashville, Chattanooga & St. Louis Railway," short globe-type, red etched globe 75

Lantern, "Northern Pacific Railroad," tall globe-type, clear globe w/raised lettering 210

Lantern, "Northwestern Pacific Railroad," short globe-type, red etched globe 65

Lantern, "Pacific Electric Railway," tall globe-type, etched clear globe 75

Lantern, "Pere Marquette Railroad," short globe-type, unmarked red globe 50

Lantern, "Pittsburgh & Lake Erie Railroad," short globe-type, globe etched "Omaha" 55

Lantern, presentation-type, all-brass, bell bottom style, red & clear tall globe-type, presentation inscription on globe "D.A. Kendall, Pine Bluff, Ark.," Handlan Co. 950

Lantern, presentation-type, all-brass, bell bottom style, tall clear unmarked globe w/unique copper arm lens protectors, Geo. M. Clark Co. 300

Lantern, presentation-type, all-brass, bell bottom style, unmarked tall clear globe, M.M. Buck & Co. 325

Lantern, presentation-type, all-brass, tall clear globe, frame & globe marked "Pullman," Adams & Westlake Co. 450

Lantern, presentation-type, chrome-plated, bell bottom style, green & clear tall globe etched w/initials & wreath, M.M. Buck & Co. 950

Lantern, presentation-type, chrome-plated, cobalt blue & clear globe etched w/initials "F.D. ORR," Adams & Westlake Co. **2,000**

Lantern, "Reading Railway," tall globe-type, frame marked "LO CO DEPT," clear unmarked globe 100

Lantern, "Richmond, Fredericksburg & Potomac Railroad," short globe-type, clear etched globe 80

Lantern, "Rock Island Lines," tall globe-type, clear globe w/raised lettering 100

Lantern, "Rutland Railroad," short globe-type, red etched globe 90

Lantern, "Seaboard Air Line Railway," short globe-type, etched red globe 100

Lantern, "Southern Pacific Company," tall globe-type, clear globe w/raised lettering 160

Lantern, "St. Louis & San Francisco Railroad," tall globe-type, Adlake Reliable frame w/bamboo handle, clear globe w/raised wording "Frisco" & "Safety First" 260

Lantern, "St. Louis & South Western Railway," tall globe-type, clear globe w/raised wording "Cotton Belt Route" 400

Lantern, "Texas & Pacific Railway," tall globe-type, clear etched globe 200

Lantern, "Wabash Railroad," tall globe-type, bell-bottom brass top type, clear globe w/raised wording "Wabash Banner Flag" 385

Lantern, "Western Maryland Railway," tall globe-type, clear matching globe 100

License Plate Attachment

License plate attachment, "Pembroke Air Park," painted metal w/reflective lettering, reads "Fly (motif of airplane) At Pembroke Air Park, Inc. On Route Five," 11" w., 6" h. (ILLUS.) 66

License plate tag, pharmacist, die-cut metal, outline of a mortar & pestle w/"RX" in white & "Registered Pharmacist" below, screw-mount, unused condition, 3 x 5" 99

Light globe, "Kentucky Fried Chicken," milk glass w/likeness of Colonel Sanders in black & white logo on rectangular red panels, 1960s, 10" h. (light wear & soiling) 110

Tracy's Coffee Light Globe

Light globe, "Tracy's Coffee," glass, top light fixture, round, white globe w/gold lettering, reads "Tracy's Fresh Roasted Coffee" soiling, minor chipping on base edges, 7" h. (ILLUS.) 281

Light or fan pull, "Wrigley's Gum," die-cut cardboard, figural Santa Claus, made to slide real pack of gum under his arm, shows packs of gum in Santa's pack, 6 1/2" h. 135

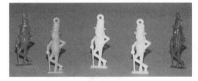

Light Pulls

Light pulls, "Planters Peanuts," figural Mr. Peanut, molded plastic, various colors, ca. 1960s, each (ILLUS.) 15

Lock, signal-type, "Missouri Pacific Railroad" 80

Lock, signal-type, "Rock Island Lines" 50

Locomotive engine builder's plate, brass, diamond-shaped, "Lima Locomotive Works Incorporated 8-1937 J7660," 9 x 16" 900

Locomotive engine builder's plate, brass, oval, "American Loco. Co. Schenectady H3-1912 50627," 8 x 11 1/2" 875

Locomotive engine builder's plate, brass, oval, "Beyer, Peacock & Co. Makers & Owners, Manchester, 1869," 7 x 15" 700

Locomotive engine builder's plate, brass, rectangular, "American Locomotive Co. 38921 Pittsburg Works January 1906," 7 1/2 x 14" 550

Locomotive engine builder's plate, brass, round, "Baldwin Locomotive Works Philadelphia USA 556," 17" d. 950
Locomotive engine builder's plate, brass, round, "Built at Mt. Clare L-2b 10-26," 8" d. 1,525
Locomotive engine builder's plate, brass, round, "The Baldwin Locomotive Works Philadelphia USA #56912," 9 1/2" d. 675
Magazine advertisement, from Saturday Evening Post, for Lionel Trains, "Gee Pop, you got 'em," late 50s-early 60s Christmas season, ads vary in price depending on size & item pictured, average price for framed Lionel ad............................... 45
Matchbook, "Keen Kutter"...................................... 15
Mayonnaise bowl, "Missouri Pacific Railroad," china, "The Eagle" patt. 75
Mechanical pencil, "Planters Peanuts," figural molded plastic Mr. Peanut on top, yellow & blue 18
Medicine chest, cherry wood w/purple felt-lined lid, brass fittings & plaque engraved "Carl's Drug Store Greencastle, PA Est. 1825," stamped "Whitall Tatum & Co. Makers" on base, includes 14 labeled clear glass apothecary jars, two Lattice & Diamond patt. poison bottles w/labels & stoppers, two ointment jars w/metal lids & one dose glass, all w/original ground glass stoppers, original skeleton key, ca. 1890-1910.. 468
Menu, "Borden," depicts Elsie the Cow, 2 pp. 14

Red Goose Shoes Mirror

Mirror, "Red Goose Shoes," counter-type, reverse-painted glass in wood frame, metal handle at top w/metal stand on sides to allow mirror to stand up on counter, logo near top, paint loss, scratches & wear to frame, very minor cracking of paint to goose, 15 1/2" w., 21 3/4" h. (ILLUS.)....................................... 303

Ceramic Horlicks Mixer

Mixer, "Horlicks," tall cylindrical ceramic body w/a small rim spout & C-form strap handle, w/metal interior mixer mechanism, white w/blue label on the side w/white wording "Horlicks Mixer," made by Alfred Meakin, England, early 20th c., 3" d., 7 3/4" h. (ILLUS.)................................... 60
Moving picture book, "Kellogg's Funny Jungleland," dated 1932, 6 1/2 x 8".............. 48
Mug, "Dr. Swett's," china, highly embossed, depicts bust of Dr. Swett on front & floral decoration on reverse, 6" h........................... 202

Cherry Brand Mirror

Mirror, "Cherry Brand," ornate gilt metal handle & rim, celluloid advertising "Fine Chocolates & Bon Bons - Cherry Brand - Cy Gousset 137-141 Prince St. New York," minor soiling & scratches, wear to gold, 2" w., 4" h. (ILLUS.)................................... 99
Mirror, "Player's Navy Cut Tobacco," depicts Player's logo of sailor & vintage ships framed by life preserver, "Tobacco and Cigarettes" below, wooden frame, 18" w., 22" h. 202

Horlicks Restaurant Ware Mug

Mug, "Horlicks," ceramic, heavy duty restaurant ware in beige w/brown script name on side, made by Shenango China, Newcastle, Pennsylvania, 20th c. (ILLUS.) **25**

English Horlicks Mug

Mug, "Horlicks," ceramic, tall swelled cylindrical form w/ear handle, white w/orange lettering, made in England, 20th c., 3" h. (ILLUS.) **20**

Lee Overalls Neckerchief

Neckerchief, "Lee Overalls," red cloth square printed in white w/pictures of buildings & vignette scenes of people wearing the jeans, ca. 1920, near mint, 23" sq. (ILLUS.) **33**

Pioneer Club Dealer Necktie

Necktie, "Famous Pioneer Club - Downtown Las Vegas, Nevada," black rayon decorated w/iridescent colors showing card, dice & the head of a cowboy, worn by a casino dealer, ca. 1950s, appears unused, 4 x 52" (ILLUS.) **88**

Needle case, A&P stores, mint w/contents **8**

Needle case, "Coca Cola," shows bottle & glass of cola & young woman holding a glass of cola w/bottle nearby, ca. 1924, overall excellent condition, 2 x 3" **55**

King's Powder Oil Painting

Oil painting, "King's Powder 'Quickshot'," gunpowder, original oil on canvas, scene of hunter near water in background, duck he has shot falling in the foreground, ca. 1890, in original ornate frame, unsigned, professionally cleaned & revarnished, overall 24 x 32" (ILLUS.) **10,010**

Borden Dairy Order Flag

Order flag, "Borden Dairy," circular die-cut cardboard insert to place in empty milk bottle to order various dairy products, center shows delivery person in white holding two bottles of milk w/"Borden's Dairy Delivery Company" around border & colored flags attached showing the various products, tab at bottom w/"For Extra Orders Turn Up Flag and Put in Top of Bottle," 1932, 5 3/4 x 7 3/4" (ILLUS.)............ **231**

Early Horlick's Advertising Pamphlet

Pamphlet, "Horlick's Malted Milk," printed paper, black & white printing on cover w/scene of a dairy maid standing beside a cow in a meadow, back cover showing a factory scene & three sizes of the powder available, late 19th - early 20th c., matted & framed open (ILLUS.) **6**

Paper clip, "Culter Proctor Stoves," w/celluloid picture.. **65**

Planters Parade Costume

Parade costume, "Planters Peanuts," Mr. Peanut, w/cane, adult sized, fiberglass w/foam padded shoulders (ILLUS.).............. **600**

Peanut dispenser, "Planters Peanuts," toy-type, molded plastic, upright style w/molded figure of Mr. Peanut, made once, used as store display, Tarco, 1978...... **45**

Pen & pencil set, "Planters Peanuts," w/"Mr. Peanut's 75th Birthday," gold-filled, Mr. Peanut engraved on clip, by Cross, rare.. **200**

Pencil, "Planters Peanuts," advertising type, green w/eraser tip, unsharpened **18**

Pennant, "Marble's," depicts gun & hatchet w/"Game Getting Gun and Specialties for Sportsman," 10 1/2" w., 33" l........................ **219**

Pennant, "Old Dutch Cleanser," cloth, downward pointed long triangular form, dark red ground w/a small section of green at the tip, partial can of the product shown at the center, reads "Safest for Porcelain and Enamel - There's nothing like it," 15 3/4 x 26" (moderate wear) **121**

Perfume sample dispenser, "Continental Novelty Company of Buffalo, NY.," painted bull's head w/directions in glass circle above, pull horns to spray perfume, ca. 1908, 14" h. **2,900**

Photograph, "Kodak" on metal plate, black & white in original frame, depicts woman taking photograph of four children & an older woman looking at a book, original label on back marked "This advertisement is the property of the Eastman Kodak Company.," ca. 1935-1945, 27 3/4" x 34 1/4" **231**

Pillow, "St. Louis & San Francisco Railway" (Frisco Lines) **33**

Pillow case, "Union Pacific Railroad" **20**

Eversweet Toiletry Pin Tray

Pin tray, "Eversweet - A Daily Toilet Necessity - For Refined People," rectangular w/flanged scalloped w/rounded fluted corners, rectangular color center scene of a scantily clad standing young lady reaching up to red roses, printed design of jewels along two sides, 3 1/2 x 5" (ILLUS.) **254**

Success Manure Spreader Pin Tray

Pin tray, "'Success' Manure Spreader," rectangular lithographed tin, wording in red around the flanged border, center color scene of farmer using the spreader, a few scuffs, 3 1/4 x 4 3/4" (ILLUS.) **105**

Pitcher, "Dr. Harter's Wild Cherry Bitters" & motif of bottle w/"Relieves All Distress of the Stomach," thermos-type, silver w/intricate raised design, stamped "E. Jaccard Jewelry Co. St. Louis, Mo Quadruple Plate" on base, ca. 1890-1910, 13" h. ... **330**

Pitcher, "Dr. Van Dyke's Holland Bitters Van Dyke Bitters Co. St. Louis," thermos-type, silver plate w/intricate design, stamped "Pelton Bros & Co St. Louis Quadruple Plate" on base, ca. 1880-1910, 13 3/8" h. **242**

Newer Horlicks Pitcher

Pitcher, "Horlicks," ceramic, bulbous body tapering to a flat rim w/wide spout, large C-form handle, royal blue ground printed w/thin red swirled lines alternating w/yellow grain heads, name printed in white, base marked "Churchill England," 4 1/2" h. (ILLUS.) **27**

Old Smuggler & Pinch Bar Pitchers

Pitcher, "Old Smuggler Scotch Whiskey," bar-type, ceramic, figural toby-style, all-white bust of man wearing tricorn hat w/wording & gold trim (ILLUS. left) **121**

Pitcher, "Pinch - The Dimple," bar-type, ceramic, flattened ovoid form w/indented sides & short flaring neck, all-white w/gold printed logo near the base (ILLUS. right) **69**

Advertising Bar Pitchers

Pitcher, "Plymouth Gin," bar-type, ceramic, figural fish w/wide open mouth forming spout & tail forming handle, embossed wording, dark green glaze (ILLUS. left) **32**

Pitcher, "Tho's. Maddock's Son's Co.," tankard-style, ceramic, depicts two portly gentlemen bowling on one side w/rack of pool balls on other, silver handle, 12 1/2" h. (slight chipping & silver loss to handle) **98**

Pitcher, "White Horse Scotch Whiskey," bar-type, ceramic, triangular foot & body w/long spout & angled handle, dark blue w/white wording & profile of a horse (ILLUS. right) **66**

Plate, "Denver & Rio Grande Western Railroad," bread & butter, china, Blue Adam patt. **20**

Plate, "Denver & Rio Grande Western Railroad," dinner, china, Blue Adam patt. **50**

Plate, "Denver & Rio Grande Western Railroad," luncheon, china, Prospector patt. **95**

Plate, "Great Northern Railway," bread & butter, china, Glory of the West patt. **45**

Plate, "New York Central Railroad," bread & butter, china, Dewitt Clinton patt. **23**

Plate, "Northern Pacific Railroad," bread & butter, china, Monad patt. **33**

Plate, "Pennsylvania Railroad," grapefruit, china, Mt. Laurel patt. **45**

Plate, "Union Pacific Railroad," china, Circus patt., scene of bareback rider, 8 1/4" d. **95**

Plate, "Union Pacific Railroad," china, Circus patt., scene of monkey w/pipe, 8 1/4" d. **95**

Plate, "Western Pacific Railroad," grapefruit, china, Feather River patt. **200**

Platter, "Chicago, Milwaukee, St. Paul & Pacific Railroad," china, oval, Traveler patt., 8 x 10" **85**

Platter, "Denver & Rio Grande Western Railroad," oval, china, Prospector patt. **25**

Platter, "Northern Pacific Railway," china, small oval, Monad patt. 60
Platter, "Pennsylvania Railroad," service, china, oval, Liberty patt. 25
Platter, "Union Pacific Railroad," china, oval, Challenger patt. 18
Platter, "Union Pacific Railroad," china, oval, Harriman Blue patt., 6 1/4 x 9" 50
Platter, "Union Pacific Railroad," china, oval, Harriman Blue patt.," 7 1/4 x 11" 70
Platter, "Union Pacific Railroad," china, small oval, Harriman Blue patt. 33
Playing cards, "Dr. Harter's The Only True Iron Tonic For The Bold," & "Dr. Harter's Little Liver Pills Cures Sick Headache Do Not Gripe or Sicken," complete set w/extra card advertising Dr. Harter's company, ca. 1892 148
Playing cards, "Dr. Van Dyke's Holland Bitters," complete set in original box w/tax stamp (some deterioration to box) 154
Playing cards, "Planters," w/Mr. Peanut, complete deck 1,375
Pocket knife, "Esso Gasoline," debossed metal, gas pump-shaped w/"Standard" on globe & "Essoline" on base, 2 1/2" l. (minor wear & scratches) 165

Early Horlick's Postcard

Postcard, "Horlick's Malted Milk," color-tinted card showing herd of cows in a wooded meadow, wording in red & blue "Homeward Bound - Original - Genuine - HORLICK'S MALTED MILK - FOR ALL AGES," reverse printed w/offer "Send 10 cents for a Speedy Mixer," early 20th c. (ILLUS.) 8

Early Hawaiian Travel Postcard

Postcard, "See Hawaii - Matson Navigation Co. - San Francisco - Honolulu - Direct to Volcano," stylized color landscape in blue, red & orange w/a guitar-playing native woman in the foreground & a steamship & smoking volcano in the distance, wording in red & white, 3 1/2 x 5 1/2" (ILLUS.) 66

1908 Ithaca Gun Poster

Poster, "Ithaca," 1908, rectangular, "Wild Gobbler" above snowy outdoor scene w/large turkey in foreground w/"Ithaco Guns - Guaranteed" below (ILLUS.) 1,540
Poster, "United Airlines," rectangular, image of skyscrapers & 1940-50s era airplane in upper right corner w/"Chicago" in upper left corner w/"United Air Lines" at bottom, framed under glass (5" tear at top center moving down between g & o in Chicago) 105

Rare Red Wing Flour Pot Scraper

Pot scraper, "Red Wing Special Flour," printed metal, blade-form w/finger hole, dark yellow ground w/red border printed w/white flour sack w/red & black printing around the sack reading "Pot and Pan Scraper - Made from the Finest of

Wheats - Scientifically Milled - Red Wing Milling Co. - Red Wing, Minn.," early 20th c. (ILLUS.) **1,155**
Punch board, "Camel Cigarettes," 1¢ play, 1940s, unused **55**

Display Punchboard

Punchboard display, "Planters Peanuts," rectangular, layered cardboard, orange, blue, yellow & black lettering, across the top reads "Planters Cocktail Peanuts," 1940s-50s (ILLUS.) **100-300**
Puzzle, "Hills Bros.Coffee," jigsaw-type, model of a black coffeepot, steam rising from spout & sitting on yellow & orange flames, can of coffee in center w/logo & "Hills Bros. Coffee," various colorful scenes of people at different times of day w/"Where's the fire?" near the handle & beneath the flames "It's under a pot of Hills Bros Coffee ...No One Can Resist That Marvelous Aroma, Copyright 1933 by Hills Bros," framed under glass, along w/original box, 14" w., 16" h. (box has edge wear & fading overall) **99**
Puzzle, jigsaw-type, "Chase & Sanborn Coffee," their famous New England country grocery store scene, colorful, complete in original box.............................. **68**
Puzzle, "Kellogg," jigsaw-type, lithographed on cardboard, depicts boy on scooter w/dog running beside, "No 3398 Corp. 1933 Kellogg Co" bottom left corner & "Printed U.S.A." right corner, matted & in newer frame, 8 3/4" w., 10 3/4" h. (minor fading, soiling, scuff mark under boy's elbow, sticker residue on glass bottom right corner) **72**
Radio, "Poll-Parrot Shoes," brown plastic cube-shaped, battery-operated w/"Poll-Parrot Shoes - For Boys And Girls" in white letters on one side, w/"Quality Speaks for Itself" on opposite side, other sides w/battery compartment, tuning & volume controls & speaker & on/off switch, colorful composition parrot sits on top on a yellow perch w/"Poll-Parrot Shoes" in black letters, radio by General Electric, 3 3/4" w., 11" h. (soiling)................. **105**
Radio, "Prestolite," countertop-style, black & orange hard rubber, white dials on

front, "Prestolite Hi-level Needs Water Only 3 Times a Year" on reverse, 6 3/4 x 10 1/8", 8" h. **226**

Early Railway Guide

Railway guide, "Atlantic and Pacific Railway Guide - May 1871," sketch of Pullman Car on the cover, nice illustrations inside, various timetables, string-bound, 24 pp., 5 3/4 x 9 1/4", spine wear, light soiling, erased writing on the cover (ILLUS.) **138**
Ribbon, "Shaker Cloak E.J. Neale & Co., Mount Lebanon, N.Y.," woven silk, rectangular w/a floral bordered reserve depicting a Shaker building & the inscription on the front w/a view of a cloaked woman on the back, 19th c., 3 x 7 1/2"...................... **259**

Columbus Flour Rolling Pin

Rolling pin, "Columbus Flour," milk white glass w/wooden handles, reads "Use Columbus Flour, Always Satisfactory and Uniform, There's No Better Flour" in blue lettering & flour sack logo, 17 5/8" l., 2 1/2" d. (ILLUS.)............................... **88**
Rug, "Buster Brown Shoes," round Acrilan acrylic, center design of Buster Brown & his dog Tige in red, orange, yellow & blue on yellow ground, blue border w/five yellow stars, marked "Carpet by Magee Pattern C189-2C SS5-8AA Permanently Mothproof, Bloomsburg, PA Perry, GA.," 47 1/2" d. **770**

Buster Brown Throw Rug

Rug, "Buster Brown Shoes," round nylon throw rug, dark blue border band w/yellow stars, center logo image of Buster & Tige in red, white, blue, brown & yellow against a yellow ground, "Buster Brown" in red under the image, overall light soiling, 54" d. (ILLUS.) 347
Ruler, "Peters Shoes," wooden............................. 18

Red Wing Gunny Sack

Sack, "Red Wing," 100 lb. gunny sack, marked "Red Wing - 35% Protein Linseed Meal, Red Wing, Minn." (ILLUS.) 75
Salt & pepper shakers, Ball Mason jar, glass w/aluminum caps, blue, w/box, pr. 160
Salt & pepper shakers, Bert & Harry Pell, mascots of Pell's Beer, dressed in black, both bald, Bert in a yellow & red vest, Harry tall figure w/bow tie, 1970s, pr. 270
Salt & pepper shakers, Blue Nun Wine, figural nun w/cobalt blue robe w/white headdress & collar, holding a basket filled w/green grapes, white base inscribed "BLUE NUN. Correct with any dish.," U.S.A., 1980s, pr. 195
Salt & pepper shakers, Bob's Big Boy, Japan, 4 1/4" h., pr. 350

Salt & pepper shakers, "Borden Company," ceramic, figural bust of cows, Elmer & Elsie, shaded brown, "C Borden" on base, 2 3/8" w., 4" h. pr. (corks missing, Elmer w/small marks on right arm) 99
Salt & pepper shakers, Handy Flame, blue gas flame, teardrop shaped, w/triangular black eyes, round cheeks & nose & smiling red lips, 1940s, impressed "Handy Flame," pr. 39
Salt & pepper shakers, Harvestore silo, cobalt blue, marked "A O Smith Harvestore System," 4 3/4" h., pr. 45
Salt & pepper shakers, Ken-L Ration dog & cat, Fido & Fifi, plastic, yellow dog & white cat, sitting up, begging, F&F Mold Works, pr. 22
Salt & pepper shakers, Nikolai Vodka Man, pr. 195

Plastic Mr. Peanut Salt and Pepper Shakers

Salt & pepper shakers, "Planters Peanuts," figural Mr. Peanut, molded plastic, various colors, each set (ILLUS.).................. 20
Salt & pepper shakers, "RCA Victor," figural porcelain Nipper the dog w/"His Master's Voice" inscription, Lenox China, ca. 1930s, pr. 85
Salt & pepper shakers, Sandeman Brandy, figure of man w/black cape & hat, probably by Wedgwood, 5 1/2" h., pr. 120
Salt & pepper shakers, Seagram's 7, plastic, red crown atop numeral seven, white base marked in red "Seagram's," unmarked, 3 1/2" h., pr. 35
Salt & pepper shakers, "Sealtest Milk," glass bottle-shaped, pr. 40
Salt & pepper shakers, Sunshine Baker, rotund figure w/mustache, in white apron, yellow bow tie, gold detailing, inscribed "Sunshine," pr. 15
Salt & pepper shakers, Tappan Chef, soft (squeezable) plastic, bell-shaped stylized figure w/goatee, flattened toque, white w/black trim, 1950s, 4 7/8" h., pr. 29
Salt & pepper shakers, Westinghouse washing machine & dryer, plastic, white w/turquoise controls & transparent plastic ports. pr. 16
Sauce dish, "Pennsylvania Railroad," china, Liberty patt. 25
Sauce dish, "Southern Railway," china, Piedmont patt. 11
Scale, "Planters Peanuts," molded figural Mr. Peanut, plastic, coin slot in top hat, originals have brass tag w/item number on back of hat, ca. 1940s, hat circumference 8 1/2" (only 8" on reproductions), 3' 8" h. 16,000

Scale, "Purina Cow Chow," rectangular, brass front, metal back, w/hanging loop at top & S-hook at bottom, "Cow Chow Makes More Milk" at top w/"Don't Guess Use This Purina Milk Scale" at the bottom, 4 1/2" w., 15 1/2" h. (minor edge wear, scratches & soiling) **66**

The Gales Bicycle Score Keeper

Score keeper, "The Gales Bicycle," trapezoidal cardboard printed w/the design of a safety bicycle, the wheels turning to show "Points" & "Games" through small round holes, advertising in black wording between frame of bicycle reads "'The Gales' - Wins The Game - The Highest Grade...," 3 x 4 1/2" (ILLUS.) **55**

Screen door, "Sunbeam Bread," painted on lettering "Reach For - Sunbeam - Bread with a Bonus" w/tin door push w/"Reach for Sunbeam Bread," wooden frame & wagon wheel trim, 34" w., 82" h. (overall wear from use, door push & handle scratched, paint loss & rust)........................ **468**

Service plate, "Baltimore & Ohio Railroad," china, Camden patt. **50**

Service plate, "Baltimore & Ohio Railroad," china, Centenary patt. **75**

Service plate, "Denver & Rio Grande Western Railroad," china, Prospector patt. **30**

Service plate, "Missouri Pacific Railroad," china, State Flower patt................... **190**

Service plate, "New York Central Railroad," china, Mercury patt. **50**

Service plate, "New York Central Railroad," china, Mohawk patt. **50**

Service plate, "Pennsylvania Railroad," china, Gotham patt. **90**

Service plate, "Southern Railway," china, Peach Blossom patt. **30**

Service plate, "Union Pacific Railroad," china, Desert Flower patt. **60**

Service plate, "Union Pacific Railroad," china, Winged Streamliner patt. **50**

Serving dish, cov., "Missouri Pacific Railroad," silver plate, by International Silver...... **140**

Serving set, "Atchison, Topeka & Santa Fe Railway," open serving dish, bowl w/handled cover & tray; silver plate; the set **275**

Sewing kit, "Stevens Firearms," cylindrical tin w/a thimble lid, made for ladies, printed w/a cream ground & black & red wording centered by a target & crossed rifles, early 20th c., some wear, 1 x 2 3/4" **165**

Socony-Mobil Ship's Flag

Ship's flag, "Socony - Mobil," double-sided rectangular nylon, printed w/a flying red Pegasus logo above a red band w/black bands at the top & bottom edges, no wording, canvas & rope mountings, some wrinkles, 37 x 65" (ILLUS.)..................... **55**

Shipping box, "Doublemint Gum," cardboard, lithographed to resemble Doublemint labels, ca. 1950s, 9 x 13 1/2 x 16" **65**

Shipping crate, "Capital Coffee," pine w/original red stain & black stenciled labels on the sides & front panel, late 19th - early 20th c., 16 1/2 x 21", 32 1/2" h. **550**

Columbia Brewing Shoe Brush

Shoe brush, "Columbia Brewing Co. - Tacoma, Wash.," rectangular wooden top w/rounded ends, premium item, ca. 1910, 2 x 8" (ILLUS.)........................... **66**

Sidewalk scale, "Planters Peanuts," figural Mr. Peanut, restored, 20 x 22" (reproductions out there--BEWARE!) **20,700**

Soup bowl, "St. Louis & San Francisco Railway," china, Denmark patt. **35**

Soup bowl, "Union Pacific Railroad," china, Harriman Blue patt. **20**

Spool holder, "Corticelli Silk Thread," spool holder, tin, rotates............................ **65**

Richfield Spray Gun

Spray gun, "Richfield - New Rapid-Atomizing Spray-Gun - Insect Spray - Surface Spray," tubular metal shaft w/plunger handle printed in red, white & blue bands w/yellow, blue & white wording, plain metal cylindrical tank w/screw-on cap, few small scratches, minor wear on plated tank, 13 1/2" l. (ILLUS.)............................ **110**

Sprayer, "White Rose Sprayer, For White Rose Insecticide Spray," pump-style sprayer, w/glass bottle & wooden handle, 12 1/2" l. (paint chips) **33**

Step stool, "Northern Pacific," metal 375
Step stool, "Panama Limited," metal 225
Step stool, "Texas & Pacific Railroad,"
metal 425

Gargoyle Marine Oils Razor

Straight razor, "Gargoyle Marine Oils," long
bone handle w/hinged steel blade etched
w/gargoyle logo & wording, soiling, some
rust spotting on blade, early 20th c., 9" l.
(ILLUS.) 165
Table, "Calumet Baking Powder," child's,
wooden body & legs w/white porcelain
top w/letters of the alphabet in a semi-cir-
cle at the top above the red & blue Calumet logo & "The Kind Mother Uses" & the
numbers 1 through 10 below, blue lettering, numbers & edge, 16" w., 20" l.,
18" h. (one leg loose, rust spotting on
edges, cracking to porcelain, minor fad-
ing, scratches, soiling & staining) 800-1,100

7Up Advertising Table Lamp

Table lamp, "7Up," a one quart soda bottle
mounted on a round wood base forming
the lamp, fitted w/a large cylindrical paper shade printed w/the red & black 7Up
logo, ca. 1950, 15 x 24" (ILLUS.) 209
Tablecloth, "Rock Island Lines," linen 40
Tablecloth, "St. Louis & San Francisco
Railway," linen 80
Teapot, cov., "Missouri Pacific Railroad,"
silver plate, "The Eagle" patt. 75

Theater slide, "Hamlin's Wizard Oil Lini-
ment, For All Painful Ailments, The Pattern Drug Store, 48 Genessee St.," glass
in blue, yellow, red & pink hand
coloring, ca. 1900-1925, 3 1/4" h. 55
Timetable, "Denver & Rio Grande Rail-
road," 1929 35
Torch can, "Atchison, Topeka & Santa Fe
Railway," metal 150
Torch can, "Missouri Pacific Railroad,"
metal 23
Torch can, "St. Louis & San Francisco Rail-
way," metal, early type 60

Rare Early Aunt Jemima String Toy

Toy, "Aunt Jemima Pancake Flour," die-cut
cardboard, string-climbing type w/a small
rectangular package of flour at the top
suspending a string w/an early image of
Aunt Jemima climbing the string, printed
in red, white & black, early 20th c., rare
(ILLUS.) 7,590
Toy, "Colt," pewter toy six-gun on original
cardboard advertising, early 45

Log Cabin Express Wagon

Toy, "Log Cabin," tin wagon pull toy for
small size syrup can, red, side marked
"Log Cabin Express," & stamped "798"
on bottom, 1 1/2 x 4 x 5 1/4" (ILLUS.) 259

Toy Greyhound Bus by Realistic

Toy bus, "Greyhound," slush cast metal w/hard rubber wheels, Realistic Toy Co., Freeport, Illinois, overall nicks & wear due to handling, 8 1/2" l. (ILLUS.).............. **121**
Toy tractor, "Farmall," cast metal painted red, marked "Farmall" w/logo on sides, 21" h. (paint chips).. **1,320**

Wood-jointed Mr. Peanut

Toy, "Planters Peanuts," figure of Mr. Peanut, wood, jointed, painted yellow, black & white w/blue top hat, ca. 1930s (ILLUS.)... **225**
Toy, "Planters Peanuts," Mr. Peanut black & tan wind-up, rare..................... **400-425**
Toy, "Planters Peanuts" Mr. Peanut, plastic windup walking figure, green, 8 1/2" h. (very light wear) **413**

Planters Toy Train Car

Toy train car, "Planters Peanuts," coal car, printed on side w/Planters advertising in red, white & yellow, Tyco, 1977, mint in original box (ILLUS.) **50**

Hubley Bell Telephone Truck

Toy truck, "Bell Telephone," painted cast iron w/red wheels & white rubber tires, Hubley, aging to tires, few nicks & rust spots, 4" l. (ILLUS.) **165**
Toy truck, "Sunshine Biscuits," metal, battery-operated, yellow w/"Sunshine Biscuits" in red lettering, Goodrich Silvertown tires, Metalcraft Corp. St. Louis, U.S.A., insert batteries through front, 12" l. (front replaced, back doors missing, lights not working) **176**
Toys, "Winchester," pewter red hunter & moose on original cardboard advertising display, ca. 1953, the set **150**
Trophy, "Stanocola Polarine," metal, engraved "Awarded To State Of Tennessee Memphis Agency as Winners Third Year 1922" on one side, "Awarded to State Of

Rare Mr. Peanut Squeeze Toy

Toy, "Planters Peanuts," rubber squeeze-type, model of standing Mr. Peanut in tan, black & white, early 20th c. (ILLUS.)... **1,870**
Toy, "Winchester," toy pewter rifle w/Winchester clown on small display board, ca. 1953 .... **45**

Arkansas Memphis Agency As Winners Second Year Stanocola Polarine Contest Year 1921" on reverse, 10" d., 10 1/2" h. **187**

Tumbler, "Chesapeake & Ohio Railroad," glass.. **11**

Tumbler, "Missouri, Kansas & Texas Railway," glass... **70**

Planters Glass Tumblers

Tumblers, "Planters Peanuts," clear glass w/Mr. Peanut decal, each (ILLUS.).................. **25**

Tumblers, "Planters Peanuts," Mr. Peanut 75th anniversary six-piece set.............. **250-275**

Umbrella, "Patton's Sun-Proof Paint Umbrella" & "The Iola Hdwe. Co." on alternating panels, wooden handle, 27" h. (some staining & holes)................................... **41**

Umbrella stand, "M. J. Ades & Company," ornate nickel-plated cast iron, half-moon shape advertising medallion in center & seven umbrella tip holes across top, em-bossed "M. J. Ades & Co. The Winner Umbrella," includes seven umbrellas w/simulated gold or mother-of-pearl & simulated gold handles, 16 1/2" l., 4 1/2" h. without umbrellas........................ **1,275**

Meredith Diamond Club Whiskey Jug

Whiskey jug, "Meredith Diamond Club," ceramic, bulbous ovoid body w/cylindrical neck, grey w/blue lettering, marked "Meredith's Diamond Club Pure Rye Whiskey - Expressly for Medicinal Use - East Liverpool, Ohio," KT & K Pottery Co., 7 1/2" h. (ILLUS.)................................. **66**

Whistle, "Planters Peanuts," figural Mr. Peanut, various colors, 2 1/2"..................... **10-15**

Yardstick, "Hi-Park Guernsey Milk, Red Wing, Minn.," wooden................................... **50**

Antique Trader Books-A Name You Can Trust

Antique Trader® Antiques & Collectibles 2002 Price Guide
edited by Kyle Husfloen

You will discover many of the current "hot" areas in collecting in this comprehensive guide to antiques and collectibles. Features more than 18,500 listings complete with current pricing and a detailed description of each item. Some added features include a listing of names and addresses of the numerous special contributors to the edition and access to a free online price guide.

Softcover • 6 x 9 • 1,048 pages
4,300+ b&w photos • 16-page color section
Item# AT2002 • $16.95

Antique Trader® Guide to Fakes & Reproductions
by Mark Chervenka

This book is your best insurance policy against getting fooled by the less valuable reproductions that have flooded today's market. *Antique Trader Guide to Fakes & Reproductions* offers a simple, but proven, identification system: side-by-side photos of authentic and reproduction items, along with a detailed explanation of how to tell them apart. Includes hundreds of items from the most popular categories of collectibles: glass; pottery; porcelain; toys; furniture; silver; advertising and much more.

Softcover • 6 x 9 • 304 pages
1,000 b&w photos • 16-page color section
Item# ATRF • $24.95

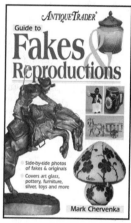

Antique Trader® Furniture Price Guide
edited by Kyle Husfloen and Mark Moran

Immerse yourself in yesteryear as you view the "period" furniture from the 17th, 18th and early 19th centuries and the late 19th and 20th century furniture popular from the 1920s through the 1960s. More than 3,000 listings with accurate prices allow you to confidently identify and value the pieces in your collection. Special sections include an introductory feature on collecting furniture, a furniture-dating chart, and an illustrated section on American furniture terms.

Softcover • 6 x 9 • 528 pages
450 b&w photos • 16-page color section
Item# AFUR1 • $16.95